# West African Popular Theatre

**Drama and Performance Studies**

Timothy Wiles,
GENERAL EDITOR

# West African Popular Theatre

Karin Barber

John Collins

Alain Ricard

*Indiana University Press*

BLOOMINGTON AND INDIANAPOLIS

*James Currey*

OXFORD

Published in North America by Indiana University
Press, 601 North Morton Street, Bloomington, IN 47404
and in Britain and the Commonwealth by James Currey
Publishers, 73 Botley Road, Oxford OX2 0BS

The paper used in this publication meets the
minimum requirements of American National
Standard for Information Sciences—Permanence of
Paper for Printed Library Materials,
ANSI Z39.48–1984.

MANUFACTURED IN THE UNITED STATES OF AMERICA

**British Library Cataloguing in Publication Data**

Barber, Karin
 West African popular theatre
 1. Theater and society - Africa, West
 2. West African drama (English)
 I. Title II. Collins, John III. Richard, Alain
 792'.0966

 ISBN 0-85255-245-9 cloth
 ISBN 0-85255-244-0 paper

**Library of Congress Cataloging-in-Publication Data**

Barber, Karin
 West African popular theatre / Karin Barber,
John Collins, Alain Ricard.
  p.  cm. — (Drama and performance studies)
  ISBN 0-253-33204-4 (alk. paper). —
  ISBN 0-253-21077-1 (pbk. : alk. paper)
  1. Theater—Africa, West. 2. West African drama
(English) I. Collins, John, date—.
 II. Ricard, Alain. III. Title. IV. Series.
 PN2979.B37  1997
 792'.0966—dc21
                       96-42321
 1 2 3 4 5  02 01 00 99 98 97

# CONTENTS

# LIST OF ILLUSTRATIONS

# INTRODUCTION

Karin Barber

The three contributors to this volume—John Collins, Alain Ricard, and I—came to be interested and involved in West African popular theatre groups in different ways.

John Collins lived in Ghana for some years as a child and returned there in 1969 to do a degree in sociology at the University of Ghana at Legon. He has remained resident in Ghana ever since, teaching, running his own music recording studio, playing guitar, harmonica, and percussion in a number of popular bands, and leading his own Bokoor Band. He met Mr. Bampoe, the leader of the Jaguar Jokers concert party, by chance at his stepmother's house when he was still a student at the University of Ghana. When Mr. Bampoe invited him to join them as a bandsman on one of their treks, Collins accepted eagerly. He wanted to learn more about Ghanaian styles of playing, having been a guitarist in several jazz bands, a blues group, and a rock band in England. He went with them several times, and it was on the third trek that he decided to write a book about the J.J.s—a project Mr. Bampoe supported—for the local Ghanaian audience.[1] He stresses the accidental nature of his meeting with the J.J.s. He did not initially set out to do a research project on the concert party, nor would anyone have suggested such a thing in those days, for the concert party was not recognized as a topic worthy of academic inquiry. However, the encounter with the J.J.s proved to be a stage in a lifelong involvement with African popular music and with highlife in particular, as a musician and as a writer, researcher, archivist, and lecturer.

Alain Ricard went to Togo as an academic. He was a research fellow at the National Centre for Scientific Research (CNRS), in the field of African languages and literatures, when he embarked on a project of filming the concert parties of Togo in the early 1970s. His first short film, *Agbeno Xevi*, was completed in 1972; a second, longer documentary, *Principe d'Asihu*, in 1982. He taught at the University of Togo and was later seconded from his institution to ORSTOM in Lomé to be a researcher in residence with the Togolese National Theatre Ensemble. He is now a research professor at CNRS. Unlike John Collins, then, his project was conceived and carried out within a well-defined and well-funded academic framework. Nonetheless, it involved him in the life and activities of the concert party in ways which exceeded and outlasted his immediate project.

I went to Nigeria in 1973 as a graduate student at the University of Ifè, and stayed on. I completed my Ph.D., on oral poetry in a Yorùbá town, in 1979, and was teaching in the Department of African Languages and Literatures at Ifè when I started a research project on the popular traveling theatre, which in the early eighties was a conspicuously successful dramatic form that had received almost no attention from the academic world. I became attached to one of these companies on a part-time basis, traveling with them and performing in a number of their stage plays as well as in two popular television series. I did this for three years, until I left Nigeria in 1984.

Although Collins, Ricard, and I became involved in different capacities—playing in the band; making a film; acting—and within different institutional frameworks—as a locally based student and musician; as a visiting research fellow; as a locally based university teacher—one experience that we had in common was the readiness with which we were admitted into the theatre groups and the extent to which we were invited to participate in practical ways—ways which actually changed the spectacle that the theatre groups offered, in however small a way.

Ricard's experience of filming Togolese concert party was one of constructive intervention. It was an intervention that affected the mode of operation of the actors. It led to a real engagement at the level of production, and brought insight into the nature of the group's relationship to the "text" of the plays. The actors made their own use of the outcome of the project—notably by showing Ricard's first film about them, *Agbeno Xevi,* as promotional material and even as a kind of curtain-raiser in actual performances. The second period of filming, in 1977, had the effect of temporarily reviving the group, which was losing its impetus. They were disappointed that his involvement stopped at filmmaking, arguing that since he had commissioned the shows that were filmed, he should go on to take full responsibility for the group on their next tour, in a managerial or directorial capacity. However, he was not able to do this, and the group did thereafter cease operations.

In Collins's case, a real exchange took place at the level of musical expertise. Collins learned more highlife, which he had already begun to play, while the Jaguar Jokers bandsmen were able to find out more about the blues and rock he had been playing in England. He was also included in the tours because he was a novelty, a crowd-puller. When the bandsmen went on their "campaign" around the town advertising the evening's performance, "I was usually taken along as I was a great attraction, taking over the guitar from Doku and introduced as an Oboroni [European] playing at that night's show. Coming right in the middle of a working day, we had an amazing effect in the villages, for people would simply stop what they were doing and start to dance: women, carrying baskets on their heads and babies on their backs, toddlers, old people, farmers; everyone within hearing distance of the speaker would gyrate."

When I went to see Mr. Adéjọbí, leader of the Oyin Adéjọbí Theatre Company, I tentatively explained that I was interested in their type of drama and would like to hang around with the company, watch their plays, record some of them, talk to the actors, and so on. Mr. Adéjọbí immediately invited me to play a part in a TV serial to be filmed the following week. Soon afterward I was trying to overcome my panic as I prepared to step onto the stage—erected at one end of the Olúbàdàn Stadium, Ìbàdàn—as a female chief in one of their live plays, Fọlájiyọ̀. The parts I played were always small ones, but the theatre company put considerable thought into composing the lines I was to speak and organizing my appearance to extract the maximum surprise value from it. Several times they sent for me unexpectedly because a performance had been scheduled and my participation in it had already been publicly announced. This openness and incorporativeness, experienced by all three of us, in itself gives much food for thought.

When we did these projects, "performance theory" was not yet considered to be at the cutting edge of humanities research. Even though ideas about participatory and dialogic research were beginning to be aired, they did not at that time seem to be fully crystalized. None of us really went into our interaction with the theatre companies with a worked-out theory which we could carry through into the analysis of what we experienced. Ricard recalls:

> The main theoretical reference for my film work was Jean Rouch: he helped me and supported my project within CNRS. I think in particular that his papers on ethnographic film, and especially his piece on "anthropologie partagée" [shared anthropology] in the book on *La Notion de Personne en Afrique Noire,* have been seminal to me. He speaks of a "permanent ethno-dialogue," and asserts that "Knowledge is no longer a secret that is stolen to be devoured in Western temples of knowledge; it is the end product of an endless quest where ethnographed and ethnographers go along the path that some of us are already calling 'shared anthropology.'" [Rouch 1973] . . . But I was too much of a positivist to let myself be led by the show. I wanted to put my Proppian "functions" on the screen. Structuralism does not go along very well with Rouchian anthropology. I had a phenomenological view of a phenomenon which I tried to describe with structuralist tools. Very unfortunate, indeed!

The line of exploration adumbrated by Jean Rouch has recently been reinforced by a strong current of theory within U.S. ethnography and performance studies. Clifford and Marcus (1986) argued that the "ethnographic encounter" should not just be participatory but should engage the ethnographer in a collaborative, open-ended, and dialogic relationship with his or her interlocutors. Margaret Drewal (1991) has enriched this argument by placing the notion of performance at the center of the study of culture. Cultural phenomena previously described in terms of rule, norm, and structure could be better understood in terms of improvisation, "restored behavior," and process, for performance is pervasive, continual, and fundamental to cultural production: "Performance is a means by which people reflect on their current conditions, define and/or re-invent themselves and their social world, and either reinforce, resist or subvert prevailing social orders" (1991:2). At the same time, "fieldwork" can be understood as a kind of performance itself: "Treating fieldwork as performance means placing the emphasis on the participant side of the participant/observer paradigm; breaking down the boundaries between self and other, subject and object, subjectivity and objectivity; and engaging in a more truly dialogical relationship with our subjects of study so that both researcher and researched are coeval participants in performance discourse" (1991:33).

Participation in performance yields forms of understanding that cannot always be reduced to verbal representation or analysis. Johannes Fabian, on a parallel tack (Fabian 1990), advocates moving "from informative to performative ethnography." This reorientation, he suggests, gives access in a new way to the constitution of cultural knowledge, because certain kinds of cultural knowledge are produced *in* and *by means of* performance. He describes in detail the production of a play by a Zairean popular theatre company—a play whose theme was sparked off by a question of his own, and whose emergence into a performed work he understands as an ongoing debate among the participants.[2]

The contributors to this volume, however, became participatory and dialogic without really thinking about it: out of interest, common sense (given the object of our interest), the sheer desire to be involved in something that fascinated us, an incipient sense that here was an opportunity to get to know people and culture in a productive and rewarding way . . . and with strong encouragement from the theatre companies themselves. But looking back, certain theoretical suggestions do emerge from our experience of participation in performance, which may make some contribution to the field of African cultural ethnography.

(1) The first question which our experiences raised—a question which is perhaps not often enough asked by ethnographers—is the one already suggested above: why are some cultural activities—like the activities of these popular theatre groups—so much more welcoming and accommodating of outsiders' eccentric desire to "participate" than others? It should not be assumed that all performance activities are equally accessible, equally welcoming, to outside participants: as if all the researcher has to

do is to go along and get involved—whether in dancing, cooking, weeding, or carving—and that a steady flow of insights will automatically ensue. On the contrary, it would seem that in some cases you might be there on sufferance, while in others your presence might be actively solicited. In some, you might be allowed only to pretend to be participating; in others, your participation might actually contribute something new and sought after to the activity in hand. A truly "coeval" and "dialogic" approach might start by asking, "What's in it for our interlocutors? In what way is this 'dialogue' of interest to them? Why are we being allowed, or encouraged, to participate? In what capacity? On what terms?"

I experienced a strong contrast between two different Yorùbá genres that I studied in two different fieldwork situations. My first research was on oríkì, a long-established genre of oral poetry, in Òkukù, a small town in what is now Òsun State. I lived there for more than three years, learned many oríkì, and often had occasion to recite them, jokingly or seriously, in conversations. But though occasions for more formal public performance were constantly arising—at weddings, festivals, funerals, house-openings, household ceremonies of all kinds—and though many people played good-humoredly along with my honorary, fictional membership in an Òkukù lineage, no one ever suggested that I should take part in these performances. My principal role was that of "researcher." This was a recognized and well-defined role which granted certain privileges (e.g., on the occasion of the ancestral masquerade festival: "Only men can enter the sacred egúngún grove—well, only men and researchers"). My main responsibility was to stand by with the tape recorder, and afterwards play back the results many times over. When, eight years later, I began the project on popular theatre, I introduced myself explicitly as a university staff member whose interest was research and whose purpose was to write a book. Nonetheless, I was immediately incorporated as an actress in the way that has already been mentioned. I was delighted at this opportunity, but it was the theatre company who took the lead in assessing my potential contribution and testing the limits of my professed eagerness to participate. In the hotly competitive world of Yorùbá popular theatre, I was a novelty which other theatre companies did not have—a selling point, as Collins was with the Jaguar Jokers.

The contrast between these two experiences may tell us something about the whole field of creativity commonly labeled "modern popular culture."[3] The role assigned to me as "researcher," rather than performer, in Òkukù does not indicate that oríkì-chanting is a closed, traditional, exclusively specialist activity or that the chants themselves are fixed, inaccessible, or strongly bounded. On the contrary, oríkì-chanting crops up in all kinds of guises and the chants are characterized by their openness and fluidity, the porousness of their boundaries, their readiness to incorporate materials from other oral genres (see Barber 1991). There are strong aesthetic continuities between genres like this and the popular theatre. But the difference in these two experiences suggests a difference in orientation and in the function and meaning of incorporation and innovation. It is not just that the theatre company was a business, bent on attracting new customers and getting the edge over its rivals. What *oríkì* chants tend to incorporate is other traditional oral genres. The popular theatre, by contrast (along with popular music such as *jùjú* and, even more markedly, *fújì:* see Waterman 1990, Barber and Waterman 1995), incorporates innovations introduced in, and emblematic of, the colonial and post-independence eras. It incorporates the texts and forms associated with Western education and the media; representations of modern life and current experience; and personalities whose aspirations were formed at least partially by colonialism — aspirations to literacy, to "modernity," to the acquisition of imported goods.

The plays of Ghanaian and Togolese concert party share this characteristic with the Yorùbá popular theatre. All three simultaneously confront and sell "modernity." All three take up a self-conscious and selective relationship to "tradition" while operating, in many respects, within the parameters of long-standing indigenous art forms. They are conscious of this problematic, and propose solutions — mixed, varied, and often contradictory ones, but ones which at some level are comfortable to both performers and audience. They have produced an innovative, hybrid, opportunistic mode of expression in which the incorporation and containment of novelty is a constitutive feature. As Ricard puts it, "The way I was warmly welcomed and the way in which a new medium — film — was used showed the tremendous adaptive capacities of the concert as a communicative medium." At some level, all the plays produced by concert parties and popular theatres in Ghana, Togo, and Nigeria are about the transformation of society wrought under colonialism (though only rarely do they represent actual European/African encounters: *The African Girl from Paris* is, as Ricard argues, a "limit" case in this respect). Thus, though the foreigner acting on stage, or playing in the band, was at one level accidental, an irrelevant and dispensable embellishment, there was a sense in which this gimmick was particularly significant to the popular theatres' projects — at least as central as Bàbá Sàlá's life-sized teddy bears and his inserted film screenings (Barber 1987). It signified the acquisition of exogenously produced novelty in an exemplary form.

Thus, the very fact of outsiders' participation may be seen as symptomatic of some general characteristics of modern popular culture in West Africa. The openness and novelty-seeking of modern popular genres can be understood as a specific, but perpetually repeated, conversation with the conditions of colonial and post-colonial modernity.

(2) A second observation that arose from our experience of working with these theatre groups concerns the idea of "text." The concert party and popular theatres of Ghana, Togo, and western Nigeria are improvised forms. No script usually exists, and each performance emerges through a collective, collaborative effort by the cast, all of whom bear some responsibility for generating, adapting, and embellishing their parts as they go along. Nonetheless, it became clear to us in the course of participating in performances that the actors themselves worked with a kind of virtual script. In the Yorùbá company that I worked with, the manager appeared to have the entire play mapped out in his head. He referred to it as to a mental blueprint, correcting and instructing the other actors as they went along. In the case of Togolese concert party, the status of the dramatic "text" became clear to Ricard in the process of working with the Happy Star concert to make the second film. The loose-jointed improvised stage action had to be captured in a limited number of six-minute film reels. The exercise encouraged the actors to adapt their normal operational habits. Using the concept of a text as a "working tool," Ricard found that "performances are texts, even though they are not written. Once written down, this becomes clear, and I decided to work from the written texts of the performance" which had already been transcribed from recordings made on his earlier trip. He found it possible to use these written texts to select and focus on key episodes *without* turning the production into a performance of a pre-given script with him as director. This was possible because the actors too sensed and recognized the essential structure of the action, which preceded and outlasted particular variations. They responded by spontaneously shortening, focusing, and tightening the scenes to match the six-minute limitation of each reel of film. "I was not filming ritual or fluidity, but potential theatre, arguing for the reconstruction of a textual object."

These concert and theatre actors' understanding of dramatic process as text must be seen in the light of the social context in which popular drama emerged, a context informed by schooling and by literacy, even when many of the actors themselves had only minimal formal education. Having gotten rid of an exclusively scriptocentric, rigidly "text-oriented" view of these plays, we need to avoid merely replacing it with an exclusive emphasis on their immediate, emergent, provisional, and improvisational character. This would be to fall back on a sentimental valorization of "orality" which the theatre companies themselves would not recognize and which would fail to account for central features of their practice. It was only by getting on stage, and hanging around behind the stage, and continuing to do so over long periods and through different phases or aspects of the process of staging a play, that we were able to get some tentative sense of the distinctive character of the improvised "text" in these theatres.

(3) "Text," however, does not mean only words, dialogue which can be transcribed and translated. Both concert party and Yorùbá popular theatre were constituted around music and still retain a strong musical component. Collins's understanding of the musical form of highlife helped to open up, in a preliminary way, the crucial question of the relationship between verbal and musical texts in concert party. By traveling with the band, seeing the same plays over and over again in different venues from his vantage point at the side of the stage, he was able to arrive at some sense of the combinatory logic, the alchemy that fuses action, dialogue, and song. In his own words:

> Unlike many western pop bands, such as the rock band I had played with in Bristol, there was no obvious "superstar," and the so-called "rhythm" guitarist for the local songs usually played a tenor or counter-melody to that of the "lead" one. Likewise the percussionists formed a tightly integrated percussion unit that did not feature long drum solos. . . . I had this point driven home to me by another concert party band, the leader of whom I stayed with for one year in Madina near Accra in 1972. This was Francis Kenya's Riches Big Sound. Any time I jammed with them in the compound of the house and I took off on an unnecessary or narcissistic guitar solo, my amplifier lead would be quietly removed behind my back. The J.J.s probably allowed me to get away with the self-indulgent solos that I simply smeared over the local dance-rhythms when I first joined them because I was such a good crowd-puller.
>
> In fact it took me some years to appreciate the musical dialogue going on, to feel relaxed with local guitar playing and generally learn something about the traditional musical sensibility. From having played African American genres such as jazz and rhythm 'n' blues I was familiar with some African musical techniques: call and response, syncopation, the use of repeated melody-rhythmic cycles or riffs, and the high degree of improvisation not found in scored music.
>
> However, there were two aspects of African music making that I was totally unfamiliar with. One was the employment of multiple cross-rhythms. The other was a sensitivity to the "hidden" or "inside" beat, as local music has a less strongly articulated main beat (or sometimes none at all) than western music, with its single emphatic on-beat that corresponds to the downstroke of the conductor's baton.
>
> The cross-rhythmic technique is in fact the very basis of the Ghanaian "two finger" style of guitar playing, where the thumb and forefinger are plucked in counterpoint to each other, and sometimes revolve around an unplayed rhythm that is only in the player's head, or clucked by the tongue, or tapped by their feet. In fact it was only after years of patient coaching from the famous Ghanaian guitarist Kwaa Mensah who, when not singing, often clucked a rhythm at the back of his throat, that I finally mastered it. . . . [Eventually] the two sub-rhythms began to summate and knit together in my mind as a single gestalt pattern of sound that made

the whole rhythmic structure easier to hold together. This subjective gestalt pattern which is not itself actually played but which helps anchor and orientate the cross rhythms is an example of what I mean by the "hidden" or "inside" rhythm. (Collins 1994:85–89)

The actors in concert party, like the bandsmen, seem to collaborate in an egalitarian way on stage. Their parts alternate and interdigitate, rather than revolving around a "star." Turn-taking is a notable feature of their acting style: the whole cast will wait while an actor completes his "riff," after which he quietly makes room for someone else. Even the villains may have their moments of pathos at the microphone. Facets of characterization also surface episodically, as if taking turns with each other, so that a figure who appears as a venal, comic, and garrulous old man in one episode may come to the fore as the voice of moral authority and wisdom in another. Sentimentality takes turns with buffoonery. These switches and alternations can be compared to the staggered, silent, and unplayed rhythms which are the key to the dynamics of the music and the invisible thread that holds disparate and cross-cutting polyrhythms together. Collins has suggested[4] that many of the characters have "silent" aspects — things about them that appear contradictory and which are neither specified nor resolved — and that there are constant reversals and time jumps in the narrative, which is not reduced to a "realistic" impression of a single linear chronicity. This intersection of musical and narrative dynamics needs to be explored much further in future work.

(4) A fourth observation arising from our experiences concerns the audience. Clearly, our interaction was not only with the performers, but also with the public who came to see them. The reactions of concert party and popular theatre audiences are easy to assess at one level. The concert party audiences weep, jeer, sing, and mount the stage to give presents to the characters they sympathize with or to the performers they admire. Yorùbá popular theatre audiences are frequently so rowdily responsive that they have to be quelled with microphones attached to a powerful sound system. Their participation in the creation of the play — intervening to make suggestions, complete proverbs, pass comments, shout warnings — is hard to miss. They supply the oxygen of public approval to new improvisations; their responses encourage the actors to expand and elaborate certain passages and to condense or eliminate others. They can thus be seen actively participating in the shaping of the show. But audiences, like performers, say that the essential thing about the play is the moral or "lesson" encapsulated and enacted in the narrative. This text — the text of the play's core philosophy — is also collaboratively and creatively co-constituted by the audience. They interpret it in their own way; "use" it in their own lives; fit it into other narratives, precepts, and experiences. But

the question of how they do this is one that, as far as we know, has hardly been broached in studies of African popular cultural forms. Studies of African performance have been very good at building the audience into a conception of the "performance-event," which includes the immediate context as well as the performer and the emergent text. But they have rarely followed audience members home afterwards. The "texts" people participate in during the "performance event" live on to resonate in their lives and in other texts they produce and recirculate from day to day—narratives, songs, reminiscences, nuggets of retold "wisdom," exercises in exegesis. Their interpretations may differ radically from each other, the reasons for their approval or disapproval during the performance may arise from different sets of interests and assumptions. It might, then, be profitable for future students of African performance to take a leaf or two from the book of British cultural studies, which assigns a central role to audience *use* of popular texts (e.g., Willis 1990, Gray 1993).

However, it is not easy to talk to "audiences" about their inner responses to a play. During the show, they are engrossed. Afterwards, it is usually very late and they all rush home. So it helps to have friends and acquaintances in the audience, people you are likely to meet again the next day, and who know you well enough to talk freely about their responses, views, and experiences. This is unlikely to be the case when you are traveling from town to town with a theatre group and never staying more than one night anywhere. The Yorùbá play I chose to include in this volume was an exception to this rule, however. It was performed one night at the Palace Hotel, Òkukù—next door to the house I had lived in for more than three years when I did my doctoral fieldwork in that town. There were many people in the audience that I had known for years. Mr. and Mrs. Akíndélé, whose commentaries inform my discussion of the play, were my landlord and landlady. John Agbéyeyè was a senior man in a neighboring compound. Indeed, I knew the audience much better than I knew the Lérè Pàímó (Èdá) theatre company who were putting on the play. These spectators' detailed and impassioned discussions of the play seemed to offer interesting insights into how particular people assimilate and transform the "lesson" of the play from their own perspective. The kind of "participation" foregrounded in the essay on Yorùbá popular drama in this volume, then, is dialogue with fellow audience members rather than interaction with the actors on stage.[5]

In this volume, then, we have theatre experienced from three different perspectives: that of a performer (Collins); that of a co-director (Ricard); and that of a member of a local audience (myself). Our approaches were quite different, and this is reflected in the different styles of our respective essays in this volume. When we were doing these projects, we did not know about each others' work, let alone plan any kind of collaborative publication. It was only after our most intensive periods of involvement with the theatre companies had ended that we got to know each other and discover each others' work. I remember being entranced when I first saw Ricard's film *Principe d'Asihu*—he brought it with him on an academic visit to Ifè—and later, the absorbing experience of reading Collins's manuscript on the Jaguar Jokers, slightly dog-eared after having languished for eleven years within the Ghana Publishing Corporation's portals. Bringing our different contributions together and reworking them for publication in their present form took a long time and was surprisingly difficult. But discovering both what our projects had in common and how they diverged was stimulating for all three of us, opening up new ways of asking questions about what we had been working on, and suggesting a broad comparative perspective that none of us had really envisaged before. The possibility of placing popular cultural forms in a historical context which embraced a large stretch of coastal West Africa had already been anticipated in John Collins's and Paul Richards's seminal essay on popular music (1982). It seemed to us that the histories and practices of the theatre companies and concert parties, based on extensive personal testimony from the practitioners and exemplified by complete transcriptions of performances, in translation, would make it possible to develop and extend that comparativist understanding. There is a real sense in which colonial coastal West Africa was one cultural zone, in which local exchanges and parallel developments were at least as important as the relationship between any one colony and its "metropolitan center." Popular theatres and musical groups from Ghana and Nigeria regularly toured each others' countries since the first decades of the century. Togolese concert party, later on, was a definite product of Ghanaian influence. Yet the three theatres developed in distinctive ways in response to the immediate economic, cultural, and political circumstances in which they had to operate. The degree to which the state intervened in popular culture; the extent and the fluctuation of personal wealth among the people as a whole; the size and number of urban centers; the degree to which the church and the school exerted a formative influence on popular culture: all these factors, and others, can be adduced in interpreting the differences between Ghanaian concert party, Togolese concert party, and Yorùbá popular theatre. It is our hope that by putting together these different texts and histories—different in themselves and described from different experiential and theoretical standpoints—we may provide the means for other scholars to carry this kind of comparative cultural history much further than we have done.

Our respective experiences and observations, however, obviously only represent a very small and tentative step in the direction of understanding what is going on when popular plays are performed in Ghanaian, Togolese, and Nigerian towns. This volume is intended only as an introduction to a field which invites much deeper and more extensive attention in future work. Nor are these written, translated representations intended to stand in for the entire experience of a concert party or a popular play. The iconic or charismatic bodily presence of the actors; their stylized or effervescent physical movement; the dance; the music; the constant interventions of the audience; the incredibly highly charged, excited atmosphere—so intense you feel the auditorium is going to explode—can only be indicated, not evoked. Nonetheless, we do think there is some value in presenting these partial "texts." The plays are *about* something, they are not just "performances." They are about matters of deep common concern and interest to the people who participate in them. Even bare, translated verbal texts do give some sense of what these concerns are, and how people propose to come to terms with them.

NOTES

1. That book was submitted to the Ghana Publishing Corporation in 1974 but because of lack of paper was never published. The essay in this volume is a condensed version of the substance of the book; much additional material may be found in John Collins's 1994 doctoral thesis.

2. Scholars of African popular culture have long been aware of the peculiar benefits of participation in performance. Much of the best work on popular music, in particular, has been done by researchers who are also dedicated performers. Their experience of learning to play, and of actually playing, African music has deeply informed their understanding of their subject matter. A fine account of the experience is given by Chernoff (1979). Participation in popular drama is rarer, but Kavanagh (1985), Etherton (1982), Mlama (1992), and Mda (1993) write illuminatingly from the point of view of participants in one particular form of popular drama—theatre for development or "conscientization theatre."

3. "Popular" is of course a much-contested and polysemic term. In this volume we are working with a broad and inclusive sense of "popular" defined in social (class) terms: popular is what is produced and/or consumed by "the people" as opposed to the wealthy and well-educated élite. But we recognize that styles of cultural production and consumption overlap and interpenetrate, and that in any case the social division between élite and "people" is extremely blurred, shifts according to context, and is impossible to define in a consistent and categorical manner. The Ghanaian and Yorùbá popular theatres both began as élite forms, patronized by well-to-do acculturated urbanites (Ghana) or "enlightened," often salaried, churchgoers (Western Nigeria). Their history is one of expansion and democratization. More useful than a model of rigid cultural stratification is Roger Chartier's model of the circulation and appropriation of cultural products within and across classes and other social divisions (Chartier 1989)—as long as one still remains alert to the emergence of a distinctive social ethos, such as the ethos of solidarity with "the poor" in Ghanaian concert party. That, however, does not solve the problem of what to do with the distinction "popular"/"traditional." This

is a distinction which on the face of it is untenable. On the one hand, it is too vague: "traditional" covers everything and anything, and is more a valorizing than an analytic term. On the other, it has a spurious air of referential precision: whether to categories of cultural production/producers—suggesting that there is a demographically identifiable "traditional" sector distinct from the "popular"—or to the *forms* of cultural products, irrespective of who produced them. No such discrete categories or sectors can be identified on the ground. But if one does away with this distinction, one still needs a way of representing "the people's" own perceptions of their cultural production: their own sense that forms like concert party, popular theatre, highlife, *jùjú*, Onitsha market literature, etc., are qualitatively *new* and *"modern"*; and that there endures something different and older, recognized by them as "our traditional heritage." See Fabian (1978); Hannerz (1987); Barber (1987), together with the four responses in the same volume, by Arnoldi, Cooper, Cosentino, and Jules-Rosette, for discussion of these conceptual headaches; see also Barber (1997).

4. In a personal communication, June 1994.

5. In a forthcoming monograph, I intend to fill out the other side of the picture, in a history and interpretation of the work of the Oyin Adéjọbí Theatre Company, drawing in part on my experience of traveling and performing with them. For introductory information on the practices and dynamics of play production in this theatre company, see Barber and Ògúndíjọ (1994) and Barber (1995).

# West African Popular Theatre

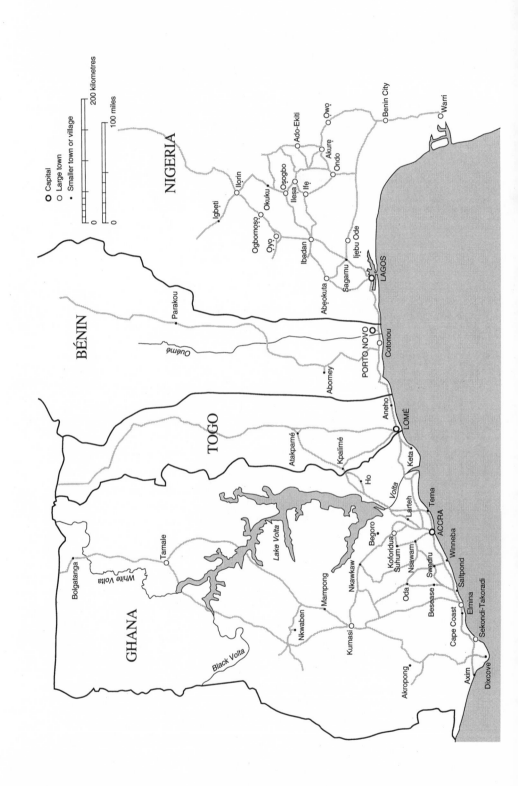

# 1

## Three West African Popular Theatre Forms

*A Social History*

KARIN BARBER, JOHN COLLINS, ALAIN RICARD

### THE CONTEXT OF WEST AFRICAN POPULAR THEATRE

The colonial period in West Africa saw the creation of a new kind of theatre: a popular, modern, commercial, traveling, musical theatre which combined elements of indigenous and imported culture in a creative and innovative fusion. The roots of this theatre were in the coastal cities where contact with Europeans had long been established: Accra and the Fanti ports of the Gold Coast, and the port of Lagos in Nigeria. But these theatres were highly mobile, traveling on itineraries that stretched far inland and sometimes into neighboring West African countries. The Gold Coast concert party, the earliest of these theatre forms, was exported to Togo. Yorùbá popular theatre did not spread beyond the Yorùbá-speaking population of Nigeria, but this area was so large and heterogeneous that it could sustain, in the theatre's heyday, more than a hundred fully professional theatre companies.

This popular theatre was a hybrid form, attuned to novelty and fashion. It emerged from areas where ancient trading cultures had operated long-distance routes crisscrossing West Africa and leading north across the Sahara before turning, with the rise of the Atlantic slave trade, to face the coast. Such cultures, Collins and Richards have suggested, were innovative and adept at the "social navigation" required to foster extensive commercial networks; with this went an open and accommodating attitude toward foreign, imported cultural elements and a willingness to invest in entertainment (Collins and Richards 1982).

The Portuguese built Elmina, a trading fort, on the Gold Coast in 1482; a string of other forts followed as Portuguese interests were displaced, in the seventeenth century, by Dutch and then British and Danish interests.

The product of this long interaction under the shadow of the slave trade was a highly localized hybrid culture in the immediate surroundings of the forts in what is now Ghana. Lagos, in what is now Nigeria, became an important slaving center in the first half of the nineteenth century, when the abolition of the slave trade made the more accessible ports further west too risky to use for that purpose. Lagos expanded and flourished on the back of the illegal slave trade and then, in the later nineteenth century, on the palm oil trade that increasingly replaced it.

When the slave trade gave way to the "legitimate" trade in cash crops, the same parts of the coast, with their hinterlands, remained commercially dominant; and in the colonial era, the Gold Coast and Nigeria continued to monopolize the trade with Europe, accounting for nearly two-thirds of the total external trade of West Africa. These two regions, then, were points of concentration of the cash economy, where exchanges with Europe were most intense.

Britain imposed a commercial colonialism on British West Africa which continued the import-export relations established at the beginning of the nineteenth century, in which primary products—mainly agricultural products grown for the purpose—were exported, and manufactured goods—mainly textiles, liquor, and utensils—were imported. But in the colonial period the volume of trade increased dramatically, and the colonial administrations laid down structures, designed to facilitate this exchange to Europe's benefit, which transformed West African society and created the new culture from which concert party and Yorùbá popular theatre arose. These structures included the administrative hierarchy, located in large towns and employing educated Africans as lower civil servants; public works, notably railway and road building, which involved the recruitment of large numbers of wage laborers, and greatly increased the speed and volume of movement in and out of the newly expanding cities; and the education system, based upon existing mission schools, which the colonial governments undertook to regulate, thus creating a national grid of institutions offering standardized curricula and qualifications. This played a major part in the enlargement of the tiny, acculturated educated élite that had dominated the social life of nineteenth-century coastal cities like Lagos and Cape Coast. As most of the schools continued to be owned and run by the churches, missionization intensified and conversion to Christianity came to be associated not only with literacy but with paid employment and the modern sector.

Colonialism thus accelerated the formation of new classes: the class of cash-cropping farmers; the small, highly educated African bureaucratic élite; and between them, an amorphous, urban "intermediate class," made up of wage laborers, artisans, traders, providers of services of all kinds, low-paid civil servants, employees of big trading companies: the domain where the formal sector dissolves into the informal sector and everyone is hustling to survive, combining two or three occupations, over-occupied yet "underemployed." It was from this intermediate sector that modern West African popular culture emerged. Popular art, popular music, and popular fiction as well as popular theatre were all products of it.

It was only in the later stages of the colonial period, however—in the late 1940s and especially in the 1950s—that the concert party and popular theatre succeeded in establishing themselves as genuinely popular forms. Four interrelated factors help to account for this moment of expansion and takeoff: the postwar economic boom, which expanded the sector of paid employees and put cash into the pockets of farmers, waged workers, and entrepreneurs alike; the enormous expansion of the cities; the remarkable growth of the education system, especially at primary level; and the wave of anticolonial popular nationalism that led up to independence for Ghana in 1957, and for Nigeria and Togo in 1960.

Until after World War II, colonialism had been run on a shoestring. The Depression, combined with a deliberate policy of financial noninter-vention, had prevented major development investment in the colonies. In the ten years after the war, however, the selling price of primary products rose spectacularly, increasing the value of exports sixfold. The volume of imports increased correspondingly. People had cash to spend. Govern-ment had the means, and also the will—with the advent of postwar so-cialist regimes in Europe—to plan development policies and to provide services. They undertook extensive public works, notably the building of railways and roads. Cash-crop farmers and commercial firms, as well as government, greatly increased their workforce of wage laborers. As the availability of paid work and urban amenities exerted a stronger attrac-tion, West African urbanization accelerated, and in the 1950s and 1960s was the fastest in the world. Between 1948 and 1960, the population of Accra increased from 124,000 to 388,000; that of Lagos, in roughly the same period (1952-1963), from 333,000 to over a million (Gugler and Flanagan 1978:41). In a little over ten years, then, both these cities trebled in size.

The city, however, was not cut off from the rural hinterland. The Yorùbá-speaking area of Nigeria had been urbanized since long before colonization; and while the cities grew enormously in the colonial period, they retained their web of relationships with smaller towns, villages, and farm hamlets. Even salaried workers in the city tended to keep a farm in the background, and interaction between urban-based and rural-based people was seamless and continuous. In Ghana, although urban workers were less involved in farming, there was continual movement between rural and urban areas, with extensive transmission of money, goods, and ideas (Caldwell 1969). As the cities exploded in the 1940s and 1950s, then, they influenced the whole population: everyone was to some degree urban-oriented, increasing numbers of rural people had close relatives living in the cities, and most people had visited or stayed there.

One reason for migration to the city was the search for the kind of work appropriate to a school-leaver. Although most migrants did not in the end manage to secure white-collar jobs, education was seen as the key to progress and to a better life. The belief in and demand for education was one of the most powerful forces of the period. One of the principal planks in the programs of both the Action Group in the Western Region of Nigeria and the Convention People's Party in the Gold Coast was the expansion of education. The 1950s saw a phenomenal increase in the numbers of children attending primary school. In Western Nigeria, the proportion of children aged 5–14 attending primary school increased from 35 percent in 1954 to 90 percent in 1960, almost reaching the proclaimed goal of universal primary education in the space of six years (Fafunwa 1974). The demand for education was so avid—in Ghana as well as Nigeria—that, when the government did not move fast enough, thousands of do-it-yourself schools were established by local communities to fill the gap (Fafunwa 1974; McWilliam 1959).

The combination of the anger and resentment of the Depression years and the soaring expectations of the postwar boom years created an active, popular, anticolonial nationalism, based on the urgent demand for self-rule and a share of the good things of life. In most of West Africa, the 1940s was a period of political unrest, the 1950s a period of swift political mobilization, formation of political parties, elections, local and regional self-government, and preparation for independence. In Nigeria, the 1950s also saw the rapid ethnicization of politics—which had previously been national and to some extent pan-African—in response to the Richards and Macpherson Constitutions of 1946 and 1951, which set up the Nigerian state on regional and ethnic lines. With this ethnicization of political identities came a strong ethnic cultural nationalism, which in western Nigeria has fueled and informed the Yorùbá popular theatre throughout its history.

Economic boom, urbanization, education, and nationalism created the conditions in which commercial popular theatres could take off; they also imprinted these theatres' outlook through and through.

The expanding cities provided both the practical base for theatre companies' activities and an ideological landscape. They were cities of migrants, heterogeneous and polyglot populations, with a bias toward youth and toward males. They were sites of entrepreneurship and innovation, the locus of new kinds of work, the only place where people with education could realize their potential. In colonial cities cash had to be spent, and people got used to paying for what had once been taken for granted: food, housing, even water on occasion. They also got used to paying for entertainment, and this was what made the professional concert party and popular theatre possible. Modern popular theatre, unlike the oral performances and masquerade theatres of tradition, sold tickets at the door. It was a commercial enterprise, bringing together crowds of people most of whom did not know each other, and who shared a common space only by virtue of being willing to pay for admission. In the hotel courtyards, community halls, open-air cinemas, and football stadiums that were the sites of this colonial popular culture, strangers collectively experienced a staging of their common preoccupations: preoccupations with modernity, money, the city, gender relations, and how to live a good life in a changed world. When Ghanaian concert shows were taken on tour to rural areas, the performers and audiences often remembered each other: the bandsmen sometimes had relationships with local women, the leader might know the proprietor of the hall, and the "pioneer" man would do research on local gossip so as to be able to include topical references in the play. Nonetheless, part of their appeal was that they were *not* part of the local community: they came from outside, brought news and fashions from the city, and addressed their audiences as a paying public rather than as neighbors and kinspeople.

Modern commercial entertainment was not only made possible by the growth of the cities with their wage-earning populations, it was also very often *about* the city, articulating ambivalent responses to the attractions and dangers of urban life.

The culture of progress through education was not confined to the classroom. Popular culture was permeated with notions of educational self-improvement. Onitsha pamphlets (which had their counterparts in Ìbàdàn, Òṣogbo, and Accra) were often written by schoolboys, for a wider audience which included "the new literate class of elementary and grammar-school boys and girls, low-level white-collar workers, primary-school teachers, literate and semi-literate traders, mechanics, taxi-drivers and, above all, . . . the numerous products of adult education classes and evening schools . . ." (Obiechina 1972:10–11). The pamphlets contained a promise of useful factual knowledge and an expanded English vocabulary. Many Ghanaian and Nigerian popular actors first became interested in theatre through taking part in school plays and concerts; in Nigeria the connection persisted in their professional lives, for most theatre companies relied on schools to provide a large proportion of their audiences. Though concert party and Yorùbá popular theatre were unscripted, improvised forms, they were yoked, ambiguously but vitally, with literacy, an orientation which had profound effects on the actors' notion of what a play is (see Barber 1995).

The concert parties of Ghana and Togo, and the popular theatre of western Nigeria, thus had their origins in the old coastal trading cultures with their long-standing flair for innovation and entertainment. But they did not spread their wings as great popular forms—accessible and magnetically attractive to large numbers of people—until they were lifted by the surging currents of urbanization, nationalism, and education in the cash-rich boom years of the 1950s. Formed by these forces, they also reflected upon them, spoke of them, gave voice to the urgent curiosity about, and the resilient will to get the better of, the drastic changes colonialism brought. In the 1960s and 70s they reached their peak of popularity and creativity. They articulated popular attitudes during the first independence regimes (which fell in 1963 in Togo, and in 1966 in both Ghana and Nigeria) and through a succession of phases of military and civilian rule. In Nigeria they were floated high on oil wealth in the 1970s and early 80s—a period when they enjoyed an extraordinary expansion, efflorescence, and diversification—only to be dropped with a crash by the collapsing economy around 1985. Those which survived put their efforts more and more into films and, recently, into videos. In Ghana and Togo, concert party has survived the economic crisis. Like other popular cultural forms (see Fabian 1978), they may dwindle as rapidly as they expanded, or they may undergo further transformations that render them unrecognizable. This volume presents one play from the heyday of each of the three theatre movements.

## CONCERT PARTY IN GHANA

### EARLY HISTORY: THE FORMATION OF A GENRE

Since World War II the concert party, a contemporary roving comic opera, has been one of the most vital and dynamic folk arts in Ghana. Like much in the country today this theatre can be considered a syncretic fusion of western and indigenous elements, in this case emerging out of the impact of western musical and dramatic influences mainly on the local Fanti culture of the coast in the first two decades of this century.

The "party" is a professional organization composed of a central core of founder members and an ever-changing periphery of "bandsmen." Until recently most of the groups were all-male, the female parts being played by men in drag. Now, however, many bands have begun to use actresses, and some a mixture of actresses and female impersonators. The concert play is basically a slapstick musical comedy, with a strong seam of pathos and a very prominent moral tone running through it. It is performed in indigenous languages and the drama is shot through with highlife music, which continually punctuates it. The lyrics of the songs are fitted to the needs of the plot, and the climax and moral of the show, which comes at the end, is usually in the form of a highlife song. The actors depict in a humorous and exaggerated way situations and stereotypes of "typical" contemporary Ghanaians, and the content of the plays relates to the everyday problems facing their audience. During the show there is a great deal of audience participation: it opens and closes with music to which the audience dances, and throughout the play itself the audience becomes extremely involved, with much weeping, jeering, and applauding. Often members of the audience will throw coins at an actor, and they may even go up to the stage with gifts of money and food, or stick coins on the moist foreheads of popular actors and musicians.

Much can be learned about the history of concert party from the memories and reminiscences of men like Bob Vans, Bob Johnson, Bob Cole, A. A. Williams, E. K. Nyame, and Bob Ansah, who were all professional performers in the early phases of concert party's history. Between them, their distinctive contributions to the genre helped to establish it as a major popular form. Their comments also reveal something of the insider's experience of concert party.[1]

In its early days in the 1920s, concert party was modeled on imported vaudeville minstrelsy. From the 1930s to the 1950s the genre became progressively "Akanized," for instance by the incorporation of an analogue of the Ananse spider-trickster character and the use of the Akan language. The highlife music with which the concert party was associated also became progressively indigenized. The story of concert party, then, is not one of evolutionary progress from a "traditional," indigenous form to a "modern," foreign-inspired one; rather, it is a story of the increasing indigenization and popularization of what were initially predominantly imported forms. But as they were indigenized, they were perceived as becoming more modern. In the end, the distinctions "imported"/"indigenous," and "traditional"/ "modern" become blurred and porous.

Four western dramatic influences appear to have been important to the emergence of concert party. Particularly significant, as the name suggests, were the school "concerts" performed throughout the colonial period on Empire Day (May 24) after a school fife-band parade around the town: indeed many famous concert actors' careers began with these shows. Second, the idea of having a raised platform as a stage, separating the actors from the audience, came both from these school shows and from "cantata," church-organized morality plays. A third dramatic influence was the silent films which started appearing in Ghana before the First World War. Particularly relevant to the birth of concert were burlesque/vaudeville films such as those of Charlie Chaplin. Fourth, just after the First World War, African American humor, music, and drama were brought to the coastal towns by the comedians Glass and Grant and by black American sailors.

Concert party in Ghana started as a one-man variety show performed for the élite. Its first generally recognized proponent was Teacher Yalley, the headmaster of a Sekondi elementary school, who started acting at his school's Empire Day concerts in 1918.[2] Yalley used to joke, sing, and dance, wearing fancy clothes, wigs, a false moustache, and makeup like a black and white minstrel's. His shows, which he subsequently took to several of the coastal Fanti towns, were in English and expensive to get into, the tickets costing between five and ten shillings each; consequently the audience was mostly the educated upper crust of the towns. The show would start with a hired brass band marching around the town, "campaigning," ending outside the theatre. Inside, Yalley then performed his comedy sketches supported by Harrison on pedal organ and a jazz drummer on trap drums; the music would be ragtime, foxtrots, and waltzes.

Other performers emerged, among them the Sierra Leoneans Colinwood Williams and Lawrence Nicol (who also in the 1920s ran a band in Sierra Leone called the Dapa Dan Jazz Band: see Horton 1984), and the Ga actors A. A. Williams and Marbel. Williams and Marbel became very well known. They retained the variety-act format, but added many new touches, inspired by visiting American vaudeville performers. There was a local entrepreneur, a Mr. Alfred Ocansey from Ada—a film distributor, and the owner of the Palladium cinema hall in Accra and Arkhurst Hall in Sekondi—who used Williams and Marbel's comedy act. In 1923 Ocansey brought over a white American tap dancer called Gene Fenneran for six months. Fenneran was extremely fat, but he could perform dexterous dances on a small round table, and he taught Williams to do the same. Even more influential, however, were Glass and Grant, a married couple who in all likelihood were African American. Ocansey brought them to the Gold Coast from Liberia, where they had been touring, in 1924. They stayed, performing vaudeville shows, until 1926, when they moved on to Nigeria. Like Teacher Yalley's shows these were high-class affairs, with a ten-and-six entrance fee, which would include a silent film before the act and a dance afterwards. Glass was made up as a minstrel, and he and his wife, Grant, would joke, dance, and sing ragtimes. Both (Colinwood) Williams and Nicol and (A. A.) Williams and Marbel understudied and performed with Glass and Grant, and continued on their own after the departure of Glass and Grant. A. A. Williams joined Glass and Grant's chorus. He considers that they had the most profound effect on his style. After they had left, he said,

> We had a troupe of twenty boys and girls of which I was the leader and the men were dressed in white flannel trousers with blue blazers, straw hats and a black bow-tie. Our plays ran for a week at a time and were mostly brought from America—I remember one we did was called "Cocoa Birthday" and we all sat down and made cocoa and everybody

had a cup drinking . . . and then all the chorus boys and girls came together to dance. Glass, he was always in flannel trousers, tailcoat and top hat or bowler—and with white paint around his mouth. The lady she rouged her lips and cheeks . . . if only you could see her—a tall slim woman. She was on the stage in the States; they came out here as qualified artists. We used a full jazz-kit—first of all on the piano was an African, and he left and Bobby Green came from Manchester, he could play the piano with the heel of his shoe . . . a damn good player. Also we had a drummer, Villas, and a saxophonist, Afuri, and the music was all ragtime pieces like "Alexander's ragtime band," "Nothing could be finer than to be in Carolina," "Hard hearted Hannah" and "Gold-diggers of Broadway." . . . It was really the same thing as music hall.

Williams said that he used to play the guitar, mandolin, and banjo and put on short plays with his partner.

He [Glass] put up a play called "I Fear No Ghosts." One man was the ghost and two of us, myself and Marbel (later replaced by Bob Banner-man), we were sitting down and I was telling him that if a ghost came I wouldn't fear—then all of a sudden a hand taps me on the shoulder—it was a ghost and I started shaking and then Marbel turned around and we ran away. The ghost was left on the stage shouting "I'll kill 'em, I'll kill 'em." Then I come in backwards and Marbel is coming backwards and we bang into one another and run away. I was thinking he was the ghost and he was thinking the same, but there were only the two of us. For this show I wore a short white piqué coat with bow tie and cummer-bund and with white around the mouth. We used the Palladium's band and later when the Accra Orchestra was formed [circa 1930] Yeboah Mensah [E. T. Mensah's older brother] came in on a trumpet. We used to do American numbers and never used highlifes (although a few were played at the dance at the end of the night's show). . . . We and Glass and Grant used background drawings which were changed up and down [i.e., scenery].

Williams also made the following comment:

I learnt my technique from the pictures and when Glass and Grant came we were able to polish up our act. Then when Bob Johnson, Dadson and Charlie Turpin used to come and see me [at the Optimism Club] they got some of their ideas from me.

This mention of films is important, as both A. A. Williams and Bob Johnson—one of the greatest early concert actors—stress the effect these had on their acting style. According to A. A. Williams, the very first motion picture was brought to the country by Mr. Sobey Quarshie in 1908, who showed it with lantern-slide shows at Azuma house in Jamestown. This was discontinued the same year due to the outbreak of bubonic plague in Accra, but silent movies appeared again during the First World War and by the early 1920s were showing at Papa Grant's cinema, Bartholomew's cinema, the Palladium, and Edward Taylor's Merry Villas—all in Accra—and the Arkhurst in Sekondi.

So by the mid-1920s concerts, in English and accompanied by dance-band music, were being staged in the coastal towns by Teacher Yalley, Glass and Grant, and Williams and Marbel. There were two foci, the ports of Sekondi and Accra. The concert parties were staged in English for a literate, affluent, and urban black audience—described by A. A. Williams as wearing evening suits, bow ties, and evening gowns. But in the same period, the 1920s, a new development was taking place, instigated by the famous concert comedian (Bob) Ishmael Johnson: the beginning of a popular concert party accessible to ordinary people.

As a boy, Johnson had tried constantly to get into Yalley's shows, only to be turned away again and again, for he was considered to be too young to attend. He finally managed to see a show in 1927, and recalls that it lasted three hours, finishing after midnight, and that the audience was "official people and gentlemen" including some Europeans. His own acting career[3] started at his Methodist school in Sekondi where he and some of his friends would stage shows after the Empire Day parades. By 1922 these schoolboys were calling themselves the Versatile Eight, the core members being J. B. Ansah, who played the gentleman role, C. B. Hutton, his "wife," and Bob, their steward and joker. Music was supplied by members of the school orchestra and Bob remembers that two of their songs were "Don't Do That to That Poor Pussy-cat" and "Minnie the Moocher." He also said that he got a lot of his ideas from the seamen who frequented the Optimism Club opposite his parents' house. Kru seamen from Liberia would sometimes sing sea-shanties and "Dagomba" high-lifes in pidgin English, accompanied by guitar and musical saw. African American sailors played on banjos, harmonicas, and accordions such numbers as the slow foxtrot "Moonlight Becomes You." According to Bob they had a deep influence on him, and "I used to copy their dancing, singing and joking." The Versatile Eight was a very different sort of affair from the concerts put on by Yalley and Williams and Marbel; it was composed of schoolboys and the tickets were a mere 3d or 6d.

In 1930 Bob finished elementary school and, with his friends Hutton and Ansah, went professional. Even then, however, they charged only one or two shillings admission, and were thus able to attract a larger and more popular audience than their forerunners. They decided to call themselves the Two Bobs, the reason being that the African American seamen in Sekondi always called them by this nickname. Hutton, the female impersonator, became known as the Carolina Girl. They took the shows on tour around the local towns. They were announced by a masked bell-ringer, who went about the town advertising by means of a sandwich board, and when the theatre was filled the show would start. The program would be as follows:

| | |
|---|---|
| 1. The Opening Chorus | a quickstep to which the three of them would dance |
| 2. The In | one of them would sing a "ragtime" |
| 3. The Duet | the Two Bobs would crack jokes |
| 4. The Scene | the play |

The first three items constituted a half-hour introduction; the play proper, which Bob calls the "scene," lasted about an hour. Their music was supplied by Kwese Nsedu, who played "jazz" (trap) drums accompanied by members of a local school orchestra, hired for the night. Bob Johnson explained to John Collins that the term "ragtime" for their music was used in the concert business to cover all the popular western dance-band styles of the time (waltzes, quicksteps, ragtimes, foxtrots, rumbas—in the 1940s—and later mambos).

The Two Bobs toured inland to rural areas, where it became necessary to infuse a certain amount of the Fanti dialect of Akan into the plays in order to communicate with the audience. The play was still mainly in English, but occasional translations into Fanti were added, and, unlike Teacher Yalley and company, the Two Bobs also sang a few highlifes in pidgin English and Fanti. This "Akanization" of the concert party was also enhanced by Bob Johnson's brilliant fusion of the American black minstrel character with that of the mischievous Ananse—the spider character of traditional Akan folklore. Akan culture has a wealth of spider stories (anansesem) in which the narrator uses different voices for the different characters and sometimes even dresses up as well. Bob Johnson himself was very definite about the effect on his career of these stories, which he used to listen to as a young boy in Saltpond. This comic combination was so successful that practically every concert comedian since then has called himself "Bob"—a stage character who, like the trickster Ananse, is an ambiguous, transgressive figure, loved and hated by the audience.

In 1935 Bob left the Two Bobs to join the Axim Trio, which had recently been formed by E. K. Dadson and Charlie Turpin. In many ways the Axim Trio was similar to the Two Bobs. They extended the Two Bobs' practice of touring inland, and continued to add elements in Fanti for the sake of those members of the audience who did not speak English. The "campaigning" was done in the same way, using a bell-ringer, but in addition they would also hire a local brass band or konkoma group.[4] They opened with the same introductory items, but their plays were longer, lasting about two hours, and covered topical social and political themes, history, and popular mythology. Some of the most popular ones, staged between 1935 and the mid-1950s, included *The Coronation of King George VI, The Bond of 1844, The Ten-Foot Man, The Downfall of Adolf Hitler, Kwame Nkrumah Will Never Die, Love Is the Sweetest Thing,* and *Nkrumah Is a Mighty Man.* Besides two trips to Nigeria and extensive tours of Ghana, including the north, the Axim Trio also visited Liberia, Ivory Coast, and Sierra Leone.

By World War II the élitist "vaudeville" concert parties had died out, whereas the Axim Trio was becoming more and more popular, and several other concert parties modeled on it had been formed. These were all Fanti, with the exception of Komega's concert, from Keta, which was Ewe and, as we shall see, influenced the development of a parallel Ewe concert party tradition in Togo.

World War II brought a wider-ranging cosmopolitanism to concert. Troops stationed at Accra brought in new ideas, and also provided some of the concerts with a new kind of audience. Bob Ansah, after the Saltpond Trio broke up in 1944, rejoined his old partner Hutton to entertain the soldiers. Concerts were even being performed for the African troops in India, for, between 1943 and 1946, an African Theatre was set up within the West African Frontier Force. Bob Vans was the leader, and with six other Ghanaians and help from other West Africans, they played at the camps and hospitals: the language they used was pidgin English and the music konkoma. Bob also told John Collins that while there he was influenced by black American comedians, in particular their tap dancing and their use of wigs for female impersonators. When Bob came back to Ghana he and some other ex-servicemen formed the Burma Jokers. It was a sign of the times that in 1948 they changed the name to the Ghana Trio, in keeping with the upsurge of nationalism that was then underway.

After the war, and even more in the boom period of the 1950s, many new concert parties were formed. By 1955 there were more than a dozen in operation. It was in the 1950s, also, that a new phase in the formation of concert party began. There were two crucial developments: the highlife band became an integral part of the show, and Akan languages became the principal means of communication.

In the early concert parties of Teacher Yalley in Sekondi and the Accra "vaudeville," highlifes were not much used; even Bob Johnson's less élite Versatile Eight used mainly "ragtime" songs, with only an occasional highlife, sung in Fanti or pidgin English. The Axim Trio, also, used few highlifes in their shows, though the brass bands and konkoma groups they hired to "campaign" for them before their shows did play highlife. Highlife music only became central to the concert play itself when E. K. Nyame formed the Akan Trio, in 1952, out of his highlife guitar band. Since then concert acting and highlife music have become inseparable.

Ghanaian highlife music and dance grew up around the turn of the century and, like the concert party, its initial locale was the coastal Fanti region. It was based on the traditional music of the area, for instance the osibi music of the fisherfolk, changed through assimilation of western musical influences. These included European instruments such as the piano, brass instruments, fifes, the guitar, banjo, harmonica, and concertina, and western musical styles such as sea shanties, hymns, ballroom dance music, and European military marches. The resulting acculturated music became known in the Fanti area as osibisaaba; but other early syncretic styles like adaha, ashiko or asiko (meaning "time": a style originating in Sierra Leone and Nigeria), and timo (a Ga style) also developed among coastal peoples.

It was only in the 1920s that these various acculturated styles became collectively known as "highlife," and by this time there were three distinct types of ensemble playing it. First, there were the brass bands with their "adaha" variety of highlife. Second, there were numerous Akan acoustic guitar bands or "palm wine" groups, the best known of these being that of Kwame Asare, or Jacob Sam, as he was popularly known.[5] Third, there was the large dance orchestra of the interwar period, which besides playing a whole range of popular western music also played highlifes.[6] These large dance orchestras created a very westernized variant of highlife which was aimed at a wealthy African élite audience. Indeed, it was in this milieu that the term "highlife" (i.e., "high class") was coined. From this tradition of large urban orchestras, the smaller postwar highlife dance bands originated, pioneered by E. T. Mensah and his Tempos dance band in the 1950s.

However, it is the guitar band that has become particularly associated with the concert party, and it was the Kwahu musician E. K. Nyame who made this link. He formed a band in 1950, and two years later, encouraged by the Axim Trio's popularity and commercial success, he decided to expand into the concert party business. He formed his Akan Trio and himself learned to play the role of the "gentleman" concert character. The result was a synthesis of highlife and concert, in which the play could be seen as a vehicle for the music at the same time that the music embellished and punctuated the play. Highlifes were already being sung in Akan languages, and E. K. Nyame's second decisive innovation was to carry the use of the indigenous language over into the dialogue of the play. For the first time, audiences who spoke no English could watch an entire play in an Akan language.

The highlife-and-Akan recipe was an instant success. Within a few years other guitar bands set up as concert parties, and, conversely, concert parties already in existence augmented their musical section of drummer and harmonium-organ to a full-scale guitar band (guitars, standing bass, trap-drums, and, by the 1950s, Afro-Cuban percussion). By 1954 (the year of the Jaguar Jokers' formation), there were ten concert parties in existence, based in various provincial towns in southern Ghana but playing throughout the country. As a result of this spread into the hinterland, the move to Akan languages was reinforced. When in 1960 a concert party union called the Ghana National Entertainments Association (GNEA) was created, all twenty-eight founder members were staging their plays in various Akan languages—and all were utilizing guitar bands to provide highlife music.

The concert party format was now established: a highlife band which would play for the audience to dance to for several hours, before the show started; an introductory sequence of dances, comic monologues, and sketches; a play, shot through with highlifes—sung by the characters and accompanied by the band, still sitting at the side of the stage—followed by a final session of highlife dance music for the audience.

The 1960s and 1970s were the concert party's heyday. In the 1970s there were at least fifty concert parties in the country, and they represented the most important development in contemporary Ghanaian drama. The vitality of the concert parties and their importance in contemporary Ghanaian life led to an upsurge of interest in them by local television producers, filmmakers, and dramatists. Official recognition of the concert party was given when the Arts Council put on a National Festival of Concert Parties in 1973. Twenty-four groups staged plays at the Arts Council's Headquarters in Accra.

The development of concert party from its earliest stages to its high point in the 1960s and 1970s can be summed up as a process of democratization with diffusion. In the early period, in the 1920s, a vaudeville-style show had been pioneered by Teacher Yalley and duos like Williams and Marbel. It was performed in English, in posh venues, for élite audiences. The second stage was the popularization of the concert party, begun by Bob Johnson in the early 1930s with the Two Bobs and continued, even more influentially, by the Axim Trio. Admission fees were lower; the concert party toured rural areas; less wealthy and less educated audiences were attracted; and to accommodate them the English was mixed with some Fanti and pidgin. The third stage in the 1950s, for which the prototype was E. K. Nyame's Akan Trio, involved the incorporation of the highlife band as an integral part of the play and the use of Akan languages throughout.

Concert party plays, in the high period of the 1960s and 1970s, revolved around permutations of a recognizable and fairly restricted set of characters and themes. The central character was often a victim—an orphan, mistreated by his or her stepparents or other relatives; a faithful wife, mistreated by a husband who is besotted by glamorous loose women; or even a well-to-do man, exploited and drained of his wealth by grasping relatives. The plot almost always involved sudden and complete reversals of fortune: from rags to riches and back; from health and beauty to repellent sickness and back; from respect and popularity to contempt and abandonment and back. Most plays had a "Bob" trickster character—a comic servant or hanger-on who cracked jokes and indulged in horse-play and buffoonery, but who often remained loyal and told the truth when others did not. Occasionally, a supernatural agent intervened to bring the story to its desired conclusion: a dead mother's spirit would act on her orphaned child's behalf, or—as in *Orphan Do Not Glance*, presented in this volume—a devil would appear, only to be defeated by a team of hymn-singing angels. But the plays were firmly planted in the everyday domestic world of contemporary Ghana, with salient reference to cocoa farms, banks, schools, and the Ghana National Lottery!

Concert party evolved a distinctive style and structure as well as standard plots, themes, and moral messages. The form is typically loose-jointed, episodic, and presentational. This can be understood in terms of the convergence of concert party's two paths of development. First there was the model of vaudeville, in which a solo or duo perform a variety of acts and turns—songs, dances, short sketches—with a musical backing supplied by musicians who are extraneous to the team. Teacher Yalley, one of the earliest proponents of Ghanaian concert party, was essentially a one-man show; the Two Bobs and their successor, the Axim Trio, increased the number of showmen but still relied on bands supplied by schools in the towns they visited. The other route was that pioneered by E. K. Nyame and his Akan Trio in 1952, where a fully constituted highlife band added a dramatic entertainment as a vehicle to show off their music. In other words, either a band was added to what was essentially a variety show made up of a sequence of acts, or a show was added to what was essentially a band playing a sequence of musical numbers. The two strands of development merged into the standard concert party which has been in place from the mid-1950s up until today: a flexible amalgam of songs, jokes, and dramatic action. The plots of the concert party plays are linear and extended, but the relationship between the songs and the dramatic dialogue is always uncertain: sometimes existing songs are slotted in even when they do not quite fit the plot. The songs may mention names of characters who are not in the play, or they may tell or allude to entire narratives which are outside the dramatic plot. In other cases, it may be said that the songs "become more meaningful" when provided with a dramatic context. The songs, then, lead the play but do not necessarily develop out of its requirements.

The loose-jointedness of the concert party pervades its entire mode. The plots, as we have seen, are full of sudden and total reversals. The characters themselves sometimes switch—for instance, from being a clown to being a mouthpiece of moral authority—without any rationalization. The representation of time and place is highly nonnatural: the stage does not represent a series of imaginary venues; rather, it remains, throughout, a site from which "acts" are projected. This is a highly opportunistic theatre in which performers may develop their "act" by playing to, and with, the audience, while the rest of the cast await their turn: as, for instance, in the scene in *Orphan Do Not Glance* where the clown Opia leads the audience in verse after verse of a well-known hymn, holding up the action (which has reached a crisis) for an unbelievably long time. The presentational style is strikingly direct: characters simply announce themselves to the audience and tell them the essential features of their character and situation. *Orphan Do Not Glance* opens with the daughter of the house saying: "Hello everybody, I'm the oldest in the family and my younger brother is called King Sam. My parents really tried for me so I managed to reach Form 1. However, since I finished, me and my friend Selena have started roaming for men." The audiences interact constantly with the characters, shouting warnings, expressing pity or disapproval. Members of the audience may—as in *Orphan Do Not Glance*—come right on stage and give money and other gifts to the character they feel most sympathy for. More than this, the audience also participates as a secondary performer. The show begins with a long session of dancing by the audience. In one performance by the City Boys in Accra, in 1990, dozens of dancers—mainly young women—climbed onto the stage alongside the band during this session and embraced the star, "Black Chinese," in order to be photographed with him by one of the professional Polaroid artists who roamed the auditorium. The band with whom the audience has just been performing remains at the edge of the stage throughout the play. Concert party, then, evolved a distinctive style, which can be understood in terms of its relationship to highlife on the one hand and to the audience on the other.

## PRESENT-DAY CONCERT PARTY

Present-day concert party has undergone further transformations under the pressure of changing musical and theatrical tastes, economic hardship, official intervention, and an internal aesthetic dynamic. The economic problems of the late 1970s and the economic adjustments of the 1980s led to a decline of concert parties and guitar bands. In 1954 there were ten concert parties in Ghana, in 1960 twenty-eight, in 1976 between fifty and sixty (the peak number), but in 1988 only around thirty. One might well ask where have all these concert people gone? Some have died and others, for economic reasons, have moved into the African churches.

In other cases the concert leaders are still around but have no equipment for a band.

Ghana's economic problems have driven a few concert parties out of the country altogether to settle in neighboring African countries, especially Côte d'Ivoire and Nigeria. Many of the Ghana-based concert parties also spend much time in these two countries. Some concert parties and concert musicians are going even further afield, on trips overseas. Since the 1980s, concert bands like Ahenfo, the African Brothers, and Konadu's have regularly toured Europe and North America, as have individual concert musicians like guitarist Eric Agyeman and trumpeter Tommy King. And there are those who stay abroad, like Nana Tuffour and Charles Amoah, both of whom obtained their musical training in Dr. Gyasi's band and who now reside in Germany, where they produce highlife records. One result of this musical exodus is that for the first time in the history of Ghanaian guitar-band highlife, a major new style of music is developing outside of the country. This is the so-called Burger [i.e., Hamburg] Highlife, a fusion of highlife and disco music that is being created by expatriate Ghanaians living in Germany—and which has become a craze with highlife fans back in Ghana.

Concert parties have made several serious attempts to unionize for their own protection and professional advancement. In 1960 Kobina Segoe, a popular magician, organized a union for concert parties called the Ghana National Entertainment Association. Twenty-eight groups were present at the foundation meeting in Accra. One of the stated aims of GNEA was "to stand as supreme promoter for all concerts in order to eliminate middlemen from this field," and the intention was to break the grip of the private promoters by forbidding members to use them without the authority of the union. Other provisions agreed upon by the member concerts show that Ghanaian concert party was conscious of itself as a profession with shared standards, goals, and interests. They undertook to attempt "to boost the reputation of concerts," "to negotiate with overseas coaches to help improve the standard of the Association," "to restrict the entry of foreign or unregistered clubs," "to ask the Ghana Government to introduce and encourage the teaching of play acting in schools and colleges," "to collect copyright of plays with a view to enhancing film acting in Ghana," "to control the theatrical profession as well as the management of affairs of artistes performing on the stage, radio, television, films, and gramophone recordings," and "to provide opportunities for intercourse amongst members and to give facilities for reading literature and delivering lectures. To give benevolent and charitable aid to the aged and distressed members of the Theatrical Profession and to organize annual competitions among its members." Detailed plans were also made for the Association to operate as a mutual aid organization, to protect members from the hardships of an uncertain profession.

Unfortunately, and after such high hopes, the union collapsed, and in 1966 it was finally dissolved by the National Liberation Council, whose policy was to proscribe all members of the Trades Union Congress, since the TUC had been affiliated with President Nkrumah's Convention People's Party. There was no concert party union in Ghana for ten years after this. Then in 1976, over forty concert parties and guitar bands came together to form the Ghana Cooperative Indigenous Musicians Society (GHACIMS), which was formally launched in 1977. For several years GHACIMS existed side by side with a re-formed Musicians Union of Ghana (which had also been dissolved after the 1966 coup) called MUSIGA. In 1979 with the reorganization of MUSIGA and its recognition by the government in 1980, GHACIMS folded and most of its members joined MUSIGA. This repeated effort to unionize reveals both the solidarity and the rivalry between professional groups competing for business.

The most popular of the concert parties operating in Ghana today tend to be famous highlife bands whose records and cassettes are better known than their plays. They draw huge crowds in the open-air cinemas they favor as venues. However, the smaller and less well known bands are facing stiff competition from "mobile spinners" — discos — which can provide an evening's entertainment more cheaply, and also give the youthful audience the original version of the reggae and rock they prefer, rather than "copyright" (foreign hits copied by local bands). This has had two effects: to drive the concert parties more and more into tours of the rural areas, where the competition is less keen; and to inject large doses of African and Caribbean reggae, disco, soul, and funk into the concert's opening session. Even very popular highlife bands (Amakye Dede, the Kumapim Royals, the African Brothers) play these styles almost as much as their own highlife compositions for which they are famous.

Concert party has diversified into television and print. In the 1970s television became a major medium for concert parties. Some established regular series, the first and most famous being Frempong Manso's "Osofo Dadzie," which stars the popular baldheaded comedian Super O.D. (Kwerku Darko). Some groups perform on television in other languages than Akan. The Adabraka Drama Troupe and the Ewa group perform in Ga, while the Tsui Shito group uses Ewe. The most popular current series is "Obra," which began in the early 1980s and stars Ghana's most famous concert actress, Grace Omaboe.

The concert parties have adapted their format and acting style to meet the requirements of television. Television plays tend to be much shorter than the live performances. They include few songs and no instrumental accompaniment, but make a much greater use of stage props, occasionally including real location shots. There is extremely rapid switching from scene to scene, with the use of different camera crews ready and waiting in the various studio mock-up locations. All the concert groups that have established long-running television series have female as well as male performers, and a number of actresses have risen to prominence through this avenue. The television-oriented concert groups never feature characters in black-and-white minstrel makeup. This adaptation to the medium of television has spilled over into live performances, so that, for example, television-oriented groups have abandoned black-and-white minstrel makeup even in their stage plays, dressing their Bobs in funny masks with false noses, moustaches, and spectacles instead. But in other ways two distinct styles are maintained. For example, the Jaguar Jokers' 1974 television play "Opia in Court" was based on a single plot idea: Opia, the "Bob" character, orders four bottles of beer in a bar; after they have been consumed by some "good-time girls" who come to his table he refuses to pay, claiming that he ordered "four bottles," and so will pay for the bottles but not the beer they contained. He is taken to court, but escapes by singing a song which induces the entire court to get up and dance. The stage version in 1976 was much more elaborate. It not only extended the play to three times its television length, but also introduced plot changes which made the story more melodramatic. Opia is accused of killing someone rather than just tricking a barman out of some beer, and he is saved not by dancing his way out of court but by two fetish priests who are able to trace the true killer. The culprit meets his doom when a spectacular ten-foot white goddess or Mammy Water appears, illuminated by dim red lights, and kills him.

Besides television, another new medium for concert parties is comic magazines, made up of a series of photographs from a concert play with the dialogue incorporated in balloon form and in a vernacular language. This innovation seems to have originated in Nigeria with the Yorùbá photoplay magazine *Atọ́ka*, dating from the late 1960s, which serialized the plays of Yorùbá popular theatre groups. The idea was introduced to Ghana in the late 1970s when Akan comic strips came on the market.

Official sponsorship of concert party hastened other changes. The use of women instead of female impersonators and a concomitant "naturalistic," "true-to-life" style of acting have been encouraged by university- or government-led "development theatre" projects as well as by television. The Workers' Brigade Concert Party, founded in the early 1960s by the Nkrumah government, used actresses from the beginning. A drama troupe named Kusum Agromma was soon afterward established to be the resident group of the National Drama Studio, set up under Nkrumah and financed by the government. In the mid-1960s the director was Efua Sutherland, the well-known playwright, who was also a lecturer at the Institute of African Studies at Legon. They modeled themselves exactly on concert party, except for two deviations: they used actresses for the female parts, and they sometimes staged propaganda plays with government-sponsored messages, for instance on family planning. When the group disbanded in the mid-1980s, several of its actresses, including the great star Adelaide Buabeng, went into television, giving further visibility to female players. The government continued to sponsor drama troupes. The Adehyeman Theatre Group, for instance, was founded under the leadership of Cecilia Anderson in 1989 to assist with an adult literacy drive. This group has nearly as many women performers as men. Some of their plays have very few traditional concert party features, being explicitly didactic (rather than merely moralistic), almost without musical episodes, and staged with an illusionistic rather than presentational style of acting (e.g., lifelike "crowd" scenes with large numbers of actors, rather than the token, stylized old man who may represent public opinion in concert party), and without the peculiar blend of pathos and buffoonery which is the hallmark of concert party. At other times, however, they stage shows which are definitely "concert party" in style.

Under the influence of these pressures and interests, concert party seems to be in a new phase of transition. Many groups use a mixture of actresses and female impersonators for women's roles, and a mixture of highly stylized and quite "naturalistic" modes of characterization. This mixture might be thought unsettling, but audiences appear to accept it. One audience member observed that actresses were better than men in drag, because they were more "perfect" and more "true to life," and he explained the presence of the female impersonators by the bands' inability to afford more actresses. Accompanying this increased, if patchy, "naturalism" has been a reduction in the frequency of highlife songs in the course of the play. The initial dance music has been increased, often lasting for four or even five hours before the play begins, but the plays themselves often boast only ten numbers instead of the thirty or forty characteristic of the shows of twenty years ago, such as *Orphan Do Not Glance.*

Another change fostered by government sponsorship has been the tentative beginning of a scripted theatre. Bob Vans, now employed by the Arts Council, specializes in writing commissioned plays for concert parties. He writes a fairly full script in English; then, he says, "I go to the group and work with them in Twi to develop it." The final performance is in Twi, and the play belongs exclusively to the group that commissioned it. Bob Vans does not go on tour with them, and they are free to add to, adapt, and vary the play as they wish; but clearly their improvisation is conditioned by the memory, or at least the notion, of the original script. Vans has a special relationship with one concert party, the Abibiman, also employed by the

Arts Council (in fact, they all live together in a sprawling compound behind the Arts Council buildings in Accra), but in the last few years he has
also written plays for the Okukuseku Concert Party, Professor Abraham's,
Senior Eddie Donkoh, Okos Band, and Waterproof Concert Party.

One remarkable change has been the tremendous elaboration and
extension of the plots of most concert party plays and the effort put into
creating amazing visual effects—especially in the form of supernatural
monsters and weird, hideous, gigantic spirits. Plots of byzantine twists
and turns, reversals and surprises, are concocted. Just when you think it's
ending—around four in the morning—a new spirit intervenes and the
plot gets a new lease on life. This greater extension has not meant a
departure from the loose-jointed, episodic style of the old concert party
with its vaudeville roots. The long plots are coherent in that they trace the
fortunes of a definite set of characters and usually—though not always[7]—
manage to end up with the good characters rewarded and the bad ones
punished. But they are not organically integrated. Changes of fortune are
entirely adventitious, usually brought about by the intervention of spirits,
and could go on indefinitely. The same basic situations are kept—the
orphan, the cruel relative, the truth-telling clown, the dead mother who
intervenes from beyond the grave—but each story is as it were doubled
or trebled.

### AFRICAN AMERICAN INFLUENCES

The hybridity that characterizes all modern popular culture in
West Africa is exhibited in peculiarly concentrated form in concert party.
Not only did highlife music itself emerge from a situation of centuries of
cultural interaction between European military and commercial visitors,
West Indian regiments, Liberian and other West African seamen, and migrants from the hinterland of the Gold Coast, but also the history of the
constitution of the concert party form is a history of continued, recent
incorporation of imported elements accompanied by an increasing dose of
the indigenous. What is most interesting about this is that the "imported"
elements the concert party founders selected were often themselves the
product of cultural hybridization. The black culture of the New World had
a formative and catalytic impact on concert party. This black influence from
the Americas completes in turn a transatlantic feedback cycle; West African
culture being transplanted in the New World during the diaspora of the
slave trade and returning to Africa in transmuted form over the last hundred years or so.[8] This feedback has had a broad effect on Africa; for
instance, the freed slaves who were returned from Latin America to Africa
in the 1880s brought with them the so-called Brazilian architecture and
musical instruments found in coastal West Africa, and black Caribbean and

African American thinkers like Marcus Garvey and W.E.B. Dubois made a decisive contribution to early West African nationalism.[9]

In highlife music, too, there has been a constant assimilation of black ideas from the Americas. Highlife reveals traces of the impact of West Indian brass band musicians, associated with the West Indian Rifles regiment, on the birth of Ghanaian "adaha" music in the 1880s; and the Ghanaian musicologist A. A. Mensah considers that certain characteristics of piano highlife were introduced to it after the turn of the century by ragtime sheet music. Then during the interwar period South American music styles were incorporated into highlife via the large westernized ballroom orchestras, and since World War II there have been the influences of swing, Afro-Caribbean music, rock 'n' roll (i.e., black rhythm 'n' blues), soul, funk, disco, and reggae.

The same sort of "feedback" process has taken place with the concert party, although this is not to suggest that it is simply an offshoot of American minstrelsy and vaudeville. As we have seen, the Ghanaian theatre has been woven out of many other strands as well: traditional Akan ceremonies, dances, and Ananse stories; school Empire Day concerts; early movies and Bible-inspired cantata plays. Nevertheless African American ideas have been a direct agent in the development of the concert party, the most obvious example being those introduced by the black American team of Glass and Grant, for even after their departure for Nigeria in 1926 their minstrel and vaudeville acts were continued in Accra by Williams and Marbel and by the Sierra Leoneans Williams and Nicol. Of the early films imported by Ollivant into Ghana, slapstick comedy had a particularly great sway on the concert actors, and through this medium influences from black minstrelsy and vaudeville percolated into the country, although, ironically enough, usually performed by white actors made up as black-and-white minstrels—for instance Al Jolson. One thus finds the paradox of Ghanaian actors copying white actors who in turn were imitating African American art and artistes; for minstrelsy and to a lesser extent vaudeville were both based on the humor, dress, music, dances, and dialect of black plantation slaves and workers of the southern United States.

Yet another Ghanaian contact with Afro-American minstrel humor and music was, as Bob Johnson points out, at the seamen's Optimism Club in Sekondi. And also of note is that all the dance music of the early concert parties was referred to as "ragtime," and ragtime is the music of American minstrelsy.

It may be that concert party was especially hospitable to elements of African American drama (e.g., the minstrelsy of both black and white Americans) because of the parallels between them. Both are forms of "lowbrow" musical comedy, performed without a script and dealing in a satirical way with the current problems of their newly urbanized and polyglot audiences. For just as Ghana has over thirty languages and became urbanized in this century, so too did minstrelsy grow up in mid-nineteenth century United States, a period when there was a great influx of immigrants from many different countries and rapid urbanization took place. Both are theatres of stereotyped characters. Minstrelsy and vaudeville have their rustic plantation "negroes" Jim Crow and Gumbo Chaff and their sophisticated urbanites Zip Coon and Dandy Jim; Ghanaian concert party has its rural "bushman" and the young urban literates like Kofi Smart and Tommy Fire.

## SOCIAL CHANGE

Heterogeneous and popular, accommodating influxes of foreign elements while continually indigenizing, concert party was highly responsive to social change and a key agent in encapsulating and disseminating the new ideas arising from it. The concert party plays spoke of the most pressing concerns of the colonial, urbanizing Gold Coast population: dealing with political consciousness, social mobility, and urban socialization.

Political commentaries and social criticism in the form of musical and dramatic satire and masquerades have long been a feature of West Africa, and this has been carried through into the new syncretic performing arts. In the case of the Ghanaian concert party, there were a number of plays that came out in open support of the independence struggle: the Axim Trio's plays *Kwame Nkrumah Will Never Die* and *Nkrumah Is a Mighty Man* have already been mentioned. Another play that the Axim Trio staged in 1950 was *Kwame Nkrumah Is Greater Than Before*, part of the gate from which went to Nkrumah's Convention People's Party's funds. In 1952 S. Sackey performed a concert called *Bo Hu Ko Ono Aba* (Wait Until Your Turn Comes) which defended Nkrumah's constitutional reforms. In the late 1950s Nkrumah's government itself began to set up guitar bands and concert parties to act as organs of C.P.P. propaganda, such as the Worker's Brigade band and concert party.

However, openly political plays have been rather the exception in Ghana, and it would be more true to say that reflections on the existing order have been in the form of social criticism and morality tales, with the plays depicting in an exaggerated and amusing way the contemporary problems of their audience. For instance, a common theme in the plot of concert plays concerns the effects of social stratification, such as poverty and unemployment, crime and money doubling, corruption and nepotism. Another theme of the plays is related to the problems caused by rapid urbanization, such as the loss of respect for traditional authority, prostitution, the breakup of the extended family (divorce, inheritance disputes, the plight of orphans) and the key role of modern education.

Indeed, one of the most popular concert parties today, Osofo Dadzie, specializes in plots of social criticism—with the support of the government. A 1970s example was its television play about corruption and inefficiency in a government institution, the hospital.

Although the concert started off as a "posh" affair of the coastal cities, within a short time it became, as already noted, also oriented toward the provincial towns and villages. Thus these roving theatres, by bringing new ideas, fashions, and the attractions of city life to even the most remote areas, acted on the rural audiences as a mechanism of urban pull. The concert party is especially important in this context of rural-urban movement when one realizes that television and rural cinema are fairly recent developments in Ghana. The concert parties represented the city ambivalently: as a dangerous place, likely to cause ruin to the unwary, but also one where "good-time girls" and other luxuries were to be found, the source of everything fashionable. The name of the Jaguar Jokers concert party captures this fascination perfectly. Mr. Bampoe, the leader of the Jaguar Jokers, chose this name because "a jaguar is a wild animal—you can't make it laugh—but we can. In those days we had Jaguar cars and to be 'Jaguar' meant to be fine or modern. For instance a 'Jaguar' man or woman was of high class." Jaguar, pronounced "jagwah," is one of the many words that have entered into Ghanaian popular language to represent the quintessence of the modern urban life.[10] Like the city itself, a jaguar is both fine and dangerous.

The concert party has an influence on urban socialization, as comic actors are popular not only in the rural areas but also in the ever-expanding cities, composed mainly of newly arrived rural migrants. So rather than playing for an established and westernized black élite audience, the concert parties now stage shows predominantly for the poor rural migrants who have flocked to the towns and cities from all over the country—and even from other countries. One result is that, although concert parties still perform mainly in the Akan languages (such as Fanti, Twi, and Akwapim), they also have portions in other languages (like Ga, Ewe, or Hausa) depending on their audiences. This was a trend which, as we shall see, was taken even further by concert parties in Togo. In the modern heterogeneous urban context, then, concerts, plays, and songs act as a humorous and cathartic means for releasing social-cum-psychological tensions and as a medium for cross-cultural communication—a dramatic lingua franca. At the same time the plays, in portraying the different characters and situations found in city life, also act as an agent of socialization for first-generation town dwellers. The concert parties educate their audiences to the complex and multiple roles met with in modern life, including the different ways these can clash, or be reconciled, with traditional life.

## CONCERT PARTY IN TOGO

In Ghana, the concert party was mainly an Akan event. Concert party songs could be heard over the radio throughout its area of diffusion, which covered the entire Akan-speaking zone (Fanti-Akwapim-Asante). But the Ewe-speaking zone, which started east of the Volta River in Ghana and extended into Togo, had its own history of concert parties.

### ORIGINS

In 1940 an Ewe-speaking concert party—Komega's Trio—was formed in Keta, and signaled the extension of concert to the eastern side of the Volta river. By the 1950s, concert party had reached the hinterland of Lomé, around Kpalime within the cocoa-growing area. The Kpalime group, the Togo Trio, was still in operation in the early 1970s. But it was through the success of a group called Happy Star in the capital city of Lomé that concert received its main impetus in Togo, as we shall see in chapter 4.

Ewe culture and Ewe language were a medium of unity among people who had been thoroughly divided. Following the German defeat in 1918, Togoland became a Trust territory of the League of Nations and was divided between French and British administrations. Britain nonetheless retained in the Gold Coast colony the coastal strip where Keta was located. The Ewe people were thus divided, until the independence of Ghana, into three territorial entities: the Gold Coast, British Togoland, and French Togoland, to which we could add the French colony of Dahomey, home of the eastern branch of the Ewe language—called Fon by the French—as described by Dietrich Westermann in his *Grammatik der Ewe Sprache* (1907). In 1940, after the collapse of France, British and French Togoland became even more divided since French Togoland was controlled by Vichy France, a declared adversary of Britain. Ewe traders found a stiffer border between their hinterland and the coastal outlet of Lomé, capital of French Togoland. Lomé was situated on the border between French Togoland and the Gold Coast, which had become their main gateway for exports to the rest of the world. Access to the Gold Coast had been made possible by the railway line, extending from Kpalime, situated a hundred miles inland. In this context of erratic divisions, Ewe nationalism was born. In the 1940s and 1950s it was to become a major movement, appealing to the world through the United Nations, which had now replaced the League of Nations as the supervisor of the Trusteeship mandate. The Ewe leaders, united under Sylvano Olympio, himself born in Dahomey, campaigned first for the unification of all Ewe under British administration, and later—realizing that this goal was unattainable—for the independence of Togo under southern (Ewe) leadership. It was too late, however: in the referendum of 1956, British Togoland elected to be united to the Gold Coast, in the hope of attaining early independence in 1957 with Ghana, under Nkrumah. French Togoland became autonomous in 1958 and an independent country—Togo—in 1960, under the leadership of Olympio, the Ewe leader. When Olympio was assassinated in 1963, power switched from the south to the north in Togo; three decades later, nothing has changed.

Intense political activity against a backdrop of cultural nationalism provided ample material for literature and drama. The main foyer of Ewe activity gravitated toward the Gold Coast. Ewe culture and language were promoted in the three years of Olympio's Nationalist government. This was enough to give an impetus to a popular drama, where a literary drama already existed.

## THEATRE IN EWE

The literary theatre in Ewe has a long and interesting history, and even though it did not directly influence the diffusion of concert party, it probably provided a context that was favorable for the appropriation of live theatrical performance by actors.

Kwasi Fiawoo, from Ho in the hinterland of Lomé, wrote two plays in Ewe, the first of which, *Toko Atolia* (1937), won first prize in the International African Institute literary competition. This play is apparently the first written and published in an African language and also in translation, since as early as 1937 a German translation appeared, soon followed by an English one. It is the story of an outcast, Agbedada, a fast-talking playboy, who is ostracized by his own village community, and who prefigures many of the characters of concert party such as Mister Tameklor or Francis the Parisian. These plays were staged by students in seminaries and in religious schools, who were thus exposed to secular drama in their own language. The plays of Fiawoo were literary and sophisticated, but they nevertheless had to be acted, and young Ewe men and women were given a practical demonstration of the potential of their language.

In the early 1940s, another style of theatre was inaugurated when the Reverend Baeta started a religious theatre group in Keta which performed Bible stories in Ewe. He called these plays cantata. In Lomé this genre began in 1946, thanks to Moorhouse Apedoh Amah, who started putting on such plays as *Isaac and Rebecca* and *Joseph and His Brothers*, derived from biblical stories. The genre evolved slowly. Plays based upon real-life situations began to be written, e.g., *Agbalevi*, a satire of the "been-to." Others were adaptations from world folklore—for instance *Ali Baba*, with an oriental setting. The biblical narratives, with their potential for political embarrassment—given their emphasis on oppression and slavery—were gradually abandoned.

So in the Ewe-speaking area of Togoland at the beginning of the 1950s three kinds of drama coexisted: the literary drama of Kwasi Fiawoo and his followers; the religious and musical plays called cantata, mainly performed by school choirs; and the occasional concert parties in Keta and Kpalime. Socially these groups were very different in their venue, recruitment, and audience. The literary plays were confined to schools having a strong Ewe program. Church choirs, made up mostly of women, performed religious plays for their congregations. Concert groups made up of men had the most eclectic public, with a predominance of school children and young urban dwellers. Whereas cantata and literary drama were almost always presented on stages, concert party more often used bars and, less frequently, residential compounds.

But if these three groups were strongly differentiated in their membership, this did not mean that a student could not attend a cantata play and perhaps even perform in a concert band in his own village. All this theatrical activity in an African language, in the standard version of Ewe, was what made the cultural possibilities in southern Togo different from those in Dahomey (renamed the Republic of Bénin in 1975) to the east.

In our investigations among concert actors we found that several of them had taken part in religious plays or attended cantata performances; a few knew how to read Ewe and had read books in their own language, which was quite an unusual phenomenon in that part of Africa. This, along with the political ferment in Togo, probably explains why concert was successful in Togo and not in Dahomey. Proximity to Ghana is not much of an explanation, since Nigeria could have played the same role in the east. On the surface, language would seem a unifying factor since, from the Volta River to the Oueme, all along the coast, people spoke languages of what Westermann described as the Ewe cluster. The Ewe spoken on the coast from Ghana to Bénin was based on the Anecho dialect—Mina—and could have helped to spread the genre to neighboring Dahomey. But there was one major difference between the Ewe spoken in Togo and the Fon spoken in Dahomey, even though they could be considered dialects of the same language: Ewe had a century-old history of writing and a sizable body of literature, while Fon did not. A translation of the Bible and a few religious texts were the extent of Fon literature up until the 1960s, whereas Ewe had a bibliography of several hundred titles, including many works of fiction and theatre.

There was thus in Ewe a theatrical activity which facilitated the diffusion of an innovation such as concert party, brought to Eweland through contact with Gold Coast groups from which Ewe groups would later trace their origins. The Happy Star Concert Band of Lomé, founded in 1965, took the name of a famous Ghanaian group of the 1960s, Love Nortey's Happy Stars, based at Nsawam, twenty miles north of Accra. Radio also played its part since many of the tunes sung in the plays came from the Akan repertory sung in the programs of the Ghanaian radio. When asked, in the course of our research in the early 1970s, Togolese actors were unable to translate the words of the songs—like their French counterparts who sing in English without the faintest knowledge of what they are saying. The songs conveyed a certain mood, and that was the important point.

Concert party in Togo, then, was borrowed from Ghana and did not become well established till the beginning of the 1960s—a very late start compared with its Ghanaian prototype. Unlike Ghanaian concert party, it remained a small movement (there were never more than eight concerts operating at the same time) and one that was totally urban: both its production and its diffusion were concentrated in Lomé, the capital. It reached its greatest output in the 1970s, and thereafter suffered a kind of paralysis and decline. In the 1980s, the greatest stars moved into one-man television and radio shows, and government repression placed limits on concert party's ability to articulate popular concerns.

In the early 1960s Lomé was a small town of 150,000 inhabitants. It had few cultural activities: two movie houses, no television, one cultural center (French) with a stage, and that was all. On stage one could often see church choirs, made up entirely of women (some dressed as men to play the male parts), performing plays totally detached from any kind of biblical reference. Some of these plays were educational, showing what happens to young people who don't listen to their parents. In the same town, on the same night, in the suburbs, which at that time were not too far from downtown Lomé, one could attend a concert party where a story with more or less the same moral lessons was being performed entirely by men, female parts being played by impersonators.

The cantata show—with women only—was attended by the church congregation, and also by the general public; the concert party—with men only—was attended by theatregoers, beer drinkers, students, and school leavers. There was clearly a class difference between the two audiences, as well as an age and a sex difference: cantata audiences were older and better off than concert audiences. Lomé was thus a kind of conservatory of old and new theatre forms. As a proper educational medium, theatre was an entertainment performed by church choirs; no respectable man would make a fool of himself in front of his colleagues and friends. Men directed, wrote, and played the music, but did not act on the stage. As a recreational medium, theatre was being performed by young men trying to use the new musical idiom of highlife to tell stories of their own lives, which were essentially the same as those told in the cantata shows. These two traditions never met on stage: there was a social barrier between the shows of the church and the shows of the bars, but as S. A. Zinsou has noted, the topics of their performances were largely the same; the same story could be treated as a cantata or as a concert. The differences lay in the style of representation: the opposition was between the dignified and the vulgar, the high class and the low class, not between two different semantic universes. Both were popular in the sense that they emanated from a community, were acted by members of that community, and left considerable leeway for improvisation. Both enjoyed singing and slapstick, even if of a higher level in cantata. Cantata and concert party were thus opposed to the literary theatre which had an author, a composer, a director. The cantata had a choirmaster, but its performance was largely a group effort, as was the case with concert party.

## THE REPERTORY OF CONCERT PLAYS

Family stories are at the core of the concert repertory. Relations between parents and children, husbands and wives are the stuff of the narrative; data presented in Alain Ricard's doctoral thesis will be used here to propose a model of analysis of family relations in the concert, which should give some general idea of the semantic universe of the genre. We will refer to texts published after being translated or adapted, but also to shows seen on stage whose plots have been collected by us from members of the group.

*Mister Tameklor,* composed by the Happy Star concert party, shows us a model of relationships between father and son. Here is the synopsis. Papa Zinsou has two sons, of whom one, Atameklo, is rich and well educated. He tells this son that he must now think of getting married. This advice irritates Atameklo. Furious, he chases his father from the house; he then hires a Yorùbá servant and asks him to find some "good-time girls" for him. Papa Zinsou, trying to return to the house, is pushed aside by his son and the Ghanaian whores who have invaded the place. The servant and his master are now competing for the favors of the girls: the latter fleece Atameklo, who is compelled to borrow money from a friend. As he cannot repay his debts, he is arrested. Papa Zinsou and his other son come to release Atameklo from prison, pay his debts, and chase away the Yorùbá servant.

Plays that feature fathers usually dramatize a father-daughter relationship. Often the daughter reacts unfavorably to wedding projects devised by the father about which she has not been consulted. Here the play concerns a male child; we can interpret his violent reaction as the refusal to be treated like a girl. Rich, with a good job, Atameklo is free from financial dependence on his father and wants to choose his own wife. However, the father did not actually choose a wife for him, but merely suggested that he get one. The son's desires leave very little room for family solidarity. He surrounds himself with strangers: Yorùbá servant, Ghanaian whores. Having broken the family ties by turning his father out, he tries to set up a new way of living and fails miserably. Unable to face his commitments, he is sentenced to carrying excrement, a job usually reserved for strangers, for a stranger he has become by breaking family ties. Atameklo is an innovator: he is the child who refuses marriage, and his venture is a complete failure.

In the other plays, daughters have no means to counteract their parents' projects except by running away. In one concert party, a father wants to marry off his three daughters: they all refuse and leave the house to lead their own life. In town they meet a young man who marries all three of them, then goes mad. A traditional priest cures him. Once cured, the young man goes to the village to see the father of the girls and remarries only one of them. Like Atameklo, the girls refused marriage, but unlike him they could not chase their father from the house. They had to leave and go to the city. In Ewe society marrying sisters is considered incestuous. The behavior of the young man who marries three sisters is crazy: having regained his mental faculties, he casts off two of his wives and finds himself reintegrated within the cultural community. Atameklo, the guilty son—not the prodigal son—is the prey of strangers; the reluctant daughters become the victims of an insane man. In the first play things are set right by the police, in the second play by a traditional priest, who restores the husband's sanity. Both plays repeat the same message: daughters must obey their parents; the city's temptations can lead them astray; it is only by listening to the advice of their parents that they can find a stable union and, in general, a monogamous one. How is it possible to reconcile the new possibilities and the freedom offered by the city with parental wisdom? The shows offer a conservative answer to this question: only respect for elders will ensure a happy life.

Another series of plays deals with a different set of characters: a young man, single or married, and the women he interacts with, including his wives. Various possibilities are presemted by two types of situations, defined by the presence or absence of wealth (signaled by a good job) and the presence or absence (or observance and nonobservance) of marriage bonds. The second play whose text is presented and analyzed in depth in this volume, *The African Girl from Paris,* deals with a rich husband and his two wives. Another play by the Happy Star, *Francis the Parisian,* can be usefully compared with it, for it reverses some of the signs from positive to negative, presenting a poor bridegroom and his two wives.

In *Francis the Parisian* Mr. John, the husband, is the prototype of the poor bridegroom. As he tells us in his introductory narration, he was once a railway engineer, so well paid that he was able to marry two wives. But he has lost an arm as well as his job in a train accident. Enter Francis, brandishing his apparent wealth and promising the two women an easy life. Mary, the younger wife, is tempted and leaves John.

A childhood friend comes to visit Elisa, the faithful wife, and gives her money to restore John's health and job. Meanwhile, Francis proves to be a phony: his creditors come to claim the money he owes them and he finds himself stripped of his rented accoutrements. A renewed John comes back on stage with the faithful Elisa. Mary, in rags, returns to ask for a job; her former co-spouse intercedes on her behalf. Francis, in disguise, is also taken in as a servant by the couple. He plans to rob them, but John and Elisa discover the plot and chase away Francis and his companion. The fact that John ends up with only one wife shows the emergence of a new style in the relationship between men and women, that of married solidarity. Thus, the unfortunate economic situation leads to the downfall of a polygamous household. Elisa, the loyal wife, supported John; she fed him, even carried him on her back, accepting the reversal of married roles. By the end of the show their trials have ended; the couple are now rich and, just as important, monogamous.

Concert stories are always a game on the links between economic and marital situations, which are usually presented as being in a state of tension. The two may be brought into harmony when the hero attains both wealth and a good marriage, but this is rare, and happens only after the hero has lost one of his two spouses. In other cases the equilibrium is reached in poverty, but with the help of a friend ready to rescue the hero from a bad situation. The economic situations of urban life—unemployment, scarcity of living space, all that John and Francis have to experience—these conditions which another John, in *The African Girl from Paris*, and Atameklo, in *Mister Tameklor,* are spared—complicate the maintenance of the polygamous marriage as it was practiced by the elders in the Ewe villages. Christianity has come, and the plays tell us: Respect your parents! Stand together with your spouse! In the family framework, which is its realm, the concert pleads for conservative solutions, even if monogamy is in fact an innovation of urban young people with a varnish of Christian education. The moral message of concert is not basically different from the message of cantata plays; the aesthetics are different, not the ethics.

Realizing that the oppositions between concert party and cantata were largely artificial, S. A. Zinsou decided to attempt a synthesis of these two genres. This has been his aesthetic project for the last twenty years and it has succeeded to a considerable extent.[11] It meant integrating the guitar of the concert with the more traditional elements of dance and music of cantata, the elaborate makeup of actresses, and the masks of comedians. The distinction between a spoken text in one language (French in Zinsou's plays, Ewe in cantata and concert) and songs in another (Ewe in Zinsou's plays and cantata, Twi in concert) was also retained. In this sense he has been able to accomplish in Francophone theatre what Wọlé Ṣóyínká did for the Anglophone theatre. Unfortunately Togo did not provide the same intellectual effervescence as Nigeria and the aesthetic creativity and sensibility of the Togolese dramaturgist has not been able to expand the way those of Wọlé Ṣóyínká and, for instance, Fẹ́mi Ọ̀ṣófisan did.

## CONCERT PARTY AS A GENRE

The origins of concert party are clearly in the Gold Coast/Ghana, but is the Togolese concert different from its parent? From a comparison with Ghanaian performances in Lomé, the Togolese show seems more rigid in its expression and more conservative in its message. It was borrowed, not invented, and even though it was thoroughly appropriated by the Togolese, it suffered from its lack of widespread diffusion, from the small number of groups in operation, and from its concentration in a single urban center. The small number of groups meant that original artists and creators were always few, and that during the decade in which his research was carried out Alain Ricard could know all the groups. It soon became apparent that Happy Star was the best group, and that there was little competition for this leadership. Within Lomé, the groups performed either in cultural or community centers, in bars, or in dance halls. Some bars, such as Chien qui fume in Nyekonakpoe, specialized in concert.

A concert party is not held just anywhere: it requires an enclosed area, lit in the center, with space for the actors. Togolese actors prefer to play on real stages, to be as separate as possible from the audiences, unlike the more relaxed Ghanaian actors who, as we have seen, freely interacted with the audience, actually encouraging them to mount the stage during the show. Since we are dealing with a first generation of actors, they tend to adhere to strict rules. Their insecurity also shows in the lack of differentiation between concert and some kinds of religious activity: concert is never played during the day. In contrast to theatre with both matinee and evening performances, concert must await nightfall. As in Ghana, there is no set time for the beginning of the show. In operation is what we have called the "*asihu* principle," which assumes that the public knows the rules of its performance: no specific time is given for the start or end of the shows, no program sheet is distributed. Like the *asihu*—the truck—in the motor park,[12] the theatre will eventually fill up quite fast, and only start when full. As we show in the chapter on Happy Star later in this volume, there is a core of aficionados among the concertgoers who know the names of the actors, the groups, and the plays, and have definite opinions on the halls and the organization of the shows—proof, in our opinion, that concert is recognized as a particular category of expression and of spectacle by the linguistic and cultural community within which it is produced. It is neither a structureless show nor a jam session: it is a distinct genre with its own form and mode of expression, recognized and understood as such by the audience.

A tension exists between the Ewe tradition and the language of concert. Concert party as a widespread urban phenomenon in Togo belongs to the post-nationalist era. The verbal text is in the language of the capital city: a lingua franca from the capital. But this lingua franca is not the language of oral tradition. In fact, the language of tales bears the mark of an older, rural environment; borrowings from French and English are less frequent. The high frequency of borrowings singularizes the concert as a particular type of expression, notable for the playful incorporation of entire sentences from foreign languages. The oral text of concert party is a mixed one, a free and popular speech which plays with the "linguistic dogmatism" fostered by the diglossic situation. This linguistic mixity has been studied in the case of the commedia dell'arte. The principle defined by Bakhtin as "linguistic decorum," which forbids mixity, does not apply to either genre. This form of intertextuality differentiates the concert from other genres in Ewe. A text such as the one we produced (*Mister Tameklor*, 1982) is not a welcome addition to Ewe oral tradition and is not suited to the teaching of Ewe. The official committee on Ewe language and literature refused in 1983 to consider our work as a suitable textbook  because of its high incidence of borrowings.

The textualization of diglossia is completed by what we can call, following Bakhtin, a carnivalization of the genres. The concert does not belong to the genres of Ewe speech recorded by F. N'Sougan Agblemagnon (1968). It was a new genre and was certainly not to be counted among the "traditional" genres of Ewe speech proudly recorded by Ewe scholars. It is a medley of these diverse forms. The opening of every show is staged in the form of a tale. Thus in *Mister Tameklor* the old "papa" comes on stage and, for several minutes, talks of meeting his wife during a buffalo hunt. This reminder of village life places the concert in the nonurban setting of the tale. The text itself is often full of proverbs, some of them contemporary: for example, "everything on the record was put there by the drummer," an allusion to the recording success of highlife and an assertion of professional responsibility. The dialogue is enriched by the use of these forms of expression. One of the most remarkable is without any doubt the mocking dueling song, ritualized in Ewe culture.  An example is found in *Mister Tameklor*: the famous (famous because the public knows and requests it) duel between the greedy Yorùbá servant and the good-time girl, between *ashao* and *anago*. It is the "battle of the songs" well known in ancient Ewe culture and still topical as a poetic form, as shown in the texts recently collected by Kofi Awoonor (Awoonor 1974).

In what way is this use of culturalized speech forms a carnivalization? Simply speaking, in the way it brings together speech forms from different performance contexts—everyday social speech (proverbs) and playful speech (songs and tales)—and the way it mixes these various forms, diverting some of them from their original functions. The tale furnishes a pertinent example. In the opening monologue of *Mister Tameklor*, each element of the narrative is transformed. The hunter returns almost empty-handed, and he describes love scenes with his wife like a radio announcer reporting a soccer game. The epic and the lyrical are transformed into burlesque.

The continuity of the narrative schemes taken from oral tradition, whose acting schemes are unchanged in the concert, is colored by an element absent in the tale, limited to the paralinguistic, and which is the discourse of objects: costumes and props. These are at the same time indices of material wealth and of contemporaneity, which the oral text could not stage with the same efficiency.

The prop is one of the essential signifiers of character. The referential character projects the text into everyday life and, at the same time, high-lights it with an evidence which the verbal element could never achieve. Thus, the fashionable young man character, the gentleman, wears a cap and glasses, carries an attaché case, and walks to the rhythm of a rapid highlife. The iconicization of the character follows a codification process which is not a mosaic but a transformation. The visual makeup of the character manifests two operational processes at work: the masks signify characters "analogically" (moustache, glasses, etc.), whereas objects taken from the everyday environment signify themselves by a contiguity of odds and ends. Everyday life is metonymized (common objects put on stage) and metaphorized (masks painted on the face) at the same time.

The stability of the form allows direct symbolic exchange with the audience: in the adventures of the gentleman and his houseboy, as in *Mister Tameklor*, they see the ancient narratives. However, these old narra-tives do not take urban society into account: the multiplicity of social roles a person can assume, the possibility for wealth but also for rapid down-fall. This incoherence is that of "fate"; this environment is that of the city, and its signifier will be visual.

Why not then retain the same narrative schemes and why not tell the stories instead of acting them? Why doesn't the staging result in the eruption of individualized characters and hence in a bursting-out from the fixed forms of the tale? The concert is no longer a tale, but its charac-ters are not yet free individuals but still behavior models.

Concert—and this is valid for Ghana as well as for Togo—is charac-terized by its mixity, both linguistic and generic. This mixity is also a trait which distinguishes it from the folklore genre *stricto sensu*. The work of professionals and semi-professionals, concert is played not to a small group but to an increasingly large public: we have attended performances before an audience of more than 700 people. Hence, the concert goes beyond the community framework of folklore and could be considered theatre. However, the repertory of a concert group is not written. It consists of a corpus of story outlines familiar to some of the actors. This, like linguistic mixity and the transformation of the tale, is typical of traditions of farce. One of the old man's speeches in *Mister Tameklor* is a good illustration: what sounds like a tale is turned into a burlesque episode and the old man appears ridiculous. Yet, at the end of the show, he will have the final word, and the son who chased him away is punished. But the entire show turns on the excesses of the son. The old discourse is not explicitly denied, it is even reaffirmed, but it is nevertheless implicitly transformed. We can't really speak of an inversion of values, only of their confusion; this can no doubt be explained by the period of rapid change in which the actors are living. The issue of the history of genres has reappeared here inside a different culture, and directs back at us pertinent questions concerning the complex emergence of theatre through the transformation of oral genre, the textualization of diglossia, and the musical melting-pot.

In the concert the characters are analogous to those we could find in a morality play or in a masque theatre. Furthermore, some of the characters are "masked": they wear a stylized coded makeup, as can be seen in the illustrations. These masks freeze them into the type they are supposed to represent: the old father, the young girl, etc. Thus the concert is a semantically closed universe: the new stories utilize the ancient schemes. Concert actors turn the narrative into a festivity by giving it a rich visual signifier. But this festivity takes place in a closed universe: they are looking for free individuals to put on stage. They are witnesses to the explosion of oral tradition of which they show us a few pieces. They have conquered verbal and gestural freedom, but they have not yet conquered the freedom to give their own direction to the stories they are transmitting. The character cannot leave the stage without taking with him the person.

## RELATIONS WITH THE GOVERNMENT, EVOLUTION OF THE GENRE

Organized with the objective of producing shows for monetary gain, the Happy Star Concert Band was not registered as a company, only theoretically as a voluntary association. When in 1973 the only political party, the RPT, became hegemonic, all voluntary associations had to register within the party or disappear. This meant the end of many theatre groups performing in French who had been for many years present in the cultural life of Lomé.

At one stroke of the pen, the government wiped out organized theatrical activity in Togo, especially theatrical activity in French. Nothing could have been better for concert party. The group, loosely organized, vaguely registered, had no complaints at being "integrated" in the loosely organized and vaguely defined youth sections of the RPT. The competition from legitimate theatre had been abolished, and concert proliferated, in the suburbs and among school-age youngsters. It seemed at that time to be the vanguard of Togolese theatre because of the quality of its actors.

It is in those years that a national troupe was created, not as a grandiose institution, but more as a training resource and as a national selection of actors drawn from existing groups. Several members of concert party groups were recruited into the National Theatre. Here the plays had to be performed in French, but the talents of these performers as singers, dancers, and clowns could be put to good use in the slapstick and singing interludes.

The New Department of Theatre and Cultural Groups, created within the Ministry of Youth and Culture in 1975, took care of training the actors and supervising the groups. It organized in 1975 a National Popular Theatre competition open to concert parties. A certain amount of official recognition came with it; the groups theoretically followed the party's leadership, while in actuality continuing to operate as independent voluntary associations. The National Division of Theatre, headed by the playwright-scholar S. A. Zinsou, kept a close watch on the activities of these groups while providing occasional training and producing its own plays in French. The years of "authenticity," the mid-1970s, were a particularly important time for these groups since the political struggle was led in the area of culture; the goal was to regain a lost Africanity. But they responded in a rather ambiguous, if not totally humorous, way—as when Francis became Fo—the Christian first name being Togolized. In many instances the powers that be appeared satisfied with not losing face rather than concerned with a true Africanization (and who knew how to achieve this?). All this, of course, was wonderful material for satire, and concert parties would exploit it at times, but only briefly: they were very soon made aware that it was not a good idea to proceed further. The favorite political tactic of the Eyadema regime was intimidation and it worked very well with concert parties, who were thus condemned to repeat the same old stories.

Television and radio shows were made available to some of the best comedians and in particular to one Kokuvito, who came to dominate concert party in the 1980s. It is significant that his group was known by the name of its leader, not by a team name: not Happy Star, but Kokuvito Concert. Verbal dexterity, visual invention, and physical vitality were the assets of Kokuvito (Sylvestre Adenyo), who had trained in Ghana before returning to Lomé to work as a mechanic and briefly to be part of Happy Star at the beginning of the 1970s. In the 1980s Kokuvito became famous for telling Ewe stories on his radio show and for the social commentaries present in his plays. He was usually careful not to antagonize the government, but in 1984 he slipped and made fun of its incapacity to provide adequate grain storage facilities. He disappeared, and reappeared only several weeks later; it was rumored he had been thoroughly beaten up by the gendarmes. Back on stage, he henceforth kept to his usual range of comments on unfaithful wives and lazy husbands. The lesson had been learned. In 1985 Alain Ricard spent a year with the National Department of Theatre. He was able to follow the day-to-day running of the Ministry of Culture. It was indeed important that the plays and sketches maintained a neutral stance toward the government and did not make fun of the general.

At the same time, it was noticeable that from the 1970s onwards concert party activity had slowed down. There were fewer groups and performances, and the only name that was quoted was that of Kokuvito. Groups had fewer members, concert relied more on music, and the audience had changed. In the late 1960s and early 1970s, Lomé had been mainly an Ewe-speaking town, more ethnically homogeneous than it was to become in the 1980s, and schooling was not universal. By the mid-1980s the population, which had reached half a million, had a large proportion of migrants from the North, and school-age children had all been taught a bit of French. Concert party using cultural resources from the Ewe hinterland for an Ewe-Mina audience was out of step with the new urban population. An important element of the work of the National Division of Theatre was culturally to legitimize concert party. By organizing festivals, by recruiting actors, by taking them to study sessions and tours, the Ministry put its stamp of approval on a previously informal activity. Moreover, S. A. Zinsou, head of the Division and himself a playwright, used several techniques derived from concert in his own plays which he staged with the National troupe. Having men play women achieved the proper distancing effect while solving the problem of the lack of properly trained actresses—for even in the National Theatre Company it was difficult to get actresses and to keep them. Songs, makeup, improvisation, and a general style of narrative fluidity in his own writing were borrowed from concert, and Zinsou himself acknowledged his debt wherever and whenever he could. When he took *La Tortue Qui Chante* to Limoges and on a European tour in 1986, the lead part was played by a comedian from Lomé, Aze Kokovivina, a main competitor of Kokuvito for the artistic leadership of concert party. Aze's photograph appeared in *Le Monde* and he was applauded as a great comedian.

This recognition was a mixed blessing for concert party. Its best comedians were drawn to theatre in French or to the one-man show. They could no longer continue to perform within the concert language, which they were gradually losing, since the actors' only formal training was by witnessing performances. Relations with Ghana were strained all through the

1980s, owing to the radical regime of Jerry Rawlings, who was feared in an almost paranoid fashion by the Togolese president. This prevented highlife bands from touring Eastern Ghana and Lomé as they had regularly done in the 1970s.

Kokuvito died in May 1988, and his funeral was attended by representatives of the government. In 1989 demonstrations against the regime started and took a more violent turn after the jailing of a young playwright, Kosi Efui. His plays were in French and it seems that the language of contestation has been largely French. Will concert party start again and bloom when speech is eventually liberated in Togo?

## YORÙBÁ POPULAR THEATRE

Lagos, like Cape Coast, was the seat of an élite culture among the Anglicized professional classes in the nineteenth century. As in the Gold Coast, the music and drama produced by this élite were based on imported forms: in the case of Lagos, British music hall and classical European music. Churches, schools, and social clubs staged concerts and variety shows that were exclusively in English, and charged high gate fees to exclude the lower classes. Unlike the "highlife" shows of the Gold Coast, however, these entertainments did not become popularized and democratized; in the words of Bíódún Jéyìfò [Jeyifo], they "did not crystallize into a viable, historically perpetuated tradition; rather they went down a historical blind alley, leaving only the memory of unconsummated hopes and aspirations" (Jéyìfò 1984:41).

However, élite dissatisfaction with the British was already strong by 1880, and it continued to grow. One of the early forms in which it was expressed was in the demand for independent churches: churches run by Africans, even though preserving most of the liturgical and ritual features of the existing mission-run churches. Churchmen with independent leanings took the lead in calling for a re-indigenization of cultural practices: the reversion to African names, the search for parallels to or precursors of Christian beliefs in indigenous practices, and a general support for "native traditions" which was given body by pioneering research into proverbs, folklore, Ifá divination, and historical traditions. This interest in the indigenous was manifested in theatrical productions in the Yorùbá language, drawing on elements of indigenous culture, put on by associations drawn from the membership of breakaway churches such as Bethel and St. Jude's. Between 1904 and 1920 at least twenty different "native dramas" were staged in Lagos (Leonard 1967). In 1910 the Lagos Glee Singers attempted to convert this new initiative into a commercial concert-party show, with dances, and songs and sketches in Yorùbá. The attempt fizzled out, however, and there was little new activity during the depression of the 1930s.

But church performances in Yorùbá survived, and these became fundamental to the development of contemporary Yorùbá popular theatre and to our understanding of how this theatre differs from Ghanaian and Togolese concert party. This style of church performance was called "cantata," as in the Gold Coast and Togo, or alternatively "Bible opera." It consisted of dramatized versions of well-known Bible stories, rendered entirely or almost entirely in song. The music was largely choral, based on hymn tunes, but adapted to suit the tonal contours of Yorùbá speech (Euba 1970). The performers were members of the church congregation—usually of the church choir—and the operas were often composed by the choirmaster. The plays were often staged in the church itself, and the acting style tended to be static and highly stylized. In the late 1930s and the 1940s a number of well-known and highly regarded composers began to emerge who were known for the superior quality of their productions. These included G. T. Onímọlẹ̀ and A. B. David. Bible operas of this type have continued—especially in Aládùúrà churches—all over western Nigeria up to the present. J.D.Y. Peel has a delightful description of one such performance—*The Fall of King Nebuchadnezzar*—staged by the Cherubim and Seraphim in 1962 (Peel 1968:188–90).

At a particular moment in this long and fairly stable tradition, however, a prodigy burst from within it, expanded, diversified, and in a remarkably short time had grown to the stunning size and shape of Yorùbá popular commercial traveling theatre. That moment came in the 1940s, just when the Bible opera tradition was reaching its zenith: in the last years of the war and the first years of the postwar boom. Although, according to A. G. Hopkins, the postwar economic revival took some years to be felt in West Africa, and in fact was not well established until the 1950s, nevertheless expectations of boom were high and demands for a better life—politically, economically, and socially—were in the air (Hopkins 1973:267–68).

The development of the commercial theatre was pioneered by Hubert Ògúnñdé [Ogunde] (Clark 1979). Ògúnñdé was a policeman, former teacher, and choirmaster of a branch of the Church of the Lord Aládùúrà in Lagos. In 1944 he staged his first production, *The Garden of Eden and the Throne of God*, a completely orthodox Bible opera performed by his church choir, much in the style of the other composer-choirmasters who had already blazed the trail. The only difference was that from the beginning, Ògúnñdé enlivened the hymn-like music with a larger dose of highlife than other composers. However, in the very next year, Ògúnñdé brought out a new production, entitled *Worse Than Crime*, which used the standard operatic format but drew on very different thematic materials. *Worse Than Crime* was a denunciation of colonialism. In 1946, only two years after his first production, Ògúnñdé went professional, recruiting a group of performers who were to be paid, full-time theatre workers. The new company's first play was *Tiger's Empire,* another political play, and their second was *Human Parasites,* a social satire. In the following few years Ògúnǹdé pioneered other themes—for instance, folk stories—and after a trip to England from which he brought back £2,000 worth of equipment (lights, sound system, musical instruments) he set the standards by which all subsequent groups were measured by the public. He also brought tap dances from the England trip, and—more significantly—elements of concert party entertainment from a trip to the Gold Coast the following year. In 1950, in *Black Forest,* perhaps the most crucial innovation took place: the inclusion of improvised dialogue between the set pieces of the learned songs. All the main components of the Yorùbá popular traveling theatre were thus in place within six years of Ògúnǹdé's first production: a wide variety of themes (religious, political, social commentary, folkloric); a combination of song and improvised dialogue; the use of a platform stage with the equipment associated with conventional Western theatre (curtains, lights, scenery); the practice of traveling to find fresh audiences, and an itinerary not only covering the Yorùbá heartland in western Nigeria, but also reaching Yorùbá enclaves in northern and eastern Nigeria and even outside Nigeria; and finally, an eclectic syncretic artistic mode, incorporating imported vaudeville elements and indigenous performance traditions into what was already, in effect, an established "creolized" cultural form, the Yorùbá Bible opera.

The subsequent development of the popular theatre was shaped by the individual responses of actor-managers to what they perceived as the audiences' desires. While it is important to stress, as Bíọ́dún Jéyìfò does, that it was the audience rather than specific "great men" who drew the theatre on and made it what it has become, it is also clear that each of the important early theatre leaders had a distinctive and strongly characteristic style which blazed the trail for later groups and which established, early on, the essential and fundamental proliferation of alternative modes, so characteristic of Yorùbá theatre and so strikingly absent in the Ghanaian and Togolese concert parties.

Ògúnǹdé himself laid down examples of a number of distinct genres: political criticism, topical satire, folkloric tales, and crime thrillers. Soon after Ògúnǹdé had established himself, several other theatre leaders began to become prominent. Three of them subsequently became extremely influential throughout the Yorùbá speaking area: Kọ́lá Ògúnmọ́lá, Dúró Ládiípọ̀ [Ladipo] and Oyin Adéjọbí. Ògúnmọ́lá and Ládiípọ̀ were both school teachers; Adéjọbí at first worked in a store and later, for many years, as a council clerk. All three began, like Ògúnǹdé, by producing Bible operas for their own churches and then for other congregations who sought their assistance. All three converged on Òṣogbo in the 1950s, and both Ládiípò and Ògúnmólá profited from the interest of the élite cultural establishment, without being taken over by it.[13] All three gradually added secular plays to their repertoires; started performing in hotels and community halls as well as schools and churches; took their plays on tour; converted themselves from charitable fund-raisers to commercial business organizations; and then, in the early 1960s, went fully professional. But while all three men had similar backgrounds in the church and teaching, and followed a similar path from Bible opera to secularized, commercial touring theatre, the styles they pioneered were deliberately differentiated.

Ògúnmólá was known for his realism: he made little use of the supernatural or of legend and myth. His plays were noted for their finely ironic attentiveness to contemporary behavior. Ládiípò established a quite different style. He was more "purist" in his traditionalism than Ògúnňdé, drawing heavily on well-known Yorùbá myths of gods and heroes, and utilizing indigenous performance modes—dùndún, bàtá and igbìn drums, oral performance repertoires such as oríkì (praise poetry), ofò (incantations), and ese Ifá (Ifá divination poetry), and indigenous dances—much more extensively than his contemporaries. Adéjobí created plays in mythical, historical, satirical and comic modes, but his great strength was witty, lifelike dialogue and tight, complex plotting, with coherent and polished interlocking of the component episodes of each play.

Although the work of these and other early theatre leaders bears witness to the vigorous growth and rapid diversification and elaboration of the popular traveling theatre, it was not until the late 1960s and early 1970s that, buoyed up by the tide of oil money, the theatre exploded into a huge movement, with more than a hundred fully viable commercial companies plying the roads. From the early 1960s, the theatres had been much involved with Nigerian television, which was inaugurated in 1959. Since the early 1980s there has been increasing involvement in filmmaking and even more recently in drama videos sold directly to customers in motor parks and supermarkets. Some groups also participated in radio shows, were featured in the photoplay magazine Atóka, and produced records and cassettes of their music. They reached their audiences through multiple media, but their primary mode was, until very recently, the stage performance, which in the case of the most popular companies attracted audiences of thousands, who packed the school auditoriums and community halls and even on occasion filled a whole football stadium.

During the period between the original Bible operas and the most recent plays, their performances underwent striking stylistic changes. The early Ògúnňdé plays, like Bread and Bullet, included improvised dialogue but relied for the bulk of the performance on set pieces, long solo and choral songs in hymnic highlife style, accompanied by stylized gestures, with only limited movement around the stage. However, as the subject matter became more diverse and, in many cases, more contemporary and domestic, spoken dialogue gradually ousted sung passages in all the theatre companies. During the 1960s it was common to use the singing mode for all the key passages: for moments of heightened emotion or reflection; for soliloquies; to express collective sentiments; to set the scene; to produce final closure with a moral summary; and—perhaps surprisingly—to lay out the key narrative elements needed to follow the plot. The songs— most of which were choral, and often sung by everyone in the company whether they were on or off stage—were like permanent landmarks, jutting up from the flow of improvisation like stepping stones which led the plot in its correct sequence from beginning to end. They were often very long and elaborate, but as the tune of the song followed the tonal patterns of the Yorùbá language more or less exactly, they were almost as easy to follow as speech. Progressively, however, improvised dialogue took over, and the landmarks became key phrases or sequences of speech rather than songs. By the early 1980s it was common to find plays with no songs in them at all. The musical component had been relegated entirely to the "Opening Glee," a curtain-raiser usually made up of songs and dances (though it could also contain comic monologues or dialogues, or short satirical sketches unrelated to the main play). The theatre practitioners themselves observe that this shedding or stripping away of songs was in part a result of their involvement in television, where programs were shorter and more accurately timed, and where pithy, individualized, "naturalistic" dialogue was preferred to stylized, static choral singing.

Yorùbá popular theatre, then, like Ghanaian concert party, began life as a specialized production for a special interest group (in the Yorùbá case, this was the Christian congregation rather than the wealthy social élite), and quickly moved out of the segregated area of its origin in response to the desire of a much larger popular audience. Both theatres very quickly adapted in form and subject matter, and developed touring skills and itineraries. Both were urban based and toured rural areas. Both maintained a tangential relationship with political movements and parties, though Yorùbá popular theatre never attracted the degree of government sponsorship that Ghanaian concert party did. Both, in their heyday, drew their performers and much of their audience from the "intermediate classes"—that heterogeneous mass of wage laborers, petty government and business employees, artisans, self-employed providers of services, and traders—though Yorùbá popular theatre was not directed specifically to "the poor" as Ghanaian concert party was: it also drew spectators from among the well-to-do, and the most successful groups often gave performances at the invitation of élite social clubs.

However, there are also striking differences between the two theatres. The form and style of the presentation itself, the interaction of the performers with the audience, the themes of the dramas and their insertion into present-day popular concerns are quite unlike. The distinctive features of the Yorùbá popular theatre, in comparison with Ghanaian and Togolese concert party, can probably best be grasped by considering the following issues: first, the continued importance, in Yorùbá plays, of the original model of drama they started with, that is, the church choir Bible opera; second, the continued strong link between Yorùbá popular theatre and the schools, bringing with it a strong orientation to literacy even though the plays were not scripted; third, the specific character of the Yorùbá commercial environment, within which the popular theatres operated as another "informal sector" business, in conjunction with a style of social mobilization and personal advancement prevalent in (Nigerian) Yorùbá areas which could be described as "big man-ism"; and fourth, the particular history of Yorùbá cultural nationalism and what J.D.Y. Peel (1989) has called the "cultural work of Yorùbá ethnogenesis."

Concert party, as we have seen, took its main impulses from vaudeville and was structured around the presence of a highlife band. The dramas were loose-jointed, formulaic, and presentational rather than representational. Yorùbá popular theatre, by contrast, had as its original and primary model the depiction of Bible stories. From the beginning, the point of the presentation was to act out a narrative in such a way as to convey its force, its completeness, and the lesson it enshrined. From very early on, other elements were added to this model: Ògúnṅdé's folkloric plays, and even his political ones, contained long sequences of dancing and singing which were not essential to the plot. In *Africa and God*, ostensibly about the benighted state of pagan Africa until rescued by European missionaries, the first half of the play is devoted to a full-blown celebration of Yorùbá royalty with all its pagan ritual and performance arts, extended to the point where it subverts the message of the play (see Barber 1988). It became very common for additional "turns" to be added as performers become available. For example, in the Oyin Adéjọbí Company's *Mo Ráwọ̀*, a new character was added at the last moment when Mr. Adéjọbí had a visitor—an old friend of his—who was a headmaster but also an excellent *ìjálá* chanter. In a scene set in an Aládùúrà church, one member of the congregation is given an elderly, pagan father who is brought to the church to learn its teaching. When the priest, seeking to convert him, says "Our father, which art in Heaven," it reminds the old man of his own dead father, and he bursts out into protracted *ìjálá* chanting in his memory (see Barber 1986). There was thus scope for extra scenes and sequences to be added as the opportunity arose, and the structure of the plays was flexible enough to carry all kinds of excursions and accretions. However, all these embellishments were extraneous, and did not disturb the narrative. Most Yorùbá popular plays paid great attention to coherent plotting. Kàrímù Adépòjù, the manager in Oyin Adéjọbí's company, once expressed his dissatisfaction with a particular new play of theirs in the following terms: "One scene should follow out of another so that everything clicks. But this one is like the plays of these mushroom companies who just throw them together anyhow." Adépòjù had a clear and developed idea of the *articulation* of the play, a sense of design and overall architecture, which was perhaps exceptional among Yorùbá theatre companies but which was present, to a greater or lesser degree—sometimes more as an ideal than an actuality—in all of them.

The pure entertainment, adopted into the Bible operas from influences such as comic films, Bobby Benson's highly Westernized vaudeville of the 1940s and 1950s, and—significantly—Ghanaian concert party itself, tended to be concentrated in the "Opening Glee," which became an essential part of every Yorùbá popular theatre's program, though varying tremendously from one to the next. In some, the Opening Glee was one long introductory song, telling the story of the play that was to follow. Ògúnmọ́lá used this style in his early productions. However, there was already a cabaret element, as the chorus which surrounded the lead singer was made up of women dressed in matching costumes. This custom continued. The Adéjọbí company used to change the women's costumes regularly, as they were an important part of their image of glamour and modernity: often, they consisted of trouser suits (quite daring in the 1970s and early 1980s) or short skirts. Lérè Pàímọ́'s chorus even wore hot pants. In the course of time, however, those companies which had begun with a song about the play gradually introduced other themes, ending up with a medley of unrelated songs on topical, philosophical, or moral themes. In *The Secret Is Out* by Lérè Pàímọ́'s Èdá Theatre Company (see chapter 7), the Opening Glee contains anachronistic remnants of songs composed to introduce another, earlier play in their repertoire, one which made Lérè Pàímọ́'s name and established his company in the public eye. It also contains another element common in many companies' Opening Glees: the inclusion of renditions of traditional oral genres, in this case snatches of folk songs and extensive renditions of the *oríkì orilẹ̀* (praise poetry of origin) of Pàímọ́'s mother's home area. Others included short sketches unconnected with the main play, or even—in the case of the highly innovative Moses Ọláìyá—screenings of short films of his own plays. In most productions, the Opening Glee was distinctly more sexy and modern than the main play: a kind of up-front enticement of assorted items, usually unconnected thematically either to each other or to the play proper.

In the play itself, the attention to completeness and coherence was reflected in the relations between performers and audience. The audiences tended to be extremely boisterous and noisy—the microphones and amplifiers, which gave a kind of electronic choreography to many plays, were often essential to the actors' survival—and, as in Ghana, were always ready to shout comments, complete proverbs, and pick up and repeat catch phrases. However, they did not go up on stage to reward either the performers or the characters they were portraying; and they did not have a period of participation through dancing before or after the show. The acting space was distinct and segregated from the audience space. Yorùbá companies tended to place importance upon the formal arrangements of the performance venue. Like Togolese concert party actors, they required a platform stage with lights, backcloth, and curtains. They would not consider performing in the round. When they mounted performances in the open air—such as those given in football stadia—they went to great lengths to simulate an indoor, conventional theatre. There always had to be some rows of chairs, and the notional space between stage and auditorium was always preserved. The coherently plotted narrative play, with its attention to motivation, consistency, and cause and effect, seems to have offered less access to the incursions of the audience. And although Yorùbá popular audiences responded with immediacy and intensity to what was presented, the solidarity of weeping that seems to occur in Ghanaian concert parties was not a feature of Yorùbá performance. The audience, rather than being overcome with sympathy for the victim in the story, is spellbound by the magnetic, radiant bravado of the star actors as they demonstrate their powers. Paradoxically, then, the plays that are more "realistic," more closely modeled on real-life motivation and action, are at the same time more of a spectacle, while the loose-jointed music-hall style of the concert party nonetheless evokes huge tides of emotional identification with the characters.

Both Ghanaian concert party and Yorùbá popular theatre are strongly committed to imparting a moral lesson. But the plots of Ghanaian concert party plays often contain non sequiturs, temporal jumps, inconsistencies of character, and unexplained motivation. This is not the case with most Yorùbá popular plays. They go to greater lengths to demonstrate, by a careful tracing of actions and their consequences, exactly how good and evil end up getting their just deserts. Every step may be recapitulated, the sequence reexamined, before the appropriate conclusion is drawn (see Barber and Ògúndíjo [1994] for an example). The attention to narrative architecture, therefore, is not merely an aesthetic but also a moral commitment. Narrative coherence and perspicuity are essential to this mode of moralizing.

The Yorùbá popular theatre's origin in the church had other consequences too. Most significant was the inclusion, right from the beginning, of women performers. Women were the mainstay of church congregations and choirs, and in the Aládùúrà churches they played a prominent and conspicuous role in their actual organization and leadership (see Turner

1967, Peel 1968). This made possible, and encouraged, a more "lifelike" style of representation than that adopted by the concert parties, where extraordinarily poignant and comic effects are produced by the female impersonators, no matter what roles they play. It may well be the presence of these young men in drag, both endearing and ridiculous, which has set the predominant tone of concert party, the compelling blend of pathos and buffoonery. Cross-dressing, as we have seen, can be a kind of "mask." The Yorùbá popular theatre was not masked in this sense. It developed a range of exuberant, polished, but predominantly naturalistic styles, in which people looked like the characters they represented, and in which the sinuous cadences of everyday speech registers were lovingly reproduced and mocked. The sheer volume of words spoken in the Yorùbá play in this collection, *The Secret Is Out*, compared with *Orphan Do Not Glance* or *The African Girl from Paris*, is an indication of the bubbling, lifelike impression created by this drama (however hackneyed the plot may be), in which the characters all chatter away and interrupt each other, rather than delivering themselves of schematic utterances alternating with emotional solo highlife songs, as in concert party. Overall, the Yorùbá popular theatre was less formulaic, less tied to permutations of standard turns and acts, and more open to experimentation and the incorporation of new elements.

The church was of course intimately connected with the schools, and with the idea of literacy, education, and progress. Ghanaian concert party, as we have seen, had strong links with school life. One of its first proponents was a teacher, whose earliest shows were staged for Empire Day celebrations. Several trios started life as groups of schoolboys earning pocket money during the holidays, just as some of the most famous bands were founded and trained in schools (e.g., E. T. Mensah by Joe Lamptey — see Collins 1986). However, once they went professional, the concert parties and bands moved away from the schools and performed exclusively at public venues — hotels, village squares, open-air cinemas, and so on. The Yorùbá popular theatre, like the concert parties, recruited many of its performers from among school pupils who had enjoyed acting end-of-year dramas. Churches recruited teams from their mission schools to take part in Bible operas and cantatas. But the link between the Yorùbá popular theatre and the schools actually strengthened over time. First of all, schools were important audiences for many theatre companies. Boarding schools, in particular, provided large captive audiences whose lesser ability to pay (tickets were sold at reduced prices) was compensated for by their guaranteed mass attendance. Survival of many of the smaller and less prosperous theatre companies was dependent on these school audiences; even large and successful companies like Lérè Pàímọ́'s Èdá Theatre used to include a fair proportion of schools in every tour until their growing fame made it unnecessary. By playing to school audiences, they in turn inspired more school productions and attracted more school-leavers to join the professional theatre.

The school connection brought with it a certain orientation to literacy. Like Togolese concert parties, the Yorùbá popular theatre, though remaining resiliently oral and improvised, inhabited a domain that was permeated by the idea if not the fact of literacy. Theatre companies framed their activities in a token writing. They often "researched" the material for their historical and mythical plays, not only by eliciting oral traditions from the "old people" but also by consulting works such as Samuel Johnson's *History of the Yorubas* and, more significantly, the widely used school reader series *Ìwé Kíkà*, from which, for instance, Dúró Ládiípò derived the plot of *Ọba Kò So* (see Ọlájubù 1978). They sometimes drew on published Yorùbá novels for their plots; for instance, the Oyin Adéjọbí production *Kúyè* was based on Ọdúnjọ's novel of the same name (see Barber and Ògúndíjọ 1994), and their more recently composed play *Ìtójúu Kúnlé* was loosely based on another novel by Ọdúnjọ, *Ọmọ Òkú Òrun*. Popular improvised plays were also published in photographic strip cartoon form in photoplay magazines like *Atọka*, a publication which began in the late 1960s and continues today, publishing each play as a four- or five-part serial, with glossy cover and added attractions such as horoscopes, advice column, and pen-pal advertisements interspersed. The coverage of each play was quite detailed, and the school child with only partial literacy in Yorùbá could make out the story—especially if he or she had already seen the play. The theatre companies welcomed this form of publication, both as a kind of advertising and as a record of their productions.

Alongside the improvised theatre there also flourished a "literary" drama in Yorùbá—plays written by well-known Yorùbá authors and intended to be read rather than performed. Among them, the work of Adébáyọ̀ Fálétí is outstanding; but there are at least thirty other playwrights supplying the school (and school-leaver) readership. Some of the written plays *are* performed—Ọládèjọ Òkédìjí's marvelous *Réré Rún* has been a mainstay of university dramatic societies for years—and the divisions and barriers between the popular theatre and the Yorùbá literary theatre are much thinner than between the popular theatre and English-language art theatre such as that of Ṣóyínká and J. P. Clark. Indeed, some popular theatre leaders have sought out published texts for conversion into a play, and have modified their improvisational technique to accommodate this process (the best-known example is Ìṣọ̀lá Ògúnṣọlá, whose production of Akínwùmí Ìṣọ̀lá's historical drama *Ẹfúnṣetán Aníwúrà* drew the largest crowds ever recorded for a theatrical performance in Nigeria). Other cultural entrepreneurs might run a theatre company and *also* publish plays for the school market, writing the play *after* it had been fully developed through improvisation, and not referring to it as a script but rather as a byproduct of their operations (an example is Lánrewájú Adépójù, better known for his neotraditional oral chanting, who published the play *Sàgbà di Wèrè* in parallel to the performances of the same play by his small theatre company).

The ambience of literacy gives rise to a notion of the play as a text. While Western scholarship strives to get away from the restrictions of this notion and to rediscover a notion of performance that avoids it, these oral, improvisatory performers aspired to the condition of literacy. They invariably spoke of "writing" their plays, though what they wrote was a synopsis (usually abandoned after the first rehearsal) as well, of course, as the posters that advertised the show. Frequent reference was made to "letters of invitation" when a company gave a performance at the request of a specific social club, and managers or bosses usually kept a book in which the names of actors and their payments were recorded. A written itinerary was also drawn up when a new tour was planned. Often, these official texts were made more authoritative by being typed up with numerous carbon copies. But this was a writing that committed them to little: schedules and plays were changed as necessary. The actual play remained a collective product, worked out through practice and assembled through the resources and skills of individual performers (see Barber 1995). The analogue to the book is the proscenium arch and the platform stage. Within its confines, as Jéyìífò has so perceptively pointed out, the action is lined up, two-dimensionally, as in a photograph, but at the same time seems continually to effervesce, to be ready to burst out of the frame.

The early Independent churches, which greatly boosted the use of the Yorùbá language in church services and dramatic performances in the first decade of this century, were a significant agent in the development of an African and Yorùbá cultural nationalism in Western Nigeria. Indeed, until the 1920s the churches were the *main* site of contestation over indigenous and exogenous identities. It was clergymen who pioneered almost all the influential work on Yorùbá indigenous history and culture (unlike in the Gold Coast, where many of the prominent nationalists were lawyers rather than churchmen: see Jenkins 1990). The introduction of plays in Yorùbá, with Yorùbá traditional music and songs, was therefore more than just a strategy to attract a larger congregation: it was part of the project of Yorùbá cultural nationalism which has continued, with immense success and sophistication, throughout this century. Bible operas were part of a movement that asserted the value of Yorùbá culture, and the popular theatre that took off from their base retained and was inspired by this orientation. Some of Ògúnǹdé's early plays took up a pan-African rather than specifically Yorùbá posture. But the prime and incontrovertible representative of Africanity in his plays is Yorùbáness. In *Strike and Hunger* —an overtly, even riskily anticolonial play—even the "stranger king from overseas" who has come to oppress the people is represented as a Yorùbá ọba, given a Yorùbá name (Yéjídé), and surrounded with the full panoply of Yorùbá regality. Culture is Yorùbá: there is no other culture worth portraying. In his later, party political drama *Yorùbá Ronú*, Ògúnmọdé does represent the enemy (the North) as utterly alien and non-Yorùbá—but through a series of direct inversions of what *is* seen as Yorùbá, not by creating an image of the North based on observation or even prejudice. Thus the aliens wear skins instead of cloth, are ruled by a queen instead of a king, and the queen roars like a leopard instead of speaking the opulent Yorùbá of royalty. That they are *not* Yorùbá is enough (Barber 1988).

The Yorùbá popular theatre as a whole was pervaded with an intense and creative engagement with the Yorùbá language. While the fascination of Ghanaian and Togolese concert party plays comes from their incipient polyglottism, their ability to communicate to non-Twi or non-Ewe speakers, through parody, imitation, and snatches of other languages, the fascination of Yorùbá popular theatre comes from its exploitation of "deep" registers of the Yorùbá language, combined with its incessant new coinages. This can be seen in *The Secret Is Out*, in which half the fascination of the criminal underworld lies in the villains' exuberant use of thieves' slang, and in which the denouement involves a struggle to the death with traditional "deep Yorùbá" incantations as weapons. One member of the audience commented that she liked the character Adéntọ̀ọ́—the cheerful and disrespectful young hero—because his command of deep Yorùbá "made the play sweet." Others observed that they particularly enjoyed the scene at the traditional shrine "because it showed the songs and dances exactly as they used to be done in the old days." While the concert party addresses itself to (and thus helps create) a cross-ethnic, hybrid, urban public of many tongues, gaining its effects through comic misunderstandings and mistranslations, Yorùbá popular theatre teaches its audience locally specific registers and idioms which, some people think, might otherwise be lost. The only foreign language prominently intercalated into the Yorùbá is English; and the representation of English speakers is typically ambivalent. English is both the emblem of "enlightenment" and the mark of pretension, ostentation, and folly. By and large, people who don't speak proper Yorùbá are rather ridiculous. Good Yorùbá is highly regarded. When Karin Barber took part in Yorùbá plays, phrases that were especially "deep" or, alternatively, especially idiomatic and demotic, would be given to her to say, in the knowledge that this would cause more amusement and gratification than if she spoke a superficial, "akòwé" (educated person's) Yorùbá. The commitment to Yorùbáness as a cultural category was often made quite explicit by the theatre companies, who would assert that their mission was to preserve and bring to the attention of the world the glorious "traditional heritage" of the "Yorùbá people" (who incidentally did not exist, conceptually, until sometime in the nineteenth century), a process which quite often necessitated investigations and inquiries among the old people who still knew these things.

The popular theatre, like the church it came from, was a significant agent in the process of creating this ethnic solidarity, this sense of Yorùbáness. Like the church, the theatres operated at a pan-Yorùbá level, traveling from one "Yorùbá subgroup" to another and adopting an accent, an idiom, and a set of assumptions which would be comprehensible and acceptable to all. The theatre, like the schools, the radio, and the Yorùbá-language press, contributed to the establishment of a "standard Yorùbá" to which all dialects of the language could relate themselves.[14] While poking gentle fun at the peculiarities of various "subgroups," they also taught Yorùbá-speakers that *all* their different local customs, religious practices, and usages were part of a total Yorùbá culture. At one level this could be seen as a dilution of local cultures, but at another it was an enrichment, for it taught the schoolboys and girls a broader range of Yorùbá cultural elements than they were exposed to at home; and it taught them to value them and acquire them *as* "cultural heritage."

This mining of the seam of cultural identity—and in the process disseminating and reinforcing that sense of identity—was only possible for the popular theatres because of the sheer size of the Yorùbá-speaking population. There are currently estimated to be about 25 million people for whom Yorùbá is the first language in Nigeria. In the time of the greatest expansion of the theatre companies, in the early 1970s, their numbers (never accurately assessed) were probably already enough to populate a medium-sized European nation state. A theatre group could tour indefinitely and never cover all the towns and villages that were eager to see it. When groups went to the north of Nigeria, they needed to make no concessions, for the Yorùbá enclaves in northern cities supplied ample audiences. This made it an economically viable proposition to invest exclusively in a mono-ethnic audience, in the way that it was not for the concert parties in Ghana or Togo. Ògúnǹdé made one attempt to adapt his style and language to Ghana, in his tour of 1948, when he staged a concert party–style show in English—but this was a lone attempt. All other groups dug themselves deeper and deeper into the linguistic experience of the Yorùbá. In the process, the ethnic loyalties that were eventually thoroughly politicized by the Action Group and its successor, the UPN, were boosted. The result, in comparison with the concert parties, was a very dense linguistic texture. The loose-jointedness of the concert parties extends to the languages in which they are performed, the brilliantly ironical juxtapositions and switches matching the shifts in character, scene, and situation, and the not fully integrated alternations between highlife songs and dialogue. The Yorùbá plays, by contrast, offered a seamless web of Yorùbáness, so much so that non-Yorùbás were rarely considered interesting enough to be worth representing.

It was not only the size of the Yorùbá-speaking public that made the difference, however, but the social and business relationships which structured it. The organization of the Yorùbá popular theatre companies, and their mode of operation as small businesses, followed the lines of other social organizational patterns in Yorùbá society. The key aspects of this could be summed up as, first, a system of "big man-ism," in which individuals (usually men) made a place for themselves by the recruitment of supporters, whose adherence and recognition gave them power; and second, an extremely old and sophisticated trading system, participated in by both men and women, in which networks of influence, and public recognition and visibility, were essential. Theatre could be seen as deriving from these features of the social system—a system founded on visibility, display, and showmanship to attract adherents and customers—as well as supporting them and feeding into them.

Each theatre company revolved around its "founding father" and was usually named, formally or informally, after him (the Lérè Pàímó Theatre, the Oyin Adéjobí Theatre, and so on). These founders were almost always male, as were "big men" more generally in Yorùbáland. They attracted "adherents" both in the form of the members of their company and in the form of a loyal public. The adherence of the company was something that was always of great concern to the founder. The relationship that bound the actor to the company was not a bureaucratic-rational one: it was not usually a legal contract, even when given the outward forms of one. Rather, it was a personal loyalty and service such as obtains between patrons and supporters in other spheres. The founder's actors are his "boys"; they are expected to "serve" [sìn] him, and in return he is expected to protect and reward them. It is well known that Ògúnǹdé married his leading ladies in order to keep them in the company. This was in fact a common practice, and its significance is that in this way the founder attaches to himself not only some valued adherents, the basis of his success, but also the source of further adherents, his children, who will also serve him in due course. Whatever financial arrangements were made on paper, in practice the founder would pay his group in an ad hoc manner, depending on the amount of the take after a performance or a tour. Some of his most valued performers might take a regular proportion of the profit, while others were notionally on a fixed salary; but since income fluctuated, in effect the latter were dependent on his good will and good sense, while the "shareholding" members, if there were any, needed bonds of personal loyalty to tide them over the lean patches. The importance placed on personal loyalty was to be seen in the way founders berated former members who had defected either to join a more prosperous group or to found a new one of their own. The founder, then, had to build himself up by surrounding himself with "people"—the more weighty and well known the better. Some founders successfully operated with a co-star: either a "manager," a right-hand man whose loyalty was beyond question (e.g., Lérè Pàímó's manager Ahmed Odùọlá, or Adéjọbí's manager Kàrímù Adépòjù), or a wife who was almost as well known and beloved by the public as he was (Ògúnñdé's and Ògúnmọ́lá's first wives). Nonetheless, the founder was the hub of the company. Ultimately, all control rested in his hands and all decisions were referred to him. He was often the principal composer of the play's music, the prime architect of its plot, and the person who allocated actors to roles and vice versa.

The centrality of the founder in every aspect of the practical and artistic life of the company means that the history of the development of Yorùbá popular theatre was, much more than that of Ghanaian concert party, indeed a story of the deeds of great men. Each leader had to create a distinctive and magnetically attractive persona in order to establish himself both with his actors and in the public eye. This led to the exploration of distinct styles, an innovativeness and invention that went far beyond the economical and elegant permutations of a handful of well-known plot situations characteristic of Ghanaian and Togolese concert party. Thus, because of the dynamics of big man-ism, the diversification of the theatre was given a tremendous boost.

It also meant, however, that the corporate integrity of theatre companies was always under threat of vitiation. All successful actors wanted to become the boss of their own company, and might leave at short notice to try their luck. The company was the big man's company, and however much mental and physical effort the members put into it, it was ultimately an extension of *his* persona. This may help to explain why the collapse, when it came, was so complete. In times of economic hardship, once the big men of the theatre could no longer bind their members to them with the radiance of their prosperity, plays disappeared from the stage. Theatre companies were intermittently cannibalized by the few, highly successful bosses who had broken into filmmaking and who could cream off the stars from dozens of other aspiring, struggling groups. The latest development is low-budget dramas made on video, for sale in motor parks and supermarkets, which recycle many of the stage plays' themes, retaining the essential improvised style (see Haynes 1994). What is missing, in both the films and the videos, is the collaborative presence of the audience, whose role in the constitution of the stage plays was so vital. It remains to be seen whether this lack can be overcome and a true indigenous cinema emerge from among the débris of the formerly great theatre of the stage.

All three theatres, then—the concert party of Ghana and Togo and the popular theatre of western Nigeria—have had a discernible rise and decline. Ghanaian concert party and Yorùbá popular theatre both began in the colonial period as exclusive forms of entertainment based on imported models; Togolese concert party was a later outgrowth and imitation of the Ghanaian form. But because of their capacity to speak of widely felt contemporary concerns in a novel and fascinating medium, these theatres rapidly expanded, indigenized, and popularized themselves. In all three cases the innovation and impetus came from the urban-focused, artisanal and petty bourgeois strata who had some education and some aspirations to self-betterment but were not themselves members of the élite. The theatres were not the products of well-meaning government arts or education policies, even though governments and educational institutions did from time to time take an oblique and ambivalent interest in them. Rather, they were self-supporting and self-directed businesses—often struggling to keep afloat—in the fluid informal sectors of Accra, Sekondi-Takoradi, Lomé, Ìbàdàn, Òsogbo. . . . Their inspiration came from themselves and their audiences.

Being largely "unofficial" arts, which attracted official recognition and sponsorship only partially and intermittently, they were not highly regarded by the élites. Even among their huge popular audiences, their public image was constantly in need of renovation and rescue from accusations of disreputable behavior. The leader of the Jaguar Jokers in Ghana felt the need to explain to headmasters that they could send their pupils to the show with a clear conscience because the plays taught valuable lessons; the members of the Èdá Theatre Company in Nigeria insisted that, far from being drunken layabouts, they were "like preachers." Their insecurity—both financial and social—was mitigated, in all three theatres, by an incipient strong professionalism, at least among the permanent core members of the companies. To them, theatre was a vocation as well as a business, and they took pride in their expertise. But their insecurity may also be considered to have attuned the actors to layers of popular feeling and popular experience to which anthropologists and literary scholars of West Africa have had little previous access. In the "In" to the Jaguar Jokers' concert presented in this volume, the comedian Yaw Bob introduces a number as "a really nice song, it's for workers and it's the sort of song that will let them forget they are hungry when they are returning home from work." The plays in this volume all, in different ways, address the theme of hardship. They present scenarios of uncertainty, poverty, hunger, mistreatment of the helpless, reversals of fortune, marital dead ends, and the spectacle of others illicitly enriching themselves. The solutions they offer are largely conservative; but the dominant impression is a sense of a resilient will to survive, a will to deal properly and philosophically with life's vicissitudes, by unleashing on them hilarious laughter as well as solemn moralizing.

All three theatre movements seem to have passed their heyday (Ghanaian concert party's was in the 1950s and 1960s, Togolese concert party's and Yorùbá popular theatre's in the 1960s and 1970s) and to have entered a phase of diminution, decline, or dissolution. However, it does not seem possible that the enormous imaginative energy of these theatres and their audiences could simply evaporate. They may prove resilient enough to reassert their distinctive popular ethos through television, film, video, or indeed through a new phase of live theatre in the future.

NOTES

1. John Collins talked to all these concert party performers, as well as many others. The information in this section of the introduction is based largely on interviews and conversations with the following, in addition to the members of the Jaguar Jokers: Kwaa Mensah (3 and 8 January 1989, 20 June 1989, 20 and 30 May 1990, 14 November 1990, all Accra); Mr. Gambia, concert party promoter (31 May 1973, Koforidua); Bob Vans, Bob Thompson, and Bob Cole, concert party "Bobs" (August 1974, Arts Council of Ghana, Accra); James "Jimmy" Moxon, in the entertainment business (several talks between 1973 and 1975); Mark Anthony, concert party visual artist (19 December 1973, Agona Swedru); Ishmael Bob Johnson, concert party comedian (March 1974, Teshi Nungua); A.A.S. Williams of Williams and Marbel (July 1973, James Town, Accra); E.K. Nyame (8 June 1975, James Town, Accra); Bob Ansah, concert party comedian (18 May 1976, Ghana Arts Council, Accra); Love Nortey of the Happy Stars (September 1969, Nsawam); Francis Kenya of the Riches Big Sound concert (a number of conversations in 1971 when John Collins stayed at his house in Madina); John Darkey, National Commission on Culture (interviewed 1982: see Collins 1982b); Nti Agyeman of Adom Internationals concert party (1988, Bokoor house, Accra: see Collins 1992); Vida Hynes (née Oparabea), former concert party actress (18 March 1990, Toronto, Canada); Adelaide Buabeng, concert party actress (31 May 1991, South Legon, Accra); Professor K. N. Bame, Institute of African Studies, University of Ghana, Legon (2 October 1991, Legon).

2. See Bame (1985) and Sutherland (1970). Bob Johnson, who was born in 1904, remembers this show of Teacher Yalley's and believes it to have been the first of its kind. However, according to Catherine Cole (personal communication 1994) archival records show that African comedy duos were performing for white audiences in the Gold Coast as early as 1903. We are grateful to her for sharing with us this information.

3. The reader who wants a more detailed account of Bob Johnson's life should consult Efua Sutherland (1970).

4. Konkoma or konkomba was an Akan highlife style popular in the late 1930s, 1940s, and 1950s. It developed as a "poor man's" village version of the "adaha" highlife music of the local brass bands. It was sung by groups of men and women, who would march, then congregate and form a circle, inside which they performed competitive dances which involved trying to bump each other over. The brass-band influences in konkoma included syncopated marching, uniforms, a baton-throwing conductor, and the "pati" side-drum of local brass bands. But konkoma groups did away with expensive brass-band instruments, substituting local per-

cussion instruments and voices. Although a variant of the name is "konkomba," this musical style has nothing to do with the Konkomba people of northern Ghana, but is part of an Akan expression "me twa konkoma na bo fum" (I cut konkoma and I fall down).

5. The first highlifes on disk were by Sam's Kumasi Trio, recorded by Zonophone in London in June 1928.

6. For detailed discussions of the growth of highlife styles, see Coplan (1978), Chernoff (1985), Collins (1976b, 1986, 1994).

7. An example of a plot that seems to leave an important evildoer unpunished is the Osei Kofi Concert Party's *Ye Pɛ Akoma Mu dɔ* (We Won't Love from the Heart), which Karin Barber saw in September 1990 in Accra. In this story, a bad older sister tries to make her good younger sister sell her share of a joint inheritance of land. When the younger sister refuses, the older sister uses spirit agents to kill the younger sister and her son. The younger sister's husband and daughter survive. The dead mother and dead brother now appear to the daughter to warn her against the wicked older sister and to advise her how to select a worthy husband. The rest of the play revolves around the competition between three suitors for her hand, and the trick she and her father play on them to expose the insincere fortune hunters among them. The wicked older sister never gets her comeuppance, as the second plot displaces the first before its resolution.

8. The earliest known example of this feedback is the introduction of Goombay drumming—a neo-African cult music of Jamaican Maroons settled in Freetown in 1800. Goombay subsequently spread through much of West Africa. In Ghana it is called Gome. It is also found in Mali, Cameroon and Ivory Coast, where it was carried by migrant workers. See also E. J. Collins (1987).

9. For a detailed account of early West African thinkers and writers, see July (1968). For further discussion of early West African cultural nationalism, see Moraes Farias and Barber (1990).

10. Other similar words that have been adopted into Ghanaian popular language more recently are "guy," "apache," "Jack Toronto," "Santana man," and "Afro."

11. See Zinsou 1975, 1987, for texts of two of his plays.

12. A motor park is a large open-air space found in every town and city in coastal West Africa, where a variety of commercial goods and passenger vehicles arrive from, and depart to, medium- and long-distance destinations. There is a wide range of these vehicles, and their local names vary. There are buses of all sizes; "mammy wagons," four- or six-wheeled vehicles similar to goods trucks except that the back part, behind the driver's cab, is arranged with benches and enclosed with a locally made, usually wooden, often partially open superstructure, carrying twenty or more people; "taxis"—often station wagons, which carry 4–8 people, ply established routes, and only leave when they are full; and small passenger vans, called "danfo" in Nigeria, carrying approximately ten people.

13. Ládiípọ̀ became known outside his local school and church circles when Ulli Beier's Ìbàdàn Mbari club of artists and writers invited him to come and perform a Christmas cantata for them in 1961. Beier's long-term support and collaboration significantly contributed to the realization of his distinctive dramatic style. Ògúnmọ́lá so impressed a visiting Rockefeller agent (again through the good offices of Beier) that he was given a grant to spend six months at Ìbàdàn University's drama department in 1962, shortly after he had gone professional.

14. For a scholarly discussion of the establishment of "standard Yorùbá," see Fágbọrún 1994.

# 2

## The Jaguar Jokers and *Orphan Do Not Glance*

JOHN COLLINS

### EXTRACTS FROM A TRAVELING MUSICIAN'S DIARY

I first met Mr. Bampoe of the Jaguar Jokers in 1969 through my father, and the three of us discussed the idea of my going on "trek" with the band. I had already begun to learn highlife on my guitar and so jumped at the notion of joining them as a musician, for I would be able to learn guitar-band music and teach them the blues and rock I had been playing in England.

SEPTEMBER 1969

The first trek I went on lasted two weeks during September 1969, and we played at many different stations in Accra, Akropong, Nsawam, Begoro, and half a dozen villages around Akim Oda. The mornings and early afternoons were usually spent traveling in a hired mini-bus, festooned with signs reading "Opia," "JJ's T.V. masters" and the name of the town we were staging in that night—all painted on with Reckitt's laundry blue. We played in all sorts of buildings: cinemas, bars and nightclubs, halls and private compounds. In the latter we sometimes had to use a crude wooden platform for a stage.

After we reached our destination came the long job of unloading the drums, boxes of costumes, wooden cartoons, speakers, and amplifiers from the roof rack and setting them up in the theatre. Then one of the speakers would be fixed back onto the roof rack and, using the smaller amplifier run on batteries, we would go out on "campaign" to the neighboring villages. One of the boys, sitting next to the driver, would make announcements through a microphone and others would play the electric guitars, congas, and claves in the back. I was usually taken along as I was a great attraction, taking over the guitar from Doku and introduced as an Oboroni [European] playing at that night's show. Coming right in the

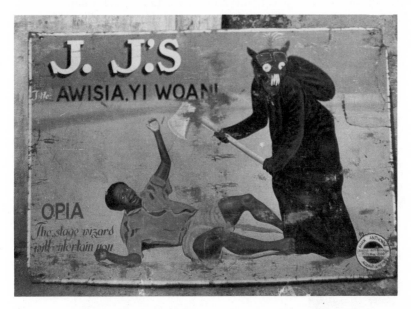

*Jaguar Jokers' cartoon advertising* Orphan Do Not Glance. *Photograph © John Collins.*

middle of a working day, we had an amazing effect in the villages, for people would simply stop what they were doing and start to dance: women, carrying baskets on their heads and babies on their backs, toddlers, old people, farmers; everyone within hearing distance of the speaker would gyrate. They were especially excited by the fast "jazz" playing of the guitarist who would be doing smooth glissando runs up and down the fret-board to an uptempo Dagomba highlife or a pachanga or congo number; they even seemed to appreciate my attempts at this. As we drove slowly around the village we were followed by a constant horde of small children screaming "Opia . . . Opia . . . Opia. . . ." We would sometimes be out for over two hours but were usually back before dark and in time for "chop."

At dusk the stage was lit, unless there was electricity, by a couple of tilley lamps (kerosene pressure lamps) which gave a fine white glow hanging above the stage. Around 8:30 and after the children who always seemed to infest us had been driven out, the amps were switched on, instruments tuned, and the show started off with the "inside rhythm." This consisted of between one and two and a half hours of Ghanaian guitar-band music: highlifes, congo numbers, pachangas, cha chas, South African patha-patha, and, most popular of all—soul music. Even in the villages James Brown was the absolute king of music, especially with the younger people. Today one can still see tro-tros (local passenger vehicles) displaying "J.B. forever."

The play itself was a three-hour affair, and always seemed to start much later in the rural areas than in the towns—at one village I remember it started after midnight! The night's show closed with an hour or so of dancing, after which we finally got to bed, sleeping on the floor of the theatre. We were up in the morning by seven, so when did we sleep? If we were lucky we would get in about three or four hours, but sometimes, when we traveled straight after the play, none at all. The bandsmen therefore invariably became good at catnapping and would fall asleep in the bus, on their mats on arriving, in fact whenever they got a chance.

I spent a lot of time during the actual plays in the anteroom, a curtained-off section or room behind the stage, lit by candles. Bandsmen in various stages of slumber would be dotted around, with Mr. Baidoo snoring the loudest; some of them knew their parts so well that they could

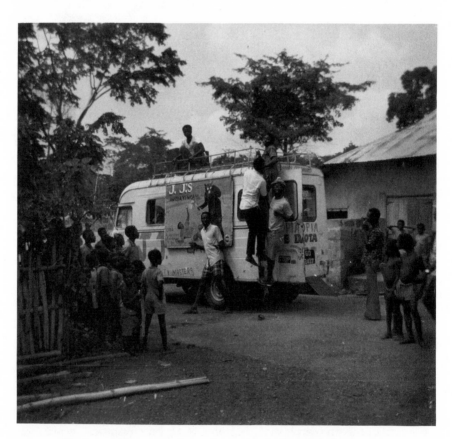

*The Jaguar Jokers preparing to "campaign." Photograph © John Collins.*

take a twenty-minute nap here and a five-minute one there, always knowing exactly when to get up and rush on stage. Other actors would be putting on makeup and changing clothes and I would sit there talking to them in between their acts. I was always struck by the difference between Mr. Bampoe and Mr. K. A. Hammond, the two principal actors, on and off stage. On stage Mr. Hammond, or Johnson as he is called, wears either a loose-fitting suit, which is just right for his loose-limbed dances, or a traditional cloth which he makes a great show of adjusting. On and off the stage his language is slow and controlled and he can speak the most beautiful Church English. Mr. Bampoe on the other hand is a short compact man, but extremely agile, who plays the extroverted and mischievous Opia character: a complete contrast to his real-life personality, which is rather retiring and phlegmatic. He used to get particularly annoyed by members of the audience who, seeing him in his ordinary clothes, would call him or accost him as Opia. This real abhorrence of recognition was the reason, he told me, that he liked his ground charcoal makeup; for off stage hardly anyone would realize who he was. The third principal actor was Mr. Baidoo, who played the matronly roles. The other female impersonators were all slim young men who would be in various stages of drag: putting on earrings and high heels, hitching up brassieres stuffed with socks, adjusting their wigs or crouched over a mirror for the final touches of pomade, red face powder, and eye shadow.

Once we were actually stoned by an angry crowd. It happened when we had just set up everything in a smart theatre-cum-cinema, built by a mining firm for its workers, in a diamond town near Oda. The chief of that area had made a declaration, a short time before, that concert parties were only to charge 20 pesewas entrance, and as we had not known this we were charging 40 pesewas, which led to an argument with the crowd outside. We would not budge, as our price was the usual one for villages and small towns, and anyway it was a question of concert bands sticking together, for if we had played for the 20 pesewas we would have set a precedent that would have ruined the business for others coming after us. We told them that we weren't going to play, closed the doors, and packed everything up. It was then that some members of the crowd threw stones over the wall at us, but they soon dispersed and left for their houses. As we drove off a little later we passed many of the disappointed villagers, some of whom had walked five or six miles to see us, but in spite of everything they all smiled and waved at us in good humor. However, we must have upset some of them, for hardly had we gone a few miles when we had a puncture. We put on the spare, started up again and had another blowout. Nails had been driven into our tires. We had to stay in the forest that night and sleep in the bus, and some of the hungrier boys managed to catch a scraggly little rat which they gutted, singed, roasted, and ate.

*Bandsmen setting up the stage. Photograph © John Collins.*

The biggest audience we had on that trek was at the town of Akropong, during the Akwapim people's yam festival. It was absolutely jammed with people dressed up in smart traditional clothes with the chiefs distinguished by their royal umbrellas spinning above the crowd. There was enough business for two concerts that night. It really gets chilly up in the Akwapim hills at that time of year, and by the time the show was about to begin the clouds descended and we were so cold that I and some of the bandsmen went to an akpeteshie (local gin) bar to warm up. Mr. Bampoe didn't come with us, as he never drinks or smokes.

## JUNE 1972

Although I visited Mr. Bampoe, Hammond, and the bandsmen from time to time, I did not go on trek with them again until June 1972, just after I had finished my degree at Legon. After finals I took a friend and went on several short treks in the Accra-Nsawam area. My friend, Peter Wilks, was also in the sociology department and a musician. We had been

*Concert poster for the Jaguar Jokers. Photograph © John Collins.*

in an Afro-beat band called Bokoor ("Cool") the year before, playing second band to the Uhurus Professional Dance Band. With the help of the J.J.s' drummer and bass guitarist we were given a spot during the inside rhythm to play some rock and Afro-beat numbers. I also played some blues harmonica, and the audience didn't know quite what to make of it. They couldn't believe that such a small instrument could make such a "thick" sound, and they kept looking around for the organ. Mr. Bampoe hadn't known I could play this instrument, and he was so excited by it that he rushed from the gate to the stage, injuring himself slightly in the process; I had to promise to buy him one and teach him to play it after that.

In the three years I had been away from the band there had been some changes. For a start, it had grown from fifteen to twenty members. They no longer depended on accumulators and gas lamps, as they had bought a compact, portable German generator. They had also replaced their rather eclectic collection of amplifiers and speakers with proper band equipment, including a decent public address system. The female impersonators were wearing Afro wigs which had since become the fashion, almost completely replacing the European-style wigs that had been most popular before. Two new styles of music had come onto the scene and had been incorporated into the band's repertoire. These were Nigerian Afro-beat, influenced by soul, and reggae, a West Indian music that had suddenly leaped into the Ghanaian limelight.

## DECEMBER 1973

Previously I had always gone with the J.J.s as a musician, but this time Mr. Bampoe and I had discussed the idea of writing a book; so I went loaded down with guitar, harmonicas, notebooks, tape-recorder, tapes, and a cloth. I had arranged to meet them at a small village near Swedru and arrived there late on a Monday afternoon. Although I had checked the venue in that morning's *Daily Graphic*, the townspeople told me that the show had been canceled and I should go back to Swedru to check what had happened. I caught a tro-tro and one of the passengers told me that he had heard they were staging at Nsaba, just north of Swedru. He told me he was going there himself, and when we arrived at Swedru and were walking over to the Nsaba motor park, whom did I see but Mr. Hammond, wearing a suit, with suitcase in hand. We were both surprised to see one another, and he told me that he had just come down from seeing his family and was also looking for the band. All three of us went to Nsaba together and on reaching there at about eight we discovered that the date had been changed from the Monday to the Tuesday. There had obviously been a mix-up so, rather than staying, we headed back to Adoagyiri where we were told the postponement had been caused by a breakdown of the mini-bus. I spent the night in the J.J.s' guest-room.

The following afternoon I joined the mini-bus with the rest of the band and we took the Swedru road for Nsaba. We arrived at the Susu Biribi nightclub at 5:30, just in time to set up the equipment before it got dark. The concrete stage was set at the back of a sunken courtyard surrounded on three sides by an open veranda—a perfect theatre. The mini-bus also got off before dark, for the campaign, and I was surprised when they didn't ask me to go with them. The reason, I found, was that the J.J.s had discontinued the old method with its live music and now just advertised with amplified voice alone. They did however try to compensate for the resulting loss of impact by slinging from the truck large wooden paintings, called cartoons, which depicted scenes from the play; but I never thought this new type of campaigning matched the excitement generated by the fast highlife and congo music with which they had announced themselves in the past. The generator was used on the campaign and when that was over and the boys returned it was connected to the electrical system which had been installed while they were away.

By nine o'clock the inside rhythm, or inside campaign as they sometimes called it, was in full swing. Doku was on rhythm guitar, Jackson on bass, with Yaw Bob playing highlife guitar and Ofei doing soul. They were supported by other members on trap drums, congas, maracas, and claves. They started off with nine or ten highlifes, pachangas, cha chas, and congo numbers. One of the highlifes was based on an Ewe agbadja rhythm and another, the most popular, was a Nigerian one called "O Yea Mama." After this it was time for "souls" which included James Brown's "Gimme Some More," "Pop Corn," "Papa Got a Brand New Bag" and numbers such as "Funky Funky," "Funky Four Corners," "Chain Gang," "Mr. Big-stuff" and one by Millie (Millicent Small). It also included some West African soul, or Afro-beat as it is called: "Akula," a Ghanaian number, several by Nigeria's Felá Aníkúlápó-Kútì, and "Music for Gong-gong" by the London-based Osibisa. This last song was by far the most popular that Christmas. We played it at both ends of the show, then again as our finale, sometimes two or three times over. The band also played reggae, with Jimmy Cliff's "Synthetic World," "Grooving Out of Life," "It's Too Late," and "I Can See Clearly Now" the favorites. Also popular was the music of the Staple Singers, a band that came to fame in Ghana through the 1971 Soul to Soul concert at the Black Star Square in Accra. There was of course a "smoochy time" when the lights were dimmed and people danced to excruciating songs like "These Arms of Mine" and "All My Sorrows." The "souls" finished on an Afro-beat number and were followed, after a fifteen-minute break, by four highlifes composed and sung by the newly arrived Obeng, songs which the J.J.s hoped to have recorded. The music lasted until 11:20, completing about two and a half hours of inside rhythm, with the "souls" taking most of the time.

When the music had finished the place was packed, at 50 pesewas a head. There were plenty of benches to sit on, brought in by small boys who would beg, borrow, or steal them to earn themselves a free ticket. They weren't allowed to sit on them however, but had to sit right up front on the floor, which was really the best place to be anyway. Scuffles were constantly breaking out among them for the best view; then they would shift around a bit and then settle down until the next disturbance. The play, which I recorded, ended at 2:40 and was followed by three quarters of an hour of dancing, after which we finally got to bed.

## 19 DECEMBER

We got up at 7:30 and by 10 all twenty-two of us had piled into the Renault and were headed for Swedru and breakfast. We stopped at a chop bar, a small wooden shack behind the main motor park, where we ate fufu or ampesi with grass-cutter stew. By noon we had reached Abbam and after passing almost through the dusty town we pulled up outside a large walled compound, inside of which there was a small raised stage with two anterooms behind. The proprietor, whose house adjoined this courtyard, had built the place especially for concerts, dances, and religious meetings.

Hardly had we got the equipment inside when a meeting of the whole band was convened in one of the anterooms. It went on for a hot and noisy one and a half hours, and two problems were dealt with. One was a question of discipline: some of the bandsmen had got into the habit of roaming the town before the show, looking for drinks and women, and weren't coming back in time for the inside rhythm. It was agreed that everyone, without exception, was to be in the theatre by 8:30 at the latest. The second matter was more serious. Just before this particular Christmas the world oil crisis, precipitated by the Arab-Israeli War, had occurred. The result in Ghana was that for a two-week period it was almost impossible to buy gasoline. The J.J.s, who were on a long trek in Brong-Ahafo at the time, had great difficulty in buying fuel for the bus and generator, and decided to return home. They hoped at least to get together a local tour for the Christmas holiday. It took them five days to get back, begging for gasoline, gallon by gallon, all the way. Although by the time I joined them the shortage had lifted, they had made no money on the Brong-Ahafo trip and this meant only a small Christmas bonus for the members. This problem was aired at the meeting and the boys consulted, for "money palaver" can be a most disruptive force in a concert party. The band boys finally agreed that the little "chop money" they had received on that trek was all they could expect in the circumstances.

After the meeting Mr. Bampoe and I, exhausted, went to sleep at a friend's house and only woke up when we were told the promoter had kindly arranged food for all of us. By the time we had finished eating it was time to play. That night huge rhinoceros beetles were out and zooming down at us from nearby palm trees—attracted by the stage lights. For some reason the turnout for the show was rather sluggish and people were only slowly trickling in, at 60 pesewas a seat. We did *Awisia Yi Wo Ani* (*Orphan Do Not Glance*). Because of the small audience, and the consequent lack of audience response, the play was condensed from the usual three and a quarter to two and a half hours, and the closing dance was also shortened. We slept long that night.

## 20 DECEMBER

The theatre at Besease (Beseadze) was a covered concrete stage in the courtyard of a large and imposing compound house. We arrived there about one. The place was like a fort with its massive iron swing gate embedded in an archway. Outside was a signboard that read:

Belongs to Kofi Boakye
   Animal and Bird Dealer
    Parrot
     Dove
      Tortoise
      Monkey

By seven the whole place was filled by residents of the house, bandsmen, small boys, and women setting up food stalls. Before we started, the children were driven out by older boys playfully wielding sticks.

The place was packed that night with at least four hundred people, and I remember being struck by their dancing. Hardly any of the couples danced together. Each one was self-contained, with a serious look of extreme dedication on his or her face, each trying to outdo the others in vigor and bluff.

The musicians were also putting on the "bluffing" look—sucking in the lips, tensing the skin around them and looking down their noses through half-closed lids. The conga player, Kwadjo Fordjour, was somehow even managing to sing and chew gum at the same time, so that whenever a note came out you could see a great red blob hanging precariously from his tongue. During "Music for Gong-gong" Ofei did a fantastic guitar break in which he somehow converted the instrument into a trumpet and played a long reveille. His favorite stance was well forward into the audience with his legs wide apart and knees bent like a crooner; he was continually scratching himself, swatting insects, picking his nose, and generally taking absolutely no notice of the audience who were weaving around him. Doku, the other guitarist, stood well back from the crowd and played with heavy eyes and a wistful smile on his face. After the souls, which lasted for one and a half hours, Yaw Bob came in to play a finger-style rhythm for Obeng's highlifes; he has very large almond-shaped eyes and a smile that splits his large face in two—a real joker's face.

For the show at Beseadze, the play itself was slightly modified, as one of the young female impersonators had to leave suddenly to visit his mother, and the role of Dansowa had to be edited out. After the show, instead of staying in the town, we packed up and headed straight back for Adoagyiri, arriving there just after dawn.

### 21 DECEMBER

I spent the Friday morning sleeping in the guest room and at 3:30 in the afternoon we were off to Somanya. When we reached the cinema where we were to stage, Mr. Bampoe and I left the bandsmen to unpack and went with a promoter to his house, where he had prepared some food for us. The crowd was small that night, dwarfed by the enormous hall, and the show finished at 2:30, without the usual closing dance.

## 22 DECEMBER

We left the town Saturday noon, but before our departure a short executive meeting was held in which it was agreed that Nyamekye was to become a full executive member from the New Year. On the journey Mr. Bampoe told me that the band had only received 80 cedis and the promoter almost nothing at all for the night. It seemed that the proprietor of the cinema had assured our promoter that the townspeople would have been paid by the previous Friday and there would have been money in their pockets; so the promoter paid him 80 cedis for the hall. We found out too late that no one had in fact received their monthly salaries and we all had to cut our losses—everyone, that is, except the proprietor.

We pulled up outside our next station, the Unity Garden Bar at Nkawkaw, in the middle of the afternoon. It was a small but pleasant place with a courtyard surrounded by trees and shrubs; the only trouble was that it was impossible to take a siesta because of the incessant racket from the jukebox and some jackpots (slot machines). Mr. Bampoe and I went to sleep at his brother's house, only a short walk away; this was the same brother who had acted with him in the early days. There was a good turnout for the evening's performance and Mr. Bampoe received the full 180 cedis that he had asked for from the three young promoters. The next morning I said goodbye to the band and Mr. Bampoe and Boahene, one of the younger actors, saw me off at the motor park. I intended to spend a few days over Christmas with my family in Legon, but told Mr. Bampoe that I would join them afterwards.

## 29 DECEMBER

I went to Adoagyiri by motorbike. When I arrived I found that the whole band had gone to Mangoase, except Mr. Bampoe, who was waiting for me. He got on the back of the bike and we took the short bush road to the town. Mangoase is a rich cocoa town, or it was before the swollen root disease destroyed most of that industry in the 1940s. This previous glory is reflected today by the large stone buildings, ornate but crumbling. It was around 7 P.M. when we arrived at this hilly town. We were headed for an old cocoa shed that was no longer in use but was given over, at 8 cedis a night, to concerts, parties, dances, and the like. I was able to drive my bike right inside this enormous stone warehouse, but since it was dark I couldn't make out then quite what the place was;

it seemed a bit like a church hall or even a small cathedral, with its two lines of square pillars going off into the gloom. Dotted around were feeble lights, glimmering islands in distant corners. Bandsmen were talking or sleeping around solitary candles. The young Boahene was with his even younger wife, resting on a mat; he had brought her along with him from Adoagyiri in the mini-bus.

Dodo and the electrically minded bandsmen seemed to spend ages adjusting the German generator outside the back end of the hall and stringing the flex down to the stage. Then suddenly there was light and the audience began to trickle in. We switched on the amps, tuned up, and started to play. By ten o'clock most of the younger people were dancing, older ones were sitting on benches, and the "smallboys" were in a tight semicircle around the stage. After a while I stopped playing and Ofei took over from me.

I went outside to buy some tea and bread from girls who had put up wooden stalls. These were lit by paraffin lamps fabricated from evaporated milk tins. The girls were selling a whole range of things: oranges to drink, P.K., Hacks, cigarettes "one one," and rice and stew. As I was sitting down finishing my drink I recognized the familiar opening chorus. The show had started, so I went back inside. All eyes were focused on the three comedians, the audience of several hundred looking like moths clustered around the stage lights. Many of them were standing and some had even managed to wedge themselves into the spacious window nooks four feet above the ground.

I circled the audience and went behind the stage and through the curtain into the anteroom. I stayed there for a time talking to the actors and then went outside into the audience. It was really hot in the building and there was no breeze as all the windows had been boarded up. On top of that the acoustics were shocking. I had intended to record the play but gave up this idea. The play finished around two in the morning, the crowd getting especially excited towards the end when Mr. Baidoo, dressed as a crazy woman, ran among them chased by Opia. The show closed with half an hour of souls, mostly "Music for Gong-gong," and then reluctantly the young dancers left.

Suddenly the place seemed empty and bandsmen were putting benches together for their bed mats. Mr. Hammond made himself a grand bed on the stage, using two thick mats and a thin rug, and Mr. Bampoe, myself, and five others made preparations to sleep on the floor of the anteroom. Some of the bandsmen weren't intending to sleep, however, for hardly had we put head to floor when we heard a tumult echoing from the direction of the door. Mr. Bampoe reluctantly got up to see what was happening. Some of the bandsmen and the driver had made a plan. The

Renault had acted as tro-tro earlier in the evening by picking up people from nearby villages who had wanted to come and see us. When it was time to take them back, the bandsmen decided only to take the men and leave the women behind to share out among themselves. There was an angry scene, as the men from the villages, who had brought their girls along and paid for their tickets, didn't like the idea at all. In the fracas the truck's back door was somehow unhinged and some of the girls were screaming that they wanted to be taken home. An annoyed Mr. Bampoe soon put a stop to the whole business when he ordered the driver to take everyone home. It wasn't really his night at all, for we hadn't earned much money anyway. Three months before, they had been hired by the same promoter but the show was rained out and to compensate for this they were only being paid chop money for the evening's performance.

## 30 DECEMBER

We got up at 6:30; already the long job of dismantling the equipment and packing it on the truck had begun. Boahene and I, on the bike, took the good road to Nsawam as he wanted to join his wife, who had taken an early tro-tro there. I breakfasted at their house and later in the day we met up with the bus; we were going to Kwaben—or so we thought. En route we stopped at a gas station at Anyinem and by sheer coincidence met the Kwaben promoter, who told us there had been a change of plan. We had thought everything settled as we had the date confirmed by that day's *Graphic*. Mr. Obobi, the promoter, told us he had sent someone up to Kwaben who had found there had been a mixup and another band was playing there that night. He therefore suggested that we should play at Osino, a town not very far away. When we arrived there at four in the afternoon we were fortunately able to arrange a show, even at such short notice.

Our stage was a roofed one in the courtyard of a fine two-storey house where, for tea, we ate some of the sweet kenkey (blancmange made from cornstarch, water, and sugar, cooked and sold in a large green leaf) for which the town is famous. Indeed the place is so famous for this that it is often referred to as Osino-Graphic, for sweet kenkey makes an early morning meal just as a newspaper makes early reading.

After playing during the inside rhythm I collapsed and slept in the busy anteroom, and by the time Mr. Bampoe woke me the show had finished and people were leaving. He and the executive members wanted to use the room. They pulled some benches together for a table which they then sat around, dividing the money. The promoter hadn't turned up so all of it was going to the band, and after paying 40 cedis for the Renault and 20 to the proprietor of the house, they only had 40 cedis for themselves. This meeting seemed to take an incredible amount of time; all I wanted to do was to go back to sleep, and the last thing I remember before doing so was being fascinated by the largest moths I've ever seen in my life. They were attracted by the stage lights, and were so heavy that even with nine-inch wingspans they could hardly flap more than a few feet from the ground.

### 31 DECEMBER

We woke up early, but the morning passed in a relaxed way. Most of our group spent their time airing and ironing clothes and eating at a local chop-bar. Mr. Bampoe and I also went out to eat and then came back to eat again with Mr. Hammond and Baidoo. The proprietor had kindly provided us a breakfast of plantain and garden egg stew. It was noon before we left. This time we were headed for Ayikuma, a village near Larteh but at the foot of the Shai Hills.

We had only gone a few miles of our journey when one of our back tires blew and we all had to pile out to let Joe Dakota and Kuma change the wheel. While we were waiting the boys plucked red ripe pawpaws from the trees along the roadside. We had a feast. We stopped at Koforidua where the blown tire was repaired, and while there Mr. Bampoe and I went to greet a promoter for the town, Mr. Gambia, whom we found behind the counter of his toy shop.

From Koforidua we climbed up to Mamfe, and coming down past Larteh we could see Ayikuma laid out below. We arrived there at half past four, outside the Garden of Eden Bar. Mr. Bampoe and I ate at the house of one of his friends, and we stayed so long we only just made it back in time for Mr. Bampoe to whiten his lips and change his clothes for the opening chorus. It was New Year's Eve and the place was full of excited people, especially at the back where the dancing was going on. Beer and spirits, including local ones, were being consumed in quantity, and one man had become so fighting drunk he kept moving from one angry confrontation to another; but before anything ever happened the crowd would close on him and he would have to move on. I dozed through most of the play and thus into the New Year—I had also drunk a lot.

When I woke up in the morning it was to find Mr. Bampoe in deep conversation with a group of men around a table littered with the previous night's enjoyment. One of them was Mr. Obobi, who was apologizing for not having come to Mangoase to tell us about the change of plan at Kwaben, for, as Mr. Bampoe told him, we were bound to follow the advertisements he had put in the paper. By 12:30 the band was on its way again and I left them to return to Accra, but arranged to meet them at Easter. . . .

## THE J.J.S' STORY: THE BANDSMEN

Mr. Bampoe was the founder and leader of the Jaguar Jokers. His interest in acting began early, as he had always been good at his school's end-of-term plays, in which biblical stories, historical sketches, and *anansesem* (Akan spider tales) were performed. However, his main stimulus came from the many groups that on coming to Suhum stayed at his grandmother's house, for she was a Fanti and many of the concerts were from that part of the country. As a young boy Mr. Bampoe saw the Two Bobs and later the Western Trio, the Dix Covians, the Keta Trio, the Saltpond Trio, and of course the famous Axim Trio.

> I was eleven years old (1946) when I really got interested in the concert business and the main influence was the Axim Trio; for whenever they came to Suhum they would always lodge at our place. I remember seeing them stage *The Coronation of King George VI, The Bond of 1844,* and *The Downfall of Adolf Hitler.* These shows were always in English and during them they didn't use instruments. . . . The songs they played (before and after the play) were mostly quicksteps, ragtimes and foxtrots and I can remember a few like "In the Mood," "Blue Skies," "Somewhere over the Rainbow," "Stepping Out with a Memory" and "Professor Man." They also played a few highlifes such as "Everybody Likes Saturday Night," "Sweet Banana," "Ama wa ye awi" and "Kwerku dada sen."

Bob Johnson, leader of the Axim Trio, recalls that Mr. Bampoe "was a real rascal and he used to carry boxes to the concert room for us. Normally we just used to sleep on the floor but as we were great friends of Mr. Bampoe's uncle we stayed at the house." But let Mr. Bampoe continue:

> The afternoons after the Axim Trio had staged in our town I started staging with some schoolmates in my house. We had no music and no name but we painted our faces and imitated the Axim Trio. Our gate fee was a stick of plantain and children used to come.

This group of schoolboys, which was soon to become known as the Yanky Trio, got its first real outdooring thanks to the promoting activities of one of Mr. Bampoe's junior uncles, who also had an eye for profit:

> He advised us to stage at Bartholomew's, a yard behind a shop used for concerts (now called Ricardo's Bar), for money instead of for food. So we started to get money but my uncle and his friends, who were on the gate, used to cheat us and they only gave us food, but we didn't care then too much as all we wanted to do was stage. Our first station away was Asuboi, on the Nsawam road and seven miles from Suhum. Again my uncle and his friends took all. So then I planned with my younger brother (who was also a member of the trio) that next time they wanted us to go

anywhere we wouldn't. So they didn't mind us and went and arranged for themselves a play at Nankese—where they were beaten up. We teased them after this, for they thought they were going to make something better and they were beaten.

There was some opposition to Mr. Bampoe's acting career from his family, for although they all enjoyed concerts this profession was held in low repute and was not considered to offer a future for a young man:

> My senior uncle disagreed that schoolboys should adopt this habit (of acting) and we were told not to make concert again; but we were so stubborn, you see. We used to go secretly and stage somewhere and when we came home we would be beaten severely. This went on until after one holiday, after a longish tour, I showed him some sandals I had bought with the money I earned: they were what we called "Achimota sandals," expensive ones like the students at Achimota College used to wear, costing £1 7s a pair. This took my uncle by surprise and so he advised me that if I could make money out of the concert in my holidays, he had no objection.

The Yanky Trio kept going for two years, performing within the Akim Abuakwa area, and Mr. Bampoe recalls that the greatest profit they ever made for one night was at Asamanskese, where they made £4 16s. In those days they would never bother with advance publicity and posters but would, as Mr. Bampoe describes, simply make their way to a village:

> When we got there we would go to the chief and give him a shilling and he would send a gong-gong beater (town crier) through the town. After that we would contact a konkoma or brass band and before the show we supplied them with gin and afterwards we used to pay the konkoma bands 10s 6d and the brass bands one guinea.

As the Yanky Trio had no musicians of their own they had to recruit these bands from the towns and villages they were staging in, and send them around the area before the show, in order to attract as large a crowd as possible; the band would end up at the compound the trio had hired for the night and the music would continue inside until the place was filled up. However, once the show had started they would stop, although the actors would borrow a drummer who would acoustically highlight the play at the appropriate moments. At that time most towns of any importance had a brass band, and the poorer villages could usually boast a konkoma group; both would play marches, waltzes, foxtrots, quicksteps, and highlifes at important functions.

The concert itself was performed in English and lasted about an hour, being divided into an introductory comedy act and then a short play. For instance, one of their plays was called *The Latrine Worker* and lasted for half an hour. It was about a tenant who doesn't pay his latrine bill to the night soil collector. After some "palaver" the collector becomes so incensed with the tenant that he starts to throw the contents of the bucket (mud) at him, at the same time singing the following song:

> Oh Dad pay me
> Make I go
> I work for you moon-die [for one month]
> You don't want to pay me.

The trio finally broke up in 1948 when the members finished their primary education at the church mission school and scattered. Mr. Bampoe, then thirteen years old, went to stay with his mother in Adoagyiri in order to learn tailoring. He was never really happy at this and the final straw came in 1952, when he had all his equipment and cloth stolen. Broke, he decided to go back into the acting business professionally.

While in Adoagyiri Mr. Bampoe had often met Bob Ansah, one of the original members of the Two Bobs, who later joined the Saltpond Trio. Just about the time of the theft, Bob was looking for a band. He and Mr. Bampoe decided to team up, and they went to Accra to recruit I. E. Mason, who had been the female impersonator of the Dix Covians. Since the foundation meeting took place in Accra, they agreed to call the group the City Trio. The leader was Bob, who also wrote the plays. These, like those of the Yanky Trio, were in English. Again like the Yanky Trio they had to use local musicians, although they did have their own jazz drummer, a Ga called Nii Otoe. The shows were one and a half hours long and the group traveled more extensively than the Yanky Trio, trekking throughout Ashanti and the Volta Region. Two years later Mr. Bampoe teamed up with two brothers, K. M. Hammond and K. A. Hammond, who had a concert called the Jungle Jokers, and the three of them formed a new group, the Jaguar Jokers.

Both Hammond brothers were brought up in Koforidua. The senior brother, K. M. Hammond, after finishing primary standard seven, went straight into Bob Cole's Jovial Jokers. He stayed with them as female impersonator from 1948 to 1951 and then from 1952 to 1954 he was a member of Bob Thompson's Fanti Trio. The younger brother, K. A. Hammond, started training as a cobbler in 1948 but changed to pharmacy in 1952, and as he explains below, it was really from this time that he began to move with concert people:

> My elder brother was in the Fanti Trio and any place they would go I would follow, with my drugs which I carried in a port-manteau. Then

early in 1954 my brother asked me if I would join up with him to form a new group. . . . I agreed to play the part of gentleman.

This band formed by the two brothers was called the Jungle Jokers. They recruited a Mr. Tetteh to play the joker. The Jungle Jokers was in existence only a few months when the Hammond brothers met Mr. Bampoe in Nsawam and they decided to join forces, although the younger brother did need some convincing.

> Bampoe tried to persuade me to join the new group but I told him I didn't want to be in show business any more as I was making money from my drugs and I had actually lost money in the Jungle Jokers. For instance we had once hired a lorry, but when we arrived it was raining, so we made no money and I had to even take my watch off (to pawn). However in the end Mr. Bampoe managed to persuade me.

They agreed that Mr. Bampoe was to be the leader, senior Hammond the secretary, K. A. Hammond the treasurer, and the name of the group would be the Jaguar Jokers. Their initial problems were considerable, as Mr. Bampoe points out:

> We had no money for posters, costumes and even transport. So we used crayons and art paper for posters and went round and borrowed some ladies' dresses for our lady impersonator and some tattered clothes for the Bob. We had to walk from three to six miles to the nearest place to perform—just for some pennies. We couldn't go to the big towns because of our lack of costumes, but later a man called Mr. Appiah Charlie from Suhum had interest in us and bought for us some nice costumes and we started performances in the big towns.

Their shows would last about two hours and as in their previous groups they recruited local musicians; however, within a short time they brought into the J.J.s Kwese Adae on congas and Otoo-Okine on the jazz drums; Otoo was also a tailor and was thus able to make many of the group's costumes. One important difference between the J.J.s and the previous groups they had been in was that the plays were staged in Twi rather than English; in this they were taking their cue from E. K. Nyame's Akan Trio.

After they had got some money together Mr. Bampoe arranged for posters to be made at £2 10s for fifty, and these were posted around the towns where they were playing. K. A. Hammond had a few words to say on these early days of the Jaguar Jokers band:

> We started (the show) with our opening chorus and then an "In" with a joker and a "duet" with two jokers; all this lasted half an hour or so. Then

came the play and we finished with "God Save the Queen." We did our own promoting and we would all go to the town for this. I remember once we went to a town in Fanti and, not then having our own transport, we took tro-tro; carrying our costumes in our port-manteaux. When we arrived the people thought we were very strange and the gong-gong was beaten that thieves were in town—so all should beware; they thought we had come to blindfold them [i.e., cheat them with money-doubling tricks]. The landlord of the place we were going to perform told us we shouldn't go out at all that night as we would be beaten. We didn't stage that night as the minds of the people had been poisoned against us.

Mr. Bampoe recalls that shortly after he formed the J.J.s there was a competition between them and his old band, the City Trio:

> I met my former people at Anyinam; we staged on the Accra road side of town and they on the Kumasi. This was no coincidence as they wanted to break us. They hired the brass band from the town that we had intended to use—so we had to get one from Akrofufu, about ten miles away. When our band came we told the bandsmen to wait on the outskirts of the town until the Anyinam band had campaigned—we wanted to surprise them. That night the people of Anyinam were happy as they had two shows; in fact they were confused as they didn't know which one to go to. We advised our bandsmen to go to the City Trio's staging area where their bandsmen were making inside campaign. Our men then started to play outside and the townspeople followed them. So we conquered the City Trio—they couldn't even pay their own bandsmen. As we left we wrote on the street "the J.J.s are supreme."

In 1956 the senior Hammond left to join Bob Cole's Ghana Trio and was replaced by Isaac Ntarmah. Within a year of Mr. Hammond's departure, the J.J.s were involved in another competition, this time with the Ghana Trio. According to Mr. Bampoe:

> Mr. Hammond left on 20 December 1956 and the Ghana Trio tried to sabotage us at Worawora, in the Volta region, in December 1957. We were already on trek in that region when we heard that Bob Cole had jumped in and had put up posters for the very same day in that town. As he had just teamed up with Onyina's guitar band he thought he was so popular and wanted us to look small. We decided that we would go by all means, and the day before we saved the money for the next day, when, I told my members, we would stage at Worawora free of charge. The next day both bands were out campaigning and collecting villagers and at eight in the evening I brought a large loudspeaker outside the house and announced "It gives me great pleasure to announce that as the J.J.s have been coming here for some years, today we are going to give you a dash—by giving you a free show." The people simply hadn't known

which concert to go to as they were being staged on opposite sides of the street; but hardly had I put the microphone down when our house was full to capacity. Bob Cole couldn't do the same and announce a free show as he hadn't prepared and covered himself. You see I did this with the understanding of my members.

Also in 1957 two important members joined up. One was Kwadjo Boye, a young highlife guitarist, and the other was Emmanuel Baidoo, who replaced Ntarmah as female impersonator and soprano singer. Mr. Baidoo had originally been a carpenter by trade but had gone into acting in 1955 with the Swedru-Agona based Ahanta Jokers, then to the J.J.s on 21 September 1957. By 1958 the group was ten strong and now had a small band incorporated into it, eliminating the need to hire local bands altogether. Also by this time they had acquired their first amplifier, a Phillips with two battery-powered microphones. For their campaign they would hire a truck for the night, costing about six or seven shillings, put inside the amplifier, congas, and guitar, and tour the town playing highlifes to advertise themselves. By 1959 they were hiring trucks by the day, so that the entire band and their equipment could travel together. This cost them £2 10s but in addition they had to pay for the gasoline and the driver's chop money.

In 1963 Enoch Doku came into the band and with his electrified guitar (acoustic guitar plus amplifier) concentrated on the western dance and pop music that was played before and after the show. Kwadjo Boye, however, still continued to play the highlifes during the show. About the time Doku came, Mr. Bampoe had just set up a second band which would use the instruments when the number one band was resting from trek. This was never a successful venture but it did give Mr. Bampoe a pool of musicians to draw on when he needed to—and once in 1963 it saved him:

> Our Kumasi tour finished on 14 February and we went back to Nsawam and were meant to start staging again on the 22nd, but it rained and there was no show. Eight of the boys asked me to give them chop money, but I said no as I had given them £8 each last 14th. . . . they had been wasting their money for nothing. I told them I would give them money after Akroso, our next station, but they planned that when we reached Kade and I did not give them something for chop, they would all break [go on strike]. When we reached there, I dropped with Mr. Hammond to get some chop and these boys asked for money and I said no. They refused to climb the lorry so I gave them fifteen minutes and if they didn't come, well . . . I move. We went without them and as we were to stage that night I moved the bus back to Nsawam and picked some of the boys I had trained in the second band. . . . I cleared eight of the number two bandsmen, but we weren't able to stage anyway as we couldn't score a

pass; the police said we did not come in time. Later my old boys said that I should take them back, but I said no. I then had palaver with two of them, Ofei and Yaw Tenge, when there was a funeral that I, with my new boys, were playing at. Ofei and Yaw wanted to play and I did not allow them to touch my instruments as they were drunk. This prompted Ofei to push me and Mr. Baidoo and Mr. Hammond forced me to report them to the police. They were arrested and had to appear before court and were remanded for one week. So I went to the court the next week and when the magistrate asked me did I want him to punish the boys, I said he should forget about it . . . so he let them free.

By 1969 (the year I joined) the J.J.s were approaching twenty strong. The year before they had acquired a complete modern guitar-band set of instruments, i.e., solid electric guitars—bass, rhythm, and lead. By 1974 the membership had grown to twenty-five. More than half the members were under thirty years of age. The three leaders—Mr. Bampoe, Mr. Hammond, and Mr. Baidoo—were among the oldest at thirty-eight, thirty-nine, and forty-eight years of age respectively. The group was also linguistically and regionally mixed: there were eight Akim, four Fanti, three Ewe, two Akwapim, two Denkyera, two Asante, one Brong, one Kwahu, one Wasaw, and one man of Nigerian extraction.

Most of the bandsmen had begun their careers as musicians and actors very young—between the ages of twelve and nineteen. It was common for them to develop an interest in "staging" or in singing from their activities at school. Thus Patrick Aikins Boahene, who was twenty in 1974 and had joined the J.J.s three years earlier, explained:

> I used to stage as a woman for my school's Founder Day concerts and when I left at about thirteen I continued staging for pesewas and plantains. There were ten of us and I was the leader; we used to watch a concert and the next day copy them in a compound house. I did this for over six months, staging in about forty villages around Dunkwa. When I was fourteen I got a job with an Italian man and wife, as a steward boy, and when they left I tried to get a job at African Timber and Plywood at Samreboi—but they wouldn't take me, so I stayed there for a year living with a friend. I then went back to my home and farmed for three years and then went back to Samreboi to try for the job again—but I failed— then the J.J.s came to town and agreed to take me.

Yaw Nyamekye, a female impersonator and singer, who was twenty-seven in 1974, became interested in singing professionally while still in elementary school:

> When I was a schoolboy I was in my elementary school's choir and later sang for Atuahene's guitar band, which was from my town (Techiman).

When the schoolmaster found out he punished me and tried to stop me. Then when the Ahanta Trio came to town I joined and went with them to Dix Cove, first as a treble singer and then as a lady impersonator.

Kwabena Mensah, a singer and actor specializing in old-lady parts, said, "I sang in my school band and always wanted to be in a concert." He joined the Prince's Trio in 1965, at the age of thirteen, and joined the J.J.s four years later.

Most of the bandsmen had worked with several other bands and concert parties before joining the J.J.s. Some had worked for the J.J.s for a time, left, and returned. More than half the bandsmen in 1974 had been with the J.J.s less than four years, but there was also a core of about ten who had been there between seven and seventeen years. It was a profession that had its committed practitioners. Kwabena Jackson, a bass guitarist who joined the J.J.s at the age of twenty-three in 1973, said: "I prefer being in a concert party to a dance band as I like the traveling. I want to stay for life and don't want to marry." However, several of the bandsmen said that if they could not realize their ambition of having their own concert, they would eventually leave the profession and do something else. Financial precariousness and social disparagement were strong incentives to leave. Yaw Nyamekye said: "I'm not married, but when I do I'll leave and become a farmer because although I can make small savings as an actor I can never get enough to have my own band." Amankwaah, a twenty-five-year-old who started his career with the Kingsters Guitar band at the age of thirteen, said:

> I've been staging since I was a boy and I like the work. Before joining the Kingsters I was a steam bender [shaped wood in house construction]. In the future I would like to have my own concert party, but if not I will start a provision shop. I am married with one child but my wife doesn't like me being with the concerts as it is not possible to make money.

Others were using the concert party as an interim measure while they tried to gather the funds to start another trade. Kwabena Mensah's real ambition was to have a "cold-store business," but he said that "the money will never reach." Emmanuel Elshun said, "I really want to be a seaman but it is difficult to get a passport or get into the Seaman's Union—as you need money." He added, "I don't think I'll stay in concert when I get older."

In general, it was clear that there was a large category of professional musicians and actors who had supported themselves exclusively by playing in professional bands from an early age, and who intended to continue. High mobility between bands caused problems for band leaders, but meant that the bandsmen gained wide professional experience.

## REFLECTIONS ON CONCERT PARTY LIFE

From my own experience I could see that the life of a bandsman was hard. I asked Mr. Bampoe and Mr. Hammond their feelings about it. Mr. Hammond replied: "If you want to be an actor you have to have love for it whether in money or poverty; do it with all your heart." I had noticed when traveling with the band that we were often shown little respect and had to sleep on the floor, and I asked Mr. Bampoe why this was so.

> It's true, people don't have any respect for concert people and I can even remember that one day somebody asked me if I'm having wife, and when I said yes he was surprised and wouldn't believe. He thought we used to go on trek for a whole year without going to our homes. . . . Bandsmen don't have money, and so can't build their own houses and have their own transport. In Ghana if you are poor, you have no respect. It's only in the last few years that people's ideas have started to change. . . . Also in the olden days people used to play guitars in palm-wine bars, where they would be invited to play and wouldn't have to buy drinks. So when your parents see you learning they don't like it.

Bands, they felt, also suffered from a low reputation because they were associated with sleazy and immoral shows. Mr. Bampoe stressed that he had constantly to differentiate his own band's plays from those low-life groups who corrupted the morals of the young:

> Some bands stage filthy shows, immoral plays, you see, or plays in which they naked the breasts or bodies of the girls. Even though the girls are played by lady impersonators it seem very peculiar to touch the middle parts of the impersonator or to dance too closely. In some towns the teachers would advise the schoolchildren not to attend concerts, and this would sometimes reduce our audience. We even planned to go to the schools and inform the teachers that we don't perform filthy shows but educative ones; we think it's good for the children to patronize our shows. . . .

Mr. Bampoe and Mr. Hammond both felt that one of the problems with concert party was the behavior of the bandsmen. Mr. Hammond complained,

> . . . when you put some of the boys into important acting positions they become swellheaded and start to bluff. . . . They are always drinking, misbehaving, and womanizing. Once we had a maracas player who got so drunk, when we were staging at Kaneshie, that he couldn't play and fell into the audience. He was sacked the following day, it was disgraceful.

Mr. Bampoe added:

Many of the band boys are rascals, their attitude on the street—this *wee* [marijuana] smoking; you can see them putting on earrings and coloring their fingers for bluffing, and they're always quarreling over girls. . . . Another problem with band boys is money. . . . One boy was poisoning the minds of the others that I should pay more. So when we got home I sacked him. The trouble with these boys is that when you say they are good or have done well, they begin to have a big head about it.

Competition between bands was also always a problem. The story of the J.J.s, as Mr. Bampoe and Mr. Hammond told it to me, was full of accounts of rival groups challenging them and attempting to steal their audiences or their actors. Loss of bandsmen to other bands was a perennial problem:

Sometimes our troubles come from other band leaders, for if you have a good actor they will come to convince him to leave, by saying that they will pay him more than we do. Because of this we have to keep training new boys, we arrange some short play for them. We have to do this for every new member, as other bands are always taking my members—it retards our itinerary.

Professional jealousy could be taken to extremes. Mr. Bampoe said that rival bands and musicians would try to spoil his performance using jùjú, and that this had put him off going into music recording:

This is what has discouraged me not to record. They [other musicians and actors] challenge each other, and when your record is playing they can make jùjú about your throat to close your throat. Many years ago a tight [close] friend of mine was poisoned through records: I even saw him the Friday before the Tuesday he died. I went to his funeral and according to his family three record needles were taken out of the throat. He was poisoned by some other bandsmen as his records were so popular on the market; so the only alternative was to kill him through jùjú. They played his records and took the needles to the jùjú man. . . . So this discouraged me and when I narrated it to my mother she advised me not to go on the record side, so I boycott it. People are so jealous. That's why I don't go to drinking bars and don't smoke, and if a bandsman called me to take some food I would never take it but give it to my boys, for in Africa if they want to poison you they mention your name and prepare the food against you, but if you don't take it and somebody else takes it, that man will never be affected.

I inquired how bandsmen protected themselves against such incidents and against bad luck in general.

I know some bandsmen who go every year to the fetish priest at Asubua, they go every blessed year so that he will bless their instruments and pour libations. . . . I know five or six bandsmen who don't like other members to travel with sugar cane on their bus—it brings rain. I once had some boys who believed this but I didn't mind them. I've also had bandsmen who won't eat konkonte as it's against their jùjú. Also some of the boys don't like people to touch their powders and chemicals in the anterooms because they have jùjú that makes the audience like them on the platform.

Both of them agreed that there was a need for a union, not only to dispense with promoters, but to create a code of conduct between the band leaders, for the constant turnover of members does interfere greatly with the band's quality, as half the time is spent in training new boys.

The last question I asked of the two actors before taking my leave of them was, what of the future? Mr. Bampoe replied first:

> For the future I will retire from the field within five years. I want to establish a farm and back the band with the profits. The problem with concerts today is that everything has become expensive. I won't go on staging because the little money you get you [have to use to] buy new instruments, do you quite follow what I mean? Transport is very dear and a new set of instruments costs between 12,000 and 15,000 cedis. . . . and to repair them we have to send them overseas. The government is now taking interest so they should help us.

Mr. Hammond had the last word:

> One should retire from concert after fifty years old. I want to become a farmer and Mr. Bampoe the same. Mr. Baidoo is going to retire in four years when he is fifty-three and he's going to buy a canoe for the fishermen in his town, Accra (in Western region). When we leave we will leave the band to the boys we have trained.

## THE CONCERT PARTY AS A BUSINESS ORGANIZATION

The Jaguar Jokers band was run by an executive committee of six members: Mr. Bampoe, Mr. Hammond, Mr. Baidoo, Enoch Doku, Kwadjo Boye, and Kwame Kede. All decisions were made by them democratically. This committee administered the band's business; hired, fired, and otherwise controlled the bandsmen; and decided on the itinerary. The bandsmen were paid a regular wage, and any profit left over after wages, transport, and equipment repair had been covered was shared by the executive members. For every day the bandsmen were on trek they were paid between 1 cedi 50 pesewas and 3 cedis, depending on their talent and length of time with the band. Most of them preferred to be given just their daily chop money out of this, receiving the balance when they returned home. Mr. Baidoo, the band's treasurer, was in charge of all money and payments.

There were unwritten rules governing the bandsmen's and the executive committee's mutual obligations. Any bandsman who defrauded or stole from the band was sacked. However, this was hardly ever done on trek, but only when the group returned to base. All musicians and singers had to be in their places by 8:30 or else they were fined one cedi. Once the inside rhythm started all bandsmen had to be about their business and not be conversing with the audience, dancing, or drinking. Bandsmen could be fined for other misdemeanors too; for instance, one actor was fined 20 cedis for tearing the shirt of an executive member during an argument. If a bandsman refused to go on trek out of laziness, the next time he would have to work three days with no pay except chop money.

The organization undertook to look after the bandsmen in difficulties, operating as a kind of safety net. Thus, if any member was sick, hospital fees and chop money were paid to him. If there was a death in a member's family, the member received a donation from the band. If a band member died, the J.J.s purchased the coffin. When a new boy joined and had nowhere to stay he would be allowed to sleep in the music storeroom at Adoagyiri, hired by the band for 1 cedi 40 pesewas a month, until he found somewhere else.

The band was not completely independent, however. For many of its tours, it depended on the agency of "promoters," who organized the tour for a fixed sum. The promoters took the gate fee, paid the band, and kept the profit, out of which they had to pay for posters, promotions, landlords, and so on. Promoters made less money in the villages, where audiences were small and the gate fees less, and consequently they paid the concerts less. In the towns the promoters' expenses were much greater, the bands demanded a higher fee, and the price of a decent theatre, say a cinema, could be as high as 150 cedis; but this was compensated for by the larger turnout and a higher entrance fee.

The J.J.s did have their own promoter or pioneer man, Kwame Kede, but he could only arrange about 20 percent of their itinerary. Whenever a promoter or Kede made a definite arrangement the date was advertised in the *Daily Graphic's* amusement column: "The J.J.s are storming . . . or shaking . . ." a particular town on such and such a date. The J.J.s also used the paper for giving their dates of breaking from trek and advertising for new bandsmen and for contacting promoters they wanted to see. The *Graphic* has been advertising concerts in this manner since the early 1950s.

However, the J.J.s would much rather have done all their own promoting, as Mr. Bampoe explained:

> During the rainy season we don't make much so promoters loan us money to bind us in the cocoa season [when there is plenty of money

around]. They will only promote us during this season as they will make money from us. . . . Promoters sometimes also buy equipment for the bands, in this case they will make deduction from you, say 50 cedis a night, against the instruments. This sort of thing is what brought us to form a union. Some promoters will even block your police permit to put on their own show. For instance once a promoter wanted us to stage for him but we did it on our own and when we got there we found another band staging at our place. The promoter had forced his way to score a permit, so our pass was rejected as they [the police] don't like two concerts to stage at one time. There are many small promoters and about twenty professional ones, some are now transport owners and rich farmers from the profits. They take thousands of cedis from us; once in Brong-Ahafo we were charging 300 cedis a night but he [the promoter] got 700 at Sunyani, 750 at Berekum, 650 at Nima and 690 at Domaa Ahenkuro. So one promoter will make more than the whole band. So now I'm prepared to tell the promoters "hands off the J.J.s." I will reject their loans. I now owe about sixteen different promoters shows, but I'm going to stage for them before the cocoa season for us to make money instead. The promoters are killing us.

As Mr. Bampoe observed, exploitation by promoters was one of the main incentives for the concert parties to form a union, the history of which has been described earlier in this volume.

The J.J.s also sought to cushion themselves from financial downturn by diversifying. Besides staging what must literally have been thousands of live shows, they performed on the air. In the late 1950s and early 1960s, they did numerous 45-minute shows for the "Radio Entertainment in Akan" program, and later they appeared on television. In fact, their television appearances resulted in Mr. Bampoe being chosen as outstanding comedian of the year in 1973:

> In May I was asked by one Kwabena Taylor, a TV producer, that the Board of Directors thought I should be awarded. I did not take him seriously, but then a few days later he came to Nsawam with four people and they asked me to write about my acting; but I still didn't take them seriously and I didn't write it. So then I was at Bubuashie (Accra), staging, when Taylor came and told me that tomorrow is the day. So I went with Mr. Hammond, Baidoo, and Nyamekye, and we staged a fifteen-minute play on the TV and I received the award.

## THE PLAYS

The typical J.J. concert has always been divided into three sections, the "inside rhythm," the opening or "comedies," and the "scene" or play. These will be dealt with in turn.

*Jaguar Jokers concert performance. Photograph © John Collins.*

## THE INSIDE RHYTHM

This is the dance music played inside the theatre prior to the main show, and it finishes when the place is adequately packed. (In the smaller towns and villages they play a short inside rhythm after the show as well.) When the J.J.s were first formed, music was supplied by their vocalists and drummer, augmented by a local brass band or konkoma group hired for the night. Later they bought an amplifier, hired guitarists, and formed their own band, and by 1968 they had a full set of solid electric guitars. Kwadjo Boye, their first guitarist, was an expert on highlife, calypso, quicksteps, foxtrots, and swing, and Lord Enoch, who came in 1963, was a specialist in pop music and congo numbers. Kwadjo Boye subsequently dropped the music side in order to concentrate on acting; his job as musical director for the J.J.s was taken over by Lord Enoch. In its heyday the music section of this concert party, excluding the vocalists, comprised half the membership and its repertoire included a cross section of music currently popular in Ghana.

## THE "OPENING"

In the early days of the J.J.s the opening lasted about an hour, was in English, and started with a foxtrot called "I've Got My Sentimental" sung by Mr. Bampoe and Mr. Hammond the younger, wearing flannel trousers, tail coats, top hats, and with blanco around their mouths and occasionally down their noses. Before 1957, when he left the group, they were accompanied by Mr. Hammond the elder, and later by Mr. Baidoo, dressed as a woman, and the three of them would sing and tap-dance. Then Mr. Bampoe would be left alone for about half an hour for the "In," during which he would sing "ragtimes," dance, and crack jokes. Finally, for the "duet" Mr. Hammond (junior) would return for more jokes.

The opening became progressively shorter over the years, and in the 1970s was only about fifteen to twenty minutes long, with the duet being cut out altogether. The opening was interesting in that the dress, music, and general style were based on the older tradition in Ghanaian concert, i.e., that stemming from the vaudeville-influenced Axim Trio, rather than the later Akan Trio. Even in the 1970s the J.J.s' opening performers still wore the white makeup and tap-danced to foxtrots; in fact Yaw Bob's song "I Want My Fufu Now" originally came from the Axim Trio.

## THE "SCENE" OR PLAY PROPER

The first few plays staged by the J.J.s were only about one and a half hours long, but since 1957 they have lasted three hours with a much shorter Axim Trio–style opening. The plays have always been in Twi, and although at first the singers were backed by just one drummer, within a short time they had a guitar band and the music and drama became inseparable.

Before going on to a discussion of *Orphan Do Not Glance*, it is worth considering some of the more general features of the repertoire. These are all basically morality plays, usually with a pronounced religious element, an influence from cantata. Although concert is a contemporary Ghanaian phenomenon, the plays include many traditional features, the most obvious being that they are performed in a vernacular language. In addition, they contain indigenous dance and music (funeral music, fetish dances) and traditional figures (chiefs, elders, and priests).

There are a number of ways in which the presentation of concert party plays differs from the mainstream western theatre's illusionistic or naturalistic portrayal of reality. There are temporal inconsistencies. In the play presented here, for example, Mr. Johnson announces that he is going to send for his friend Opia from a distant town. Opia instantly walks in, without any break in the flow of action, in response to a summons that could not yet have been delivered. Another non-naturalistic feature is the constant use of actors' direct statements to the audience, introducing themselves and providing essential plot information. Thus in *Orphan Do Not Glance,* Mr. Johnson presents himself with the words, "I'm such an unhappy person. I'm a sand and gravel contractor and was once married to Akua Nyame who became sick in the stomach and died. I had one son by her, Kofi Antobam, and he doesn't even know who his real mother is. After this I married again, to Akua Awotwe, and had a boy and a girl with her. . . ." The non-naturalistic nature of the concert party is further enhanced by the exaggerated and stylized behavior and dress of the characters: crotchety old people, berobed chiefs, semi-literate policemen, besuited teachers, flashy "good-time girls" and playboys, and the formal utterances of the "gentlemen."

As in traditional Ghanaian dramatic performances such as *anansesem* there is a great deal of audience participation, usually in the form of applause, weeping, jeering, and throwing coins onto the stage. Spectators may be so moved that they will go up on stage to stick coins onto the moist foreheads of popular actors and musicians. Food, too, may be brought on stage, as with the bread, bananas, and kenkey given to the orphan Kofi Antobam in *Orphan Do Not Glance,* in response to his lament that he is hungry because his stepmother does not feed him. Just as the audience may mount the stage, so the actors may enter the audience space. In *Orphan,* Mr. Johnson kicks his shoe into the audience; in other plays in the J.J.s' repertoire an actor may achieve a dramatic effect by bursting off stage into the auditorium—e.g., to indicate madness.

The actors sometimes deliberately instigate audience participation. In *Orphan,* the clownish Opia almost takes over the climactic scene of the play, where the hero is threatened by evil spirits sent by his stepmother and then saved by three hymn-singing angels. The audience join in the hymns, but when Opia comes in he takes over and eggs them on to repeat the verses of "Let Us Praise Him"—a popular Ghanaian Apostolic hymn—again and again. The dramatic action is suspended as he leads them through verse after verse, while Antobam, the principal character in that scene, can only stand by waiting for it to resume. It is Opia, too, who incites the audience to shout responses to catch phrases and slang, some of it coined by the J.J.s themselves: e.g., the made-up expression "potete" (meaning a henpecked husband) and the response "podowdow" (a meaningless comeback), which he applies to Mr. Johnson.

When the concert party genre was "hijacked" from the urban coastal élite in the 1930s, the makeshift stages of the more humble venues did away with the proscenium arch, the picture-frame stage, and the orchestra pit that separates the audience and performer in western-type theatre, which was the design of the school and cinema-cum-theatre concert party stages of the Gold Coast upper class. Stages in poorer and more rural areas usually jut out into the audience, so that the spatial distinction between performers and audience is reduced.

The J.J.s' plays, like many concert parties, are linguistically diverse. Mr. Bampoe told me that he and Mr. Hammond both use a variety of languages in the plays, depending on the location, although they prefer to use Twi. Thus in Accra they often use some Ga; in the Côte d'Ivoire where there are Akan-speaking people they perform in Twi; in the Northern and Upper regions they speak a mixture of Hausa, pidgin English, and Twi; in Togo and Ghana's eastern Volta Region they use a combination of Twi and Ewe. Since Mr. Bampoe is the only leading actor who speaks Guan, in the towns of Larteh, Anum, and Kyerepon he both performs in this language and translates for the audience some of the more important lines by the other actors. The polyglot texts mirror the ethnically mixed composition of the performers, the regional range of their treks, the urban mix created by inmigration to the cities from all over the country, and the internal hybridity, heterogeneity, and incorporativeness of the concert party style.

The plays are consciously modern and innovative. They set out to bring new ideas to the rural population. For many years, concerts have trekked into even the small and isolated villages in southern Ghana — places where rural cinema has only recently been introduced. The performances give a glimpse of urban life and its problems to the rustic audience and introduce new styles of speech and dress. They may be educational: for instance, many Ghanaians are familiar with the coronation of King George VI in 1936 through the Axim Trio's reenactment of this event. New political ideas were also introduced in this dramatic way, and a considerable number of plays expounding nationalist and pro-independence themes appeared in the late 1940s and early 1950s; later there was the C.P.P.'s use of the Brigade concerts as a vehicle for propaganda. Mr. Bampoe was insistent that his plays were nonpolitical, but even so at least one of them, *Go Back to the Land,* had a very overt message which was, incidentally, in line with the "Operation Feed Yourself" campaign being run by the National Redemption Council at the time. Mr. Bampoe recalls that the play went over particularly well on one occasion at Cape Coast, after a seminar organized by the Farmers' Union and the C.P.P.; the following day the group was given a pleasant reception at the residence of the Regional Commissioner.

Mr. Bampoe made the following comments on this question of concerts and new ideas:

> We purposely send new styles of dress into the villages and new songs. We give information about what is going on, say in something like "Operation Feed Yourself," we can tell the villagers to join. . . . We educate

people that it is better to stay in the bush to farm than look for a job in town because in the future we won't have food and people who go there [i.e., to the towns] come back wretched as they don't cut their coats according to their size, and their monthly salaries don't reach, so they go and steal. . . . We also give information about the government, but we don't do politics, for when you support one party, the opposition members will never come to the show and this decreases our crowd . . . but I can really say that our shows are very educative and understandable.

The characters in the plays represent a cross section of stereotypes found in Ghana today, including rural ones like bushmen and illiterate farmers, Opanyins (elders) and chiefs, and urbanites such as doctors, lawyers, and teachers, speaking partly in Twi and partly in English, and dressed in the latest European clothes. At the time I was traveling with them, the young urban male characters dressed in "Apache"-style natty suits and drain-pipe trousers, subsequently replaced by the bell-bottomed "Afro" or psychedelic look. The younger female impersonators play the roles of adventurous "good-time girls," usually treated in the stories as hopelessly spoiled. Different ethnic groups are also represented, the northern policeman speaking a mixture of Twi, Hausa, and pidgin English, the Lagosian with a strong Yorùbá accent, and Accra people speaking in Ga.

The plots of the nine plays I have collected are all permutations of a fixed number of standard components. At the center of each is "Mr. Johnson," always played by Mr. Hammond junior. "Mr. Johnson" is always a senior figure, through whom the other characters meet or are interrelated in a determinate number of patterns: whether as his children (in several plays he has two daughters, one good and one bad); his wives (again, in several plays he has two, one good and one bad); his friends; or his employees. "Mr. Johnson" thus always occupies the same structural position in the narrative, but the depiction of his worldly status varies: he may be an old, poor farmer, a wealthy man, a trader, a timber contractor, or a pensioner from the U.A.C.; he may be married or a bachelor; he may be wise throughout the play, or given to foolish whims which are only mitigated by good advice from his wife or friend. His associate is often Opia, always played by Mr. Bampoe, or a loose variant of this character called by another name (e.g., Saka, in *Kashelee*, "O.C.K." in *Go Back to the Land*). Opia, similarly, is sometimes represented as Mr. Johnson's servant, sometimes as his friend, and in one play as a poor suitor to Mr. Johnson's daughter, whom Mr. Johnson takes on as his employee. But he always displays the same mixture of good-heartedness and greedy impudence. He is a trickster-like character much beloved by the audience.

The plots, similarly, tend to revolve around a number of well-established moral themes. A key contrast is that between urban and rural life. At some point the stories usually are concerned with the plight of young single men and women who leave their homes to go to the cities. They may turn to crime, drunkenness, or prostitution, and when they return home they are full of new ideas and have little respect for the old ways. The city, though associated with glamour and the good life, is often represented as impoverishing those who go there. Thus in *Go Back to the Land*, Mr. Johnson is a farmer with two daughters, the elder of whom, Sapona, goes off to the town while the younger marries a farmer and stays on the farm. Sapona doesn't prosper in the city and after a while is forced to return home, in rags, in debt, and chased by her creditors. Her father, who is old and has had no one to help him, has very little money, but fortunately the younger daughter and her husband turn up, and as they have been doing well they are able to pay off Sapona's debts and advise her that it is better to farm than to roam about. They are so affluent that they are even able to buy her a whole new wardrobe of clothes.

The rural/urban opposition is closely associated with the themes of generational strife and changing sexual norms. The modern tendency for children to show disobedience and disrespect to their elders is seen as being aggravated by the bad influences of city life. The city is the focal point of rapid modernization, and, while being successful in the modern world is encouraged, the pitfalls—emblematized in the figure of the disobedient, loose-living son or daughter shaking off parental restraint and living it up in the city—are pointed out and the audience is directed to look back to more idyllic days. Similarly, the increasing emancipation of women is treated with cautious conservatism. Independent, western-educated, city-oriented women who reject polygyny, adopt family planning, and become economically powerful through trading seem to scare the life out of the concert party men, and the plays invariably take the rather reactionary line that the old ways, when the men had more control over the women, were better.

The concern with disrupted kinship norms, associated with city life, is clear in *The End of Our Greedy Women*, in which Mr. Johnson is a rich trader with two daughters still at school. The elder one, Ama, bolts away to Tema, enticed away by a "good-time girl" friend of hers called Georgina. Her father and younger sister, Ekua, disapprove, but Ama's mother has always encouraged her to do whatever she pleases. Opia, a poor man who lives in Tema, falls in love with Ama and proposes marriage, but she rejects him and goes off instead with a rich chief. They are not heard of for a considerable time, and the now worried Mrs. Johnson goes off to look for her daughter. It turns out that the chief is not human at all; he is a spirit, and has killed the girl. When the mother turns up he kills her too. The spirit later reveals to Opia that he killed them because they were headstrong and wicked and richly deserved it; the good, obedient daughter, who has also disappeared, is restored unharmed to her family.

The plays almost all deal with the themes of inequality and the impact of new wealth from cash crops. Unemployment and poverty in the cities is portrayed, and in the struggle to obtain wealth and prestige the humble hard worker is contrasted with the greedy man who will betray his friends and even resort to magic in his scramble for money. New wealth has led to divisive tensions emerging within the extended family, manifested in inheritance disputes (especially among the matrilineal Akan people), and other types of "money palaver." These tensions are often aired socially and therefore portrayed for instance as witchcraft accusations and poisonings. *Kashelee*—Mr. Bampoe's humorous way of saying "Ka kyere no" (tell or warn him/her) with a thick Lagosian accent—shows a local good-time girl cheating a rich Lagosian who has settled in the Gold Coast, and getting away with it. *Adofo Enne Ye Atomfos Okyena* (Friends Today, Enemies Tomorrow) portrays a rich man, Mr. Johnson, whose domestic harmony is disrupted by a false friend, a poor man who approaches him for accommodation, employment, and help, sows discord between Mr. Johnson and his two wives, and then goes off and becomes rich himself. He is ultimately punished by the poor servant, Opia. In *Ebe Ye Dwe*, Mr. Johnson is a bachelor and well-to-do timber contractor who lives alone with his servant, Opia. Opia, fed up with doing all the cooking and shopping, tries to persuade his master to get married, but Mr. Johnson says he will only marry a girl who can sing and dance well. A dancing competition is therefore arranged by Opia, and Mr. Johnson picks out two wives, a young one and an old one who is nonetheless the best dancer. In the next scene, a smart and charming taxi driver tries to seduce the younger wife with money and high living and fails, but does succeed with the older, second wife. The older wife is further corrupted by Selena, a good-time friend of hers, who incites her to poison the younger wife in order to take over the position of first wife. Caught out by Opia in the very act of poisoning the first wife's food, she is so ashamed that she takes some of the poison herself and goes mad. The closing song is a highlife that warns husbands not to marry more than one wife as jealousy will lead to trouble.

## ORPHAN DO NOT GLANCE

The play presented here is typical of the repertoire of the J.J.s as it was in the early 1970s. The plot revolves around Mr. Johnson, in this case a sand and gravel contractor who means well but is dominated by his second wife. She spoils her own two children and mistreats Mr. Johnson's son by his first wife, now dead. Sam and Dansowa are typical examples of youth gone astray. Dansowa has dropped out of school and become a "good-time girl" who goes about with her friend Selena "roaming for men." Sam is still at school but spends most of his time drinking and playing truant, and ends up by failing all his exams. Kofi Antobam,

the "orphan"—for losing your mother makes you an orphan in a matrilineal society such as the Asante—is so maltreated by Mrs. Johnson that
Mr. Johnson, in despair, eventually sends him away to be looked after by
a friend of his at Cape Coast. There, Kofi does well at school, gets a good
job as a postmaster, and marries a beautiful wife. The couple return,
obviously prosperous and successful, to distribute gifts, receive congrat-
ulations, and lecture the hapless Sam.

Kofi Antobam is the epitome of the downtrodden: he wears rags and
goes hungry while his half-brother and sister eat sardines and bread, drink
Fanta, and wear fancy clothes. Kofi's poverty is not the result of class
exploitation but of familial tensions, underlining the message that suffering is part of the human condition and can happen to anyone. The poignant figure of the orphan, which evokes such sympathy from the
audience, can be seen, however, as more than a comment on the increasing
fragmentation and breakdown of extended family structures in modern
Ghana. The orphaned condition may be a way of describing the acute
loneliness, rootlessness, and loss of primary social relations encountered
by many newcomers to the big city—a poetic way of expressing urban
anomie. It is no accident that the orphan should be such a prominent
theme in concert party, the dramatic form created and watched above all
by the poor, semi-employed urban youth.

Mr. Johnson represents the authority of age and tradition, in contrast
to the disrespectful loose manners of his children Sam and Dansowa. Yet
Mr. Johnson is ineffectual to the point of being ridiculous. Opia raises a
great cheer when, under cover of helping Mr. Johnson to sit down, he tips
him onto the ground, shouting solicitously "Hold him—he's somebody's
old man." Similarly, going away to the city, usually associated with the
"good-time" life condemned in Sam and Dansowa, is here inverted, for it
is only by going away to Cape Coast that Antobam can realize his potential. He not only lives in a city, but marries without consulting his father
and takes a typical city job. Yet all this is represented as a triumph. It is
consistent with the play's overall loose-jointed structure that any latent
contradictions or ambiguities are left unresolved.

## WRITING AND REHEARSING A PLAY

All the J.J.s' plays were created by Mr. Bampoe, who after getting
the initial idea for the plot would sit down and make a short rough sketch
of it. Then, in a hall hired for the purpose in Adoagyiri, the whole band
would spend about three months working on the story. During this time
the characters, songs, and sub-plots were developed and composed by all
members of the group. As the J.J.s' actor and musician Nyamekye said,
everyone was encouraged to put in their own ideas: "If the boys bring in
new ideas for the play, manager will accept them, although he always has

the last word. As for the music, some of the songs are written by manager but it is the musical director who arranges them. Also myself, Doku, Obeng and Yaw Bob compose some of the songs."

Once the play had been adequately rehearsed and the music worked in, the J.J.s polished it by staging about twelve times in the surrounding villages at a reduced entrance fee. The plays were performed from memory, which enhanced extemporization, momentary effects, and the gratification of the particular audience. For instance, with *Orphan Do Not Glance* the actual town where the performance represented in this volume was taking place (Nsaba) was mentioned several times, a common stage trick of the J.J.s.

Because the actors were given so much room to improvise around the main plot, it was an easy matter for them, when the need arose, to shorten and edit or lengthen and embellish the play under Mr. Bampoe's direction. This happened with *Orphan Do Not Glance* at Abbam on 19 December 1973 when the play was shortened from the usual three and a quarter to two and a half hours because of the small and unresponsive crowd. Then at Besease the next day, the role of Dansowa, the good-for-nothing daughter, had to be edited out as the actor who had been playing this part left the group without notice.

In this volume I present an "Opening" and the play *Awisia Yi Wo Ani (Orphan Do Not Glance)*, recorded on 18 December 1973 at Nsaba near Swedru. The written version was put together by obtaining a running commentary during the play, interpretations afterwards from the various actors, and finally a transcription from a tape-recording. In the translation much of the humor and depth has obviously been lost, but I have tried to keep the spirit of the play intact using a synthesis from the above sources put into colloquial English, rather than a literal translation. It should be remembered that music and sounds from the band accompany most of the action. Finally, the division of the play into scenes is of my own making. The plays are in fact continuous, but for ease of reading I have separated them into discrete sections at convenient points.

# 3

## Text of *Orphan Do Not Glance (Awisia Yi Wo Ani)*

BY THE JAGUAR JOKERS

### THE OPENING ("COMEDIES")

#### OPENING CHORUS (11:25 P.M.)

*Music starts and then Bampoe, Baidoo, and Hammond file on stage and introduce themselves by dancing and singing a quickstep, pointing at one another as they sing:*

> This is J. B. Bampoe
> This is K. A. Hammond
> And this is E. C. Baidoo . . .

*Bampoe and Hammond are wearing Russian/Canadian arctic caps, red waistcoats, and white trousers with a blue stripe running down each leg. Both have blackened their faces. Mr. Baidoo, the female impersonator, is wearing a European wig, glasses, a beautiful long Ghanaian evening dress, and high-heeled shoes. After the quickstep the three of them go straight into a fast Dagomba highlife:*

> A thief stole 5 pesewas[1] from a trader
> And the townspeople blamed me for it.
> Still, I knew I hadn't done it,
> So I didn't really mind what they said.
> Now the thief has been caught,
> And these people are ashamed.

---

One has to fear human beings in this world
As they will always get you into trouble.

*The three comedians leave the stage.*

## THE IN

*Yaw Bob enters with whitening around his mouth and dressed in
old rags, singing the following highlife:*

I am afraid of the world, look at all the suffering,
     people trying but dying in poverty.
I am sorry for myself, for all the difficulties in this
     life only lead to one thing—death.
Still, after you're dead you never come back, so it's best
     for a person to stop thinking about poverty.
As the elders have said, you don't suffer in the afterlife,
     so why worry about poverty now?
When you are born it is not known what you will have in life,
And even if you are poor it's best not to worry
     as everyone (rich and poor) is going to die.
Nobody is better than anybody else. . . .

YAW BOB: *(In Fanti)* Talking by me, talking by you, listening by nobody.[2] Some time ago I went to the G.B.C. Two[3] offices in Accra, as they were having a big competition there. . . . But first let me tell you how I got there.

When I got to the motor park at Oda[4] I didn't have any money so I had to sneak into the back of a tro-tro[5] and as it was loaded up with bags of charcoal and only the last two benches were free, me and the other passengers were all squeezed up together, like sardines. We were really uncomfortable, and the driver wasn't around either. He finally came after a long time, a tall lanky man who drove so fast that I was praying to God that we would make it to Nsawam.[6] When we did reach there the driver stopped so we could eat some bread, and some of the passengers bought 10, 20, and even 40 pesewas' worth from the sellers who were clamoring around us. I was sitting pretty still though. However, when the driver asked whether we were all satisfied I was the one who shouted out the loudest that I had finished.

We left Nsawam and as we were passing through Pokuase one of the tires burst POOM *(with drum accompaniment)*. We were coming up to a bridge and capsized into the river POOM. I was at the back of the lorry so I was able to jump clear. After I had picked myself up I heard one of the lady passengers shouting out to me in Ga, "Oh gentleman, gentleman, my kenkey[7] has fallen into the river so please retrieve it for me." I tell you, why should I have saved her kenkey when she hadn't even been injured?

She shouted out again, and I replied, "Mammy, you are a fool, why aren't you thanking God that you haven't been injured like the others? Why should I, who have also just missed death, jump into the river for your things?" I said, "Am I your mother to save it for you?" I didn't pay her any attention.

As luck would have it a G.B.C. van was passing and the driver recognized me and asked why I was late in coming to Accra, so I pointed out the accident to him. We got to Accra just in time for the competition. I sang a really nice song, it's for the workers and it's the sort of song that will let them forget they are hungry when they are returning home from work.

I'll sing it for you, first in Twi and then in English. However, the English version's fairly difficult, so if you don't throw me enough dash after the first one I will put the rest of the song into my pocket and walk away. . . .

*Yaw Bob then goes on to sing the song with the assistance of a drummer:*

My wife beat my *fufu*[8] now
My wife beat my *fufu* now, now, now
My wife beat my *fufu* now
My wife beat my *fufu* now, now, now
It's twelve o'clock, I feels hungry
I want my *fufu* now
There's a boom boom yerede
A boom boom yerede
I want my own,
My wife beat my *fufu* now, now, now. . . .[9]

*Finishes at 11:45 P.M.*

## THE "SCENE" OR PLAY PROPER: *ORPHAN DO NOT GLANCE*

### SCENE 1 (11:45 P.M.)

*The band starts playing congo music and two "good-time girls" enter, dancing. They are wearing slacks, wigs, large earrings, and high-heeled shoes.*

ABENA DANSOWA: Hello everybody. I'm the oldest in the family and my younger brother is called King Sam. My parents really tried for me so I managed to reach Form One.[10] However, since I finished, me and my girlfriend Selena have started roaming for men.
SELENA: Good evening. I'm the daughter of the popular Appiah Nana and my house name is Akosua,[11] but my Christian name is REAL SELENA.

DANSOWA: Selena, my parents don't like me going out like this, enjoying myself.

SELENA: Oh don't worry, I'll go and explain to them that it's good for you to have a boyfriend.

### HIGHLIFE SONG

*The two girls sing a song about how lonely they are as their boyfriends have left town, so they have to find new ones. King Sam enters, dressed in a khaki school uniform.*

KING SAM: Dansowa, you must leave your friend right now, you know our parents don't approve of her, and anyway you've been out too long.

DANSOWA: Go back and tell *your* parents that Selena doesn't want me to move an inch, as what we're doing . . .

DANSOWA AND SELENA: . . . IS REALLY GREAT!

SELENA: Listen to me a moment.

KING SAM: Why should I? It's none of your business.

DANSOWA: Oh go away. *(To Selena)* Don't mind him. I've told him to go, if he just wants to stand there let him do what he likes.

KING SAM: Hey, why are you hitting me with cassava?[12]

DANSOWA: Are we eating cassava?[13] Look Sam, you're here and my friend's here, so why don't you greet her?

SELENA: Yes, why haven't you said hello to me?

KING SAM: O.K., how are you?

DANSOWA: That's better. Now, Sam, have you bought those trousers you promised me for Christmas?

KING SAM: Be patient and don't worry, I'm going to make sure this Christmas is going to be a really nice one.

SELENA: *(Picking up the mention of presents)* Hey Dansowa, your brother is really nice. *(Knowing laugh from the audience)* Tell him that I love him.

DANSOWA: Sam, are you listening? Selena says she wants to befriend you.

KING SAM: *(Laughing)* I always have money for girls and drink.

SELENA: *(Enticingly)* King Sam, are you going home now? Let me lead you.

DANSOWA: Can I come as well?

SELENA: No, this is just between Sam and me.

*They all leave the stage, Selena and King Sam hand in hand.*

### SCENE 2 (11:55 P.M.)

*Mr. Johnson, wearing a hat, suit, and tie, enters singing a quickstep.*

### QUICKSTEP

Cry baby cry
Cry baby cry
Just today you left home
And you broke my heart
Cry baby cry . . .[14]

*As he finishes, in come Selena and Dansowa.*

MR. JOHNSON: I'm such an unhappy person. I'm a sand and gravel contractor and was once married to Akua Nyame who became sick in the stomach and died. I had one son by her, Kofi Antobam, and he doesn't even know who his real mother is. After this I married again, to Akua Awotwe, and had a boy and a girl with her. . . . What shall I do about this girl? *What shall I do about this girl?* WHAT SHALL I DO ABOUT THIS GIRL? *(This is accompanied by a drum roll.)* If I tell her to keep still she just jumps over me. *If I tell her to keep still she just jumps over me.* IF I TELL HER TO KEEP STILL SHE JUST JUMPS OVER ME. *(Another drum roll.)* So what shall I do with this girl? What shall I do with both of them?—For they are both spoiled. *(Mrs. Johnson enters.)* Akua, my first wife, gave me one child and you have given me two. As for Abena she's just roaming about, but thank God the two boys are still at school. But there's one thing I have to ask you, who's going to look after Antobam when I go off on business?

MRS. JOHNSON: Well, I'm not going to keep on looking after him. *(Just at that moment King Sam arrives.)*

MR. JOHNSON: So, Sam, you've finally come home. Where is your brother Kofi?

KING SAM: He was delaying on the way so I left him.

MR. JOHNSON: WHAT! Is he trying to rule me in my own house? Tomorrow he won't get any chop money. He really is too bad trying to teach *me* how to live. Surely it should be the other way round?

KING SAM: You're right, he's too disobedient, you should check him.

### HIGHLIFE SONG

*Antobam's plaintive voice comes from behind the stage*
*(i.e., outside the house). He is singing that he never sees*
*his mother and that he is being badly treated in the house.*

MR. JOHNSON: Sam, go and call Kofi into the house, he shouldn't be playing in the road like this.

*Sam goes off and comes back with Antobam, who is wearing*
*extremely ragged school clothes. He goes to greet his father.*

MR. JOHNSON: Go you! Is this the sort of time you come back from school?

ANTOBAM: Oh father, my teacher sacked me from school because my uniform was torn, and he told me not to come until it was mended. I was so upset that I went and sat under a tree and fell asleep.

MR. JOHNSON: I thought you were playing around. Weren't you?

ANTOBAM: No, I wasn't.

MR. JOHNSON: Sam, didn't you just tell me that Kofi has been playing around all day?

KING SAM: Actually I didn't see this myself but a friend told me. *(Audience starts hooting at Sam.)*

MR. JOHNSON: So you didn't see him yourself. Well, next time only tell me what you see with your own eyes, you liar. *(Turning to his wife)* You'd better go and get a school uniform for Kofi and then there will be peace. Don't they have any khaki in Nsaba?[15] Now I've got to leave for work, or my men won't do anything today. Kofi, your stepmother will buy you a new uniform, so don't worry.

### HIGHLIFE SONG

*Mrs. Johnson laments the fact that she has to look after all
the children when her husband goes away.*

MR. JOHNSON: *(Giving his wife some money)* Here, take this and send the boys to buy some food for themselves.

*All leave the stage.*

### SCENE 3 [12:10 A.M.]

*Mr. Johnson enters, wearing a suit and an old battered khaki hat. He has just
come home from work. He is followed by King Sam and Mrs. Johnson.*

MR. JOHNSON: Sam, why were you so long in getting the food?

KING SAM: Oh, Kofi was delaying as usual.

MRS. JOHNSON: *(Interrupting to defend Sam)* I didn't even send Sam, I only sent Kofi.

MR. JOHNSON: *(Confused by these two contradictory stories)* For goodness' sake let's forget the whole thing, my head's spinning.

### HIGHLIFE SONG

*Mrs. Johnson sings about how upset she is, and as she
nears the end Sam joins in, whistling.*

MR. JOHNSON: What the bloody hell do you mean *[in English]*, whistling when your parents are singing? A pepper like you, where do you think you come from?[16] *(To wife)* By the way, where is Kofi's uniform?

MRS. JOHNSON: How many times are you going to keep asking me this? Haven't I told you that I'm sewing one for him?

MR. JOHNSON: I'm sure people will think I can't look after my children properly. Can't you see how it looks with one son properly dressed and the other not—already the teacher has been giving me funny looks. What have you done with the 16 cedis I gave you?

MRS. JOHNSON: You think I've chopped the money?

MR. JOHNSON: I didn't say that exactly.

MRS. JOHNSON: Well stop trying to disgrace me then, I've just been too busy, that's all.

MR. JOHNSON: All right, all right, let's stop this palaver. If you find housework so much I'll bring somebody in to help you. In fact I've got just the person, he's my friend Opia from Teacher Okai.[17]

MRS. JOHNSON: Well if he tries to boss me around I'll leave.

MR. JOHNSON: *(To audience)* You see how she is?

### HIGHLIFE SONG

*Mrs. Johnson sings about the quarrel she is having with her husband.*

### SCENE 4 [12:20 A.M.]

*Although nobody leaves the stage there is meant to be a break in time, for Opia enters, face blackened and wearing baggy yellow trousers, a checked shirt, and a brown cap.*

MR. JOHNSON: Hey, Opia, come in and put your bags down. This is my wife, I think you already met some time ago in Swedru.

OPIA: Yes, that's right. *(He greets everybody.)*

MR. JOHNSON: Opia, do you like the idea of staying here with us instead of going back home?

OPIA: At Teacher Okai I owe 16 shillings to a kenkey seller called Auntie Akweley, and every time she sees me she asks me for it. Now I can't get any more kenkey, and as I'm always hungry it would be great to stay here. Also, back home there's another woman called Ajala who sells rice balls, and she's getting annoyed as I owe her money. The only food I could get was Accra Passport,[18] and now I even owe the Ewe girl who sells that. . . . Wait, I haven't finished yet. A few days ago I was in my room when I heard a knock. It was one of Auntie Akweley's children coming to collect the money *(he mimics her Ga speech)* and I told her I would only give it to her mother. A few minutes later the gari[19] seller's daughter *(he mimics her Ewe)* came so I threw her out. Then believe it or not Ajala's daughter came, greeted me *(mimics her Hausa)* and asked me for the money, and I had to send her packing. After all this knocking I was beginning to think the radio had done something.[20]

MR. JOHNSON: *(Puzzled)* What do you mean by the radio did something?

OPIA: Ah, I'm glad you brought up the topic of radios as I really have reason to thank them. You know this signature tune that is played on

G.B.C. first thing in the morning? *(He sings it accompanied by drums)* Well, this song is really handy for people who owe money as it wakes them up early, so they can get away quick, before their creditors come. In fact this is what I did this morning, although funnily enough as I opened my door to run away my neighbor across the road, Mr. Ofori, also started running. I suppose it was for the same reason. . . . Let me tell you all here tonight that there is nothing to be ashamed of in having debts, as everyone owes money to someone or other. I'll also tell you the best thing to do whenever you get into this situation. After you've had your evening bath, refill your bucket and leave it outside your door with towel and soap. I seem to remember now that I tried this trick on a woman from Akroso. I left my bucket out overnight and was woken up by the G.B.C. song *(He sings it again)*—Dah . . . dah . . . dah. However, instead of going back to sleep[21] I leaped out of bed, ran out, and hid. When the woman came a little later she saw the bucket and thought I was in the room. She waited and waited but of course I never came.

MR. JOHNSON: Well, I don't care what happened to you at Teacher Okai, but I do want you to stay here and look after my children as if they were your own. You see the problem is I can't stay around all the time as I have to keep going back and forth to my job-site.

*Mr. and Mrs. Johnson exit. Antobam enters.*

KING SAM: Opia, if you think you're just going to sit around you're wrong. I'm not going to do anything, you are going to have to fetch water, pound *fufu*, everything in fact, do you hear?

ANTOBAM: Sam, can't you show respect to one of father's friends? Opia, don't listen to him, if you want anything done I'll help you.

*Mrs. Johnson comes in carrying a small table and two stools.*
*She turns to Sam.*

MRS. JOHNSON: What would you like to eat?

KING SAM: Oh, some bread, rice, and sardines.

*As Mrs. Johnson turns to leave, Opia starts to slap the now seated Sam.*
*With each blow there is a crash on the drums and a single note on the guitar.*
*Mrs. Johnson sees what's going on out of the corner of her eye.*

MRS. JOHNSON: Opia, what do you think you're doing?

OPIA: Sam asked me to show him how to box.

MRS. JOHNSON: What! He asked an old person like you?

KING SAM: Don't listen to him, mother, he's telling lies, he just came up to me and hit me.

> *Mrs. Johnson briefly departs and returns with some food,*
> *to find Opia up to his antics again.*

MRS. JOHNSON: Stop bullying Sam and get on with the housework.
OPIA: What do you think I am? A machine?
MRS. JOHNSON: Are you trying to be rude?
OPIA: No, you didn't hear what I said, I said I was going to find a machine to sew my shirt.

### SAD HIGHLIFE SONG

> *While Sam is sitting down eating, Opia and Antobam sing about their*
> *suffering and the fact that whenever Mr. Johnson is away they don't eat.*
> *Members of the audience are moved by this and throw money on stage or come*
> *up bringing kenkey, bananas, and bread. By the time the song is finished,*
> *Antobam is literally weighed down with food, but Mrs. Johnson comes and*
> *snatches it away. The audience really gets angry and jeers at her, and she*
> *taunts them back. As she leaves with the food she turns to King Sam.*

MRS. JOHNSON: Sam, if you want anything done, make sure Opia does it for you.

> *Boos from the audience. While Mrs. Johnson is away Opia jumps on Sam's*
> *back and starts hitting him again. There's great excitement, with the drums*
> *and guitar playing and the audience cheering, but Mrs. Johnson soon returns.*

OPIA: We're only playing leapfrog. Hey Sam, now it's your turn to jump over me.

> *Opia leaves sheepishly and an unhappy-looking Mr. Johnson appears.*

MR. JOHNSON: Oh life, life, life, life.[22] Akosua, has everybody eaten now?
MRS. JOHNSON: Yes. (*Audience boos and hisses.*)
MR. JOHNSON: What did you eat?
KING SAM: Bread, rice, and sardines, and now I'm completely full.
MR. JOHNSON: (*Turning to wife again*) What about Antobam? He's still wearing his old clothes. How long is it going to take you to sew, two years?
MRS. JOHNSON: My dear, why do you keep bringing this subject up?
MR. JOHNSON: (*To Antobam*) Have you eaten today?
ANTOBAM: No. (*He begins to cry.*)
MR. JOHNSON: Hey, why are you doing that?
ANTOBAM: Because I'm hungry.
MRS. JOHNSON: (*To Antobam*) Are you sure you haven't eaten?
ANTOBAM: No. I mean . . . oh, I don't know.
MR. JOHNSON: Really, Kofi, make up your mind.

> *Opia enters to a great cheer from the audience.*

MR. JOHNSON: Look, what's been happening here since I left, Opia?

OPIA: Although it was Kofi who went out to get the food, he didn't get any himself. Your wife and Sam were sharing it among themselves.

MRS. JOHNSON: Stop gossiping, Opia, or I'll fire you and drive you out of the house. Kofi, you say you haven't eaten, all right, I'll give you some food.

ANTOBAM: *(Timidly)* Oh it's O.K., I have eaten.

OPIA: *(To Mr. Johnson)* You see how scared he is?

MR. JOHNSON: I don't know who has or hasn't eaten, *(to Mrs. Johnson)* so you'd better give everyone food.

### SAD HIGHLIFE SONG BY MR. JOHNSON

> You are the woman I've married
> But if I say anything you won't listen
> I'm telling you today, be very careful
> For wickedness is not good
> Be kind to the children and let's have peace.

*The stage clears.*

### SCENE 5 [12:45 A.M.]

*King Sam, Antobam, and Opia enter, followed by Mrs. Johnson carrying a pestle and mortar containing ampesi.*[23]

MRS. JOHNSON: I've cooked some cassava, come and make *fufu* so that Sam can eat.

### SLOW HIGHLIFE SONG

*Antobam starts pounding and Opia sings the following lament:*

> I'm afraid of this woman
> Because of the way she treats us
> I'm beginning to regret that I ever came here
> To a house where the wife rules the husband.

*Antobam complains that he has a headache and Opia takes over.*

### FAST HIGHLIFE SONG

*As Opia starts pounding, a new and faster highlife starts up. Everything gets faster and faster, the crowd starts roaring, and Opia begins to do a crazy dance culminating with his hitting Mrs. Johnson's hand with the pestle ("accidentally on purpose").*
*Suddenly Mr. Johnson reappears to find his wife howling in pain.*

MR. JOHNSON: What's happened?

OPIA: *(As if butter wouldn't melt in his mouth)* I accidentally crushed her fingers *(he ostentatiously hops about)* and anyway she knocked my leg with the mortar.

MR. JOHNSON: Well, you'll both need medicine won't you? From now on there won't be any more *fufu*-pounding in this house. If you want some you'll have to get it from a chop bar. *(He leaves the stage.)*

OPIA: *(Smirking at the audience)* Auntie, I'm sorry, I'm sorry. *(Audience laughs.)*

OPIA: *(Turning to King Sam)* See how I have injured your mother, let this be a warning to you. *(To Mrs. Johnson)* I have some information for you, but first you'll have to give me some food before I tell it.

MRS. JOHNSON: Here, take some of this bread. . . . Now, what is it?

OPIA: I saw a spirit last night and it asked me why you weren't feeding Kofi properly, and I said I didn't know.

MRS. JOHNSON: Take the rest of the bread.

OPIA: *(After gobbling up the bread)* I was only joking.

MRS. JOHNSON: Opia, you shouldn't say things like that because it might annoy Kofi's real mother. Don't you know that she's dead?

> *Mrs. Johnson and King Sam leave. Mr. Johnson's sister enters to find Antobam weeping. Opia tells her what's happened.*

OPIA: *(To Antobam)* I didn't know your mother was dead, did you?

ANTOBAM: I always thought Auntie here was my mother.

AUNTIE: No, no, I'm not your mother although we've always let you think so. I really am your aunt, your mother died just after you were born.

ANTOBAM: *(Wailing)* I never knew, I never knew.

### TRADITIONAL FANTI FUNERAL SONG

*Opia and the Aunt sing, accompanied by drums.*

> In this world we come to work and suffer
> But Kofi, your mother has passed away
> We pity you, for you didn't know she was dead.

> *As they sing this, Opia tries to console the weeping Antobam. Mr. and Mrs. Johnson come in with King Sam.*

OPIA: Today Kofi has found his right path.

MR. JOHNSON: *(Understanding this proverb refers to Antobam's dead mother)* Who told Kofi this?

OPIA: King Sam told us she had passed.

MR. JOHNSON: I suppose you mean passed away. Well Sam, you'd better pack your things and get out of here, I never wanted Kofi to know about this.

OPIA: Oh forgive him, forgive him, let him stay, as from now on I will make sure he changes his ways.

*Mr. Johnson departs, upset.*

MRS. JOHNSON: Cheer up, Sam, what do you want to eat? You can have anything but *fufu*, as my hand is still hurting, thanks to Opia.
KING SAM: *(Demurely)* Bread, sardines, and a Fanta please.

*Mrs. Johnson goes and brings the food and they both begin to eat.*

OPIA: Sam, don't you feel any pity for Kofi? Give him some food.
KING SAM: Why should I do anything for him?

### SAD HIGHLIFE [NIMPA REBRE[24]] BY OPIA

My mother, you said it, that people are bound to suffer
People are suffering in this life
People are suffering in getting their daily bread
People are suffering before they go to their graves
Auntie Ofuriwa is the one who said that people will
  suffer
And it's true, people are suffering before they get their
  daily bread.

CHORUS: Mother, you said it
People are bound to suffer.

*Opia slips away and returns with Mr. Johnson, much to
the audience's delight. There is cheering and drumming, and
the bass guitarist does glissando notes up and down his instrument.*

MR. JOHNSON: Well, seeing is believing. (He starts to slap his wife, the drummer emphasizing the blows, and Opia chases her and King Sam around the stage.) Both these boys are my sons yet you treat them differently. (Then in slow and precise English) I'm telling you that you will go back to your town. (Crowd roars approval.)

### FAST DAGOMBA HIGHLIFE[25]

*Opia and Mr. Johnson dance and sing, and Opia whistles:*

I have not married a good wife at all
For she is too troublesome
I will let her go to her parents and remain alone.

*As they sing members of the audience come up and give them money.
Everyone leaves except Antobam.*

ANTOBAM: I'm so sad, for now I understand the character of women. I wish someone would come and take me away from all this.

### SAD HIGHLIFE SONG

*Antobam sings and audience members bring up money.*

I Kofi Antobam am suffering
My dead mother, please come and take me away
My father has tried for me
But because of this woman[26] I can't prosper
Someone please come and take me away.

*Opia returns singing a highlife.*

### SAD HIGHLIFE SONG

In this world there is hardship and trouble enough
So if you meet a person who has lost a parent
You should pity them
Feel pity for the sorrow of Kofi Antobam.

### ANOTHER SAD HIGHLIFE

*Antobam, accompanied by Opia sings:*

Why is it that I came to this world
And the river of life took my mother away so soon?
I was too young to have lost my mother . . .

OPIA: Kofi, I feel so sorry for you . . . so sorry. *(He leaves.)*
ANTOBAM: Christ help me. *(Audience responds, "We pity you.")*

### SCENE 6 [1:05 A.M.]

*Suddenly the main lights go off and three dim red lights are switched on.
A devil appears, making animal noises and waving an axe around. He is
completely covered in black cloth, is wearing a mask, and on top of his head a
sparkler is burning. Antobam falls to the ground in fear, and just as the devil
is about to pounce on him three peals of thunder sound from the back of the
stage (made by clanging three gong-gongs). On the last peal, the curtain is
pulled open to reveal three angels, dressed in white and wearing European
masks. They have their hands outstretched, and moving forward they sing in
Twi the Presbyterian hymn "The Spirit Is Willing." The audience joins in.
After they finish, one of the angels goes to the devil who has taken up
a frozen attitude and speaks to him.*

ANGEL: Devil, who are you? Are you not afraid of this world? You don't have any power here, get up and go.

*The devil leaves, whimpering. The audience sing a second Presbyterian hymn,*
*   "I Am an Orphan," and then one of the angels speaks to Antobam.*

ANGEL: Antobam, get up in the name of God and pray to him, for he will
help you and cast evil spirits away.

*The audience responds "Amen." The angels sing their last hymn, "Naomi,"*[27]
*   moving backward with their hands outstretched as they do so:*

> Today here I am, Naomi
> When the rain is falling I always walk in it
> When the sun is shining I also walk in it, just like that.
> I shall keep on walking like this until I die.

*As the hymn ends, the curtain slides across and the main lights go back on.*

## SCENE 7 [1:20 A.M.]

*Antobam, who is still on stage, wrings his hands and cries out in joy.*

ANTOBAM: God has helped me, let us praise him.

### APOSTOLIC HYMN, "LET US PRAISE HIM"[28]

*Antobam and the audience sing this popular Ghanaian hymn together.*
*   Toward the end Opia comes in.*

> Praise our God
> For his only son that has been our comforter
>    and savior today
> We praise him, we magnify him, we thank him.
>
> In the morning of the third day he rose up from
>    the tomb
> Death could not hold him
> We praise him always.
>
> He has overpowered death
> He has delivered us from our sins
> And for his sake, we are now at liberty.

OPIA: Kofi, why are you singing?
ANTOBAM: I went to sleep and dreamed that a devil was trying to kill me,
but I was saved by three angels.
OPIA: Kneel down, for God is with you. Let us praise him.

### APOSTOLIC HYMN, "LET US PRAISE HIM"

*They all sing it again, and after they finish Opia says "Na wu da ho" (So you*
*were sleeping), and this phrase sparks off the song again. This happens five*
*times. Each time they conclude the hymn, Opia teasingly starts it up again,*

*each time getting more excited. After the fifth rendition, Opia just mouths the phrase and the tantalized audience shouts it out for him. The hymn is then sung for the last time. Mr. Johnson enters looking grim.*

MR. JOHNSON: This world is so full of trouble. There is now gossip that Kofi is the cause of the disagreement between me and my wife. *(Turning to Antobam)* Kofi, I think I'd better send you away from here. You can go and stay with my friend Mr. Nkansah, in Kumasi. I've already seen him about this and he said you can finish off your education there with him. Now listen, when you get there make sure you behave yourself. Don't steal, don't go and eat outside the house, and if an elderly person sends you on an errand don't squeeze your face, do everything they tell you to do. In this suitcase I have packed two sets of school clothes, a pair of canvas shoes, a sleeping cloth and a Sunday suit. Here, also, take this 16 cedis,[29] and if there's any balance left when you reach Kumasi give it to Mrs. Nkansah and she will look after it for you.

OPIA: Hey, so you're going to Kumasi. . . . The only thing I can give you is some old clothes and 5 pesewas *(he is torn between his greed and his friendship for Antobam)*, but I can give you some advice. If you spend 3 of these 5 pesewas, give the rest to a poor person, for if you do, it will surely come back to you.

*(Audience applauds.)*

MR. JOHNSON: Kofi, wait and say goodbye to your stepmother. I know women, if you don't say goodbye to her she will always hold it against me.

*(Mrs. Johnson enters and her husband explains his decision to her.)*

MRS. JOHNSON: If you're going to divorce me why bother telling me any of this?

MR. JOHNSON: Look, I'm not going to divorce you.

ANTOBAM: Goodbye everybody.

*Mrs. Johnson ignores his farewell and turns her back on him, muttering that he is no good. As Antobam leaves he sings:*

### SAD HIGHLIFE SONG

My stepmother thinks I am of no use
I'm leaving so that someone else can replace me
So that my stepmother can have peace
I'm sure her family are devils.[30]

MR. JOHNSON: As I've sent away one son, it's only right that I should send away the other as well. Sam can go and stay with my friend Kwamena Williams in Oguaa.[31]

OPIA: *(To Mr. Johnson)* Well, if Kofi's gone to Kumasi and Sam's going to Oguaa, then your wife had better go to your job site where she can watch the quarrying and the WALA TU WALA SA.[32] *(The whole audience joins in this phrase.)*

MRS. JOHNSON: I don't want Sam to leave.

MR. JOHNSON: Don't tell me what to do or—*[in English]* I'll show you my mental powers.

MRS. JOHNSON: *(Slapping her husband)* All right, show me your powers, show me. *(Slaps him again)*

MR. JOHNSON: I suppose I'd better let him stay, you are his mother.

OPIA: What! I've never seen such spineless behavior in a man before! If I had a girl who tried to push me around like this I would beat her, and then she wouldn't think she was so wonderful. When this sort of thing starts with women and a man doesn't check it, and even starts trailing around after her, it means he's POTETE![33] *(For four or five minutes Opia prances around the stage shouting "Potete," with the audience responding "Po-dowdow." The drums and the guitar, bending a single note, follow the tone of the audience's reply.)*

MR. JOHNSON: What's happening here? Everyone shouting "Potete, potete."

OPIA: Well, we haven't mentioned any names, have we? We're just doing our own thing. *(He sneakily mouths the word "Potete" again, and the audience screams back the reply.)*

### FAST HIGHLIFE

*As the music is playing, Opia and the audience keep shouting out to one another. Opia starts to do a scatty dance, and then Mr. Johnson, although he doesn't really know what's going on, gets so roused that he too joins in and ends up by kicking one of his canvas shoes into the audience. The stage clears.*

### SCENE 8 (1:35 A.M.)

*A number of years have elapsed. King Sam comes in wearing "Afro" clothes (bell-bottom trousers, a flowery shirt, and a head-scarf). He is accompanied by Selena and Dansowa wearing slacks and wigs. The band begins to play rock 'n' roll, and they start coolly to dance to it. Sam sits down at a small table he has brought in, and the girls open some bottles of beer. As they are drinking and smoking Mrs. Johnson enters.*

MRS. JOHNSON: Hey Sam you do look nice, and you too, Dansowa. *(She leaves.)*

### SOUL "FUNKY FUNKY"

*Sam and the girls dance and sing this number. King Sam's schoolteacher, dressed in suit and tie, joins them.*

TEACHER: Sam, where's your homework?
KING SAM: I haven't done it, sir.

*Teacher leaves, annoyed, and Sam and the girls continue to dance to "Funky Funky." Almost immediately Teacher returns with Mr. Johnson.*

MR. JOHNSON: Sam, you're just too bad. You are just a small boy, you don't work, yet you seem to have enough money for beer-bars. Now I know why I'm always losing money around the house. Whenever I said anything about this before my wife would get angry.
DANSOWA: Sam, why do you sit and let him shout at you like that?
TEACHER: Shut up! What do you mean, "shout like that"?
DANSOWA: I mean my father implying that Sam has been stealing his money to buy drinks. If so, say so. . . . *(To Teacher)* You Saamia.
MR. JOHNSON: *(To audience)* Look how she's behaving. Teacher, please, what does Saamia mean? *(He and Teacher repeat the word three times, the audience thinking it a great joke that they don't know the meaning of the word.)*
TEACHER: Old man, I'm sorry I don't know, it's not in the dictionary.
MR. JOHNSON: Opia, what does it mean when a girl calls you Saamia?
OPIA: It's rather better to die than hear that word. If they say this it means you are the slop-water left over from making kenkey. *(The audience gets hysterical at this point.)* Dansowa, how can you say this to a respectable man?

*He grapples with her and in the confusion knocks Teacher down. The pushes and blows are emphasized by the drums. Dansowa shouts over and over again that she will get Opia. The audience is loving the whole show. Teacher gets up off the floor and, trying not to be annoyed with Opia, he speaks English:*

TEACHER: Don't worry, don't worry, Opia, I wasn't standing properly.
OPIA: *(Feigning concern)* Well said, teacher, I'm glad you didn't hit me back, for it was a mistake.
TEACHER: *(To Mr. Johnson)* You know that Sam hasn't been to school since we reopened?
MR. JOHNSON: Sam, if you don't learn now how will you get promotion later on?
TEACHER: *(Speaking to Sam in English and trailing off into Twi)* You must be very careful, because of you ma do de blows wo ha [because of you I have received some blows].
OPIA: *(Pointing to Teacher)* I tell you this man has sense, you can see he has training, for he knows all about *etiquette, civilization,* and *politeness* [English].
MR. JOHNSON: I'm sure this boy will spoil all the other children.
MRS. JOHNSON: What! Are you trying to disgrace him in front of all these people?

MR. JOHNSON: You want me to say nothing? You want him to stop school and go drinking instead?

*Just at this point, a bell rings from behind the curtain.*

MR. JOHNSON: *(In English)* Who's that, come in and enter with love, enter with pleasure. *(A messenger dressed in a suit comes in.)* Good evening, I am Johnson, what can I do for you?
MESSENGER: I've got a telegram for you. *(He hands it over and leaves. Mr. Johnson opens it and reads it. Every time he makes an exclamation, Opia echoes it.)*
MR. JOHNSON: Oh!
OPIA: Oh!
MR. JOHNSON: No.
OPIA: No.
MR. JOHNSON: Ah! Thank God!
OPIA: Ah!
MR. JOHNSON: *(Turning to Opia)* If you want to read it take it.
OPIA: I don't want it, you read it.

*The audience laughs at this because they suspect he can't read properly.*

MR. JOHNSON: *(In English)* Listen to the contents of the letter. It is from Kumasi and it reads, "Your son Kofi Antobam has successfully passed the Common Entrance Exam." *(Applause and cheers.)*
OPIA: Isn't that just what I said? Sure . . . sure . . . sure.
MR. JOHNSON: All right, what did you say?
OPIA: The price of cocoa has gone up.

*The crowd is in uproar over this. Mr. Johnson then reads out
the telegram again, this time in Twi for the non-English speakers.
He also explains to them what this exam is, and that passing it
will enable Antobam to go on to secondary school.*

OPIA: Hurrah, Kofi's going to Sekondi![34] *(More laughter.)*

**HIGHLIFE SONG**

*Opia and Mr. Johnson praise Antobam for doing so well and making them
happy. Mr. Johnson leaves.*

OPIA: *(Teasing Sam)* Antobam's passed but I'm sure you'll fail.
MRS. JOHNSON: *(Angrily)* Hey, Opia, stop that.

*They all leave the stage.*

## SCENE 9 (1:55 A.M.)

*A few more years have passed. Opia and Mrs. Johnson enter
to find King Sam sitting down sadly.*

MRS. JOHNSON: What's wrong, Sam, are you sick?

KING SAM: No, I'm all right, but I just heard I failed my exams.

OPIA: How did you manage that?

KING SAM: The teacher said I failed because I haven't been going to school enough.

OPIA: *(Making a great pretense)* Oh . . . what a shame!

MRS. JOHNSON: Oh Sam, you've disgraced me. *(Waves her arms about and sings a lament:)*

#### SAD HIGHLIFE SONG

> How can I prosper
> When my enemies are prospering
> I have failed in life.

OPIA: *(To Mrs. Johnson)* Hey stop crying, I've just seen the teacher and he gave me a certificate that says Sam passed with a hundred percent. Here it is, Sam, but let me give it to your mother so that she can frame it.

*Opia gives some bread and a tin of sardines to her, much to
the audience's amusement. He then torments King Sam by
singing a parody of the soul number "Funky Funky":*

#### "FUNKY SARDINES"

> Funky sardines
> Funky brodo [bread]
> Wow . . .
> I'm soul brother number two.

*Mr. Johnson hobbles in using a stick and wearing a cloth. He is now old with
white hair under his hat and a white beard [indicated with powdered chalk]*

MR. JOHNSON: *(In English, pronouncing each syllable carefully)* Ladies and gentlemen, now you can see by your own eyes that I am old. As we all know that every blessed day sends us nearer our graves; now is the time for these my children, whom I have spent a lot on, to repay me for what I have spent on them . . . because I am old . . . *(Crowd applauds)* . . . I feel to do hard business but mind you my age at the present moment won't permit me to do any hard business today. I have wished for life but I can't do it. The soul is willing but the flesh is weak.

*The audience joins in this last utterance and applauds him. He repeats the
speech in Twi. After finishing, he makes a great flourish with his cloth and*

*starts to sit down, but as he is lowering himself laboriously into
the seat Opia rushes up to help him and sings out:*

OPIA: Monso no mu . . . oo, obi na kwakura [hold him . . . oh, he's somebody's old man]. Monso no mu . . . oo, obi na kwakura, monso no mu oo, obi na kwakura.

MR. JOHNSON: *(Now seated)* Sam, is it true that you failed your exams?

KING SAM: *(In English)* Please father, I failed.

MR. JOHNSON: *(In English)* You failed, my dear son, I am telling you that because of your failure I am doomed.

OPIA: Dooooooomed!

MR. JOHNSON: *(Stands up. In English)* My dear son, why didn't you try your best possible to pass this your final examination? You know that opportunity comes but once, and you have lost your chance.

*He then translates this into Twi, and again as he sits down Opia, much to
everybody's delight, sings out "Monso no mu . . ." etc.*

MRS. JOHNSON: We should let Sam try again, I'm sure next time he'll pass.

OPIA: The old man doesn't have enough money.

*Suddenly a bell rings, and in comes a messenger bringing a telegram
for Mr. Johnson, whose eyes by now have become weak.*

MR. JOHNSON: *(In English)* Sam, go and get my reading spectacles. *(King Sam brings them, and his father continues in English.)* Listen to the contents of the second letter. It's from Kumasi again and it reads "Your son Kofi Antobam—" Oh, I thank the Omnipotent God!

OPIA: *(Trying to mimic him)* Oh, I thank the Superintendent God! *(Much laughter.)*

MR. JOHNSON: *(Annoyed, he hands the letter to Opia)* O.K., as you're so interested, you read it.

OPIA: *(He has to say something, so he says:)* Pim praa timi timi nyama li.[35]

*He repeats this several times, with the audience and drums
responding "Nanaa timi timi nyama li."*

MR. JOHNSON: *(Exasperated)* All right, give it to me and I'll read it. *(In English)* Your son Kofi Antobam successfully secured job at Kumasi. Will arrive at Agona Nsaba today with wife. *(Loud cheers.)*

OPIA: Isn't that just what I said?

*Mr. Johnson gets up and sings:*

### HIGHLIFE SONG

Here we are in the world
And if you respect yourself the future

will be a happy one
Now Kofi has completed college and is working
He is also married and is coming to show
his wife to us
In this world if you are patient you will enjoy
For God works mysteriously
You have to suffer to gain.

SCENE 10 (2.15 A.M.)

*Enter Kofi Antobam, in a smart suit, with his wife bewigged and wearing a long sequinned dress. They all greet one another.*

MR. JOHNSON: Come and sit down.

ANTOBAM: I can't sit while you're still standing up.

MR. JOHNSON: This boy really has got respect. (*He sits down and once again Opia, joined by the audience, shouts out "Monso no mu . . .," etc. Opia then starts to ogle Antobam's wife and starts raving about how beautiful she is: "E ye fefefe."*)

ANTOBAM: Father, you remember how you sent me off to Mr. Nkansah's? Well, that very day we went round to see a headmaster and luckily there was a vacancy at his school. I studied there and after I passed my exams Mr. Nkansah got me a job as postmaster. (*Applause.*)

OPIA: My brother is now a postmaster. (*He chants the following phrases four times. The audience joins in the last couple of times:*) Me sua [I carry] letter . . . postmaster!

ANTOBAM: Later Mr. Nkansah asked me if I was considering marriage at all, and I told him there was a girl I liked. We went to her parents and after we were married Mr. Nkansah suggested that we should come to visit you.

ANTOBAM'S WIFE: I come from Akim Oda but I sell children's clothes and groundnuts[36] in Kumasi . . . in fact that's how I first met Kofi, I was selling groundnuts one Saturday afternoon. He said . . .

OPIA: (*Interrupting her*) If you were selling groundnuts and somebody wanted 5 pesewas' worth but gave you 20 pesewas, how much balance would you give back?

ANTOBAM'S WIFE: Oh Opia, 15 pesewas of course, now be quiet and let me finish. Kofi said he wanted to marry me and asked me whether I already had a husband, and I told him no. So then he went to see my parents, we got married and now I'm here.

MR. JOHNSON: Well, you are most welcome.

ANTOBAM'S WIFE: May I give some advice to my sisters here? It's this: if a young man is in love with you, you should stop roaming around and have patience. In this way the two of you will come to understand one another.

MR. JOHNSON: *(Who has been ogling his daughter-in-law)* Not only young men I hope. *(Audience laughs.)*

ANTOBAM: I couldn't come empty-handed, so here, father, take this cloth to keep yourself warm. *(Applause.)*

MR. JOHNSON:.*(In slow, ponderous English)* In fact and in truth this is my tears of joy; my son Kofi has done what Napoleon could not do.[37] Kofi I thank you very much and I say to the Lord Almighty may your ship sail to the distant shore. *(Much clapping. He then repeats the speech in Twi.)*

OPIA: *(Impatient for his present)* Oh come on, come on, hurry up.

ANTOBAM: Opia, I've never forgotten the help you used to give me, so take this bag and go and look inside.

OPIA: *(Incredibly coyly)* Oh no no, I can't take it.

ANTOBAM: Well if you don't want it I'll keep it. *(At this Opia snatches the bag and rushes out amidst a lot of laughter.)*

ANTOBAM: King Sam, how ever did you manage to fail your exams?

KING SAM: My mind was all messed up.

ANTOBAM: Look Sam, father is old now so we have to look after him . . . so you'd better mend your ways.

> *Mr. Johnson's sister, Auntie Aba Yaa, comes in and is introduced to Antobam's wife. Selena comes in looking mean.*

SELENA: Ah—so there you are, Sam. I've been looking for you. What do you mean telling me to go and collect those shoes you promised me when you didn't even pay for them? Now it's my palaver, so give me the 10 cedis.

MRS. JOHNSON: How can he pay, he's only a schoolboy.

SELENA: He may be, but that didn't stop him taking me out for drinks.

MRS. JOHNSON: You really have no shame. *(The audience jeers at her for always supporting King Sam, no matter what.)*

ANTOBAM: Let's stop this. Here's the money for the shoes. Sam, if you don't have money you shouldn't put someone else into debt.

KING SAM: O.K., O.K., you're right as usual.

> *(Audience hoots at him. Opia reenters wearing blue trousers and hat—the present from Antobam.)*

OPIA: *(Abusing King Sam)* As for Sam, he's stolen all the khaki shirts in Nsaba.

> *Antobam gives a 10-cedi dash to his aunt and 15 cedis to his stepmother.*

OPIA: *(Annoyed)* Kofi, how can you give your stepmother this money? Don't you know that it was she who told me that your mother was dead?[38] *(Audience boos him, as now is the time for byegones to be byegones.)*

MRS. JOHNSON: Thank you Kofi. You know, although people used to think I didn't like you, I always tried to treat you and Sam the same. *(Audience hisses.)*

ANTOBAM: I think it would be a good idea if Sam came back to Kumasi with us to finish his education. Then later we'll get him a job . . . I think it's time for us to leave now.

OPIA: Let me give Sam some advice first. Sam, make sure you pound the *fufu*, sweep the floors, and wash all the clothes for Mr. Antobam.

KING SAM: I agree.

OPIA: Wait, there's one more thing yet. Kofi, whatever you do, never mention the word "sardines" in Sam's presence or he will fail in whatever he is doing, and especially never let him eat them again. *(Laughter.)*

KING SAM: *(Emphatically)* I won't.

### FINAL HIGHLIFE SONG

*All the characters join in for this last song, with Mr. Johnson singing the lyrics and the rest the chorus:*

> Let this concert be a warning to you
> There is always trouble if you marry two wives
> For one wife will never look after the other
> wife's children properly
> And here is some advice for wives
> Never discriminate between your children
> For they all belong to your husband.
> To the children here I say this
> Young people should give respect to their elders
> They shouldn't steal or go to beer-bars
> In this life if you don't succeed
> It may be best to leave and try elsewhere
> Antobam didn't succeed until he went to Kumasi
> As you can see my wife wants Sam to succeed
> So she is now letting him go away
> But in the long run only God knows who will
> succeed in life.

*Play closes (2:40 A.M.)*

NOTES

1. Pesewa: smallest unit of Ghanaian currency: one-hundredth of a cedi. Usually translated as "one penny."

2. Talking by me, etc.: i.e., "Everyone should be quiet and listen." This opening is intended to make sure the audience is settled down and paying attention.

3. G.B.C. Two: Ghana Broadcasting Corporation, Channel 2.

4. Oda, or Akim Oda: a town in southern Ghana.

5. Tro-tro: a local passenger vehicle, so called because the fare on these vehicles used to be threepence: "tro" was the name for the old lobular-shaped Gold Coast threepenny bit (thus, "threepence-threepence," i.e., "threepence a ride").

6. Nsawam: a town about twenty miles north of Accra, close to where the Jaguar Jokers were based.

7. Kenkey: Cooked, half-fermented corn dough, a staple food in Ghana. One type of kenkey, wrapped in corn leaves, is the staple of the Ga people; another type, wrapped in banana leaves, is eaten by the Fanti.

8. *Fufu:* boiled yam, cassava, or plantain, pounded to a smooth paste with a pestle and mortar.

9. This song was part of the Axim Trio's repertoire, and was written by Quayson, their organist.

10. Form One: of middle school, after six years of primary school.

11. Akosua: born on Sunday.

12. "Why are you hitting me with cassava?" means "Why are you insulting me?"

13. That is, "I am not insulting you."

14. "Cry baby cry . . .": This is a reference to his "good-time" daughter who has been out of the house for many hours.

15. Nsaba: Agona Nsaba, the town where this performance took place.

16. "A pepper like you": He means Sam is small fry who thinks too big, i.e., a small pepper from an important market.

17. Teacher Okai: A town near Nsawam.

18. Accra Passport: a nickname for a mixture of gari (cassava meal) and beans.

19. Gari: cassava meal, often eaten with water or milk as a light meal.

20. The radio had done something: i.e., had broadcast the news of his debts around the town.

21. "Instead of going back to sleep . . .": A pun on the Twi word *da,* to sleep.

22. "Life . . .": He is referring to his domestic troubles.

23. *Ampesi:* Boiled yam, cassava, or plantain.

24. *Nimpa Rebre* was a popular highlife of the early 1970s composed by C. K. Mann and made popular by the Ogyatanaa Show Band of Kojo Donkor. The translation from Twi is by Osei Ntiamoah. This highlife shows the way popular songs may be included in the play for their overall ambience even when the words don't fit the dramatic situation exactly. "Auntie Ofuriwa," mentioned in the song, is not a character in the play. But the general melancholy mood and the theme of suffering is appropriate to this moment in the play, when Antobam is again being denied food and care by his stepmother.

25. The term "Dagomba highlife" does not refer to the Dagomba ethnic group of northern Ghana. It is an early style of highlife introduced to Ghana by Liberian Kru seamen and stevedores in the early part of the century.

26. "This woman": his stepmother, Mrs. Johnson.

27. An Apostolic/Charismatic church song with a highlife beat. This text was translated from Twi by Osei Ntiamoah.

28. A hymn in Twi translated into English by Osei Ntiamoah.

29. Cedis: a cedi is currently worth less than one cent, but in 1972 when this play was recorded it was worth about 75 cents or 50 pence.

30. Antobam believes it was probably his stepmother who sent the devil to him.

31. Cape Coast.

32. "Wala tu wala sa": An expression made popular in 1973 by the record of that name composed by the Ga highlife band Wulomei. The words are Twi and mean "you are digging it and shoveling it away." The song continues, ". . . onipa baako" (all on your own). The song's composer, Nii Ashitey, told me that it was written in support of the then new regime of Colonel Acheampong, which was initiating and encouraging a number of self-reliance programs, such as "Operation Feed Yourself" and the "One-Man Contractors," or public-spirited individuals who, of their own accord, repaired street potholes. This was also a time when large numbers of workers were employed by the government to build drains in Accra. However, the workers who were doing these various digging works did not like the expression Wulomei had coined, as they claimed that members of the public interpreted it to mean "if you are removing what you have already dug then you are making double work for yourself and therefore must be an idiot." "Wala tu wala sa" became transformed into a patronizing term directed at the laboring class. Denigrating manual labor in this fashion is not generally found in traditional Ghanaian societies where most people at some point undertake farming, porterage, and other physical work. The customary greeting in Southern Ghana to someone working, "Ayekoo," carries no suggestion that the person toiling is inferior. "Wala tu wala sa" is therefore to be understood as part of the evolving Akan vocabulary concerned with modern class distinctions.

33. "Potete": One of Opia's own words for a man who is controlled by his wife. "Podowdow," the audience's reply, is another word coined by Opia, and is apparently meaningless.

34. Sekondi: a seaport on the Fanti coast.

35. *Pim praa* is a popular children's game throughout southern Ghana. The players sit down in a row or circle with their legs outstretched singing the song and pointing to each of their legs in turn. The person whose leg the last word of the song falls on pulls it back. The winner is the first person to remove both legs and the loser is the last person in the game. The words of the song, "Nanaa timi timi nyama li" are a nonsense phrase used by Akan children.

36. Groundnuts: peanuts.

37. A slang English phrase, popular all over Anglophone Africa. What Napoleon could not do, according to one explanation, was to overcome all his problems.

38. Opia blames Mrs. Johnson for revealing the secret that Antobam's mother is dead because Antobam was brought up thinking his aunt was his mother. Mr. Johnson's second wife—Antobam's stepmother—let out the secret in a brutal way when she was annoyed with Opia, causing Antobam pain.

# 4

## Concert Party in Lomé and
## *The African Girl from Paris*

Alain Ricard

The concert story in Lomé begins with the Happy Star Concert Band. Through this original group, which successfully adapted a style imported from Ghana, we are able to judge the difficulties that a voluntary association experienced in meeting the widespread demand for shows which had started to develop at the beginning of the 1970s. While providing some income to its members, how was it to transform itself into a professional company, always on the road, always ready to put on a new show? The story of Happy Star of Lomé tells us how this group was unable to undergo the change and how others were left to carry it out.

The distinction between professional and amateur acting runs throughout my whole argument and should be clarified from the outset. It is taken from the historical sociology of drama by Jean Duvignaud, and especially from his book *L'Acteur, esquisse d'une sociologie du comédien* (1965). He opposes the actor (i.e., the amateur performer) to the comedian (the professional). His argument is that only in certain historical situations does the professional performer find an environment conducive to this activity. My contention is that in Togo, Happy Star has been performing at the very juncture between amateurs and professionals. This is especially what I try to demonstrate by a microanalysis of the economics of the concert business. On another level and to pursue further Duvignaud's argument, I would suggest that the existence of an institution with a professional image-producing capacity (a theatre), run as a private business, is living proof of a certain amount of freedom of expression within a society as well as of critical distance from their own actions by its performers. It has a cathartic dimension. Can this critical dimension free itself from the repetition of fixed plots? I will anticipate my conclusion and say that I do not think it is possible without the participation of a metadramatic criticism which is usually produced by the director or the author; these two characters were not part of the universe of concert party in Togo, while Hubert Ògúnǹdé became both in Nigeria.

The way in which the group functioned explains how shows were supplied; and through the study of the halls and audience we understand how demand was expressed. A real concert market existed; this was the novelty introduced by the concert party in Lomé.

## THE STORY OF THE GROUP

The group which made up Happy Star was not united by what sociologists would call primary ties or the solidarity of common ancestry. On the contrary, it was recruited on the basis of the complementarity of members when it came to organizing shows. I was able to reconstruct the initial stages of the group from talks I had with its three founding members: Pascal, Lucas, and Benjamin. In 1962 Pascal returned from the Belgian Congo where he had been a musician, and was now playing with an orchestra in Lomé. A native of Aneho, he belonged to the eastern Ewe group, the Mina. Lucas, after having worked in Ghana, finished his apprenticeship as an automobile painter. He belonged to the Ewe group from Alfao, a village near Lomé. As for Benjamin, he was an Ewe from Denu in British Togo. That is where he went to primary school before coming to Togo to work with the Bénin Breweries, the top company in Lomé before the port was built in 1965.

Born of three Ewe sub-groups and coming from three social environments, the founders of the group complemented each other when it came to concerts: Pascal was a guitar player, Lucas a singer-composer, Benjamin an actor. All three were living in the western neighborhood of Lomé, Nykonakpoe, a short distance from each other, and naturally it was in one of the neighborhood bars that they began performing after they had put a group together.

The first people to join the group were neighbors from the district—young apprentices left to themselves, as apprentices often are in Lomé, or students who had become aware of the theatre through school and who were happy to demonstrate their skills on a stage of their own.

The real backup came from a group of carpenters from up-country brought in by Téo, who had been spotted by Pascal at a show in the neighborhood and had agreed to join Happy Star, bringing his group to Lomé. After Téo arrived with three new members, the group further increased its size toward the end of the 1960s by admitting students and apprentices. The latter saw the concert as a means of getting food and sometimes money, something which very often was denied them by their

*A concert party trio. Photograph © Alain Ricard.*

apprenticeship masters. Among this group were Daniel and his friends. They were boys of the same age and background who were introduced by friends but who did not live in the original concert neighborhood. Simon's approach was more original. After having roughed it in many West African countries, in Ghana in particular where he was with a group also called Happy Star, he returned to Togo and joined the group which had chosen to call itself by the same name as the one he was with in Accra, due to that group's wide popularity both in Ghana and in Lomé.

From 1965 to 1974 the company operated a bit like a goumbé, the voluntary association of young men in Ivory Coast for mutual help and merrymaking. The titles—president, manager, etc.—used by the members were in keeping with their concern to copy modern commercial and administrative structures in a company which brought together, without any form of written contract, young people with a definite objective: in this case, the production of theatrical shows. The titles "president" and "controller" indicated a division of labor which assigned to each and every one a precise role. The office of president was not an honorary one. It distinguished the title-holder from the actors who worked under a manager. The president had capital at his command, such as electronic equipment, while the actors worked. The association had no legal status. As far as the authorities were concerned, the company existed only through its leader, the president, who signed the applications for performance authorization at the city hall and had to answer to the police for his members if for example there was a brawl. The only contacts with administration were with the local council which charged a fee agreed beforehand for the authorization of all performances, to which must be added a 10 percent tax on tickets sold. There are several details to be noted in the accounts. There was often no need to obtain authorization. This was true for remote areas out of town and in other cities; if they could start the show without attracting official attention, it would be too late to call the police after the performance. And even when the authorization application tax was paid, the cashier would find a way of cheating the inland revenue by selling the tickets, stamped by the municipal controllers, several times over. All these transactions were skillfully carried out and gave the group a strong feeling of solidarity.

Relations with administration were the responsibility of the president and the accountant. The latter was in charge of revenue, whereas the president dealt with the municipal officers. Relations with all managers were more the duty of the president, assisted in this case by the actors' manager. Halls were rented at a fixed price. Bargaining was out of the question; the only consideration that had any weight with the hall proprietors was to obtain a proper mixture of musical groups, in order to alternate dance orchestras and concert parties.

The issue of halls went hand in hand with publicity and the material organization of the performance for which the actors were responsible. One actor took care of radio advertisements, another placed announcements in the paper, a third drove around town in a taxi equipped with a loudspeaker which announced the evening performance. The higher the rent of the hall—and the rent was high if the hall was central and very popular with the public—the more it became necessary to advertise, because this was what would bring in more revenue. An afternoon, sometimes a whole day was devoted to advertising. The members who did not have a profession, or the apprentices, took charge of it, and they knew from experience that they were playing an important role: in the group's finances, the advertising bill was often higher than the hall rental fees.

There were various kinds of material and operational costs. Musical instruments, amplifiers, and loudspeakers had to be maintained. The climate, transport conditions, and installation made the equipment suffer. One member of the group was in charge of testing it and having it serviced. However, repairs were expensive. Since the group would not be able to perform without a microphone or an amplifier, it was sometimes necessary to rent expensive equipment. Unlike in Accra or Lagos, electronic equipment was scarce on the Lomé market. Costumes and stage accessories were not often replaced, but all the same they needed maintenance.

Once the equipment was taken care of, the members had to be catered for. All had to be supplied with food on the evening of the performance. The actors had to be helped when in difficulties, and their health taken care of. Finally it was important to guarantee the spiritual welfare of the group by making offerings to the voodoo priest, known as the "charlatan."

## CONCERT AS BUSINESS

I studied the group's production budget from figures taken from the treasurer's books. They do not include monies paid to the actors, the amount of which was fixed and automatically paid out of the takings after every performance. The various entries imply that there had to be some initial investment and working capital for which the president was responsible. After analyzing the group's accounts, I saw that the same entries were made for six months. I studied the respective proportions of these entries. Taxes rarely exceeded 2,000 francs (100 CFA francs = 2FF), thanks to the various tricks already mentioned. The rent of a hall was always between 1,500 and 3,000 francs. Advertising costs varied considerably depending on whether or not the entire range of mass media had been used or if the group was satisfied with sending somebody around the neighborhood ringing a gong. In the latter case, expenses did not exceed 200 francs, whereas a radio announcement cost at least 1,000 francs, a paragraph in the paper cost just as much, and a taxi charged 200 francs an hour to drive around the neighborhood with a loudspeaker. Therefore money spent on advertising had to be invested judiciously; the highest expenditure was always incurred for performances in the central, well-known and comfortable halls which attracted spectators not only from the neighborhood but from the whole town.

The actors' costumes, the "rig-outs" as they were called, were generally borrowed, or made by one of the group members if he happened to be a tailor. The item "equipment" also included the maintenance of instruments, which could turn out to be very expensive.

Under "sundry" expenses we find:

- one accident                                 1,000 francs 3/8/74
- purchase of gasoline and engine oil            945 francs 3/9/74
- purchase of articles for voodoo priest         475 francs 3/9/74
- 2 packets of medicine                          175 francs 4/9/74
- 1 anti-tetanus injection                       150 francs 1/3/74

Sundry expenses thus included anything that contributed to the moral and spiritual health of the group.

The average investment for a performance in a concert or dancing bar hired for 1500 francs plus taxes, publicity, and sundry expenses, was about 5,000 francs. For a performance in a specialized hall, you have to multiply this figure by two or three, but profits will also be higher. Thus the cost/benefit ratio is very clear. The greater the money to be earned the more one is prepared to risk, so you spend more money on a good hall. This sort of calculation turns out to be right, because the biggest takings generate the biggest profits. By playing frequently in the same hall you attract a regular audience and avoid moving around, which is an advantage; the disadvantage is that you are asking too much from an audience

Performing in a courtyard. Drawn by Bérénice Ricard. Used by permission.

which is already paying one and a half times the guaranteed minimum wage per hour for a concert.

After each performance, the actors received a gratuity, fixed once and for all depending on their seniority in the company: this was known as the fee. On extremely successful evenings they received a bonus which might be higher than their normal salary. Finally, the stars who managed to move the audience with their songs pocketed the coins thrown to them or placed directly on their foreheads by the spectators. For good singers, these gifts might amount to 500 francs, doubling or tripling the evening's profits.

Thus each evening a good actor earned a minimum of 150 francs, the average fee, plus some coins. Since he normally performed three or four days a week, this meant that he earned close to 500 francs a week, or 2,000 francs a month. I cross-checked this information with the actors, and half of them confirmed that they earned 2,000 francs a month. A sum of 2,000 francs a month, to which one could add 1,000 francs' worth of coins, might seem a ridiculously small amount of money. But in 1974 it corresponded to a third of the minimum wage of a civil servant and represented more

*Performing in a community center. Drawn by Bérénice Ricard. Used by permission.*

Tonyeviadji

*Performing on a traditional stage. Drawn by Bérénice Ricard. Used by permission.*

than the average income per inhabitant in Togo. Therefore, by Lomé standards, it was not an insignificant sum of money, and the activity of concert actors can be considered to have been part of the economic circuit which made them professionals (or comedians), not amateurs in search of pocket money. They were also professionals in the sense that they were dedicated to the work. Naturally there were some amateurs, but most actors committed themselves to the concert intellectually and with devotion. Small as their earnings might have been, it was money earned doing something they loved, through group activity which provided considerable advantages in kind: drinks, trips, and also food, in addition to the prestige of being an actor.

The company became a profitable enterprise. But how was this activity seen by the public it wished to reach? I decided to carry out a survey on the social origin, age, and sex of the spectators. I wished to discover if the audience, which turned out in great numbers, irrespective of where the performance was taking place, was familiar with the companies and their repertoire. The assumption I wished to test was that an activity as well

Ambassador

*Performing on a patio. Drawn by Bérénice Ricard. Used by permission.*

organized as this one would certainly have a public who knew and appreciated it—in contrast to those who disparaged it as trivial entertainment and ignored it in writing the history of literature and the theatre.

I looked for the answers to these questions by conducting a questionnaire-based survey in 1975 in three performance halls of Lomé. The average age of the audience was around twenty, almost the same as that of the actors. The concert was a style performed by young people, thus attracting a young audience. At this point it is worth considering the demographic composition of the Togolese population. In 1970 half of the population was under 24 years of age. Youth were in the majority in the towns, and this was reflected in the concerts, both among the actors and among the audiences.

More than a quarter of the respondents to the questionnaire were women, and this, in my opinion, is very important. The actors saw their audiences as being predominantly female. They were wrong, but on the other hand men were overrepresented in the survey because it was difficult to obtain an answer directly from the female members of the audience. In a couple, it was always the man who spontaneously answered even if the questions had been put to the woman first. Having taken this into account, I estimate that just over a third of the audience was made up of women.

The survey gives only a rough idea of the social composition of an audience made up of school pupils and employees. The objective was not to establish a socioeconomic profile, but rather to show that there was an established audience, in the sense of a constituency that recognized and welcomed the concert shows as an organized, recurrent feature of the cultural life of the towns. This activity, apparently improvised and even disorganized, left to the whims of the impromptu, was in fact a cultural phenomenon followed and understood by groups of spectators. I think it is important that there was an interaction between actors and audience, and that this interaction was based on the understanding of the concert style by the audience. In this way the audience was able to evaluate the style and determine whether or not it could evolve.

I then proceeded to draw up concert knowledge indicators. My first assumption was that if I were to obtain correct answers to four specifically chosen questions I would be able to evaluate the knowledge people had of concerts; my second assumption was that the actors constituted a group of experts and that they should therefore have been able to obtain a maximum of correct answers to these questions.

The first question asked for the names of concert troupes; the second whether the Ghanaian origins of the concert were known; the third asked for play titles; and finally the fourth asked which hall was most suitable for concerts in Lomé. I attached the same importance to each question (a good answer was equivalent to one point) in drawing up my scale. As expected, the actors obtained nearly 3 points (2.9) whereas the audience got only 1.6 points; but if we look at how points were distributed within the audience, we see that a fair group of spectators was as familiar as the actors with the way a concert functioned. Of course this was a minority, but an important one. In short there were connoisseurs, showing that the concert had become a true institution in Togolese cultural life. It had its specialists, its repertoire, its areas, its audiences; it could not be anything else but a theatre, as will be confirmed by the study on concert dramaturgy.

## CONCERT AS THEATRE

Dramatic improvisation, in Togolese concert party, cannot be described as disorderly at all. The use of space and time was governed by definite rules, accepted by the group members and recognized by the audience. If the concert was in the process of becoming a theatrical performance, the question is whether one can talk of concert dramaturgy, of a dramatic composition of all the elements brought into play, complying with a general view of what a good, or successful, show should be. The principles of this dramaturgy cannot be sought in stage directions, a director's book, or the printed texts of plays, for concert shows were oral shows. The text was not recorded and there was not even an outline for beginners to use. The only written documents that the company kept and used were the schedule of shows and the places where they were performed, together with regular statements of accounts and a list of the company members. There was also a list of show titles, but it did not contain a summary of, or information on, the subject matter. Writing was used for managing the company and not for recording texts.

Among the duties that the company members assumed, I noted that the president served as impresario and boss. He was neither the author of the plots, whose origin was in fact unknown, nor—by a long chalk—the best actor. In the company that I met in the early 1970s, the manager was the best actor, artistically responsible for the show. Even if a company did not have a specific name for its director, it knew precisely what his duties amounted to. However, as one can imagine in an oral theatre of recent tradition and introduction, the role of the director was very different from the one that is familiar in Europe. It was not a matter of interpreting a text laid down in writing in which the general organization is spelled out: in the case of the concert it was a matter of creating a dramatic situation which would help the actors enter their roles and carry them through the story.

The steering committee members, who were also actors (namely the manager, assistant manager, and controller) had to be familiar with concert traditions and in particular the plots. The manager had the final say on the performance. He was in charge of the show, and thus was equivalent to a director.

From the show summaries that I collected, I discovered that the president was not familiar with most of the stories and in fact was only interested in the material aspect of the show. It was the manager who decided which play to perform, depending on the schedule and availability of players. Moreover, since in this case he was the leading actor—not to say star—he had to lead the show and monitor the pace and sequences. This instantaneous staging obeyed not a written model, but a model learned from watching other shows. It was adapted to the actors' and audience's means. Staging took place literally on the stage. There was some preparatory work during group meetings, but this did not take the form of rehearsals. In this type of show there is no difference between a rehearsal and the actual performance. The rehearsal is part and parcel of the actual performance concept and cannot be separated from it; to perform is to repeat a handed-down plot. All that is required is the means with which to repeat it—in particular a sufficient number of actors—and care to repeat it according to the rules.

*Happy Star of Lomé: a "Bob." Photograph © Alain Ricard.*

The way in which the stage was set depended on a model imposed by the place where the performance was to take place. The show was always performed in the open air and the actors had to use a microphone. In actual fact, in many localities the microphone could have been dropped. But its function was twofold: it was used to amplify the voices of the singers and musicians as well as those of the actors. If a singer accompanied by a guitar did not have a microphone, his voice would not be heard. Electrical amplification had become a must for all bands, and the concert party bands did not wish to appear like the poor relatives of show business.

However, the microphone was positioned in such a way that it did not allow for full use of the stage: placed in the middle, it attracted actors and singers who rarely made use of the rest of the space on stage. Stage action was dependent upon the microphone, which meant that it was limited to interaction between three or at most four players who grouped around

*Happy Star of Lomé: a "gentleman, young lady, and old father."*
*Photograph © Alain Ricard.*

the microphone. In general, lighting consisted of just a light bulb or even —in areas where there was no electricity—a hurricane lamp. Often, because there was no platform, the audience was on the same level as the actors and could only see their faces and torsos next to the microphone. No use was made of space to consciously create split levels. The stage had no depth, or rather the depth was not created by the scenery, but by the band which formed the background. The band was at the beck and call of the players gathered around the microphone. Only on rare occasions was it brought in to the heart of the show. In one of the plays we recorded, there was a character who mentioned the presence of the band on the stage, but this type of comment was very rare during performances.

The actors' entries and exits traced a path which went from the wings to the microphone, passing in front of the band. But the dancing parts of the show were an opportunity to leave the microphone and make greater use of the stage space—and, as we shall see, these sequences were rather frequent. The only items of decor were a table, some chairs, sometimes a few plates, glasses, food, and drinks. If the table was laid it was usually beneath the microphone, close enough for the actors to reach it effortlessly. The manager had to make arrangements to obtain any props which the company did not own itself. He had to hire the table, chairs, and place settings, and send one of the "kids"—i.e., the new arrivals in the group— to buy a plate of *fufu* and a few bottles of beer from a street vendor (it was always real *fufu* and beer). The manager was to a certain extent the stage manager, for obvious reasons: since he was the one who chose the play, he was the one to know in advance what materials would be required to perform it.

The distribution of duties to the actors, like setting up the stage and collecting the various props, might have been part of the manager's job. But there was another activity which in our eyes was more central to production itself, and that was the assignment of roles. The staff or group of members was made up of young people who often did not have any theatrical experience. The method used to prepare actors, or "train" them as they called it, was through observation and imitation. However, this did not determine whether an actor had the right physical and intellectual characteristics to perform the roles he aspired to. Someone had to evaluate the dramatic qualities of an actor in terms of what he believed a concert required: and it was the manager who decided which part an actor was to play. It is easy to draw up a list of potential parts. There were male and female parts; among the female parts, the young women were distinguishable from the old; among the male parts, the young men from the old men. Actors who acted the part of young women had to have a light voice and an ability to sing; by contrast, an actor with a deep voice would be chosen to play the part of an old man. Thus each group member stuck strictly to his specialization. The parts of old man, young gentleman, and young woman would always be assigned to the same actors, and these parts constituted the central characters of the show. The actors' manager was responsible for assigning parts: for example, to a handsome newcomer with little experience he would give the part of a young woman, requiring the new actor simply to smile and sway in time to the music. It was only the manager who could make these choices and have them accepted by the group.

In making these choices he would take into consideration the actor's stage capabilities as well as his improvisational and singing potential. In this theatre of improvisation, sequences were decided upon by the actors. Their own verve, and their storytelling talent, were taken into account when evaluating their ability. The manager would choose a play, briefly explain the plot to the actors who "looked like" they could play the required parts, and insist on the need to introduce a certain number of songs at key moments, especially during transitions. He would also play the leading role and would be on stage most of the time. When on stage, he was in control of the narrative progression, i.e., the plot, and the theatrical dynamics, i.e., the interaction with the audience. He had to make sure that these two functions worked in harmony. On the one hand, he had to mark the narrative development with songs which represented intense dramatic moments, during which the audience expressed its approval or disapproval at the course of events. On the other hand, interaction with the audience, characterized by several verbal exchanges which I have transcribed and translated in *Mister Tameklor,* could not be allowed to result in total loss of the story line. It was the manager's duty to keep the play on its narrative rails and to synchronize with the lead guitarist who was also the band leader. If there was no understanding between these two group members, the show would not run smoothly. "You always keep your head down when you're playing the guitar and so you can't see when you're being told to stop," said Benjamin to a new guitarist when he was manager in 1977. He was reproaching the guitarist for not following the acting carefully. The actor-manager would direct the guitarist and through a series of gestures signal him to stop or start playing. A good guitarist, conversant with the plots, the dramatic style of the actors, and the mode of interaction with the audience, would be able to introduce a song at the appropriate moment and sometimes might even suggest the musical emphasis which would ultimately provide the highlights of the concert.

Originally in Happy Star, the president was the lead guitarist and because he got on so well with the manager the shows were a tremendous success. Music introduces the various points of the show: it backs up the "comic acts" (prologue) and announces the play. It also sets the internal pace, as long as this pace is controlled by the band conductor.

The whole structure of the show is held together by just a few people, first and foremost the manager; only he can impose a pace on the play and control its development by speeding up entries and exits. However, there is nobody waiting in the wings with a stopwatch to call the singers or players. The twenty-four musical interventions that we counted in *Mister Tameklor* always occur at more or less the same moment in the show, but never exactly at the same point. The manager knows that after the girls have entered he has to lead up to the fight with the cook, then the duel; that after the duel, he has to try and borrow some money from his friend, etc. He knows this and he acts exactly when he is supposed to and knows when to speed up the action or slow it down; and yet he never consults a written script. This theatre of improvisation relies entirely on the actors. The main actor is the star, prompter, director, and stage manager all in one. The system cannot function if between him and the other group members there is no longstanding team work similar to that uniting the players in a jazz band who are in the habit of improvising together.

To be a concert actor you have to abide by the plot and at the same time provoke the audience; you have to stick to the thread of the story and at the same time take advantage of the emotions triggered by a song

*Happy Star of Lomé: the orphan and the clown. Photograph © Alain Ricard.*

to pocket the money which the audience will throw to you on the stage. The show advances according to the plot: since there is no scenery, scenes are easily changed from one locality to another according to what is being said. There is no higher unit than the sequence to organize the major moments of the play; the scenic duration of an event is often without any bearing on its importance in the plot. In other words, drama is under the control of narration and does not yet quite exist as such, despite modest attempts made by the manager to set the pace of the show and stop it from getting bogged down in cabaret talk or dancing exhibitions.

There is no rule governing the use of the narrative *time*. In relating events different manners of speech are freely used, and it is up to the players to transform them into stage play. The skill of a concert actor consists in achieving this transposition.

The delivery of a speech is bound by specific spatial and temporal constraints which, to a certain extent, are constitutive rules of the concert, insofar as it actually is a dramatic action. As a narrative, the concert uses some transformation models which are very similar to those of the tale. Bound by narration, the concert nevertheless is a dramatic genre, whose subject matter is not so much Togolese society but rather the spoken language, as we shall see in the following section where a foreign language is staged.

## FILMING CONCERT

In 1972, a friend and I had shot a twenty-minute film on concert party. Using borrowed equipment, in the absence of continuous synchronous sound, we were able to bring to life the plays of Happy Star. We even managed to achieve synchronous sound with a 16-mm Beaulieu and a UHER for exactly three minutes, the length of a film cartridge.

This produced the interview with Pascal d'Almeida, then leader of Happy Star, who in his poor French explained his own career and the workings of the group. The film *Agbeno Xevi* was—and still is—shown in Togo, especially at the French Cultural Center, which was the only proper theatre in Togo at that time. Without exception laughter would burst from the audience when Pascal appeared. Happy Star were even able to turn this weakness of the poor performance of their leader into an asset, and at times used the film in their own show as a kind of introduction. It was good publicity, good music. The only problem was the lack of a suitable projector. They could only find one when they were performing downtown in the French Cultural Center.

A few years later, in 1977, I went back to Lomé and Happy Star with a much more ambitious project. I wanted to produce a faithful record of entire plays. In today's age of video, the obvious solution would be to

*Happy Star of Lomé: Mister Tameklor and his girlfriend. Photograph © Alain Ricard.*

record the entire three-hour performance and edit it down to an acceptable length afterwards. At the time, I refused to shoot in video because of the lack of proper facilities in sound editing. Twenty years ago, sound editing was not only more difficult than today, but the cost of digitalizing and computerizing would have been prohibitive.

Granted that the performance lasts three hours, that you have only one camera equipped with film cartridges six minutes long, and that you have a limited budget, how do you reconstruct a meaningful sequence from such short excerpts? One that not only follows the story line but also conveys the atmosphere and rhythm? This question forced me to consider the possibility that the concept of text, of textual production, might not be a volatile entity, but a working tool. Performances are texts, even though they are not written. Once written down, this becomes clear, and I decided to work from the written text of the performances. First, I had to convince the actors to accept our interference and decided to try to use our camera not only as a recording instrument, but also as a stimulus.

On the basis of my theoretical assumptions, I proceeded to choose three plays, already transcribed and translated, and I asked the group to perform only these plays. We proposed to furnish the appropriate lighting and sound equipment; we would then intervene selectively to record the key moments of the play. We discussed our proposal at length with the actors. It seemed to them a poor way of doing things, since some of their new plays were, of course, so much better than those we had selected. They also resented our proposal to fall back on the past and not to project them into the future, with their new repertoire. But in the end, they agreed to our project. I should say that our system proved very efficient. Since the plays had been translated, in addition to being transcribed and typed, we knew them quite well and were able to verify that five years after the original recordings their structure was basically unchanged. We were able, without too much difficulty, to control the principal moments of the show in order to record them. It was indeed a novel experience which brought us on the stage along with the actors.

A good song, an effective slapstick interlude, were scheduled to appear and we had to get ready for them by being on the stage in advance. When it was time, and once the filming had started, we knew we had only six minutes ahead of us; after that we had to reload, which took one or two minutes, but that was enough effectively to terminate the recorded sequence. So, gradually, the actors started to fit our implied prerequisites: not too much, not too long. The process was accomplished gradually and freely, without any explicit instruction from us. We refused to put ourselves in the capacity of stage manager or of director. This would have been the next logical step to take to be sure of controlling the performance. It would have meant standing backstage, following the script, and telling the actors what to do to be in total conformity with the published version of the play. This drift toward taking control of the group was also happening in other areas: since we had commissioned the shows, the actors did not quite understand why we did not want to take full responsibility for them for their next tour.

Once the film was released, in 1982, it was shown in Lomé and became at times a substitute for a live Happy Star performance that no longer existed. I had been able to revive the group for the time of the shooting of the film, over a month. The question is why they could not continue on their own. They had been shown that a real possibility existed to do things in a new fashion: use film to introduce the performance, choose more songs to enliven it, shorten the plays, tighten them. This was clearly the responsibility of a director, but none was to appear. My role had ended and could not be carried over that far. The way I was warmly welcomed and the way in which a new medium—film—was used showed the tremendous adaptive capacities of the concert as a communication medium. Moving pictures were brought into the show and became part of it. One performance I witnessed was particularly interesting, since our first film was shown with an actor commentating with a voice-over on what was happening on the screen. More pictures, even moving pictures, were what the shows needed, because after all concert party is as much images as sounds. Taking a historical or genetic perspective on the genre, it is clear that it has at its core the need to produce images of contemporary life, images that represent objects of desire. And that is what we were doing.

An important aspect of the production of concert parties for filming purposes was the changes we had to make in the texts to suit the new mood of the times. When we recorded the plays, in the early 1970s, the "authenticity" policy was not yet in vigor. Characters could bear French names like Francis or Jean. But in the late 1970s, after the dramatic change of names imposed by President Gnassingbe (Etienne!) Eyadema of Togo, it was considered seditious to use Christian names. Students and priests had been jailed for such a crime! Therefore, when I presented the actors with the text of a play called *Francis the Parisian,* I posed them a major headache: what could they do to retain the flavor of the original work while not attracting the wrath of the vindictive general? This was instinctively and neatly done, as it had been in real life: Francis became Fo, "mister" in Ewe. As in real life, a vague euphony presided over the choice of the new name. Reminiscences of the old name remained in the new which functioned like a kind of a trigger for the memory. The actors had found a solution to our little problem and, as one of them put it: "the name will change, but not the situation." Nothing could have been clearer!

It is interesting to note that while the film could be appropriated within the context of performance without any difficulty, this was not the case for the book, containing two plays *Francis le Parisien (Fo Parito)* and *Mister Tameklor* (Akam and Ricard 1981). The book was an object that had no place in the universe of the concert. There is a certain degree of paradox here, since many of the actors were literate, and some of them had read classics of Ewe literature and were interested in reading in their own language. We also know that they kept a written record of their repertory, of their tours, and of the scenario of the plays. But a book with a translation was not an adaptative commodity for their performance, while a film was. Had the book been printed and published in Togo like a chapbook, would it have been more successful? I doubt it, since it was not the habit of the actors to use any kind of written medium.

The experience of directing a concert party was not new to me, since in 1973 I had had to run the same group during a tour at the Nancy Drama Festival. There the situation was quite different. I had already done a short film on the group and thanks to that film managed to get them an invitation to France. They arrived having no idea of what to do, even thinking that they had to perform in French, since they were in France. When we finally managed to convince them that theatre in France did not mean "in French," and that the Japanese for instance would perform in their own tongue, it made them feel much better!

Nonetheless, this uprooting of concert, transplanted onto a different stage, was somewhat traumatic. Plays had to be timed, even shortened, and controlled staging was necessary, while in Lomé everything lasted as long as it could and was sung or spoken around the microphone, the only spatial reference and focus of the whole play. Simple transposition to a large stage did not work, and they suddenly, probably for the first time, felt the need to have a director, somebody with a general idea of what the show should be like. Up to that moment this general idea could only be reconstructed through the different points of view of each one of the different actors. But it is one thing to realize a lack and quite another to know how to fill it.

This was especially so since their activity was still conceived in half-religious terms: for instance, no rehearsal was ever held; the performance itself was considered enough of a rehearsal. There was even opposition to the very idea of rehearsing, and especially the idea of rehearsing during the days, which were spent idly during the stay in France. Why was this so? Because as one actor one day pointed out to me: "masks only go out at night. . . ." Performing was still an activity needing some spiritual endorsement. One could not go around during the day, posing as a girl or an old man, under the pretence of making "theatre." It literally made no sense. On the other hand, letting the masks "go out at night" was not an organized ceremony having a specific position within the Ewe Pantheon, the voodoo cult. It was, I think, only an amateur actor's problem: to become a professional, as some of them eventually did, they had to understand that their activity was freed from religious overtones. They had to free themselves from the fear that comes with making ghosts come alive.

The relationship which ghosts have with death is at the center of the play *The African Girl from Paris*, as I shall explain below. As a producer I had to pay my dues to the ancestors before embarking on the shooting of our film. But it was not a mere propitiation. It was a more important ceremony. The band leader and actor Lucas had just died. His absence was felt, since he was by far the best singer and an excellent actor; however, the "show must go on." Yet his colleagues refused to go on without being sure that Lucas was happy where he was, and that he would not come back unexpectedly in the middle of a play, thus sending his unfortunate partners directly into the kingdom of death, which they were not yet ready to visit. So the actor chosen to stand in for Lucas asked for a special propitiation ceremony where we all—including the technical crew—addressed the spirit of Lucas and promised to avenge his death, if it turned out not to have been natural. The ceremony cost us several bottles of whiskey and gin and a few chickens, which we, along with the fetish priestess, ate once the business of sending messages to the other world was disposed of.

## L'AFRICAINE DE PARIS (THE AFRICAN GIRL FROM PARIS)

Each culture has its way of exorcising its inner beings. Social conditions permitting, some cultures turn this exorcism into dramatic art. This applies not only to the Yorùbá but also to the Ashanti and Ewe. Today we are lucky enough to be able to read and reread some of the texts which mark this strange rite and herald the advent of theatre into a society. One of these very texts is *L'Africaine de Paris*, which features among the first shows performed by the up-and-coming Happy Star in 1965 and which I was able to record in 1971. My various surveys showed that this show was among the first, if not the very first, that the group staged. Several actors even insisted on this point, which for me was an excellent example of the importance of this text in the concert world. The fact that this text, original in many ways, is often quoted and not brushed aside proves that it expresses very deeply and in no uncertain terms the founding myth of the concert, what I call its paradigmatic nature. It is the extreme limit of creativity achieved by the group, beyond which it cannot go. It is as if we found ourselves in front of the first and last play created in Togo by a group called Happy Star, but a group which was unable to find a new form with the input of a great creator such as Hubert Ògúnndé in Nigeria.

Here is the plot outline of *L'Africaine de Paris*, taken from the transcription of the show which I attended in 1971, published by the University of

Bénin the same year and translated shortly after by S. A. Zinsou, and recently published (1987).

Mr. John, upon his return to Lomé after a twelve-year stay in Paris, meets with Cecilia again, who has given birth to his child and waited to marry him. But in Europe Mr. John has married an African girl, Monique, who has followed him against his will. Mr. John asks Cecilia to accept the situation and she does. Mr. John entrusts his two women to Youki, the cook, and asks Cecilia to prepare a very spicy stew. The dish does not agree with Monique, and she dies. Cecilia no longer wishes to stay with Mr. John; she is afraid of Monique's ghost, which returns to haunt the place. Mr. John remains alone and tells us he is going to commit suicide.

The text is interesting partly because of its apparent simplicity. A young man is betrothed to a fellow countrywoman, goes abroad, returns with a new wife, and tries to make two women live together in a country where polygamy is traditionally accepted. The venture fails because the foreigner dies; her death and above all her apparition in the form of a ghost terrorizes the first wife, who runs away, leaving the young man helpless. Here we have the story of an individual, John, who is the victim of a tragedy—the loss of his two wives—and who cannot live with it. Instead of ready-made solutions from traditional tales, we have an opening toward the unknown.

Monique, the Parisian wife, speaks French throughout the play. The other characters are not supposed to understand her, nor she them. There is more to this than just a comical motive: what is at stake is the staging of the French language, a language of prestige in the bilingual environment typical of West Africa.

The concert players build a theatre with cultural beings who live in the inner space of the group. But they know, more or less, what they are doing in becoming "somebody else." The end, which is not really an end, is surprisingly uncertain.

Characters like Mr. John, with a past and a future, come alive before our eyes. Mr. John is an orphan who was helped by his future mother-in-law; he spends twelve years in Europe without returning home. The fact that he is an orphan, coupled with his fierce determination to succeed, makes him the typical hero of concert party. Cut off from his roots, catapulted into the White Man's world, he then returns to his country. Today Mr. John is an important civil servant. He works in a different world; he needs friends; he has to please his boss and be a model executive. He also has to educate his Togolese wife if he does not want her to be a social handicap in the new life he intends to lead. Mr. John has been a success in Europe and wishes to be equally successful in Togo.

The unexpected arrival of Monique, the African girl from Paris, introduces an element of disorder in the wonderful world that he was planning for himself. But John is a coward; he does not know how to introduce this other wife. To John's great surprise, Cecilia is steadfast in the face of adversity. She sees in this companion her chance for advancement, thereby demonstrating her strong desire to become "European."

From the point of view of characterization, Monique is a success. She is a total stranger in the world around her; she does not speak the native language, does not wish to learn it; she does not understand the local customs, although she does try to learn how to dance. Her arrival, which is presented as unexpected, could in fact have been the result of an invitation from John. Monique followed him without knowing that the place of first wife was already taken. John is relieved to see that Cecilia accepts Monique and does not think of asking Monique to return to Paris. He tries to find a modus vivendi for the two wives, but he is unable to hide a strange resentment against Monique. The incarnation which she represents to his dreams is no doubt too ordinary.

He urges her to learn Ewe and subjects her to a test—swallowing strongly spiced stew. Using her common sense, Cecilia realizes that John is overdoing it, but her warning goes unheeded.

Monique's arrival has enhanced John and Cecilia's desire to lead a European style of life. Her death plunges them into a dream which puts them out of touch with reality. At the end of the play, John discloses to us that he is "under the impression of living in a dream." He no longer knows what to do and finds himself blaming Cecilia for Monique's demise. The apparition frightens John out of his wits, causing Cecilia to make sarcastic remarks about her husband's manliness before she leaves him.

Mr. John is now truly living in a dream: he no longer knows whether he is a man or a woman. He wants to take his own life and then changes his mind. He decides to become a vagabond—in other words he goes crazy, since vagrancy is typical of madmen in a society which does not lock up the demented in an asylum.

## AN ORDINARY DREAM

The play begins with an account of John's life and ends with his maunderings, after a death which has all the characteristics of a murder. For the actors this text is a chance to fulfill their desire to master the predominant language and gain access to the higher class: the language is Parisian. But at the same time this desire is suppressed, since the Parisian girl is sent to the land of the shades from where she returns to haunt the world of the young Togolese.

This representation of cultural beings who haunt the inner world is similar to the seance of hakka shown in the film *Les maîtres fous*, by Jean Rouch, in the Gold Coast: they call into the world the beings which haunt them in order to exorcise them. Their ritual practice seeks to master possession ritual. The actors do the same. But in Lomé what makes them professionals is the ability they have to provoke their obsessions and act them so as to free themselves of them.

What in Rouch's film is a barbaric and at the same time peaceful ceremony, is in this case a show. What then is the difference between a ceremony and a show? I believe it to be the acceptance of the other's presence; the integration of this presence as a constitutive rule of the event. The show is not self-contained; it accepts the other as an essential component. When Rouch films *Les maîtres fous* he turns their ceremony into a cinematographic show; Genet, in order to make a show out of a ceremony, includes in the staging of *Les Nègres (The Blacks)* the presence of a White Man. There has to be a White Man and if one cannot be found, a Black Man will have to wear a mask.

By making a show out of their major obsession, the concert players run the risk of displaying their inner world to the gaze of the other. They reveal themselves, and it is precisely this in my opinion which makes this text defy what the semiotician Yuri Lotman, applying the concept to folklore, called "identity aesthetics": the repetition of scenarios borrowed from oral tradition. For in this case, the text ventures into something new, which the actors do not master and which leads to the final mental distress of the character.

A theatre is born when the presence of the spectator is deliberately sought, when he is not a voyeur and no longer a participant. Therefore the cultural beings that inhabit the inner world must be sufficiently understood by the actors for them to play them in front of the audience without getting carried away by them or by their own sensitivity, which would otherwise send them to the world of the mad.

Concert actors know that they are going to stage the mythologies of everyday life, that they are going to speak the language of cultural domination and represent the cultural and linguistic alienation of their coastal cultures. This is not an easy venture; others jeopardize their sanity in doing do, as shown in Rouch's film. The actors must therefore prepare themselves for the task. They wait for nightfall because "masks only go out at night." They mask themselves; they protect themselves against the spells cast by dead actors. A sort of symbolic armor is constructed which will allow them to withstand the shock of representing cultural beings from their inner world. In my opinion, the use of female impersonators can be linked to this need for symbolic protection by creating a distance between the actor and the character he is bringing to life.

Cecilia and Monique, like all the female roles, are played by men. The theatre group as a whole—the true producer of the plays—is confined to the universe of male identity and is clearly separated from the practical and symbolic rituals of women. Women are often the mediators in the possession cults of coastal cultures. Being male, the actors are protected against the risk of being possessed and, at the same time, create a distance between themselves and the female characters they impersonate. The public knows that the women on stage are actually men; everybody knows that they are watching a show, not a ceremony. If women started to play ghosts, would the distinction be as clear? Female impersonation is a second mask. The actors create a universe which must be different from everyday life in order for them to risk representing some of their obsessive fears. In Lomé, women are spectators but not actors. Dramatic art seeks to control the processes of identification. These must be avoided in order to preserve the margin for play and hence, theatre. Female impersonation guarantees this margin by preventing any sliding toward identification.

The continued use of female impersonators in concert plays clearly distinguishes concert from Yorùbá popular theatre, which, as we have seen, employs actresses. The roots of Yorùbá theatre account for this difference. The Christian influence shown in the biblical adaptations was no doubt sufficient to avoid identification of the show with ritual practices. Theatre originating from ancestor cults is more cautious. Even today, Apidan theatre, described by Kacke Götrick (1984), does not use actresses even though the actors are masked. Is this because two precautions are better than one? The biblical adaptations of Ògúnmdé were too far removed from reality to lead to confusion, so he could permit himself to hire actresses. A show as direct, as simple, as violent as *The African Girl from Paris* could easily be confused with ritual practices, so that the actors had to protect themselves by impersonation and the use of masks.

### THE THEATRE OF DOMINATION

The staging of language through "masks" and female impersonation is a peculiarity of concert. Here, language is also the area where cultural alienation is revealed. Linguistic domination is expressed through multiple clues: in this particular text, it is made strikingly clear in the staging of the dominant language. Incredible boldness, astonishing acting, since the actors are unable to speak French correctly. Through their role-play, they express a clear awareness of the sociolinguistic hierarchy with which they play so often in their shows.

To represent one's everyday mythology, one's own alienation, requires boldness and strength, but also control. However, the group has never theorized its practice; its shows are extemporaneous, in direct contact with daily culture, with all the pertinence and violence of "art brut." Creation requires tearing away from one's universe in order to produce something else, an object, a text, a show able to surpass yet express the essential dimensions of the world. The greatness and the strength of the *African Girl from Paris* lie in its ability to evoke Genet, through the acuteness of its perception of cultural and linguistic domination, through the ritualistic simplicity of its staging and, most curiously, through its opening toward the unknown.

In the treatment of the essential dimension of their existence, the dominated condition, the group has no solution to propose. They do not know what their character should do: the madness of the protagonist is a kind of freedom. Liberated from society after twelve years in Europe, liberated from desire by the death of his Parisian wife, the main character literally does not know to which saint he should pray. The Parisian girl belongs to the world of cultural beings which haunt the imagination of young people from coastal cities. This educated young woman, who speaks French, inhabits the inner world of the young. Contact with other cultures has triggered the rise of new religions. In the new pantheons appear new gods. In *Les maîtres fous*, these include British authority figures of the Gold Coast—the Governor and the Queen. In Niger, the wife of an administrator belongs to the new genies; in Lomé the Parisian girl is a concert character. She is "the dead woman"—another title of the play; in other words, she returns from the world of the dead: a ghost. The African girl from Paris, the ghost, belongs to the world of cultural beings. She is not an ordinary character who becomes a ghost. She is a character who comes from the world of the shades, who incarnates the desire of the young, who gives body and language to this desire but whose presence they cannot bear. They send her back to the world of shades, but she returns to haunt them, thus showing her real nature.

The Parisian girl is a genie, like the "hakka," as Rouch's friends would say; she speaks French, she has come back from the dead. In materializing this genie, the actors have gone as far as they can in their search for truth. The Parisian incarnation is an act of personal lucidity. They have materialized what haunts them. This is done in the form of drama, but their theatre is not yet solid enough to integrate what would be a novel way to represent the subconscious. It goes astray in search of new paths and the theatrical discourse sinks into incoherence.

In short, this truth from the realm of the unconscious totally dominates the moralism of the story. To bring the face of desire on stage reduces to shambles the usual narrative schemes with their easy moralism. The simplicity of the play's structure highlights what I consider to be a truth of the unconscious that results in the production of an everyday myth. The story has none of the twists and turns of the other shows. It stages a domestic scene—a man and his two wives—in which the duration of the show nearly coincides with real time, thus increasing the relevance as well as the ordinary aspect of the topic. Instead of slackening or digressing, the narration is concentrated on the fate of the Parisian girl, in actuality the central character.

The simplicity and familiarity of the plot are typical of concert. As I pointed out earlier, concert is theatre because its actors are professionals. They produce texts which are the staging of actions, and they use characters to tell a story. All the shows have all the formal features of the theatrical text, but the text we present here has something more: the end of the play is an opening into the unknown, a signal that the universe of repetition and of identity—what could be called the universe of tradition and ceremony—has been abolished in favor of something else, not yet understood but definitely different.

Theatre is born from a disruption of the ceremony, of the need to say something different, to let other subjects speak and to let them hold discourses which are not those of tradition. It is born of acculturation, encounters with other societies and with this Other which has been responsible for upsetting the coastal societies of West Africa: the Christian West. This encounter has been an enslavement. African societies are dominated and their cultures have become those of domination. Hierarchies have been established which always place the European and his language and culture at the top. Everyone knows that. The actors know it. Cultural domination is one of the main subjects of their theatrical enunciation. Yet it is rarely shown on stage. In *The African Girl from Paris*, domination, along with its corollary, aspiration to acculturation, is the subject; but the text has nothing to say beyond describing the situation.

In order to become a theatre, that is to say, in order to create original texts, a concert party group must exist as an independent agent. The group which produces the stories should be responsible for its own history, like Ògúnǹdé, who was able to free himself from ancestral and biblical masquerades to produce a personal artistic and political message, like Wọlé Ṣóyínká and others, able to invent a dramaturgy of freedom. In short, concert party has marvelous professional actors but has nothing original to say; on the other hand, many writers and dramatists have something to say but can't find the actors. For it is true that concert party confines itself to the universe of repetition, in spite of the unique example I have just given. *The African Girl from Paris* is the only text in which the ambiguous subject of Happy Star's theatrical enunciation—domination and its corollary, the desire for assimilation—is confronted; it is the only play in which this central reality, which propels tens and hundreds of boys on stage to become accomplished professional actors, is faced, but with no concrete results. The group has nothing to say when its representative finds himself facing the image of his desire. His identity, as well as that of the group, is in danger. Mr. John no longer knows who he is. The boldness of the confrontation opens up an immense horizon which intimidates the group; it doesn't know where to go. All of concert and much more is contained in this text. Theatre is already present. The group has pushed its capacity for independent speech to its extreme limit, but nothing comes out of this adventure.

Oral tradition produces a theatre. The concert party is indeed an oral genre: it belongs to the "mixed" orality which coexists with written sources and notes which Paul Zumthor has so judiciously described (Zumthor 1983). But this oral theatre is not, as is too often believed, a feast or a ceremony: we are in the presence of an original text, which has a viewpoint on language and society, and which is also an artistic creation. Concert party tells of cultural alienation, of respect for elders, and, in *The African Girl from Paris,* it tells of the incapacity to confront innovation, that is, to denounce and go beyond cultural domination. Concert party is a witness to a situation but does not help change it. Its power is that of direct speech, in contact with its society, capable of subtly indicating the myriad of linguistic and cultural alienations but incapable of indicating how to go beyond them. Ògúnm̀dé had to meet concert party in order to rid himself of his grand biblical machineries, to let direct speech take the forefront. Ògúnm̀dé had an aesthetic and political project, and could therefore create a theatre. Concert actors had a theatre in search of a project.

The Parisian girl is a ghost: she is a dramatic character and not a person possessed. Our actors are characters in search of authors.

# 5

## *The African Girl from Paris*

BY HAPPY STAR OF LOMÉ

MR. JOHN: Well, friends and spectators, good evening! Let me introduce myself. I am called "Monsieur Jean." As you can see, "je suis un grand parisien." First of all, I have something to say. So: I was brought into the world, I must have been barely three years of age when my mother, she who gave birth to me, died.

Then my father, the author of my days, my father who worked on my mother to bring me into the world, after spending several years with me—I was about twelve years old—he too left, he too went "en touche."[1]

And so I found myself facing the problems of life all alone. I divided my time between the well, the beach, and the fields.

Then I found myself at school, yes, I started school.

I was in "le troisième classe"[2] when I made "l'amour"[3] with a girl.

That girl, her mother had so much money that, well, she couldn't even count it all. So that this girl, all I had to do was to go and see her, and tell her "here is my 'besoin',"[4] and we understood each other. And as time passed, she ended up by paying all my school expenses. It was she who bought my books, she paid for everything. So I was able to go right up to the "certificat."[5] Then, thanks be to God, I was able to "passer," yes to "passer un concours,"[6] and I obtained a "bourse"[7] to study in Europe.

That's right, to study with white men!!

---

*Note:* The text on which the present translation is based was recorded by Alain and Bérénice Ricard in the Festival Bar, Glidji, Anecho District, Togo, on Sunday, 30 May 1971. It was then transcribed by Messrs. Afeli, De Souza, and Gavlo, at that time students at the University of Benin, Togo, where I was then teaching. The text was later translated into French by Mr. Akam and myself, and into English by myself. I should add that Senouvo Agbota Zinsou, also a student at the time and now a major playwright, became interested in the text and produced a French adaptation, *L'Africaine de Paris,* published in 1987.

But what to wear? Because with what I had, they wouldn't even have let me on the docks.

So I spoke of my problem to my girlfriend. Her name was . . . uh . . . Cecilia. Well, I told her my problem and she answered that she had been waiting for me to bring it up and that she would speak to her mother.

That's right, tell her mother everything!

No, she shouldn't say anything to her mother!

I suggested that we do as we had always done, even if it took a long time, until we had saved enough money for my trip. She said no, that as things were, she would take me to her mother, explain everything and she was sure that everything would be all right.

Okay, but she would have to do the talking.

She said okay.

So we went to her mother, and she told her everything. And her mother said that that was fine and that she was happy for me and that she would take care of everything.

I could only say: "okay, fine."

Right away she sent for a tailor who took my measurements and made me some suits, some of these suits—I don't need to insist, you can judge for yourself. Then, the day of my departure arrived and I left for Europe. I stayed twelve years, then I had short vacation and I returned home.

But before my departure [for Europe], I had promised my fiancée not to marry another woman in Europe, that she would be my only wife. But I must tell you that she had never been to school, she didn't know what school was all about; but so what, the important thing is to lead a happy life.

Well, this young lady, I am going to call her and introduce her to you. Because when I returned here, I found her waiting for me. She wouldn't marry anyone else but me. *(Aside)* Could you have waited? Twelve years, I say? Could you?

SPECTATOR: Yes.

MR. JOHN: We'll see! I'll call her . . . Cecilia! Where is she, Cecilia? Oh Cecilia, do you think you're still at home with your mother?

> *(Enter Cecilia, who does not appear to appreciate what*
> *Mr. John has said. He continues, aside:)*

Admit it, darling, I have struck home.

My Rosina.

CECILIA: Fo.

MR. JOHN: Sissi.

CECILIA: Fo. So, tell me, what's life like here?

MR. JOHN: Do you know that when I was in Europe, I thought only of you? Now that I am back, I don't think I'll ever return . . . What! Find you only to leave you again? Never! Your entire life is going to change. Now then, I have something to tell you—it's about what we said—what we promised each other —uh—if you still agree, we'll get married . . .

CECILIA: Keep going, I'm listening.

MR. JOHN: Do you want me to go on?

CECILIA: Yes.

MR. JOHN: So, you did all you could to help me, you promised to wait for me, and now that I am back I can find nothing to make me doubt what you said and I can't tell you how happy that makes me. So, if you accept me, I will be so happy.

CECILIA: Ah, Fo John. . . .

MR. JOHN: Yes?

CECILIA: What you say warms my heart.

MR. JOHN: Does it?

CECILIA: I wasn't expecting you to say such beautiful things upon your return, because . . .

MR. JOHN: Yes?

CECILIA: After your departure . . .

MR. JOHN: Yes?

CECILIA: . . . you know I never went to school . . .

MR. JOHN: Yes . . . yes . . .

CECILIA: I am illiterate.

MR. JOHN: That's true.

CECILIA: At the marketplace, my friends all told me that you would have nothing to do with me when you came back.

MR. JOHN: What? They want to kill me!

CECILIA: It's because you have become a big man. But me, I told them that since I was lucky enough to have a child by you, I would wait for you. And now you tell me that the only wife you want is me! I am filled with joy and don't know how to express it.

MR. JOHN: Ah, my darling! You know, I hired a servant, a boy named Youki.[8] Yes, Youki will take care of you, my darling, when I am at work. *(To audience)* Yes, I will call him and introduce him to you. Youki! Youki! *(Enter Youki.)*

YOUKI: Boss!

MR. JOHN: Youki . . .

YOUKI: Boss, you're already here?

MR. JOHN: Yes.

YOUKI: So that's it, we are off!

MR. JOHN: Like I said . . .

YOUKI: Yes . . .

MR. JOHN: You see this lady?

YOUKI: Yes.

MR. JOHN: Well, she's my wife.

YOUKI: Yes, she wanted to marry me.

MR. JOHN: So . . . wait a minute . . . What are you saying?

YOUKI: Yes, yes, she wants to marry me if I'm still free this year.

MR. JOHN: Listen: I'm asking you if you see this lady?

YOUKI: Yes.

MR. JOHN: You really see this lady, Cecilia?

YOUKI: Yes.

MR. JOHN: Cecilia, do you see her?

YOUKI: Yes.

MR. JOHN: She is my wife.

YOUKI: What is your wife like?

MR. JOHN: *(To audience)* What a boy! But wait, I know how to get him. *(To Youki)* This lady, I'm telling you that she is my wife and . . .

YOUKI: Yes?

MR. JOHN: She's the one who will take care of you, she's the one who will cook for you. Do you understand?

YOUKI: Ah, you want to marry her! (give her your hand [in marriage])

MR. JOHN: That's it. I want to marry her! (give her my hand [in marriage])

YOUKI: Ah, she has fallen into a well and you want to give her a hand! [to get out]

MR. JOHN: What are you talking about? Listen, Youki!

YOUKI: Boss . . .

MR. JOHN: Pay attention! What I'm telling you . . .

YOUKI: Yes.

MR. JOHN: Try to understand.

YOUKI: Yes.

MR. JOHN: She wants to make "marious" with me.

YOUKI: Oh I see, she wants to make "marious" with you?

MR. JOHN: That's right.

YOUKI: She wants to be united with you?

MR. JOHN: Yes!

YOUKI: That's very good.

MR. JOHN: That's right. So . . .

YOUKI: Yes.

MR. JOHN: I want you to work for me.

YOUKI: Okay.

MR. JOHN: You are going to wait on her a bit.

YOUKI: Boss.

MR. JOHN: Yes.

YOUKI: And after I prepare her bath, will I scrub her back?

MR. JOHN: No, no, no, she knows how to take a bath herself.

YOUKI: Oh.

Mr. John: So you have to . . . Hey, Cecilia!

Cecilia: Fo . . .

Mr. John: Like I said, I no longer want to leave and I have to find a job here. And as a matter of fact, a young man asked me to see him and I have to go right away. Can you prepare something for us in the meantime?

Cecilia: You know, Fo, you are no longer in the country where everyone turns like a tap. You've just come back and already you're running around to see people; stay with us until you can leave when the offices open.

Mr. John: Oh, but you know that everything is a matter of "appui." I need his answer to see if I can find a job. So you see!

Cecilia: Okay, come back quickly.

Mr. John: As fast as I can.

*(Mr. John leaves and returns immediately.)*

Youki: Welcome back, Boss!

Mr. John: Youki . . .

Youki: Boss . . .

Mr. John: So you smoke!

Youki: No, it is "Komora."[9]

Mr. John: Komora?

Youki: Yes, and you're supposed to smoke without inhaling.

Mr. John: Listen, I don't want you to smoke in front of me. Understand?

Youki: Yes.

Mr. John: Well, Sissi . . .

Youki: *(Pointing to a passing airplane)* Boss, look at the bird!

Mr. John: Siss . . .

Cecilia: Fo . . .

Mr. John: I'm leaving for work. But as you know, we whites,[10] we have money; so I'm going to give you some, you will go to the market and you will buy what is needed to prepare a good meal.

Cecilia: Don't worry about the money for the meal, I'll take care of it.

Mr. John: No such thing, I'll give you what you need. I'll . . . I'll give you the money.

Youki: Let me get in on it too.

Cecilia: Wait a minute . . . If you won't let me take care of the household expenses, you are insulting me.

Mr. John: Not at all, I'll give you the money, that's all.

Cecilia: No, I'm telling you that I'll take care of everything.

Mr. John: Is that true?

Cecilia: Yes.

Mr. John: Oh, in that case, I'll see you later.

Cecilia: Return quickly.

Youki: Boss, there's no oil in the lantern.

Mr. John: What?

YOUKI: I said there's oil in my lantern.

MR. JOHN: Oh . . . And so what?

YOUKI: So, will you bring me some candy? *(Exit Mr. John.)*

CECILIA: *(To audience)* So you see, my friends, women often claim that men are liars, but I don't think so: if we do what they ask, we can be sure to live in harmony with them. When my husband was in Europe, my friends told me that since I was illiterate, I should find another man: he would never marry me. My husband is educated, he even went to Europe. If his friends came here and found me, they would be surprised. But I've already told myself that I wouldn't worry about that. I promised to be his and his I will remain. And then, when he returned, he said he would have no one but me. That made me very happy. I'm sure that if women always did what their men wanted, they would be faithful.

YOUKI: Auntie, the boss told me to scrub your back after I got your bath ready. *(Music. Mr. John returns.)*

MR. JOHN: Hello Youki.

YOUKI: Welcome home, boss!

MR. JOHN: Did anybody come while I was out?

YOUKI: No, no one came.

MR. JOHN: No one came looking for me?

YOUKI: No.

MR. JOHN: Good.

YOUKI: All that happened was that I got Auntie's bath ready but she wouldn't let me scrub her back.

MR. JOHN: And that's what's making you sweat so hard?

YOUKI: No, I was just practicing for the domestic games.[11] I'll be playing soccer.

MR. JOHN: Oh? That's good. But now . . . Tell me, you didn't even sweep the house.

YOUKI: But of course I swept the house, Boss! But . . . uh . . . I want to tell you something.

MR. JOHN: I'm listening.

YOUKI: Were you blind to marry this woman?

MR. JOHN: You're asking me if I was blind to marry this woman?

YOUKI: Yes, because . . . primo, she doesn't understand French.

MR. JOHN: That's true . . . So when she returns . . .

YOUKI: Yes . . .

MR. JOHN: When she returns, I'll tell her.

YOUKI: Yes.

MR. JOHN: Good. *(Cecilia enters.)*

MR. JOHN: *(To Cecilia)* Ah, you're here?

CECILIA: Yes.

MR. JOHN: O.K.

CECILIA: Youki, go get something to drink for your boss.

YOUKI: And the money?

CECILIA: Here, and come back quick. (*Youki leaves and returns immediately.*)

YOUKI: I went to UNELCO[12] but it wasn't open yet.

CECILIA: Don't kid me; go get the drinks.

YOUKI: I'm telling you I went to UNELCO and they didn't have any. Right, boss?

CECILIA: Hurry up and fetch the drinks. (*Exit Youki.*)

*Music. The couple sit down at a table.*

MR. JOHN: Darling . . .

CECILIA: Fo . . .

MR. JOHN: Hello . . . *[In English]*

CECILIA: Hello . . . *[In English]*

MR. JOHN: (*Observing Cecilia's problems with her fork*) Don't worry. I'll teach you how to use it.

CECILIA: You know, with fingers . . .

MR. JOHN: Yes, I know that here we eat with our fingers but I want to teach you what I learned in Europe, all right?

CECILIA: Yes, that's fine.

MR. JOHN: Ah!

CECILIA: Youki, Youki!

MR. JOHN: (*Watching Cecilia struggle with her fork*) Ah, you see, you're learning fast!

CECILIA: (*To Youki*) Come clear the table.

MR. JOHN: Cecilia . . .

CECILIA: Fo . . .

MR. JOHN: Now I'm leaving. I have to return to work.

CECILIA: Already?

MR. JOHN: Well yes. Do you want to tell me something?

CECILIA: You just got back and you're leaving already.

MR. JOHN: Do you want me to spend the whole day with you?

CECILIA: Okay, okay, go ahead and leave.

MR. JOHN: I just started work and you know that anything new is exciting. (*To audience*) I went to Togo Metal, I filled out a "demande" and I was named "sous-directeur." Because, paper is what I know! And then our "directeur" told me he was taking his "congés" soon and that perhaps I would replace him.[13] (*To Cecilia*) So I have to be enthusiastic. I'm going to be the first at work in front of the door before it's open.

CECILIA: That's a good idea.

MR. JOHN: So I'll see you soon.

CECILIA: Come back quick.

MR. JOHN: Yes.

CECILIA: Bye-bye! *[In English]*
MR. JOHN: Yes, see you soon. *(Exit Mr. John.)*
CECILIA: My problems are over! If I had listened to my friends, I wouldn't be so happy today. You reap what you sow, I'm enjoying my own handiwork.

*Song:*

> Bird from the heavens, take my "lettre"[14] to Adzi.
> I wanted to come myself but night surprised me
> And I had no flashlight . . .

*(Exit Cecilia. She returns immediately.)*

YOUKI: Welcome home, Mistress!
CECILIA: Youki, hasn't the boss returned yet? *(Enter Mr. John. He appears depressed.)*
CECILIA: Fo John. What's the matter? What has happened? Answer me, what's the matter with you?
MR. JOHN: Life is so hard!
CECILIA: Did you hear something bad about me?
MR. JOHN: Oh no! *(Aside)* I'm lost.
CECILIA: Youki, go to the kitchen and set the table.
MR. JOHN: I can't tell you what is bothering me.
CECILIA: Youki, I'm telling you go set the table! Fo John . . . please, tell me what's wrong. Perhaps someone said something bad about me, is that it Fo John?
MR. JOHN: Cecilia, I know it, I know that as soon as I tell you, you will pack your bags and leave me. It's inevitable, I'm sure that when I've spoken, you'll pack your bags and go.
CECILIA: Fo John, what can you say that's so terrible, to make me leave? Are you sure that you're not the one who wants to put me out?
MR. JOHN: Don't make me say it.
CECILIA: You're pressing me, you want to leave me?
MR. JOHN: I know, I'm going to call a "taxi," yes a "taxi" . . . no no, not a "taxi."
CECILIA: Fo John, at least tell me what you mean! I've already told you that while you were gone, my friends told me all kinds of bad things. I wouldn't be surprised if they told you wicked things about me. So please Fo John, tell me. I'll never leave you. If I wanted to leave you, I wouldn't have waited seven years for you.
MR. JOHN: What you're saying reassures me, but it's not all that simple.
CECILIA: Tell me what's the matter. I swear I've done nothing wrong.
MR. JOHN: Oh God, oh Cecilia, if I open my mouth, everything will collapse.

CECILIA: Fo John, I swear I won't leave.

MR. JOHN: All right, at any rate the saying goes that whatever the news, it comes through the mouth. I'm talking, I'm going to tell you and even if you leave, that's all right. You see, when I left to go to Europe . . .

CECILIA: Yes?

MR. JOHN: I really did go to Europe. But for a man, to live all alone like that in Europe, yes, to live in Europe all alone for twelve years, I can tell you that it's very hard. So, while I was in Europe, uh . . . I mean, uh . . . I met a European. She was black but she was born in Europe and she doesn't speak our language, only French. So we studied together, what we called "leçons de choses" and we ended up by finding the "résumé." And when we found the "résumé," we followed up with a few "feintes du corps" and in the end, she came to live with me.[15]

So when I returned here, I lied to her, I told her that I would be gone only a few days, that there were a few people I had to see but that I would return to her. But when I saw you again, I realized that you were the one for me and I decided to stay.

I told myself that she would tire of waiting for me and would end up understanding that our story was finished.

But this morning at work, I received a telegram saying I was needed "à l'aviation."[16] Who would need me "à l'aviation"?

It was she, the woman I married in Europe.

But I don't want to be stuck with her. Yet I can't leave her at the airport. Believe me, it's a problem that bothers me a lot and I don't know what to do, so I thought I would tell you, maybe you could help me.

And if you say you want to leave me, there is nothing I can do but send her home.

CECILIA: Fo John, you know very well that I've never been to school and that I don't speak French: you're saying things that I don't understand, speak clearly: only words can ease your heart.

MR. JOHN: I'm glad that you want me to explain everything. But no doubt you want me to explain everything so that you feel better about leaving me.

CECILIA: No, explain to me so that I can tell you what I think.

MR. JOHN: And you'll tell me what you think at the same time that you leave. All right, so be it!

I was saying that when I was in Europe, I met a girl. This girl, I led her to think that I would marry her and she believed me. So we lived together, then I left her to come home. I thought I was free of her but she has just arrived saying she wants to know my country, she arrived this morning and her name is Monique.

I wanted to tell you so that you could give me your opinion: if you accept, I'll bring her home; but if you don't, I'll send her back.

CECILIA: So she's your wife?

MR. JOHN: No, of course not . . .

CECILIA: Tell me if she's your wife.

MR. JOHN: Well, you know, if she came all this way, it's for me.

CECILIA: Fo John . . .

MR. JOHN: Yes?

CECILIA: It's funny that you should be afraid of me.

MR. JOHN: Here we go.

CECILIA: I'm the one to be afraid of you and I'm very much afraid of you. I don't know why but I fear you very much. I was even thinking just today to talk to you tomorrow at the crack of dawn.

I feel that I'm not good enough for you and I was going to suggest that you marry an educated woman.

MR. JOHN: That's it, that's it!

CECILIA: I'm not educated like you.

MR. JOHN: I knew that!

CECILIA: Bring her home. I'm sure that she would help me become an educated woman. What a happy coincidence that what's happened is what I was thinking. Bring her home, I will love her like . . . I love you.

MR. JOHN: Hurrah! I've won a "million" jackpot! I'm holding a "million." How marvelous! See, unspoken truth is the source of headache. *(To audience)* So you see, if I hadn't confessed, I would have fallen sick.

YOUKI: Boss, if you bring this woman home, we could do "partagement un à un"?[17]

MR. JOHN: What? What are you saying? Watch it! Cecilia, Sissi . . .

CECILIA: Fo.

MR. JOHN: I'll drop by the "aviation" and I'll be right back.

CECILIA: How can we ready the house to welcome her? She's someone important.

MR. JOHN: Oh yes, O.K. I'll give you some money . . . here.

CECILIA: I think we should buy more chairs, don't you agree?

MR. JOHN: No, it's for food . . .

CECILIA: For the food . . .

MR. JOHN: She will sit on the chairs we have. And if she won't . . .

CECILIA: But you can see the nails sticking out . . .

MR. JOHN: She'll sit on them anyway.

CECILIA: Okay, go get her, go get her quick.

MR. JOHN: Good, let everything be "bien,"[18] huh, you know how proud Europeans are! So, the food must be "bien." *(Exit Mr. John.)*

CECILIA: Youki, here take this money and buy a few chairs to fix up the house before they arrive. You, you went to school for a few years, you must know what to do; so go quick. *(Exit Youki. Cecilia is alone.)*

CECILIA: I'll never understand men. But I loved him and I was sure that my love would be forever. And what does he tell me today? That he had a wife in Europe and who knows what else. So what, I'll accept everything. If I complained people would say her husband went to Europe; she's jealous and doesn't want a co-wife. So let him bring her home, I won't try to take her place, I'll only take what belongs to me.

*Music. Mr. John returns, accompanied by Monique.*

CECILIA: Fo, welcome!

MR. JOHN: Yes, greet her, welcome her.

CECILIA: Madame, Madame, welcome. *(To Mr. John)* Fo, I am greeting her but she doesn't look as though she is going to answer.

MR. JOHN: That's all right, speak to her anyway . . .

CECILIA: *(To Youki)* Youki, Youki, interpret for us. *(To Monique)* Madame, welcome.

MONIQUE: Alors Monsieur Jean, alors Monsieur Jean.[19]

MR. JOHN: Alors?

MONIQUE: Qu'est-ce qu'elle dit?

MR. JOHN: Monique, elle dit bonne arrivée.

MONIQUE: Merci.

CECILIA: Welcome Madame.

MONIQUE: Alors Monsieur Jean, elle continue toujours . . .

MR. JOHN: Elle dit "bonne arrivée," je te l'ai déjà dit!

MONIQUE: Alors, merci . . .

CECILIA: How is everybody in Europe?

MONIQUE: Alors, Monsieur Jean?

MR. JOHN: Oui?

MONIQUE: Qu'est ce qu'elle dit?

MR. JOHN: Elle dit bonjour.

CECILIA: How is everybody in Europe?

MONIQUE: Bonjour . . .

CECILIA: And how are the children?

MONIQUE: Bonjour . . .

CECILIA: Is everybody in good health?

MONIQUE: Bonjour . . . *(Cecilia pauses in order to receive greetings from Monique.)*

MR. JOHN: *(To Monique)* Bien, main'nant il faut lui saluer quoi.

MONIQUE: Bonjour Madame . . .

CECILIA: Fo John, what did she say?

MR. JOHN: She said . . .

CECILIA: Yes?

MR. JOHN: She says hello.

CECILIA: Oh . . . *(To Monique)* Hello; how is everybody in Europe?

MONIQUE: Bonjour . . .

CECILIA: Is everyone in good health?

MONIQUE: Bonjour . . .

CECILIA: How are the children?

MONIQUE: Bonjour . . .

CECILIA: Welcome to this country.

MONIQUE: Bonjour . . .

MR. JOHN: Hey, Youki! Youki! Youki!

YOUKI: Boss . . .

MR. JOHN: Come, come greet the lady.

YOUKI: You want to kill me.

MR. JOHN: So Youki, weren't you the one who boasted that you could speak French? You were making fun of a certain lady who didn't know French; so let's hear you speak French.

YOUKI: But I only went to night school.

MR. JOHN: So speak night-school French. Speak to her in night-school French.

YOUKI: "Monsieur, bonsoir."[20]

MONIQUE: Pardon, je ne suis pas un monsieur.[21]

YOUKI: Oh, I think she's refusing what I said.

MR. JOHN: Don't go away; she's telling you that she's not a man but a woman and that you have to start your greetings over again.

YOUKI: Oh. "Bonsoir d'moiselle."[22]

MONIQUE: Bonsoir Monsieur.

YOUKI: Oh, she answered me!

MR. JOHN: *(To Youki, who is leaving)* Hey Youki, come back, you're not done yet! Ask her how everybody is in Europe, ask her for news of Europe! She answered once and that's all?

YOUKI: Yes, you're right. *(Aside)* What a carry-on! *(To Monique)* "Mon vieux hein, elle dit que hein, la France-là, euh . . . Yeurope . . ."[23]

MR. JOHN: Hey Youki, "elle dit que la France-là . . . yeurope . . ." What is the meaning of that? I told you to ask her to tell us about the beautiful things in Europe! Or greet her correctly and ask her for news of people in Europe, her sisters, her brothers, her children or nephews, ask her if everybody is in good health and wait for her answer! *(To audience)* This Youki, he's more like a whiskey. Let him show us how he can say hello in French! Didn't he boast of his French? So let him speak!

CECILIA: Fo, drop the matter, let's take care of the new arrival, she must be hungry. *(Everybody exits . . . Cecilia returns soon after followed by Mr. John, Youki, and Monique.)*

CECILIA: Welcome to you both, Fo John.

MR. JOHN: Thank you.

MONIQUE: Alors Monsieur Jean, qui est cette Madame?[24]
MR. JOHN: Ah oui, Monique . . .
MONIQUE: Monsieur . . .
MR. JOHN: C'est ma première femme quoi.[25]
MONIQUE: Votre femme?
MR. JOHN: Oui.
MONIQUE: D'accord.[26]
CECILIA: I don't understand what you're saying . . .
MR. JOHN: *(To Cecilia)* She said . . . she said . . .
CECILIA: Yes?
MR. JOHN: She said . . . listen, she asked if you were well and I said you were.
CECILIA: That's good.
MONIQUE: Alors Monsieur Jean?
MR. JOHN: Hello!
MONIQUE: Et le garçon?[27]
MR. JOHN: Oh yes, c'est mon petit frère.[28]
MONIQUE: Votre petit frère? O.K. . . .
MR. JOHN: She asked . . .
YOUKI: Yes?
MR. JOHN: She wasn't insulting you, you know?
YOUKI: Yes.
MR. JOHN: She asked how you were.
YOUKI: Thank you, I'm fine.
MR. JOHN: *(To Cecilia)* Good, now I'm going to rest, I need to talk to my whiskey bottle. So call Whiskey, call Monique too and what you feel like saying to her, have Whiskey say it. Let him translate the news from Europe, I'd like to hear that.
CECILIA: Do you think that Monique will teach me the language?
MR. JOHN: Of course! But let's not talk about dawn before nightfall.
YOUKI: *(Trying to change the subject)* Boss, I think we'd better put Auntie's purse away so that it won't be stolen.
MR. JOHN: Ah Cecilia . . . now I'm going to give you some money, Cecilia . . .
CECILIA: Yes?
MR. JOHN: You'll go the market; I'll give you 1,000 francs for shopping . . . no, 500 francs and you'll buy something she likes, that is, hot pepper! She loves it.
CECILIA: I've never heard that there are whites who love hot pepper!
MR. JOHN: Yes, so with the 500 francs, buy 250 francs' worth of hot pepper. Buy 60 francs of meat, also some gombo, but she doesn't like gombo very much. To buy the rest of the ingredients, use 100 francs but don't forget, 250 francs' worth of hot pepper. With the rest of the money, buy

whatever else you need and you do the cooking, you prepare the meal for my return.

YOUKI: Boss, you say she's white but I see that she has black skin.

MR. JOHN: What I meant, uh, what I meant . . .

YOUKI: Yes?

MR. JOHN: She's black but was born in Europe.

YOUKI: Oh I see . . .

MR. JOHN: And she has never visited her country.

YOUKI: Oh I see . . .

MR. JOHN: And she doesn't speak our language.

YOUKI: Oh I see . . .

MR. JOHN: And since this is her first trip here, she knows nothing of our customs, she has black skin but that's all.

YOUKI: Oh I see.

MR. JOHN: Do you understand?

YOUKI: Yes.

MR. JOHN: She's not white.

CECILIA: But Fo, didn't you say that you don't like hot pepper? 250 francs' worth of hot pepper? Do you plan to open a restaurant? And even for a restaurant, do we need so much hot pepper?

YOUKI: Oh, you need that much for "akpama" sauce.[29]

CECILIA: Let me prepare the sauce my way.

MR. JOHN: No, no. I see you don't trust me; I'll have her come and she'll tell you herself.

YOUKI: Ah, if the boss hadn't gone to Europe, he would never have seen such a thing.

MR. JOHN: Monique, Monique!

MONIQUE: Monsieur.

MR. JOHN: Tu n'as pas faim?

MONIQUE: Oui, j'ai faim.[30]

CECILIA: What did she say?

MR. JOHN: She said "oui."

CECILIA: Ask her if she wants 250 francs of hot pepper in the sauce.

MR. JOHN: That's what I asked her!

CECILIA: And she said "wui"?

MR. JOHN: Yes.

CECILIA: I think maybe I didn't quite understand what she said.

YOUKI: What did she say? What did she answer?

CECILIA: (To Mr. John) Would you mind asking her again?

MR. JOHN: Est-ce que tu vas manger?

MONIQUE: Oui, je vais manger.[31]

CECILIA: She said "éwuii, éwuii, éwuii," or in other words, "that's too much, that's too much"![32]

MR. JOHN: No, she didn't say "éwuii" but "oui," she didn't say it was too much.

CECILIA: I won't listen to you, she said "it's too much" and don't try to fool me.

MR. JOHN: What?

CECILIA: Nobody can eat 250 francs of hot pepper!

MR. JOHN: Who's in command here? If you don't want to do the cooking . . . Whiskey, come here, take the money and go get the ingredients.

MONIQUE: Alors, Monsieur Jean . . .

MR. JOHN: Yes?

MONIQUE: Est-ce que vous vous querellez?[33]

MR. JOHN: Non, non, non.

CECILIA: She's going to think that we are arguing.

MR. JOHN: Isn't that what we're doing?

CECILIA: Okay, give me the money. I'll do the cooking.

MR. JOHN: Good.

YOUKI: Boss, boss . . .

MR. JOHN: Yes?

YOUKI: Why don't we cook "dzogoli"?[34] Maybe she would prefer that.

MR. JOHN: "Dzogoli"? Is there a lot of hot pepper?

CECILIA: That's enough! Fo John, give me the money and I'll prepare what you want.

MR. JOHN: But if I return from work and I don't find . . .

CECILIA: Don't worry, everything will be done as you wish.

MR. JOHN: . . . you'll have me to deal with . . . *(To Monique)* Bon Madame . . .

MONIQUE: Monsieur . . .

MR. JOHN: Je viens tout suite; je m'en vais au service.[35]

MONIQUE: D'accord.

MR. JOHN: Bon.

MONIQUE: Alors, Monsieur Jean . . .

MR. JOHN: *(To Cecilia)* See you later.

CECILIA: Bye-bye . . . *[In English]*

YOUKI: Good-bye boss!

MR. JOHN: Yes, yes . . . *(To Youki, who's gesturing)* What is it?

YOUKI: Bring us a goat, bring us something nice.

MR. JOHN: Yes. *(Exit Mr. John.)*

CECILIA: Youki . . .

YOUKI: Yes Auntie . . .

CECILIA: Go get . . .

YOUKI: Holala, here we go again!

CECILIA: Whiskey, ask her . . .

YOUKI: Yes?

CECILIA: Uh . . .

YOUKI: Yes . . .

CECILIA: Markets, are there markets in Europe?

YOUKI: *(To Monique)* Uh, Madame . . .

MONIQUE: Monsieur?

YOUKI: Uh, en Europe, l'Europe-là, est-ce qu'y a de grands voitu, voitu-là?[36]

MONIQUE: Oui, il y a de grandes voitures en Europe.

YOUKI: *(To Cecilia)* She says that in Europe, markets are very tall buildings with many storeys!

CECILIA: Whiskey . . .

YOUKI: Auntie . . .

CECILIA: Bravo, how well you speak; the boss's presence must have made you shy, no?

YOUKI: At school, a long time ago, when the teacher spoke, I answered him.

CECILIA: Good, now ask her . . .

YOUKI: Yes?

CECILIA: Ask her . . .

YOUKI: Yes?

CECILIA: If they have trains like ours?

YOUKI: *(To Monique)* Elle dit que hein, vous êtes couillion.[37]

MONIQUE: Whiskey!

YOUKI: Oui . . . Allo, 008![38]

MONIQUE: Alors la mad . . . la madame a bien voulu m'insulter?[39]

YOUKI: Hola, non . . . elle dit que hein, y a en France le cocotier-là?

MONIQUE: Il y a des cocotiers en France.[40]

CECILIA: What did she say?

YOUKI: She said you can find everything there.

CECILIA: Say Whiskey.

YOUKI: Yes?

CECILIA: You say a lot to each other but you only tell me a little.

YOUKI: You should go to school yourself.

CECILIA: If that's all you can say . . . leave us alone. I'll talk to her by myself.

YOUKI: All you have to do is to go to school.

CECILIA: Monique . . .

MONIQUE: Madame?

CECILIA: *(To Youki)* Here, take this money, go do the shopping for me and set the table. Monique . . .

YOUKI: Auntie, you haven't given me enough money, the boss gave you two bills.

CECILIA: All right, here . . . Monique, when the "patron"[41] comes back from work, what should I say? When the "patron" returns, how do I greet him?

MONIQUE: Comment?

CECILIA: When the "patron" returns, how do I greet him?

MONIQUE: Madame, Madame . . .

CECILIA: Yes?

MONIQUE: Mais je ne comprends pas.[42]

CECILIA: I'm asking you what I should say to the "patron" when he returns, yes when he returns from work?

MONIQUE: S'il revient, dites "bonne arrivée Monsieur."[43]

CECILIA: What?

MONIQUE: On dit: "bonne arrivée Monsieur."

CECILIA: "Gbon dzive"?[44] And to tell him to sit down?

MONIQUE: Comment?

CECILIA: And if I want to tell him to sit down?

MONIQUE: On dit: "asseyez-vous."

CECILIA: What?

MONIQUE: "Asseyez-vous."

CECILIA: "Assevi"?[45] And to tell him to come and eat?

MONIQUE: Bon, on dit: "mangeons."

CECILIA: What?

MONIQUE: "Mangeons."

CECILIA: "Amadji"? Fine. In Europe, do you dance? Do you dance?

MONIQUE: La danse?

CECILIA: Yes . . .

MONIQUE: La danse européenne.[46]

CECILIA: What?

MONIQUE: La danse européenne.

CECILIA: I'm talking about dancing.

MONIQUE: Oui, c'est ce que j'ai dit, "la danse européenne."[47]

CECILIA: Yes?

MONIQUE: Oui; on fait cette danse européenne.

CECILIA: Show me. *(Music. Monique dances.)* Is that all, is that all you know how to do? You should feel it in your entire body. Wait a minute, I'm going to ask the orchestra to play us some local music and you'll see. *(Music. Cecilia dances.)* You see; the whole body participates.

*(Mr. John returns.)*

MONIQUE: Monsieur Jean . . .

MR. JOHN: Ah oui?

MONIQUE: Soyez la bienvenu.

MR. JOHN: Ah merci.

CECILIA: Fo John . . .

MR. JOHN: Yes?

CECILIA: "Gbon dzive" . . .

MR. JOHN: What? "Gbon dzive"? The goat has given birth to two baby goats? What goat? We don't have a goat! Where did this goat who had two baby goats come from?

YOUKI: Welcome home.

MR. JOHN: Thank you, Youki.

CECILIA: I wanted to welcome you.

MR. JOHN: Is that what you wanted to say?

CECILIA: Of course!

MR. JOHN: You were saying "welcome"? I didn't understand. I heard "gbon dzive" and understood that the goat had given birth.

CECILIA: I spoke to you in French!

MR. JOHN: Ah!

CECILIA: Yes, I was speaking to you in French.

MR. JOHN: I didn't understand . . . Who's taught you this French?

CECILIA: Monique did.

MR. JOHN: Aren't you ashamed of yourself to lie like that? How could Monique say "gbon dzive," she doesn't know a word of Ewe?

CECILIA: What should you say then?

YOUKI: Maybe auntie feels like eating a goat sauce.

CECILIA: What do you say?

MR. JOHN: Euh, Monique, euh . . . je crois, elle dit quelquechose, elle dit que c'est toi, c'est toi-même qui l'a a dit ça.[48]

MONIQUE: Quoi?

CECILIA: "Gbon dzive" . . .

MONIQUE: Alors, qu'elle répète encore une fois.[49]

MR. JOHN: Quoi?

CECILIA: "Gbon dzive" . . .

MR. JOHN: That's it! Tu entends main'nant?[50]

MONIQUE: Vraiment hein, mon vieux, elle veut dire: "bonne arrivée"![51]

MR. JOHN: *(To Cecilia)* Oh, so you wanted to say "bonne arrivée"? Look, you were right . . . "Bonne arrivée" . . . Come here, I'll teach you to say it, you can't roll your tongue correctly. Listen to me: "bonne arrivée" . . . Repeat.

CECILIA: "Bonn . . . "

MR. JOHN: Bonne . . .

CECILIA: "Bon ve" . . .

MR. JOHN: Non, it's not "bon ve"! You say "bonne arrivée"!

CECILIA: "Bonne . . . "

MR. JOHN: "Arrivée!"

CECILIA: "Ar . . . arrivée."

MR. JOHN: Very good. Once more.

YOUKI: Boss, if she doesn't succeed, give her a whack on the hand.

CECILIA: "Bonne arrivée."

MR. JOHN: Again!

CECILIA: "Bonne arrivée."

Mr. John: That's very good! "Bonne arrivée . . . "

Cecilia: "Assevi" . . .

Mr. John: Listen, is that what I just taught you?

Cecilia: "Bonne arrivée."

Mr. John: Very good! And what's this "assevi"?

Cecilia: "Assevi."

Mr. John: "Assevi"? Are you talking about the cat?

Cecilia: No, I was telling you to sit down.

Mr. John: And what has the cat have to do with that?

Cecilia: I wanted to tell you to sit down.

Mr. John: Sit down? And how do you say that? "Assevi"?

Cecilia: Yes.

Mr. John: Peculiar . . . Monique, qu'est-ce qu'elle dit?

Monique: Elle dit "asseyez-vous."[52]

Mr. John: Cecilia, come here; you don't say "assevi" but "asseyez-vous."

Cecilia: "Assé-vous" . . .

Mr. John: Not "assé-vous" but "asseyez-vous."

Cecilia: "Asseyez-vous."

Mr. John: Ah, this child is gifted in French.

Cecilia: "Amadji"[53] . . .

Mr. John: Listen, I'm beginning to get tired! What are you saying?

Cecilia: "Amadji" . . .

Mr. John: "Amavi"?

Cecilia: Non, I want to tell you to eat.

Mr. John: And you say this: "amavi"? *(To Monique in Ewe)* Monique, you're her teacher; what did you teach her?

Monique: Elle dit "mangeons."

Mr. John: What?

Monique: "Mangeons."

Mr. John: "Mangeons"! And how do you say "mangeons"? Listen: you say "mangeons"! Repeat!

Cecilia: "M . . . Mann . . . "

Mr. John: "Mangeons"!

Cecilia: "Mmanch . . . "

Mr. John: "Mangeons"!

Cecilia: "Mmanchions."

Mr. John: No, not "manchions," but "mangeons."

Cecilia: "Manchions"!

Mr. John: No, not "manchions," but "mangeons"!

Cecilia: "Mangeons"!

Mr. John: That's it, "mangeons"!

Cecilia: Mangeons!

Mr. John: All right; let's start again. Repeat everything I've taught you.

Cecilia: There is also the word "Monsieur," the words "Monsieur, Madame, Mademoiselle" that I don't understand.

Mr. John: First repeat what I've taught you.

Cecilia: But if . . .

Mr. John: First repeat what I've taught you.

Cecilia: All right, Mons . . . Madame Jean . . .

Mr. John: Is that what I taught you? I asked you to repeat what I just taught you!

Cecilia: "Bonne arrivée!"

Mr. John: Very good!

Cecilia: "Assey-vi!"

Mr. John: No, "asseyez-vous"!

Cecilia: "Asseyez-vous!"

Mr. John: Very good!

Cecilia: "Mangeons!"

Mr. John: That's it!

Youki: That's it, she's done it!

Cecilia: And who do you call "Monsieur," who's "Madame," and who is called "Mademoiselle"?

Mr. John: You want to know that too?

Cecilia: I know how to say the words, but I don't see the difference.

Mr. John: I'll teach you. You see, you are "Madame" and I'm the one who "damé"[54] you. A "Mademoiselle" is a woman who is not married. But "Monsieur" is someone like me; I, I am "Monsieur." And someone like— *(pointing to Youki).*

Youki: "Célibatai"![55]

Mr. John: Non, you can also refer to Youki as "Monsieur" but since he's young, it would be better to call him "jeune homme."[56]

Cecilia: I see.

Mr. John: That's it . . .

Cecilia: Youki!

Mr. John: But . . .

Cecilia: *(To Youki)* You can serve the meal now.

Youki: Right away!

Mr. John: One moment! Did you put the hot pepper in?

Cecilia: Yes.

Mr. John: All of the hot pepper?

Cecilia: Yes.

Youki: That's the truth.

Mr. John: So bring the meal! *(Music. Dance.)*

Mr. John: *(To Cecilia)* That's it, is it ready?

Cecilia: Yes.

MR. JOHN: Good, speak French now.

CECILIA: "Monsieur Jean . . . "

MR. JOHN: Yes?

CECILIA: "Mangeons!"

MR. JOHN: That's very good . . . And you, Monique, you've been here a while; tell us in Ewe to come and eat. When you go to a country where people wear black cloths, you must do as they do. It's your turn to speak: there is no longer any question of your leaving, so you'll have to learn Ewe.

MONIQUE: Monsieur Jean . . .

MR. JOHN: Yes?

MONIQUE: Que dites-vous?

MR. JOHN: I don't know but I'm telling you to come and eat.

MONIQUE: Moi je ne comprends pas.

MR. JOHN: I'm telling you that we're going to eat. If you don't understand, that's too bad for you, you'll die of hunger. Don't gesture that you don't understand! You were the one who wanted to come; I didn't ask you, you came by yourself.

MONIQUE: Monsieur Jean . . .

MR. JOHN: What?

MONIQUE: Faites tout ce que vous voulez.[57]

MR. JOHN: "Faites tout ce que vous voulez," is that Ewe? *(To Cecilia)* To shame her tell her in French to come and eat.

CECILIA: "Madame Jean, Madame Monique . . . "

MONIQUE: Madame?

CECILIA: "Mangeons!"

MONIQUE: D'accord. *(She begins to eat with appetite.)*

MR. JOHN: *(To Monique)* Aren't you ashamed of yourself?

YOUKI: "Ventilatai"! Boss, while you eat, I'll be the ventilator for you! *(Music. Youki dances around the table.)*

MONIQUE: Monsieur Jean, Monsieur Jean . . .

MR. JOHN: Yes?

MONIQUE: Avec la main, j'ai . . . je ne suis pas bien . . . [58]

MR. JOHN: You really want to eat . . . . *(To Monique, but still in Ewe)* You should eat more slowly.

YOUKI: Boss, strike a pose, I'm going to take your picture.

MONIQUE: Monsieur Jean, Monsieur Jean!

MR. JOHN: Alors?

MONIQUE: Qu'est-ce qu'elle a mis dans la nourriture?[59]

MR. JOHN: Hein?

MONIQUE: Qu'est-ce qu'elle a mis dans . . .

MR. JOHN: C'est du piment—non?[60]

MONIQUE: J'ai chaud mon vieux, je vais mourir![61]

YOUKI: Here we go!

MR. JOHN: *(After giving some water to Monique)* Ça va un peu?

MONIQUE: Oui, ça va un peu.[62]

MR. JOHN: Ah bon, ça va.

YOUKI: Boss, you were saying that I should wish her a nice trip on your behalf.

MR. JOHN: Huh, what are you saying?

YOUKI: Didn't you tell me to wish her a nice trip? ·

MR. JOHN: Come quickly and mop up this water!

YOUKI: Wait a minute, first I'll wipe up the water on the table.

MR. JOHN: Cecilia, now . . . Monique, viens . . . now . . .

YOUKI: Have you finished eating?

MR. JOHN: *(In Ewe to Monique)* Come, come here next to me, come sit here . . . Now, I'm off to the office, hein . . .

YOUKI: *(Who has taken the place of his master in front of the dish)* It's not true! I'll never be able to do that!

MR. JOHN: . . . hein, do you hear me? I'm leaving for the office, be good until I return . . . answer me!

MONIQUE: Whiskey . . .

MR. JOHN: What do you want whiskey for? *(To Youki)* Don't answer her. *(To Monique)* Answer me quick, I must leave.

YOUKI: He's caught the "pas de temps,"[63] he's not at all free.

MONIQUE: Whiskey . . .

MR. JOHN: What, Whiskey? You're just an idiot! My dearest Cecilia . . .

CECILIA: Monsieur . . .

MR. JOHN: Euh . . . main'nant je m'en vais au service, je viens tout suite, hein.[64]

CECILIA: "Quand est-ce que tu vas revenir?"[65]

MR. JOHN: *(To Monique)* See how the illiterate speaks French! And yet she never set foot in a school!

YOUKI: "Nou touzou débrouiller pour parler français mais zeuropéen zamais parler ewe."[66]

MR. JOHN: Je viens dans deux minutes, hein.

MONIQUE: Dans deux minutes?

MR. JOHN: Oui.

MONIQUE: Bon, c'est peu.[67]

MR. JOHN: Bon, Monique . . .

MONIQUE: M'sieur . . .

MR. JOHN: No Monique, you say "Fo." Monique . . .

MONIQUE: M'sieur . . .

MR. JOHN: No, say "Fo." Monique . . .

MONIQUE: M'sieur . . .

MR. JOHN: Peuh . . . too bad for you. Hey, Whiskey!

YOUKI: Boss, I . . .

MR. JOHN: Always with your nose in a plate, eh?

YOUKI: No, I . . .

MR. JOHN: See you later. And take good care of Monique.

YOUKI: Yes.

MR. JOHN: Don't take advantage of the fact that she doesn't understand Ewe to make fun of her. Understand?

YOUKI: Monique could have given us a present when she arrived . . .

MR. JOHN: Ask her for it, you have to ask her.

YOUKI: She's not very nice, this white lady.

MR. JOHN: I say, see you later.

CECILIA: "Bon, revenez vite."[68]

MR. JOHN: Thank you. *(Exit Mr. John.)*

CECILIA: Monique . . .

MONIQUE: Madame . . .

CECILIA: Whiskey . . .

YOUKI: Boss . . .

CECILIA: Come clear the table.

YOUKI: The bottle of whiskey, shall I leave it here or what shall I do with it?

CECILIA: Monique . . .

MONIQUE: Madame . . .

CECILIA: Alors main'nant on va aller au marché.[69]

MONIQUE: Comment? Au marché?

CECILIA: *(Laughing)* Yes.

YOUKI: *(Eating again)* I'm not going to touch the plate of the white woman.

MONIQUE: Madame, madame . . .

CECILIA: Oui?

MONIQUE: Moi je ne suis pas venue pour faire de la commerce ici![70]

CECILIA: Quoi?

MONIQUE: Je ne suis pas venue pour faire de la commerce au Togo!

CECILIA: Tu n'es pas venue pour faire de la commerce, mais tu es venue pour manger au Togo?

MONIQUE: Je suis venue chez Monsieur Jean, non?

CECILIA: Tu es chez Monsieur Jean, Monsieur Jean est . . .

MONIQUE: C'est lui qui me nourrit.

CECILIA: C'est lui qui te nourrit! C'est lui qui va au marché pour acheter les choses?

MONIQUE: Alors, c'est lui qui donne l'argent, non?

CECILIA: C'est lui qui donne l'argent?

MONIQUE: Oui.

CECILIA: L'argent lui-même va marcher a . . . av . . . a . . . o . . . Le marché n'est pas loin, à peu prés dix kilomètres seulement.

MONIQUE: Alors, on y va avec taxi, non?

CECILIA: On y va avec taxi . . . Ton papa n'a jamais acheté même une . . . un vélo. . . .

MONIQUE: Mais alors on y va avec un cheval.

CECILIA: On y va avec un cheval? Tu es venue au Togo, où est-ce que tu as trouvé au moins deux cheval?

MONIQUE: Vraiment vous brillez hein.

YOUKI: Auntie, you said that during your absence, I should tidy the house, isn't that right?

CECILIA: Yes, tidy the house.

MONIQUE: Mais vous dites que le marché est loin de dix kilomètres! Alors?[71]

CECILIA: Autrefois, c'est dix kilomètres, main'nant on a diminué, quinze kilomètres.

MONIQUE: Alors je ne suis pas un cheval pour faire quinze kilomètres à pied.

CECILIA: Alors tu n'es pas un cheval, tu n'as qu'à rester, moi je m'en vais.

MONIQUE: Allez-y revenir.

CECILIA: Bon, Monique, je m'en vais.

MONIQUE: Madame . . .

CECILIA: Yes?[72]

MONIQUE: J'ai mal au ventre.[73]

CECILIA: What are you saying?

MONIQUE: J'ai mal au ventre.

CECILIA: I don't understand . . . Whiskey, what is she saying?

YOUKI: I don't know, ask her yourself.

CECILIA: Whiskey, what is she saying? I don't understand what she's saying.

MONIQUE: Madame, Madame, Madame . . . Je mouris![74]

CECILIA: Whiskey! What is she saying; I don't understand her any more.

YOUKI: She says she has a stomach ache.

CECILIA: (To Monique) Oh, so you have a stomach ache?

MONIQUE: Mais je te dis que . . .

CECILIA: So you have a stomach ache?

MONIQUE: Je te dis que . . . my stomach hurts.

CECILIA: Whiskey, maybe we should take her to the hospital.

YOUKI: No.

CECILIA: Yes, we have to take her to the hospital.

YOUKI: My boss doesn't want me to touch her.

CECILIA: Monique, shall we go to the hospital?

MONIQUE: Allons, allons . . . comment?

CECILIA: Let's go to the hospital.

MONIQUE: Il y a du comprimé dans les boites de Monsieur Jean, non? Du compriééi . . . [75]

CECILIA: I'll run and get them so that Whiskey can choose some for you.

MONIQUE: Aie . . . aie . . . aie.
YOUKI: Holala . . .
MONIQUE: Aie!
YOUKI: Oooh!
MONIQUE: Ouille!
YOUKI: Aie!
MONIQUE: Cécile, Cécile, je mourai!
YOUKI: Aie, tu mouraaas . . . [76]
CECILIA: Whiskey . . .
YOUKI: Yes?
CECILIA: Go quick and look for a taxi, we're taking her to the hospital right away.
MONIQUE: Madame, Madame . . .
YOUKI: The taxis are on "grève."[77]
CECILIA: Help me support her then.
MONIQUE: Madame, Madame, âie, âie, âie. *(Exit Monique supported by Cecilia and Youki. Return of Cecilia and Youki.)*
YOUKI: *(Searching through Monique's things)* What is this? A white woman who gives me nothing when she arrives? Let her die. I could make a "ravage" in her purse: Look, expensive cloth, a "mouchoir," a lamp . . . That makes "trois."[78]
CECILIA: Whiskey!
YOUKI: Let's put this aside . . .
CECILIA: Whiskey!
YOUKI: Auntie?
CECILIA: Go see if she's feeling better and if I can bring her some porridge. *(Youki runs out and returns right away.)*
YOUKI: She's still alive . . . I'm telling you that what I just saw at the hospital isn't funny . . . Hihihi . . .
CECILIA: Is she very sick?
YOUKI: Her eyes are glassy.
CECILIA: Her eyes are what? Whiskey, Whiskey?
YOUKI: Hihihi!
CECILIA: How is she?
YOUKI: The whites of her eyes are showing; like this, hihihi . . .
CECILIA: What are we going to do? You, you stay here; I'll prepare some porridge and take it to her. *(Return of Mr. John.)*
YOUKI: Here's the boss himself back.
CECILIA: Welcome.
MR. JOHN: What's happening here?
CECILIA: Go get the "patron's" meal quickly.
MR. JOHN: Where's Monique?
CECILIA: *(To Youki)* Go get . . .

MR. JOHN: Where's Monique?

CECILIA: First sit down.

MR. JOHN: Where's Monique?

CECILIA: *(To Youki)* Go get the meal! *(To Mr. John)* Eat first. *(To Youki)* Go get the meal!

YOUKI: Patience, I think you were asked a question.

CECILIA: *(To Mr. John)* Come eat, I'll tell you later.

MR. JOHN: I have to eat first?

CECILIA: Yes.

MR. JOHN: I ask you where Monique is and you want me to eat before you answer.

YOUKI: What . . . what did you tell me to say to the doctor?

CECILIA: Bring me what I asked for.

MR. JOHN: Eh? Where are you sending him?

CECILIA: What?

MR. JOHN: Where are you sending him?

CECILIA: I . . . I'm sending him, I'm sending him . . .

MR. JOHN: I'm asking where you're sending him!

CECILIA: Nowhere . . . For a promenade . . .

MR. JOHN: And Monique, she went "for a promenade," Monique?

CECILIA: Yes.

YOUKI: Promenade zhôpitaux . . . promenade zhôpitaux . . .

MR. JOHN: What? Moni . . . and anyway, who does she know here to go with for a promenade?

CECILIA: Eat first and I'll explain later.

MR. JOHN: And if she wants to go "for a promenade," you should accompany her.

CECILIA: Eat!

MR. JOHN: Really?

YOUKI: "Podologie avant tout."[79]

MR. JOHN: Do you really want me to eat first?

CECILIA: Yes. *(Mr. John sits down at the table.)*

YOUKI: *(Commenting on Mr. John's meal)* Goal! Bravo Kalala and Tsinambu![80]

MR. JOHN: I'm finished, I've eaten enough!

YOUKI: My boss usually eats more . . .

CECILIA: Is that all you're eating?

MR. JOHN: Yes.

CECILIA: Too bad . . .

MR. JOHN: What's too bad? Where's Monique?

CECILIA: She's gone out.

MR. JOHN: And where did she go?

CECILIA: She went to the plage.[81]

MR. JOHN: To the plage?

CECILIA: Yes.

MR. JOHN: Does she know how to get there by herself?

CECILIA: Uh . . . a white man came to get her in a D.S. . . . [82] it seems they have known each other for a long time and he took her for a ride.

MR. JOHN: Well . . . So it's a life like that that Monique wants to lead here? Go quick and look for her!

CECILIA: But I don't know where . . .

MR. JOHN: Go out and bring her back!

CECILIA: I don't know the way to the plage.

MR. JOHN: And you let her go there all alone!

CECILIA: Since I've been living with you, how many times have you come back from work without finding me at home?

YOUKI: Monique went to 'S Trois Saisons . . .[83]

MR. JOHN: Go look for her and if you don't find her, don't come back here!

CECILIA: My God, my God where . . .

MR. JOHN: Quick!

CECILIA: Wait a minute, I'm going to tell you.

MR. JOHN: What?

CECILIA: She went . . . she went . . .

MR. JOHN: I'm telling you to go look for her, you hear?

CECILIA: But that's not necessary.

MR. JOHN: Yes it is, go ahead!

CECILIA: I'm going to tell you where . . .

MR. JOHN: And if you don't find her, don't come back either!

CECILIA: Do you really want me to tell you where she is?

YOUKI: As for me, I'm going to lengthen this dress and take it to her.

MR. JOHN: So you were lying to me! Weren't you?

CECILIA: Shortly after you left, she began to have stomach pains. I wanted to call you but she told me that wasn't necessary, that there was medicine in your suitcase she was used to taking and that would be enough.

MR. JOHN: And her stomach ache went away?

CECILIA: Yes.

MR. JOHN: And then she went to the beach?

CECILIA: She took the medicine but I was afraid it was serious so I took her to the hospital. I was going to prepare some porridge for her when . . .

MR. JOHN: Monique is in the hospital and you're telling me all these stories?

CECILIA: We thought you would lose your appetite if you knew what had happened.

MR. JOHN: Ridiculous!

CECILIA: You wouldn't have been able to eat if you had known what had happened.

MR. JOHN: I'm going to visit her and then I'll come back.

CECILIA: No, I'll go myself to bring her the porridge.

MR. JOHN: No, I'm going because I haven't seen her yet.

CECILIA: Okay; come back quickly. *(To Youki)* So? Tell me now how she is.

YOUKI: I swear, when I saw her, her eyes were bulging out of her head.

CECILIA: And the doctor wasn't doing anything?

YOUKI: There's nothing we can do for her, they say she's dead. Besides, let her die! Let her die. You are stupid to pity her.

CECILIA: She's still young! And don't talk like that of a dead person! . . . Monique . . . You know that it was thanks to Monique that I learned French? What will happen if she dies? I haven't finished learning!

YOUKI: What, he brings a white woman home and now nothing is left on the plates after the meal!

CECILIA: If it's because of the left-overs, let the subject drop; it would be sad if Monique died.

YOUKI: *(Turning toward audience)* So! Drummers, are you ready? Are you ready? We are going to a wake! *(Return of Mr. John.)*

MR. JOHN: Cecilia . . .

CECILIA: Welcome home, Fo.

MR. JOHN: Thank you.

CECILIA: So is she better?

MR. JOHN: No.

YOUKI: Welcome home, Boss . . . What about her stomach ache?

MR. JOHN: *(To Youki)* Show some patience, you. Uh . . . Moni . . . Cecilia, ever since I've lived with Monique, I've never seen her sleep like that.

CECILIA: How is she sleeping?

MR. JOHN: You're going to come with me, you'll see how she's sleeping and you'll tell me what you think, yes, what you think.

CECILIA: Let's go!

MR. JOHN: When we arrive . . .

CECILIA: Let's go right away!

YOUKI: *(Searching in Monique's handbag)* Look at this!

MR. JOHN: I'll wait for you at the door, you go and see her by yourself.

CECILIA: Come along! *(Exit Mr. John and Cecilia.)*

YOUKI: *(Searching in Monique's handbag)* She even has a few grains of *gari* in her bag! I would never have believed that a yovo's purse could be so empty . . . Let's wait for the others to return. *(Return of Mr. John.)*

YOUKI: Welcome home Boss! *(Music—crying—screams)* What has happened to her? Tell me Boss, what has happened to her?

MR. JOHN: "La terre est descendue"![84] To whom will I tell of this misfortune?

YOUKI: You can tell me . . .

MR. JOHN: *Song of desolation:*

> "To whom will I tell of this misfortune?"
> Ah Monique! Ah Youki!

YOUKI: So she finally ended up, "mouri"!

MR. JOHN: Youki . . .

YOUKI: Boss . . .

MR. JOHN: Go see Pastor Akpeteshi[85] . . .

YOUKI: Pastor Alcohol, yes . . .

MR. JOHN: Tell him that . . .

YOUKI: Yes . . .

MR. JOHN: Tell him what misfortune has befallen me and ask him to help me bury her.

YOUKI: What misfortune has befallen you? Was I also a witness?

*(Youki leaves and returns.)* Boss, I went and they told me that because the Pastor saw me, I have to be baptized! *(Music. The Pastor enters, stumbling to the sound of church music.)*

MR. JOHN: Monique, my dearest Monique . . .

PASTOR: Silence!

MR. JOHN: . . . n'est plus.

PASTOR: Silence, for Pastor Akpeteshi is going to preach! For where there is mourning, there is our joy!

YOUKI: Amen, amen.

PASTOR: For at that time, there is alcohol and plenty for all!

YOUKI: Amen!

PASTOR: Let us open the Book of the five times Corinthians or of the Germans[86] and read: "Verily, verily, I say unto you," rejoice for you have lost a loved one today and let the *sodabi*[87] flow in abundance and for all!

Let us open this book to the First Chapter, for it is there that Jesus said: "If men didn't die, when would the hungry eat?"

O most holy Saint Kalaba, if *kalaba*[88] didn't exist, where would pregnant women find strength?

O Saint Akassa, if there were no *akassa*,[89] what would the Nagot eat?

Let us sing the cantique where it is said: "If there were no *akassa*, what would the Nagoti eat?"

Courage, courage, believer,

If there were no *akassa*, what would the Nagot eat? *(Church music.)*

MR. JOHN: Monique, my dearest Monique . . .

PASTOR: Let us ask for God's grace! If He wants to be compassionate, let Him rid us of the second one!

YOUKI: Amen.

PASTOR: Now I think that it is time: the body has waited too long and if I tarry any more no one will want to follow it.

And I hope that the co-wife will not be long in following so that we will have our bread.

YOUKI: Wait, let me do her "geographie."[90]

PASTOR: I think we can finally start the burial procession! Let us sing a few hymns! Let us sing the 500-franc hymn right up to the first verse! *(Religious music.)*

MR. JOHN: Monique, my dearest Monique!

PASTOR: Let's go out and get started!

YOUKI: Wait a minute, wait a minute! Tell me if a dead man can fart . . .

MR. JOHN: Ah, Monique Monique, you have left me! Ah, my Monique is no more!

PASTOR: Let's finish with the body and let's leave! *(Church music.)*

ALL: Alleluia. Jesus will be King!

YOUKI: *(To audience)* My boss is a real "cochon."[91] He returned from Europe with a European wife and when I told him "partageon une à une," he said no! And when she was hungry, he prepared for her a sauce with 250 francs worth of hot pepper!

Music—hymn:

ALL:
        Death has surely struck my house
        In my distress, I trust in God.
        Death has surely struck my house . . .

YOUKI: *(To Mr. John)* My poor boss, she is dead and there is nothing we can do . . . They say that the great do not listen to others, here's the proof!

MR. JOHN: What, what are you saying?

YOUKI: When that woman arrived . . .

MR. JOHN: Who?

YOUKI: If you had agreed to let me have one, you wouldn't be in so much trouble today.

MR. JOHN: Do you mean to say that you wanted to take one of my wives?

YOUKI: From the moment you decided that we would get her at the "aviation," I had her on screen, me "008"!

MR. JOHN: It's a sad story.

YOUKI: That's right, this idea of hot pepper . . .

MR. JOHN: Listen, don't provoke me . . .

YOUKI: Oh, anyway, you have never paid me for the work I've done for you.

MR. JOHN: So you want to leave?

YOUKI: Yes, I want to leave you.

MR. JOHN: Hum . . .

YOUKI: *(To Cecilia)* Auntie, my boss has been behaving badly, so I am leaving you . . . Take care of yourself . . . One of these days, it may be you . . . *(Exit Youki.)*

*Music—song:*

ALL: "Afi will not marry you!"

MR. JOHN: So Monique is really and truly dead?

CECILIA: Yes and we have buried her.

MR. JOHN: I feel as though I'm living in a dream. And then there are her parents—she didn't even tell them she was coming here! What will I tell them?

CECILIA: These things just happen . . . You see, we're like plants of God. We grow and bear fruit and God picks the ones he likes. Today God wanted Monique near Him and called her. Let's not complain. Her death touches me more than you. With Monique's arrival, I became . . . oh, I wouldn't say educated but when people speak, I understand and can respond. That upsets me very much, but let's stop complaining and get on with life.

MR. JOHN: It's sad . . .

CECILIA: What has happened has happened; we can't change anything.

MR. JOHN: But what bothers me most, is what I can say to her parents.

CECILIA: Does her father live where you met her?

MR. JOHN: Excuse me?

CECILIA: Do her father and mother live where you met her?

MR. JOHN: She has a father and a mother, but what can I tell them? That's the question. Put yourself in my shoes; what can I say to them?

CECILIA: What are we going to to?

MR. JOHN: There is nothing we can do.

CECILIA: Fo John, what misfortune!

MR. JOHN: What can I say to her parents when I find myself in front of them?

CECILIA: Oh Fo John . . .

MR. JOHN: Monique! Her case is a riddle to me.

CECILIA: Fo, stop your lamentations: Monique is dead and buried; have you thought of what you would do if she returned?

MR. JOHN: No; don't say that, she was loved by others.

CECILIA: She was loved as you say; but everyone must die one day.

MR. JOHN: And I am the miserable one who might pay with his life.

CECILIA: These things happen, cease your lamentations.

MR. JOHN: No . . .

*Entrance of Monique's ghost—Cecilia screams
like a mad woman, audience screams too.*

MR. JOHN: (*To audience*) You see, just a few days ago, my wife, one of my wives died and today, the other one goes crazy; what will become of me?

CECILIA: Fo John, has she left?

MR. JOHN: What?

CECILIA: I beg of you, let's leave this house.

MR. JOHN: Leave this house? My own house? We're staying!

CECILIA: It would be better to rent another one.

MR. JOHN: What, rent a house? Own my own house and go live in a rented house? No.

CECILIA: Do you prefer living here in fear?

MR. JOHN: Jamais pas! You know that very well. When you see her, why don't you tell me so that I can face her?

CECILIA: I shouted to tell you!

MR. JOHN: Shouted? You just stood there trying to scare me. (*Mr. John in turn sees the ghost.*)

CECILIA: So, what were you able to do to her?

MR. JOHN: It's because I didn't have my rifle with me that she jostled me.

CECILIA: What, you forgot to take your rifle?

MR. JOHN: Look, I have a rifle.

CECILIA: And you could have destroyed her with a rifle?

MR. JOHN: I have a double barrel rifle and when I empty it on her, she will die twice! I'm going to get it and wait here without trembling! Let her come again to play the fool and she'll see how I welcome her. C'est moi, I'll show her . . . I'm going to force her "à gauche!"[92]

CECILIA: Fie! you who have never even shot at a bird, you want to shoot a ghost?

MR. JOHN: Just stand over there and you'll see.

CECILIA: You really want us to trust in this rifle? Don't you prefer to pay to rent another house?

MR. JOHN: Look, you see this rifle, have confidence in it, have confidence in it: you will see how I destroy her, me the strong man.

CECILIA: No, I don't agree with you.

MR. JOHN: What?

CECILIA: I prefer to move.

MR. JOHN: Leave? No I'll stay here and wait for her.

CECILIA: And how will you manage to shoot her?

MR. JOHN: Well, I'm already in position, she should come now. My rifle is in my right hand, I'm telling you you don't have to be afraid. She's supposed to be dead, right? Well she'll die a second time. Be brave! I'll destroy her with one shot, you'll see. (*The ghost appears again.*)

CECILIA: You see, we should have left this house.

MR. JOHN: To go where?

GHOST: I have come to tell you that I died from eating too much hot pepper.

MR. JOHN: Let her dare come any closer and I'll shoot! (*The ghost approaches: in fear, Mr. John drops the rifle.*)

MR. JOHN: You're the one who disarmed me; you're the one who tore the rifle from my arms.

CECILIA: I believed you were a man.

MR. JOHN: I'm not a woman!

CECILIA: Perhaps, but I have nothing more to say to you.

MR. JOHN: You have nothing more to say to me! Listen, if you try to provoke me, I'll kill you! Do you remember that you cooked something for us the other day in this house?

CECILIA: What?

MR. JOHN: I'm asking you if you remember giving us something to eat the other day in this house?

CECILIA: Yes.

MR. JOHN: Well, they say she died from eating too much hot pepper; so it's your fault.

CECILIA: Is that all you can say? You think that because I love you so much, I'm crazy? I'm not crazy, I still have a head on my shoulders. You told me to prepare a hot sauce, I told you that I wouldn't do it and you forced me to do it, when you saw that I didn't want to. An argument broke out and because I didn't want the other woman to see us quarreling I yielded. Didn't I eat the same sauce? Didn't you eat it, too?

MR. JOHN: Yes . . .

CECILIA: And didn't Fanta eat some?

MR. JOHN: Yes . . .

CECILIA: Everybody ate some! And why aren't we all dead? The sauce simply didn't agree with her stomach! But you have already dragged me into evil and evil has been done. I've gone far enough with you, you can still drag me into another crime.

MR. JOHN:                              *Song:*

> Misfortune has struck me.
> I am in pain
> My wife is dead.
> My heart is in pain.

Cecilia . . .

CECILIA: Yes, Fo John?

MR. JOHN: You were saying something that I didn't understand very well.

CECILIA: Yes.

MR. JOHN: What did you say?

CECILIA: What?

MR. JOHN: What did you say?

CECILIA: What did I say? I mean what I just told you, what you heard is what I said. I don't know how I can love you more: I helped you, I sent you to Europe, you came back and you had become someone; I can do no more. Adieu . . . *(Exit Cecilia.)*

MR. JOHN:          I have fallen
                   I have no one to pick me up
                   No one wants to help me.

Yes I have no other choice, the best thing to do is to put an end to my days. If I had known what was going to happen, I would have acted differently. But it's too late.

*Music — song:*

If I had known what was going to happen, I would have acted differently . . .

It's not easy to commit suicide, yet I'll do it, I'll do it and I'm not wasting any more time. I'm wasting my time, the only solution is to kill myself. But it's difficult: Can one commit suicide with a cool head? At any rate, it's difficult. It's better to live in suffering than to commit suicide. But I might see her in the streets and meeting Cecilia would double my shame.

The beach is not far from here, it's better to drown myself in the ocean. The rifle might not kill me; yes I might miss and end up in the hospital; and I don't want that.

I'd better go to the beach: I'll go "plunger dans la mer"[93] and everything will be over.

Yes, I'm going to commit suicide alone, let no one follow me. I'll shoot at the first person who tries to follow me. I'm telling you that no one should follow my trail. But I have not a cent to pay my way . . .

Or . . . No, I'm not going to commit suicide, I'll become a vagabond . . .


NOTES

1. *En touche:* to throw the ball out of bounds, from soccer. It is used as a metaphor for dying (cf. to kick the bucket). Notice that, due to the diglossic situation, there are particular domains of activity in which French is mostly used. In school, of course, it is used in the written form; it is used orally in radio commentary on popular sports such as soccer.

2. "Le troisième classe": the third grade. He has used the wrong gender. The correct form would be "la troisième classe."

3. *L'amour:* love.

4. *Besoin:* need.

5. *Certificat:* Primary school certificate.

6. *Passer un concours:* take a competitive exam (to go into the civil service).

7. *Bourse:* scholarship.

8. Youki is the name of a popular non-alcoholic drink. The servant boy is metonymically related to food and drink—he is always hungry and thirsty!

9. *Komora:* a brand of cigarette.

10. *We whites:* In Ewe John is a *yevu,* a white man, because he says he lives like one.

11. *domestic games:* a recurrent figure of speech. The metaphor for having sex takes its elements from sports.

12. UNELCO: a popular supermarket in Lomé.

13. Many French borrowings belong to the domain of the office. *Demande:* application; *sous directeur:* assistant manager; *congés:* leave.

14. *Lettre:* letter.

15. *Leçon de choses:* physics class. *Resumé:* short paper. *Feintes de corps:* dribbles (in football). This is another recurrent figure of speech: the metaphor uses elements of French vocabulary from school as well as from sports for talking about sex. Quotation marks around such words and phrases, as with "taxi" earlier, indicate that they were not translated, unlike the rest of the sentence, which is in Ewe.

16. *L'aviation:* the airport.

17. *Partagement un à un:* Pidgin French meaning "sharing one by one," i.e., one girl for each of us. The verb root is suffixed wrongly with *-ment.*

18. *Bien:* well.

19. Monique starts speaking French (or what the actor playing this part believes is French, marshaling his meager linguistic resources in the language of primary school education). The French dialogue, translated into English, goes:

> Monique: So, now, Mr. John, so, now . . .
> Mr. John: So, now?
> Monique: What does she say?
> Mr. John: She says welcome.
> Monique: Thank you.
> Cecilia: *Welcome, Madame.*
> Monique: Now, Mr. John, she keeps on . . .
> Mr. John: She said "Welcome," I already told you that.
> Monique: So, thank you.
> Cecilia: *How is everybody in Europe?*
> Monique: So, Mr. John?
> Mr. John: Yes?
> Monique: What does she say?
> Mr. John: She says hello.

The rest of the dialogue is self-explanatory.

20. "Good evening, mister."

21. "Excuse me, I am not a mister."

22. "Good evening, young lady."

23. "Buddy, she says that France, Europe . . . " Youki has a lot of trouble finding his words. He claims to speak French and to act as an interpreter, but he can't. Mr. John has to speak French (since he spent twelve years in France!) but the actor playing Mr. John does not have much knowledge of the language either.

24. "So, Mr. John, who is this lady?"

25. "She is my first wife."

26. "O.K." This is more an expression of embarrassment on the actor's part, since he has to find something relevant to say, than a comment on the situation.

27. "What about the boy?"

28. "He is my little brother."

29. *Akpama sauce:* Akpama is boiled ox-skin, sold as a poor man's food. The main taste comes from the spices in the sauce.

30. "Aren't you hungry?" "Yes I am."

31. "Are you going to eat?" "Yes I am."

32. This plays on the homophony between the Ewe expression *wui* (too much) and French *oui* (yes).

33. "Are you quarreling?"

34. *Dzogoli:* Bean dough steamed and pounded, usually eaten with *gari* and palm oil.

35. I am coming right now; I am going to work.

36. Youki is struggling with Pidgin French: "This Europe, has it got big cars?"

37. "She says you are an idiot" (lit. "you have big balls").

38. James Bond was only 007; Youki is one step ahead.

39. "Did the lady want to insult me?"

40. "Certainly not . . . she said well, are there coconut trees in France?" "There are coconut trees in France."

41. "Patron": the boss.

42. "But I don't understand."

43. "If he comes back, say 'Welcome'."

44. *Gbon dzive* in Ewe means literally "the sheep has brought forth two lambs."

45. "Asseyez vous": sit down. *Asevi* in Ewe means "the little cat."

46. "European dance."

47. "Yes, that's what I told you, European dance."

48. "Monique, she said something, she said that it is you, you yourself who said so . . . "

49. "Let her repeat it one more time."

50. "Do you hear now?"

51. "Truly, she means 'Welcome!'."

52. "Monique, what did she say?" "She said 'Sit down'."

53. "Amadji" has only a vague homophonia with *mangeons* (let's eat), and does not mean anything in Ewe.

54. *The one who "damé" you:* neologism derived from the word *madame*, where *dame* is heard as a root verb meaning marry.

55. *Célibatai:* Youki mispronounces *célibataire.* It means a bachelor.

56. *Jeune homme:* young man.

57. "Do as you like."

58. "With the hands" (i.e., Youki's fanning or "ventilation") . . . "I am not feeling well . . . ": here Monique has started to feel very sick; she is on the point of collapse.

59. "What did she put in the food?"

60. "It's hot pepper, isn't it?"

61. "I'm burning, my friend, I'm going to die!"

62. Mr. John: "Are you feeling a bit better?" Monique: "Yes, a little bit."

63. "Pas de temps" means "no time." Never to have time is a white disease. As far as the servant is concerned, his master, John, has been infected while in Europe. Notice that no one seems to care about Monique's illness.

64. "Right now I am going to work, I won't be long."

65. "When are you coming back?"

66. "We always managed to speak French, but Europeans never speak Ewe": a nice comment from Youki! The intended irony is that his sentence is pidgin French with, for instance, complete deletion of articles which are an indispensable feature of spoken and written French.

67.     Mr. John: I'll be back in two minutes.
        Monique: In two minutes?

Mr. John: Yes.
Monique: O.K., that's not long.

68. "Come back soon." Cecilia has already begun to master French!
69. "Now we'll go to the market."
70. The following passage could be translated thus:

Monique: I did not come to do business here.
Cecilia: What?
Monique: I did not come to do business in Togo!
Cecilia: You did not come to do business, but you came to eat in Togo?
Monique: I came to Mr. John's place, didn't I?
Cecilia: You are at his place, Mr. John is . . .
Monique: He is the one feeding me.
Cecilia: The one feeding you! Is he the one going to the market to buy things?
Monique: He gives the money, doesn't he?
Cecilia: He gives the money?
Monique: Yes.
Cecilia: The money will walk to the market by itself . . . The market isn't far, it's only ten kilometers.
Monique: So can't one take a taxi?
Cecilia: Take a taxi . . . Your Daddy (Mr. John) never bought even a bicycle . . .
Monique: So, one can take a horse.
Cecilia: A horse? You have come to Togo, where did you see even two horses?
Monique: You really are having fun, aren't you? [lit. "you are shining"].

Suddenly Cecilia speaks French continuously. The acrimonious tone of the dialogue is striking, despite the obvious limitations in the French linguistic repertoire of the speakers. The African girl from Paris has come to eat in Togo . . . Is eating the mark of power, since we know from the Mufwankolo group in Zaire that "power is eaten whole" (Fabian 1990)?

71. The following passage of dialogue could be translated thus:

Monique: But you say the market is ten kilometers from here.
Cecilia: Before, it was ten, but now it's got less, it's fifteen. [Very rough sense of humour!]
Monique: I am not a horse to walk ten kilometers.
Cecilia: If you are not a horse, stay here, I am going.
Monique: Go and come back. [Syntactically incorrect French construction.]
Cecilia: All right, Monique, I am going.

72. Cecilia goes back to speaking Ewe (English in our translation).
73. "I've a stomach-ache."
74. "Mrs., Mrs., I am dying!" Very erratic conjugation of French verbs!
75. "There are some pills in Mr. John's boxes, aren't there? Some pills . . . "
76. MONIQUE: "Cecilia, Cecilia, I'm dying!" YOUKI: "Oh, you're dying . . . "
77. "The taxis are on strike": an outrageous statement. Strikes were extremely rare under the authoritarian Togolese regime, and taxis are a service that is provided all round the clock. Youki suddenly shows a certain clever nastiness.
78. "A 'ravage' in her purse": He "storms" the purse, stealing a cloth, a handkerchief [*mouchoir*], and a lamp: in all, three [*trois*] items.
79. "Podologie before all." An interesting compound, from *podo* [belly] in Ewe, i.e., the science of the belly (cf. the "politics of the belly," also a Togolese specialty).

80. *Kalala and Tsinambu:* taking food becomes a sport. Kalala and Tsinambu were popular Zairean soccer players.

81. "To the plage": to the beach.

82. D.S.: a luxury Citröen car in the seventies (phonetically similar to "déesse" [goddess]).

83. "S Trois Saisons": notice the play on words, modelled on S GGG (S trois G), which stands for Société Générale du Golfe de Guinée: a popular department store.

84. "The earth has fallen down!"

85. The pastor's name, Akpeteshi, is an Akan word for a drink made from a distillation of palm wine (like *sodabi* in Ewe). It evokes his strong devotion to this drink.

86. The letter to the Corinthians becomes a letter to the Germans, because they were the foreigners who happened to have brought the Bible to Togo.

87. *Sodabi:* spirits made from the distillation of palm wine (*akpeteshi* in Akan languages).

88. *Kalaba:* a kind of clay eaten to compensate for mineral deficiencies.

89. *Akassa:* a kind of pudding made from beans, eaten by the Nagots, i.e., the Ànàgó [the Yorùbá].

90. *Géographie:* Youki, a school-leaver of course, is obsessed with the recitation of lessons. Geography is an important subject in primary school.

91. "Cochon": pig.

92. *To force her "à gauche":* to put her on the bad side, i.e., to kill her.

93. "Throw myself in the ocean" (Lomé has a beach).

# 6

## The Ẹ̀dá Theatre and *The Secret Is Out*

KARIN BARBER

### HISTORY OF THE Ẹ̀DÁ THEATRE GROUP

Like all Yorùbá popular theatre groups, the Ẹ̀dá Theatre is inseparable from its founder, director, and star actor, Lérè Pàímọ́. The history
of his group begins with him.

Lérè Pàímọ́ was born around 1940 in *ilé* Ìkòyí Ọ̀dàn, Ògbómọ́ṣọ̀ọ́. His
father was a tobacco and yam farmer, the leader of the local farmers'
organization. His mother was a trader. Pàímọ́ was sent to primary school
in Ògbómọ́ṣọ̀ọ́, but then left for the Gold Coast with a younger brother
of his mother. This was a common pattern in the 1930s and 1940s in
places like Ògbómọ́ṣọ̀ọ́ which were beyond the northern fringe of the
fertile cocoa belt. He continued his education in the Gold Coast right up
to teacher training college. When he returned to Nigeria he went to
Òṣogbo where he worked as a teacher in a Baptist missionary school,
Newton Memorial School.

Òṣogbo in the 1950s was the seedbed of the extraordinary cultural
flowering that took place in the next two decades. It was here that numerous artists, musicians, and dramatists, including Dúró Ládiípọ̀ [Ladipo],
Oyin Adéjọbí, and Kólá Ògúnmọ́lá, three of the greatest actor-managers
in the history of Yorùbá theatre, established their careers. Lérè Pàímọ́, like
many of the other actors of the time, came to the theatre through his
experience of acting at school. Theatre, he says, was "in his blood." He
took part in school productions, so successfully that up to this day his
family still call him by the names of the characters he played. In about
1960, while working as a teacher at Òṣogbo, he joined Oyin Adéjọbí's
company, which was still an amateur organization performing plays for
the church, schools, and cultural and social clubs. A year later, Dúró
Ládiípọ̀ invited him to come to the Mbari Club—the cultural center

founded by Ulli Beier—to take part in art production. He was interested in painting as well as in theatre, so he accepted the invitation. While at Mbari, Dúró Ládiípò told him about a story he had in mind, which he wanted to turn into a play. They worked together on the production, which became Ọbá Móṛò and which, in 1962, was taken to the University of Ìbàdàn and other big centers. After that they did Ọbá Wàjà and Èdá (for texts, see Ijimere 1966 and Ladipo 1970).

From the beginning, Pàímọ́'s talent as an actor was recognized, and he was given leading roles. In Èdá, a Yorùbá version of Everyman, he played Everyman himself, so memorably that up till today his nickname has remained "Èdá," and his own theatre group is known as the Èdá Theatre Company. Gradually Dúró Ládiípò's company became established as a specialist organization which toured neighboring towns. The actors gave up their other occupations to concentrate full time on theatre work. The company's greatest success was Oba Kò So, based on the legend of the life and death of an early king of Ọyọ́, Ṣàngó, who became the god of thunder and lightning (see Ladipọ 1972). This production, through Ulli Beier's good offices, was taken on tour in 1965 to the Berlin Arts Festival and to the Commonwealth Festival in London, Cardiff, and Glasgow.

Pàímọ́ regards Dúró Ládiípò as a formative influence on his career, and up to this day refers to him as "my boss" (Dúró Ládiípò died in 1978): "I benefited a lot from our collaboration. I learnt a lot. That's where I learnt how to speak eloquently and project my voice, how to dance, how to act with the body, how to sing, how to play traditional drums . . . how to wear cloth." It was Dúró Ládiípò who imbued Pàímọ́ with a sense of "tradition" in theatre, who showed him how to use indigenous arts in the construction of plays:

> Not all theatre groups used Yorùbá instruments or wore Yorùbá cloth. At this time, Ògúnǹdé had been doing his plays for about twenty years. Well, we all started in the same way, by doing Bible stories, but in due course we began to diverge, and we concentrated more on indigenous forms. Ògúnǹdé tended to do plays about what you could call "current affairs" . . . not that he wasn't interested in indigenous themes too, but sometimes characters in his plays would wear coats, and play trumpets and guitars. None of this kind of thing could appear in Dúró Ládiípò's plays. I followed Ládiípò's example.

However, he also took a leaf from Ògúnǹdé's book, in adopting an Ògúnǹdé-style "opening glee" to begin the show—a feature absent from Ládiípò's theatre, but almost universally copied by other theatre companies that were formed during the 1960s and 1970s.

Pàímọ́ stayed with Ládiípò for more than ten years. He became Ládiípò's manager and right-hand man. However, he began to want to set up his own company, and Ládiípò did not want to let him go. Typically of these theatre groups, the company members played the role of sons to the actor-manager father. Although they were paid a salary, their relationship was cemented as much by personal loyalty as by contractual agreement. Every actor-manager strove to keep his stars around him, while every star actor wished sooner or later to become the center of his own organization. As Pàimọ́ put it:

> He just didn't want me to go. But I wanted to set up on my own, to try it for myself, to use my own brain. He did a lot for me. He married a wife for me, he did everything for me. But that's not the same as if I am on my own, thinking things out for myself. He didn't agree to this. I said to myself, If I keep attending to him, he'll say "Just stay another year . . . another year . . . another three years. . . ." That's why I left suddenly, so he'd know I meant it.

That was in 1972. By 1973 Pàimọ́ had established his own theatre company.

These were the boom years when numerous new theatre companies sprang up and old ones went fully professional and commercial for the first time. Pàimọ́ had the advantage of being already well known through his work with Dúró Ládiípò—so much so that aspiring actors had been writing to him offering to join his company even before he founded it. Recruitment was not a problem. Word got around that he was starting his own group, and people flocked to join him. He began with about thirty members—only reducing this number when he realized that it was too expensive and unwieldy for touring. From the beginning, he expected his actors to be full-time professionals, giving up their former jobs and receiving a salary from him. They also began touring right from the beginning.

Since setting up on his own, Pàimọ́ and his company have produced a repertoire of plays including *Ògbórí Ẹlẹ́mọ̀sọ́, Ìdájọ́, Ìrìnàjò Ẹ̀dá, Ayé N Yí, Ayé Gbegẹ́, Gbangbá dẸ̀kùn, Àkúkúù-Bí, Aago Aláago, Gba Díẹ̀,* and *Eré Ògún.* Some of these derived directly from the "traditionalist" style of Dúró Ládiípò, being based on traditional oral narratives and making extensive use of indigenous arts such as drumming, song, and dance. Plays of this type have been kept in the repertoire, and new ones have been added, throughout the life of the company. An example dating from the early 1980s is *Eré Ògún,* a mythological drama about the Yorùbá gods. Others, however, struck a distinctly contemporary note, commenting satirically on such new phenomena as the "been-to," as in *Ayé N Yí (The World Is Changing).* A young man goes to Europe and comes back despising traditional customs: clothes, food, even customary politeness to other people have become "dirty things" in his eyes, and he will not even go to see his own father. He goes and lives by himself. When the Orò festival begins, people tell him not to go out at night, but the young man replies "What Orò? There's no such thing as Orò." He goes out at night when it is taboo, and the Orò spirit blinds him. Another play critically portraying modern mores is *Akúkúùbí*, which shows a son so deracinated that when sent for from abroad because his father is ill says he has no time to come back. Sent for a second time, he says he has no money. Only when he is told that his father has died does he come home to hold a lavish funeral. However, the death is a trick; the father is not really dead, and the "corpse" is only a bundle of cloth. The father appears to the son in the middle of the "funeral" and curses him: "You bastard, useless child, *akúkúùbí*. All the time I was sick you didn't come, but when you thought I was dead you killed a cow. Your own child will do the same for you."

Lérè Pàímó participated fully in the extraordinary creativity and innovativeness of the Yorùbá popular theatre. Like all the first-rate theatre leaders of the 1970s and early 1980s, he introduced not only new themes and styles, but also new theatrical techniques. Unlike Dúró Ládiípò, he used colorful backcloths which were changed from scene to scene, and more elaborate lighting effects. "We can't keep doing what we used to do."

## ORGANIZATION OF THE COMPANY

Lérè Pàímó's Theatre Company was based in Ìbàdàn, and its headquarters was Pàímó's own large house on the old Ìwó road. This is where meetings and rehearsals were held, and where the theatre vehicles, scenery, and other equipment were kept. The members of the company lived in their own houses, but reported to Pàímó's house every day during the weeks when the company was not on the road. The company belonged exclusively to Pàímó. When he recruited his first members in 1973, he already had the equipment he needed to start the company off: the drums, a generator, the cloth used for curtains and scenery. He also provided less tangible capital in the form of plots and ideas for plays. The other members, therefore, all came to him as employees and accepted a salary from him.

In 1988, there were eighteen members, of whom eight were women. Two of the women were Pàímó's wives, the remainder "came from outside," and were neither related to Pàímó nor from the same town. Some of them, however, were married to other men in the company. One problem all theatre companies encountered was opposition from the families of the women they employed. Parents often forbade their daughters to act; and in the case of married women, as Pàímó said, "It's difficult to carry other people's wives about the country." One sure sign of success, often cited by successful actor-managers, was that parents began to allow their daughters to join the company, showing that it was now perceived as a profitable venture rather than as a risky and disreputable one. Despite the difficulties of recruitment, women had been prominent in Lérè Pàímọ́'s company from the beginning.

Companies were held together by interest and loyalty. There was always an inner circle of senior members whose reliability was established and whose ability to carry the core narrative of the play was known. In the Ẹ̀dá Theatre, such core members included Ebenezer Ògúnwọlé, who was one of the people who urged Pàímọ́ to found his own group, and offered to join it when he did. When I talked to him in 1988 he was in his fifties. He had been with Pàímọ́ from the beginning and was completely devoted to the company. Another long-standing member was Ahmed Odùọlá, who served as Pàímọ́'s manager and right-hand man from the time he joined, in 1974, to 1984, when he left to establish his own group. Three women members—Níkèẹ́ Àsùnmọ́ and Pàímọ́'s two wives, Abíọ́lá and Mojí—were also long-standing members. But there were also people who came to see if they liked the life, and stayed only a few months or only weeks before going off to pursue some other occupation. There were those who attended all the rehearsals, but when the time came for the tour they absconded, unwilling to abandon other business in the city.

The committed and long-standing members of the company played a larger role in the running of the company and the creation of plays. They were paid more than the untried newcomers, were assigned the more important parts, and were consulted more in the running of the company. Responsibilities such as lighting, costumes, setting up the scenery and curtains, and so on were divided among the company. There were also musicians and drivers.

When live theatre was at its height in the 1970s, the company went on regular tours for two weeks out of every month. The itinerary would be planned in advance, and the member who served as the "booking manager" would be sent ahead to book the halls and put up posters announcing the time and place of the performance. Up till about 1980, their tours included a large number of boarding schools, which were guaranteed to supply a captive if low-paying audience. Pàímọ́ regarded it as a sign of his success that in the 1980s the general public supported the shows so well that there was no longer any need to go to schools.

Only in big cities would they perform two consecutive nights in the same place. Otherwise, they would move on every day to a new town. Touring involved perpetual traveling. The company would arrive at the place sometime in the afternoon and set up the stage. A party would then go out in the company truck to "parade," that is, drive around the town playing drums and announcing the show over the loudspeaker. Other members of the company would have established a camp behind the scenes. The women often brought their young children with them, whether or not they were needed in the play. Mats would be unrolled, and the women would sleep, cook food, or plait their hair as they waited for evening. Other members might stroll down to the market to see what the town had to offer. Toward evening, the musicians would begin to play—or recorded music would be played—to attract the audience. Undecided members of the public would hang around outside, sometimes dancing to the music, sometimes just waiting to see if there would be a reduction in the price of the tickets if they held out long enough. Much later—sometimes as late as ten or eleven in the evening, depending on how quickly the hall filled up—the "opening glee" of singing and dancing would inaugurate the evening's entertainment. The plays often ran for as much as three hours. In the early hours of the morning, then, the company would dismantle the set, pack the sound and lighting equipment, and establish their sleeping places for the night. It was rare for them to eat into their profits by hiring accommodation. The usual pattern was to sleep at the place where they had performed, either in the lorry or in the hall itself on mats and mattresses. The next morning they would drive on to the next place.

Itineraries were usually planned so that distances from one town to the next were reasonably short. They did not follow fixed routes, but explored new possibilities on every tour, constantly in search of fresh audiences. Someone might have heard that a certain town could provide large audiences, or they might just go because they had never been there before, to see what it was like. Sometimes they received invitations from social clubs around the country—particularly at Christmas time—and they would then build that town into their itinerary. They might also abandon places that they had visited on earlier tours if they heard that the road was no longer good: "Unless they repair the road, we are unlikely to go there again, because it ruins the vehicle."

The background of the theatre company members was typical for the popular theatre. Pàìmọ́ was like several other leading actor-managers, including Kọ́lá Ògúnmọ́lá and Dúró Ládiípọ̀ himself, in having been a schoolteacher before becoming a full-time professional theatre leader. Ebenezer Ògúnwọlé, one of the founding members, had originally trained as a goldsmith; Ahmed Odùọlá had trained as a tailor; Mojí and Abíọ́lá Pàìmọ́ had trained as seamstresses. Thus the actors were of skilled artisanal backgrounds, with at least primary education and sometimes a few years of secondary education, while the leader was better educated and associated with state employment.

Many of the actors said they joined the profession because they loved drama at school. This was Ebenezer Ògúnwọlé's story:

> I am a native of Ìbàdàn. My father was a medicine-man, he used to pluck leaves to make infusions. My mother was an èkọ-seller, she also collected

cocoa leaves and firewood to sell in the town. I was born in a village outside Ìbàdàn, not in the city itself—because all Ìbàdàn people have farms. I went to school in the farm, Wákájayé Christ Apostolic School, but schools in those days didn't go far, Wákájayé didn't go beyond Standard II, which I completed in 1952. After that I worked on the farm. But then my elder brother took me to Lagos to live with him, and I went to the Salvation Army school in Ọdúnlámì Street. My brother was a goldsmith. It was in the goldsmith's shop that I slept, ate and drank. So I came to know more about goldsmithing than people who actually learnt the trade. So when I left school I took it up as my trade. I worked as a goldsmith for five years, and got to the point where I had my own apprentices and was beginning to do well.

But I'd always loved the theatre. I used to go a lot to watch it. I loved it. It wasn't because of money. I just liked it, when I saw people acting I felt like doing it myself. I'd be so happy I would invite the actor and treat him. Whenever I saw Lérè Pàímọ́ I'd say to him, why don't you establish your own group, I'll join you. If you found a company, I'll abandon my other work, I'll be with you. I knew him because I used to see him on stage. I was impressed with his acting; it was I who went to meet him, not the other way round. He is gifted. Everybody would be mobbing him, "Ẹ̀dá, Ẹ̀dá, Ẹ̀dá," but I managed to find a way of getting near to him, to talk to him and move with him.

I joined him in 1973 right at the beginning and have stayed with him ever since. I have never performed with any other group, nor have I done any other work since I joined the company. It's full-time, travelling up and down. And we made a success of it, and got a good reputation. When we go on tour it is sheer pleasure. The public wants to know us, and they see us as the character that each of us is playing. I was Àsàfá, Ahmed was Déntọ́ọ́, and so on. When we arrived people would receive us generously, before the play; some would give us watches, others would give us cloth, or they'd give us so much to drink we could hardly perform in the evening! That's how it was.

Abíọ́lá Pàímọ́, the leading lady, encountered more obstacles:

I grew up in Ìdùnfá-Ìgbọ́rọ́ in Èkìtì. I went to school up to Standard VI before we came to Ìbàdàn in 1953 [?]. The whole family moved to Ìbàdàn. My father worked in the Secretariat, my mother sold dried fish in Dùgbè market. I didn't learn any trade, I worked for my mother for about five years. After that I moved to a relative's house in order to learn sewing, which I did for two years. But I didn't complete the training. Instead, I ran away to join Fúnmiláyọ̀ Ránkò's theatre group. She was from Ilésà; she made acting her profession. I acted with her for about a year and a half. My parents didn't like this, the whole family was against it. They kept coming, whenever I was going to perform, and eventually they caught me and brought me back to Ìbàdàn. But acting wasn't something I could give up. It was in-born, it couldn't be hidden.

I'd always liked drama. Whenever I heard the drums, I'd always wanted to be there, from childhood onwards. I performed at school. From Primary 2 onwards, they'd put me in all sorts of plays, end-of-year plays and so on. I would play the ọba's wife, sometimes I'd play a man, all kinds of roles. It was in my blood. I went to see plays as well—Ògúnǹdé, if they came to our town, Jímọ̀ Àlíyù, Isho Pepper, and so on. I would watch them, before God united them and me.

That is how I met Bàbá [Lérè Pàímọ́]. One day, there was a disturbance near the house where I was staying, my mother's older sister's house. There was a fight and my aunt was injured. So I took her to Adéòyọ́ Hospital and brought her back afterwards. In those days there were not many vehicles on the roads—transport was scarce—so we were going on foot and we passed in front of his house. He was standing upstairs on the balcony. He called "Hello sister," and we greeted each other. He asked where we were going, and I said we're going home but we can't get a taxi. He came down, he went and called his driver, and took us home. That's how it began. That was in 1965 [?]. After I married him my parents accepted that I should be on stage. Now Bàbá knows my father and mother and my whole family. They have accepted it.

## THE CREATION OF A PLAY

Like most Yorùbá popular plays, Lérè Pàímọ́'s were not scripted. The creation of a new play began with the selection of a story. According to Pàímọ́, "We do a lot of research for our stories." Some of the stories he used were drawn from traditional Yorùbá mythology. In these cases, he went to elders with a reputation for historical knowledge in order to get the "true" version from them. The events portrayed in *Eré Ògún*, for instance, "all took place in ancient times before I was born," and he therefore had to rely on narratives passed on to him through oral tradition. Other plays, however, were based on "little stories I'd heard before," a humorous anecdote, a proverb turned into a narrative, a folk tale or an account of something that really happened. *Gbangbá dEkùn (The Secret Is Out)*, according to Pàímọ́, was based on events which really took place in Ìbàdàn during the time that he lived there. Often, the stories were drawn from the rich contemporary subculture of anecdote and recollection, well-formed folk motifs being blended with observations of contemporary urban life among the intermediate classes, and quoted as documents of real experience. For instance:

Ìdájọ́: someone told the story to me. It's about a friend who betrays a friend. They were real friends; they had no money, they were poor. But in due course one of them gets rich. He doesn't forget his friend, he commissions him to build a house for him, and then goes abroad. Before his return, the friend has completed the building of the house and taken up residence in it, claiming it as his own. When the case came before the ọba, the ọba devised a test. He told each of them to carry a coffin to the river and back. Each was to take his wife with him. What they didn't know was that there was someone inside the coffin.

As they were going—you know wives will talk about all kinds of things. So as the treacherous friend was going, his wife said "Don't let that thing [the coffin] drop, you know we're using deception [ìrù] to get prosperity, so carry it [rù] well, don't get tired. . . ." The person inside the coffin was writing it down. It was a true story, it really happened. As the rich man was going, his wife said, "After all, you were doing your friend a good turn, and he's caused you to be tired of doing good turns."

The case came before the elders and they said it's all settled. How? They opened the coffins, the listeners climbed out and read out everything the wives had said on the way. They were astonished. They couldn't deny what they'd said. It had all been written down exactly.

Here a well-established narrative motif (the hidden listeners in the coffins) and problematic (friend betrays friend; women talk) are given a characteristically modern emphasis with the insistence on the veracity and irrefutability of the written word. The theme of the man who has become rich being betrayed by his long-time friend who has remained poor is a theme that has occurred in many other popular plays including one by the Adéjọbí Theatre Company, *Lániyọnu* (see Barber and Ògúndíjọ 1994). The theme of house-building, both as a sign and as a source of wealth, also recurs frequently, in *Gbangbá dEkùn* among other plays. Thus a thick soup of allusion, memory, and habit is poured into a plot that is felt to be nonetheless a reflection of real experience: a narratized experience shared by a whole popular culture.

Sometimes, when he was ready to create a new play, Lérè Pàímọ́ called a meeting of the company and asked for ideas. Anyone who had come across a good story would contribute it. Stories were selected either because they preserved Yorùbá traditions or "because they have a strong central point, a moral which people can learn from, such as 'don't steal', 'don't be promiscuous', 'don't be cruel'." To the core narrative demonstrating this lesson, the director and actors added other materials to build it up into a full-blown drama. "Sometimes I'll ask them to make suggestions. They may add things or take things out. I ask their advice and write it down, showing what each character will say—but only the gist." This written plot synopsis had symbolic if not practical importance in the creation of the play, and Pàímọ́ insisted, "Every one of my plays exists in a written form: without exception, from the beginning, I've written every one of them down."

The actual realization of the play in action and dialogue, however, was developed orally, in rehearsal, through trial and error. The director and his manager took the main responsibility for working it out. They often had a clear idea of sequences of speech and events, to the extent that they could instruct actors step by step in the creation of their parts. They did this most often for newcomers, as a form of training. Once an actor had become experienced, he or she was expected to know how to play a part without much instruction. From his or her repertoire of skills and characterization, s/he drew a suitable personality, contributing to the substance of the play as well as fitting into the director's guidelines. "When we start 'practising' [rehearsing], everyone can add to their own part." Actors, especially the well-established and experienced ones, tended to have a composite stage personality on which they drew for their various parts, all of which had something in common. Pàímó himself, for example, specialized in strong, tough characters. "I don't like parts where I have to sit in state like an oba—I like parts where they fight me, drive me into the river . . . When other companies are making films, they know the parts I can do well." He also had a flair for comedy which was an original contribution to the work of the Dúró Ládiípò company, not otherwise noted for its humor. Ebenezer Ògúnwọlé described the continuity between his own various stage presences in the following terms:

> I was Àsàfá . . . it was a character in Ìrìnàjò Èdá, friend of Everyman. We did another play that had Àsàfá in it—Ìdájọ́. It was the same Àsàfá, the same character. In all the plays we did, they kept the part of Àsàfá, with the same behaviour. In Ògbóri Elémòsó, which was about the traditional history of Ògbómósòó, he [i.e., Àsàfá] was the Elémòsó . . . then this name almost eclipsed Àsàfá. Everybody knew me as Elémòsó. Elémòsó was also a trouble-maker, a bad-tempered person; he quarrelled with everyone in the town, he disturbed everyone, he looked for trouble, he didn't live in the middle of town amongst people, he caused disturbances, he killed people's children and their animals, he drove them from the farm path and the river path, blocked them into their houses and into their farms.

As Ògúnwọlé's comments made clear, he thought of his roles in terms of an overall mood or *Gestalt* rather than in terms of their specific location and function within the plot. Thus the character in Ìdájọ́, a contemporary parable, was "the same Àsàfá" as the friend of Everyman in the adaptation of a medieval morality play. The Elémòsó in the historical drama Ògbóri Elémòsó was essentially the same personality as Àsàfá, though perhaps even more compelling in realization, to the extent that the audience, which had hitherto hailed all his roles as Àsàfá, now began to hail them as variants of Elémòsó. Michael Etherton has commented on the way this semi-fictional persona of the star actor shapes his future roles (Etherton 1982: 42–44). The audience hailed the actor, as he walked onto the stage but also when they met him on the street, by the name of his dominant role. He responded by living up to their expectations. This consolidation of an area of specialization was encouraged further by the method of production. The director and manager knew what parts their actors were good at, and continued to assign roles to them that allowed them to mine the seam. Once an actor was experienced, he would often be left to create his own performance out of his established fund of characterization skills.

The ability to project such a composite character/personality was seen by Ògúnwọlé as both a gift and an acquired skill. A good performer must have a command of song, dance, and "deep Yorùbá" which are both *àbímọ́* [inborn] and *àbùdá* [learned, acquired during upbringing]. The creation of a play draws simultaneously on spontaneous talent and conscious planning:

> When an actor is creating a part, it's in the blood, he won't have to sit and think. It will just come to him. Only the Boss will set time aside, go into his room, lock his door, stay up all night, to get the materials for the play together, and fit things so that the parts will suit the actors. We don't have to do anything except be the character—and that's an innate gift.

The operation of the actor's "innate gift" has to be developed through the application of "thought" and "intelligence" in the creation of a role:

> . . . we make additions. In my case, I think up a song that will suit the action, I write it down, and when they play the music I'll dance to it. For instance, in Ẹ̀dá, when Ẹ̀dá and his wife are quarrelling, we'll admonish the husband, he won't listen, we'll speak to the wife, she'll turn a deaf ear. Then I'll burst into song:
>
> > Two Afọfun married to each other
> > A feeble husband, a stupid wife
> > Two Afọfun married to each other!
>
> They'll drum it, we'll dance, then I'll be leaving and they'll call me back and ask me to make peace between them. The way it fits in—that takes thought and intelligence.

Ògúnwọlé laid much emphasis on the theatre as a professional skill. A bad play is one that gives the audience the opportunity to pass comments:

> "Oh, what's this one doing like that for?" So that someone who's not a player would be able to mount up upon the mistakes of a player! Saying "Have they just hired this one, or why is he doing like that?" "Speak up!" and so on—it's not good. "And you, you're not laughing when you're supposed to!" That someone who hasn't learnt the trade should be correcting someone who has—all that kind of thing. It depends on how intelligent each individual actor is.

Actors did not speak of observation of behavior as part of their preparation for a role. While plots and themes were assiduously collected from the environment and felt to come from "real experience," characterization was treated more as something that came from within, but which also took on a life of its own. Performance seemed to be seen not as mimesis so much as the bringing into being of a personality the potential for which already existed within the actor. In this representation of the creative process, there is a sophisticated and flexible balance between ideas of the planned and the spontaneous, the dispositional and the contrived, the innate and the learned. Each actor was conscious of his or her contribution to the whole, while deferring to the greater thought and larger view of the director. Even a seasoned actor may need teaching, as Abíólá Pàímó pointed out: "The boss knows everybody's talents, and plans the play accordingly. It's not just when we practise, he knows in advance. Anyone who is not up to scratch, he'll teach them again. It can happen even to me. If he tells me, then I'll work on it until it's good."

A thoroughly seasoned team works so well together that nothing goes to waste. Pàímó explained that in the early days, it used to take them a month of "practising" to mount a new play. By the time I met them in the 1980s, however, they could produce one in a week. Plays were rarely completely abandoned, even though new ones were periodically introduced. Pàímó liked to have several plays available in his repertoire on any given tour, though a new play would be performed much more often than one that most people had already seen.

## ACTORS' ASPIRATIONS AND REFLECTIONS ON THE LIFE OF THE THEATRE

Reflecting on their experiences in the theatre, the performers combined two idioms. The first time I talked to Lérè Pàímó, he told me:

> Theatre has always existed amongst us: our ancestors drummed, sang and danced; they entertained people at naming ceremonies, house-openings and family gatherings, and all kinds of meetings. Funerals, weddings, and so on would take place continually. And when we became more enlightened, these kind of [theatre companies] came into being, often founded by highly educated people. We are very glad when we come across people who will convince others that our work is worthwhile, valuable, respectable and beneficial. We've seen lots of books that have been written about other kinds of work, so ours should be covered too. We need someone to convince people that we do theatre work not because we are out of a job, but because we have chosen to do it. Above all, we don't want our traditional customs to fade out. The traditions of Yorùbáland. That's all.

Here, Pàímọ́ stressed that the modern traveling theatre was the product of "enlightenment," associated with Christianity, school education, and modernity. He insisted that the new forms of theatrical entertainment were often run by "highly educated people," and he was anxious that their work should be recognized, in the official sphere, by other highly educated people. He was keen to recruit me in this struggle for recognition; I was to help persuade other educated people that the theatre belonged in their sphere by writing a book about it. The aspect of the theatre stressed in this speech is its value as a preserver of *àṣà ìbílẹ̀* (traditional customs): a phrase which apparently came into circulation at the same time as the notion of a pan-Yorùbá identity, in the second half of the nineteenth century. It speaks of a position of some detachment from the cultural practices it seeks to preserve and valorize in the face of colonial encroachments. The emphasis on education, enlightenment, a pan-Yorùbá identity, and the value of traditional culture all go together and form a recognizable and pervasive cluster of ideas, originally put into circulation by the educated élite, but quickly adopted and reinterpreted by the "intermediate classes" that patronized the popular theatre, popular press, and popular music. The mystique of literacy, already alluded to, is thus part of a larger image of the theatre as a modern, progressive, educational force, a respectable profession to which people are called much as they may consider themselves called to the church or to teaching or medicine. Only Lérè Pàímọ́ expressed these ideas in full; but Abíọ́lá Pàímọ́ emphasized that she came from a Christian family and that the plays teach moral lessons; Ahmed Odùọlá, like Pàímọ́, spoke of "writing" his plays; and Ebenezer Ògúnwọlé, even while giving a vivid account of how the plays grow through collaborative improvisation, insisted with fervent admiration on the image of the boss as lonely author who will "go into his room, lock his door, and stay up all night" to write a play.

Other actors endorsed the ideal of a profession in the modern, educated sector without asserting that the popular theatre in fact belonged to it. Mojí Pàímọ́, for instance, said that she had no other work than acting, and did not ever want to do anything else. However, although her children were good actors, she did not want them to go into the theatre; she wanted them to go through higher education and then become doctors and lawyers.

But the idiom of enlightenment and education was not the dominant one in performers' discussions of their work. Much more salient was the discourse of travel, trade, and networks of personal contacts. Lérè Pàímọ́ said that the great advantage of the stage, as opposed to television and film, was that "you get to know towns all over the place, mix with all kinds of people, buy things that aren't available here. You tour all around, that's the advantage. All kinds of food, clothes, utensils—we'll buy them. Sometimes, we find things to buy for use as stage props in faraway places." Touring involved going out, making profitable contacts, and coming back to base with something special acquired on the journey. This could be either a purchased object or some kind of social knowledge—knowledge of "all kinds of people" and their knowledge of you. Social knowledge is the basis of social success. If you know people and are known by them, you can operate successfully. Pàímọ́ gave the following example of the advantages of being known:

> People know you. If you're asking for something, you can go—people will recognise you. For example, there's a boy here now, I took him to the Poly[technic], for them to give him a place. It's not that his papers weren't good—all the same, though, it was a matter of them "seeing someone." If I approach four people, about three of them will say "Ah! So-and-so!" That's one of the advantages of our work.

Just as traveling enabled the theatre people to buy special things which they could use as props in their plays to enhance their glamour, so appearing on stage in many different towns made actors socially visible in ways that benefited their lives outside the theatre. There was a cycle of reinvestment: more visibility meant more social success, more social success meant further visibility.

If travel was seen as the heart and soul of the theatrical life, trouble with transport was its bane. Ahmed Odùọlá, speaking of the difficulties of starting his own company, said,

> We haven't yet got all the equipment, that's what's difficult. We did try to buy a vehicle, but it began to give problems before we'd finished paying for it. That's what's hard: if you have one, it gives problems, but if you don't have one, that's a problem too. But to have equipment, without any debts or problems—that's when it's good. But there's never any end to needing things.

As well as a vehicle, the theatre company needed "instruments": props, costumes, musical instruments, stage scenery, microphones, sound system, loudspeaker, lights, and generator. All these things had to be bought, and almost all were imported goods. Without them, a play was not regarded as complete, or even feasible. The theatre was thus in a sense a setting for a display of things "brought back," whether literally or metaphorically, from networks of contacts beyond the immediate locality. The theatre companies' constant touring was an economic necessity. No single town would yield audiences enough to support a theatre company for more than a few nights a year. But the stress they laid on the joys and advantages of travel, of "knowing people" and of "bringing things back" shows that touring appealed to a deep sense of what made life satisfying. While deeply attached to locality, what makes life worth living is the capacity to extend beyond a local base into constellations and networks of other localities, in the process establishing profitable contacts, becoming known, and bringing things back.

All the theatre practitioners said their greatest ambition was to make a film. The way they described it confirms that travel does not mean the actual pleasures of the open road. Many actors, in fact, found touring exhausting. Being in a film lessened that hardship, because "once you get to the place, you don't need to set up the stage or get up and perform; you just show the film and move on." But more significantly, "film can go further—from one country to another—because we've heard about Ògúnṅdé films with subtitles being shown in Europe." Film, then, constituted the ultimate in travel. The performer could extend his visibility right overseas, throwing out a potentiality for knowing and being known into regions he had never entered. Film, therefore, like television, "advertises you better" than stage performances. The metaphorical, as well as actual, conjunction between traveling and the establishment of the self in the public eye could not be clearer.

The two idioms—that of enlightenment and that of travel—are clearly linked, for enlightenment itself is one of the things people acquire and bring back to their community. This may be the way to understand how the popular theatre, so conscious of its own modernity and its distinctness from masquerading and other traditional forms of spectacle, nonetheless was so comfortable with the older idioms and assumptions of the uneducated people who made up the bulk of its audience. Enlightenment and modernity, as acquisitions brought back by traveling entrepreneurs, fitted into the patterns of an ancient trading culture.

### THE SECRET IS OUT

The performance of the play that this translation was made from took place in the Palace Hotel, Òkukù, on 23 December 1981. This was a busy time for all the theatre companies, as farmers and traders returned to their home towns for Christmas celebrations and social clubs invited groups to give command performances. The Palace Hotel in Òkukù was a normal family compound, built of earth in a rectangular courtyard shape, which the owner had decided to turn into a bar and eating place run by himself and his two wives, who continued to live there. It was on the outskirts of the town, but since Òkukù is small, it was within easy walking distance for everyone. The theatre company arrived in the afternoon and began to set up the scenery along one side of the courtyard,

*The Èdá Theatre: Wúrà and Asíndẹ at home. Photograph © Elio Montanari. Used by permission.*

making use of the slightly raised concrete platform that ran right around it. The backcloth and curtains were rigged up by suspending them from the end walls of the courtyard, and the standing scenery was then put in place, along with the powerful sound system. Around seven o'clock at night, as it got dark, the company members began to play the drums and clusters of children began to gather outside the entrance. They hung around for a long time, perhaps hoping that the ticket price would be lowered if they held out long enough. Meanwhile over the next few hours adults and older school pupils gradually arrived and took their seats on the rows of chairs and benches inside, in the open-air space in front of the stage. The drumming, alternating with popular recorded music, continued until about eleven, when the play finally started.

The audience was fairly small, but it filled up the Palace Hotel's courtyard. The people who came were predominantly young, but—either be-

*The Ẹ̀dá Theatre: Fosko (Lérè Pàímó) in his hunter's gear.
Photograph © Elio Montanari. Used by permission.*

cause it was Christmas, or because the Palace Hotel belongs to a nephew of the late ọba—there was a more "respectable" atmosphere, with more adult women and salaried workers (for instance, teachers, bank clerks, and local government workers) than in many popular theatre audiences. Though they made continual loud comments and laughed a lot, they were attentive.

People I talked to afterwards all insisted that what they liked most about the play was the valuable "lessons" it taught. John Àgbéyẹyè, a farmer from Ilé Olúawo Oníṣeègùn in Òkukù, expressed this vividly when he said:

> Yesterday's play was wonderful. It wasn't actually "play," because its purpose was to impart a lesson. Because if you're really intelligent, really smart, well, the wisdom that you can manage to pick out of that play is

no joke. Somebody who isn't intelligent will just watch it vacuously, and laugh. But the whole evening I just kept quiet, I watched the play, because I found wisdom to pluck from it.

In discussions afterwards, people took the "lessons" of the play to heart, seeking ways to expand them and apply them by relating them to anecdotes of their own experience and observation. Several of them remarked that what the play portrayed was true to life: that the events it depicted were exactly what was happening nowadays, and that times were changing for the worse. The play, clearly, captured a vision of contemporary moral crisis which the audience recognized, and offered a solution which they warmly endorsed.

*The Secret Is Out* shows a beautiful but spoiled and discontented woman, Wúrà, leaving her wealthy, good and generous husband, Asíndẹ, for another man: an admirer who wears magnificent robes, spends money freely, and boasts of being far richer even than Asíndẹ. But the man is revealed in the next scene as the robber-chief Fosko, dressed in hunter's gear and in charge of a gang of thieves. On his orders, Wúrà is robbed and driven away when she arrives to take up residence as his new wife. Meanwhile Fosko and his gang, disguised as Aládùúrà preachers, have visited Asíndẹ's house and taken an impression of his keys under cover of a prayer session, with the intention of coming back to burgle the house. But one of the assistant robbers is a novice, Adéntòọ́, who reveals that he only joined the gang because he was destitute and Fosko offered him work. The other two assistant robbers—nicknamed Oríejò (Snakehead) and Rẹ̀sònà (Rexona, a popular brand of soap)—persecute, cheat, and abuse Adéntòọ́ until he decides to run away.

On the day that the robbery of Asíndẹ's house is planned, Adéntòọ́ slips off—taking some of Fosko's magical war-charms with him—and goes to the sacred grove where the townspeople are celebrating their traditional Elékóto festival in honor of youth and fertility. There the priest and priestess, surrounded by devotees ritually dressed in white, are presiding over the performance of cult songs and ceremonies associated with purity and honesty. Meanwhile the townspeople bring in reports of an ever-increasing spate of robberies and beg Olúọde, the head of the hunters, who is also the chief priest at the festival, to help them. At this point Adéntòọ́—who now turns out to be the son of a respected traditional chief himself—breaks the news of the planned robbery of Asíndẹ. Olúọde, Adéntòọ́, and other townspeople go to Asíndẹ's house to lie in wait for the robbers, and there follows a pitched battle of a type very common in popular Yorùbá theatre, where the principal weapons are incantations and charms. After a long, dramatic struggle, Adéntòọ́ and Olúọde between them overcome the robbers, even Fosko who remains defiant to the last.

Wúrà appears on the scene, dejected and in rags. Asíndẹ tells his rescuers her story, and Adéǹtọ́ọ́ lectures her and the world at large on the consequences of running after riches without first asking about their origin.

In this narrative, two characters or groups of characters err and are punished: Wúrà, who leaves her kind and generous husband to run off with an apparently more glamorous stranger; and Fosko and his gang, who live by robbery and trickery and who are eventually brought down by communal forces of righteousness. The audience perceived two main "lessons," one drawn from each of these narrative outcomes; but they also linked the two in an overall diagnosis of the ills of modern society.

Several people, commenting on Wúrà's story, observed that it held an important message for women. Wúrà makes a foolish choice, arising from her own greed, discontent, and impatience. She chooses ill-gotten wealth—because it is offered by a flashy, ostentatious character—over honestly acquired wealth offered by her mild, unassuming, but generous husband. She is punished for this the very moment she leaves her husband for Fosko, and ends up in poverty, without the benefit of either man's house and money. The men in the audience stressed this lesson particularly. Mr. G. A. Akíndélé, the chairman of the Odò-Ọ̀tìn District Council and a retired primary headmaster, expounded it with great fervor:

> The lessons that this play of Lérè Pàímọ́'s teaches us are extremely important. Especially for you wives of ours. You should purge yourselves of greed, you should purge yourselves of discontentment in your marriages, those are the things that lead you astray, that make you lead a bad life, and end in destruction. May God not let us come to destruction, amen.

He was particularly critical of Wúrà for being attracted by Fosko's superficial and deceptive glamour instead of showing gratitude for her husband's real generosity:

> He [Asíndẹ] was a rich man who did his utmost to please his wife. There was nothing he didn't do for her, he bought cloth for her, even a car, he bought a car for her, like the passenger car he drove himself, but all the same, because he wasn't flamboyant, and didn't change his clothes like a chameleon, this woman—she liked display, anything flashy or glittery—but this man, this robber baron, he deceived this woman: he told her to look at the clothes he wore, the cars he owned, he said he had a Mercedes and a Peugeot, he was terribly arrogant, to the point that he turned this woman's head, and she insisted on moving to his house.

Mr. Gbénga Adébíyìí, who worked at the National Bank of Nigeria, stressed Wúrà's insatiable greed for money: "The play teaches women to be contented in their husbands' houses, and not to run after outsiders who are prepared to spend a lot of money to attract their love. Love of money leads to regrets—that's what this play teaches women." Mr. Samuel Agboọlá, a local government worker, put it slightly differently: "Women shouldn't try to use their beauty to obtain instant riches."

These reflections on the lesson imparted by Wúrà's story show that it is inseparable from the lesson imparted by Fosko's. Fosko's story teaches us that ill-gotten wealth brings retribution. The continuity between the two is especially clear in the interpretations offered by women members of the audience, who understandably were not so keen to dwell on the importance of contentment in one's husband's house, and more interested in linking Wúrà's greed with the broader theme of illicit gain, exemplified by Fosko. Mrs. Bísí Adésóyè, a teacher, agreed that the play taught women that they should be contented with what their husbands could provide, but quickly went on to develop the theme as follows: "It teaches us that we shouldn't be impressed with big spenders, because we don't know where their money came from. Before you run after a man, you should investigate him and the work he does."

Mrs. Rebecca Akíndélé, a trader, having summarized Wúrà's story, concluded with a general observation that applies equally to men and women: "People should not be envious of each other; you should be content with what you've got, and be satisfied with it, as what belongs to you, and may God not allow other people's possessions to fill us with desire more than our own, amen."

Even when I asked whether she thought that there were many greedy and ungrateful women like Wúrà around, she continued to speak in general terms—indeed, her answer seems more applicable to the robbers than to Wúrà:

> They are many. The reason why they are many nowadays is that everyone is going after other people's property, they are not going after property that they have gained by their own hard work. People like us who have worked as hard as we have and got where we have today, if we'd been going after other people's property, we'd have—by now I too would have got four, five, six cars. But someone who waits for the fruits of his labour, if God wants that person to ride in a car, there is nothing to stop them riding it modestly about, there's nothing to stop them, provided they trust in God, and trust in their own hard work, and invest the money they earn to bring in more work, money will come! . . . But if a person takes shortcuts, if a person uses magical commands to get money, there's nothing to prevent it from vanishing. When it's not earned by the sweat of your brow.

In this statement, Mrs. Akíndélé moves from Wúrà's greed and impatience to what she sees as a general malaise of present-day society, in which everyone is taking shortcuts to get rich quick instead of working hard and waiting for God to reward them in his own good time. She affirms that patience and hard work will be solidly rewarded, while ill-gotten wealth is not to be trusted. Other members of the audience shared Mrs. Akíndélé's disapproval of contemporary "money love." Mr. Agboọlá developed the theme of greed as follows:

> They're running after instant riches, they don't want to work, they don't want to wait—with the idea that you prepare, you cook the soup, you make the fire, and only after that do you eat—they don't want that at all, they want to eat ready-cooked soup nowadays. In the world of today, the "enlightenment" that has arrived, there doesn't seem to be anyone who wants to do more than just start riding a car straight off—as soon as they start off, they want to have a car, they want to show off in a 504, that's what's destroying them. . . .

These commentaries seized on what I also perceived as the principal theme of the play: the distinction between well-gotten wealth, acquired by hard work, and ill-gotten wealth, acquired by fraud, robbery, or magic. I thought the play worked this distinction out in great detail. Asíndẹ is a good rich man who came by his wealth honestly and remains modest and generous. He is rich on a grand scale; he has already built fourteen houses, and Fosko comments sourly, "Asíndẹ has money all right. He's building houses like mad. He's building houses like a nesting ant." Though he wears lace and damask on stage, he is supposed to be too busy to worry about dressing up for social occasions, to the chagrin of his wife. Asíndẹ himself points out that earning money is not easy: "Don't you know that my work gives me a lot of trouble? Think of the day I went to supervise that building, remember what time I got home!" He is generous and trusting; when Wúrà pesters and criticizes him, he does not take offense but instead gives her everything she asks for, even a car; he presents the keys to her a few minutes before she walks out on him. To steal from a man like this would be the act of a mean, envious, vindictive person. The play stresses that Asíndẹ doesn't deserve such treatment: for example, when Adéǹtòọ́ breaks the news of the robbers' plans to burgle Asíndẹ's house, the townspeople feel the injustice keenly, commenting, "What! That nice Mr. Asíndẹ, what have they got against him?" "They said he's rich," explains Adéǹtòọ́. "Oh, the world is hard," say the townspeople.

Asíndẹ is contrasted explicitly with Fosko, the possessor of illegitimate and baseless wealth. Fosko wears magnificent clothes to dazzle Wúrà. She complains that her husband never dresses up to go out, and Fosko replies, "He's not a chameleon like me, always changing colors," and later boasts: "I wear all kinds of clothes, I drive all kinds of different cars, I'm well respected by the public." He is a parody of the kind of wealthy man that

The Èdá Theatre: Wúrà and Rẹ́sọ̀nà. Photograph © Elio Montanari. Used by permission.

Wúrà wants to be associated with, because of course his remarks are ironical. He "wears all kinds of clothes" when he dons different disguises to trick his victims, appearing successively as a fine man-about-town, a soldier, and a preacher. He presents the appearance of being even more magnificently generous than Asíndẹ, brushing aside Wúrà's thanks for a lavish gift of money with the words "How many hundred [naira] did I give you when we went out? After all, when we walk, we stumble and we drop a few coins"—meaning that to him, the gift of hundreds of naira was like dropping some small change from his pocket. But Fosko's generosity, like the money itself, is obviously a fake, paraded only to deceive his victims. His wealth is a fake in another sense too. Because it is based on rotten foundations, it cannot last; instead, it will bring down inevitable destruction on the owner. There are hints that Fosko is much less wealthy than he pretends. Despite his claim that he "drives all kinds of different cars," when Ṛẹ́sọ̀nà goes to collect Wúrà's luggage she has to go on foot, pretending that she has parked the van around the corner. If Fosko is living on borrowed time, it appears that it is already running out.

The key opposition between well-founded and ill-founded wealth seemed to me to be supported by two other equally explicit contrasts. Real work is contrasted with fake work. Asíndẹ is an honest, diligent man, always busy about his houses. But Fosko and his gang are engaged in a parody of work. Great play is made with this notion in the scenes set in the robbers' headquarters. Adéǹtọ́ọ́ is an "apprentice" who has to be "trained" before he can be "promoted." After he has been beaten up by a man whose pocket he tried to pick, Adéǹtọ́ọ́ complains, "This work of ours is hard." Fosko agrees: "Yes, it's a hard kind of work. It's hard. But lucrative work is never easy." The positive values associated with *iṣẹ́* (work) and *owó* (money)—and their conjunction in the popular slogan "Work to have money"—are here mocked by the robbers, who are doing fake work and getting fake wealth.

In addition, real, traditional medicine is contrasted with dubious medicine acquired by purchase. Although there is no explicit reference to money-medicine in *The Secret Is Out,* charms and medicine are part of Fosko's stock-in-trade as a robber and swindler. As he boasts, "He [Asíndẹ] is not as important as I am. . . . I've got money; I've got medicine; I've got status." Medicine, then, is an essential aspect of his power. But in the final confrontation, the young novice Adéǹtọ́ọ́ overcomes Fosko's medicine with his own. This is partly because, before he left the robber's headquarters, he stole Fosko's most powerful secret charm. But there is more to it than that. As Adéǹtọ́ọ́ points out, "You bought yours, I inherited mine." Time-honored medicines inherited from a powerful father are stronger than concoctions bought from strangers. Inherited medicine, it is suggested, has an intrinsic fidelity to its owner. During their struggle, Fosko tries to seize Adéǹtọ́ọ́'s jùjú, and Adéǹtọ́ọ́ says contemptuously "You can have it—it's mine," meaning that because it has an inner relationship with himself it cannot be used against him; instead, it will turn on whoever tries to take it over. The charm that he stole from Fosko, on the other hand, does not appear to have that property: it does not help Fosko at all. Just as money obtained fraudulently will not stay with you, so medicine acquired through a slippery and impermanent commercial relationship will not be faithful to you, but will work for whoever gets their hands on it; by contrast, money acquired through bodily effort, and medicine passed down from the father whose body engendered yours, will stay at your side.

Adéǹtọ́ọ́'s medicine is associated with the values set up in the religious shrine scene: they are traditional, inherited, rooted in a past where people were pure in heart and feared to transgress the laws of the òrìṣà, and therefore they are effective. Fosko's medicine, "got with money," may temporarily dazzle, but in the long run it is only a reflection of his own bravado, not of real power.

Thus well-founded wealth, real work, and inherited medicine are contrasted with ill-founded wealth, fake work, and bought medicine. Wealth acquired by fake work unsupported by community and tradition is a mirage pursued by the modern world; it can only lead to shame and destruction. Wúrà's mistake, which led to her downfall, was—as Mrs. Adésóyè pointed out—that *she did not inquire first* into the origins of Fosko's wealth before running after him. She failed to distinguish between solid and illusory wealth.

So the play shows a good rich man being rescued from a bad rich man by the forces of traditional morality. It is interesting to note, however, the dramatic treatment of the actual agent of his rescue. Initially an innocent *poor* man, extreme destitution drove Adéǹtòọ́ to join the robber gang. At this stage he is presented as a bit of a clown and a scallywag, but still an endearing character. But once he reaches the sacred grove, he becomes *omọ* Jagun, the respected son of the late chief Jagun (a warrior or hunting title). It is Adéǹtòọ́ who leads the rescue operation, and it is he who represents the authority of traditional morality at the end, when he executes the robbers and lectures Wúrà on the error of her ways. The issue of his poverty is simply dropped, and it is clear that it was introduced only as a mechanism to get an innocent insider into the gang in order that it can be betrayed. The play is not at all concerned with the condition of the destitute or with the moral problem of the poor man driven to crime. As soon as is convenient, the character of Adéǹtòọ́ is simply *rewritten* in such a way that it would be inappropriate to ask whether he managed to overcome his poverty, or whether he was ever brought to justice for his implication in crime. (It is interesting to note, however, that some members of the audience did have strong views on Adéǹtòọ́'s character. Mr. Akíndélé saw him as the embodiment of the lesson that repentance and reform are good. John Agbéyeyè, more skeptically, said, "Once a thief, always a thief," and maintained that a person driven to crime by poverty cannot be forgiven on that account, for theft is theft, whatever the reason for it.) The play itself, though, appears not to be very interested in the moral problems concerning crime and poverty; it concentrates on the distinction between good and bad *wealth*.

However, both in the play itself and in the reactions of the audience, there are strong indications that the interpretation of modern wealth proposed by the play is not fully realizable. Within the play itself, there is a curious weakness in the representation of the good wealthy man Asínde. For the contrast between good wealth and bad wealth to succeed, his wealth would have to be justified by evidence of his capacity for vigorous hard work: but he appears feeble and insubstantial beside Fosko. This is only partly because the role of Fosko is played by the star, Lérè Pàímọ́ himself, and —like Satan in *Paradise Lost* —is far more exciting dramatically than the role of the good character. It is also —perhaps mainly —because of the inability of the text to specify where Asíndẹ's wealth really came from. Asíndẹ apparently builds houses, and he talks of the immense trouble and effort his work requires. But what does he actually do on his building sites? He is never seen working. He always appears wearing expensive and immaculate robes of damask, lace, or hand-woven linen; he talks vaguely to his contractor—to whom he gives 2,000 naira with only the most cursory inquiry into its intended use—and stays at home until the late afternoon. The rich man's stereotypical representation is flowing robes of immaculate white and a cool, languid, even limp manner, denoting precisely the absence of arduous physical effort. How could this fabulously wealthy figure be represented as an honest toiler? The text cannot speak of the real foundation of "honest" wealth. Indeed, in his closing remarks, speaking as himself, Lérè Pàímọ́ acknowledges, obliquely, that no great wealth can be regarded as good wealth: there is no such thing. He says:

> If you see people building one house after another, buying more land every day, [remember that] at the root of riches is a shameful secret. Don't you go that way, let us wait our turn, the good things of life that are due to us will not pass us by, God willing. . . . They may shine [with wealth] every day; by the power of God, we too will be blessed in our time.

Though he is reaffirming the lesson that one should not envy the rich or attempt to take shortcuts in acquiring one's own wealth, his formulation is very strikingly undermined from within. The proverb he quotes, "At the root of riches is a shameful secret," applies to *all* wealth. It claims that there is no good wealth, despite the play's attempt to demonstrate the contrary. Even more significant is the phrase that leads up to the proverb, "If you see people building one house after another, buying more land every day. . . ." After all, it is Asíndẹ, the representative of good wealth, who builds houses every day, not Fosko. The proverb seems to be directed at him.

This contrary subtext was clearly endorsed by the audience. At the point when Asíndẹ asserts, in the face of Wúrà's nagging, that he has to work terribly hard at his house building—"Don't you know that my work gives me a lot of trouble . . . ?"—Mrs. Akíndélé, who was sitting next to me, said with good-humored scorn, "What trouble does *he* have to go to?" When Asíndẹ returns from his visit to the houses he is building, in scene 3, someone else in the audience greeted him ironically, "Greetings for the trouble of making money." The opening of the last scene, where Asíndẹ, ignorant of the huge battle about to take place on his doorstep, complains fretfully about a malfunctioning air conditioner—as if this were the worst trouble he ever had to encounter—drew loud laughter from the audience. One woman commented, "It's because his wife has left him [that's why his domestic arrangements are breaking down]." His generosity to Wúrà, similarly, drew contemptuous comments.

Commentaries from people in the audience confirmed this interpretation explicitly. John Agbéyeyè picked out the proverb "At the root of riches is a shameful secret" as the central message of the play, and like Lérè Pàímó cited prolific housebuilding as the prime example of excessive, unnatural wealth:

> You see, the play shows modern behaviour exactly as it is. You'll see people building one house after another, houses with three storeys, and wearing all kinds of sumptuous cloth, and you who have worked and worked and worked and haven't got a penny, you might think "Ha! wasn't this person born the same way I was, how come oceans of money just flow to him like that"—you won't know that it's through robbery, he waylays people on the road, takes things from people who have little enough in the first place, that's how he's risen in the world. That's the meaning of the play last night. Because it taught us that "At the root of riches is a shameful secret." "At the root of riches is a shameful secret"—that was the title of the play, and it's true. That's it.

Mrs. Akíndélé was of the opinion that most wealthy people today get their money illicitly: "Most people nowadays use human beings to do money magic, their wealth is not gained by the sweat of their brow." She went on to endorse the play's evocation of the past and tradition as a standard by which modern mores could be judged:

> It didn't happen in the old days. In the days of our ancestors/grandfathers, there was nothing like that, only hard work. In those days they didn't set much store by book-learning, they were farmers, and they made a good living from it. Those who managed to make some money and knew how to use it, their wealth didn't evaporate. Not many people were wealthy in the old days, there are more people nowadays using other people's lives to make money-magic than there were rich people in the old days. But nowadays, what's most common is to put someone in a room, put a calabash on their head, take someone else's child and use it for money medicine. That's what they do nowadays.

By assimilating Fosko's illicitly gotten wealth to the contemporary myth of money-magic (not actually mentioned in the play) Mrs. Akíndélé evokes a powerful popular explanation of sudden, enormous wealth: the kind of overnight fortunes that became common and conspicuous in the age of the petro-naira (see Barber 1982).

But while audience members picked up and elaborated this central equivocation of the play's message—its concealed admission that there *is* no well-gotten great wealth, and that Asínde is an unreal, impossible figure—they also affirmed with great conviction that hard work *is* rewarded, and that lasting wealth *can* be gained by honest toil. Mrs. Akíndélé said:

> [Hard work] will bring in results, if you find the right line of business. If you are prepared to work hard, you'll make a profit—you definitely *will* make a profit! The profit you make will depend on how much you invest. And how much do I have to invest? I might want to grumble, but since my profit is in proportion to what I put into the trade, how can I complain? Now if you invest a hundred pounds with luck you might make £30 profit. If you say that's not enough, that you want a hundred pounds profit, do you think it can be as much as that? Of course not. A hundred pounds outlay can't even bring in thirty pounds, that's the kind of amount you can expect—as opposed to a person who traps a human victim in a room, who'll pour out money in floods . . . the person who does that will spend the money just anyhow, and it won't finish, he'll spend it without caring, but in the end his time will be up—it could be after ten years, or after six months—and he'll die.

This statement combines a muted discontent with the amount of capital she has at her disposal (possibly a hint directed at her husband, who was present at the time), a realistic sense of how much a given outlay can bring in, and a fervent affirmation that hard work *does* bring in money, while the illicit acquisition of wealth *will* be punished by death. The last element—the affirmation—sounds more like a wish than a statement of fact: it is a resounding statement of how things *should* be.

The play itself, like Mrs. Akíndélé's narrative commentary, may be read as an affirmation of how things ought to be. The very act of affirmation may be felt to help bring this desirable state of affairs about. Thus, indirectly, people's interpretation of the play could be seen to be a denunciation of the flood of petro-naira that engulfed Nigeria from the early 1970s onwards, and which in 1981 was at its height. This was a time when unprecedented numbers of politicians, contractors, military top brass, and business people got fabulously rich, virtually overnight, while the majority of farmers, workers, and small entrepreneurs continued to struggle to make ends meet. By repudiating all wealth except that which is earned "by the sweat of our brow"—a phrase used by several members of the audience—they affirmed the value of labor and their distrust of the modern Nigerian economy of extraction and embezzlement. They asserted that labor ought to be rewarded with wealth and that trickery and corruption ought to be punished by shameful exposure, loss, and death. In this case, the general conservatism of the popular theatre becomes a kind of critique, and a kind of repudiation, of a deranged economy and society.

# 7

## The Secret Is Out (Gbangbá dẹkùn)

BY LÉRÈ PÀÍMỌ'S ÈDÁ THEATRE COMPANY

### OPENING GLEE

*The company women, dressed in miniskirts, come on stage and sing:*

CHORUS:    Here we are
           This is all of us
           We are the ones who do remarkable shows[1]
           When the world has time [to watch us]
           We will have things to say
           If you like, listen
           If we talked and talked far more than we do
           Those people with flat ears
           Would never listen.

           "Oh my husband
           All your games with the girls
           Have come to an end"[2]
           "Oh my husband

---

*Note on the Text:* The performance represented here took place on 23 December 1981 in the Palace Hotel, Òkukù. It was recorded by myself (KB), and photographs were taken at the same performance by Elio Montanari. Subsequently the tape recording was transcribed by Báyọ̀ Ògúndíjọ, who was then a colleague in the Department of African Languages and Literatures, University of Ifè, and also my research associate, and is now a member of the Institute of Cultura! Studies at the same university (now renamed Ọbáfémi Awólọ́wọ̀ University). I then translated the transcribed text, with Báyọ̀'s advice, listening again to the taped version to remind myself of the effects of music, laughter, audience comments, and so on. I recorded the interviews with Lérè Pàímọ and members of his company, and the opinions given by members of the Òkukù audience; Báyọ̀ Ògúndíjọ transcribed them, and I translated them. The translation of the play presented here follows the scene breaks that were clearly marked in the performance by the use of recorded music and the curtain, as well as some minimal changes of scenery.

*The Secret Is Out* is copyright by Lérè Pàímọ and the Èdá Theatre Company, from whom permission must be obtained before the play is performed or reproduced in any way.

All your games with the girls
Have come to an end.
If you have a gun
It does not spell death
If you have arrows
It does not spell death
If you have a cutlass
It means nothing.
But on the day that you have words with a woman
On that day you have seized hold of death!"

What is the matter with you
You people, tell me
My laughter that brings long life
My laughter that brings joy
We have brought a play
We have brought joy
This is a work we have given much thought to.

Today's play goes like a proverb
Today's story goes like a warning.
It's time to begin the play
So get down to business
To sing for us.

Onílé-Ọlá had two wives[3]
In his young days
Lánínhun was the senior wife
Òréńté was the junior.
One of the two left him,
And became a wanderer.

SOLO:     Èdá went away, but Èdá has come back![4]
CHORUS:  We have arrived.
SOLO:     The *igbegbe* bird never stays long in the place where
               it finds its food
CHORUS:  We have arrived.
SOLO:     We went away, but here we are again
CHORUS:  We have arrived.
SOLO:     Thanks be to God in Heaven
CHORUS:  We have arrived.
SOLO:     Haa
               Fire never kills the kite.
               Kite,
               Greetings for escaping the danger.

> "The bellows controls the forge fire" in the house
> of Olúfón[5]
> If we do eight dances bending low
> We'll do eight standing tall
> When we've done all the home dances
> We'll go and do the dances at the back of the house
> of Olúmọ
> Èdá went away, but Èdá has come back!

CHORUS: We have arrived.

SOLO: Èdá went away, but Èdá has come back!

CHORUS: We have arrived.

LÉRÈ PÀÍMÓ: *(Speaks to drum accompaniment)* Good evening. We are very happy to be among you again this evening. Thank you for coming. The New Year is coming, and by God's grace we'll celebrate it in joy. We'll be alive and well, by the grace of God. *Gbangbá dEkùn* is the title of tonight's play, and we want you to settle down so that you can enjoy it fully. We hope you won't hold it against us that for some time now we've been promising to come but haven't been able to. We were tied up with some other work. Praise be to God. May we continue to prosper. Thank you, and thank you for spending money [on tickets]. God will amply refund the money that you've spent. *(Speaks to a member of the audience)* Mátègò, "am I safe?" [English]

MÁTÈGÒ: "You are safe."

LÉRÈ PÀÍMÓ: *(Chants very rapidly and with great intensity)*

> My mother's house is Òpó [Housepost][6]
> Òpó Dewúré
> Children of Àyánfijàbí
> Ìwàlè Òpó
> I was not there to see
> I was not there to see the house of Mọjà-Àlé-Òyun
> "Forest comes to the house"
> Child of innumerable cloths
> One who stands by his word and is ready to fight
> Cloth is the covering of the skin
> I am the child of the brothers of the locust
> Child of the brothers of curses
> The child of one who uses curses to fight with
> When the curse doesn't fight any more
> I'll go and find other ones.
> Our house is Mọjà
> Àyánfijà goes in search . . .
> That's the wife of Òpó

They call their husbands Òpómúléró
[Housepost holds the house up]
The post wears a wrapper
The post ties a sash[7]
And what if a goat goes missing at Okun Apèrán?
Don't blame me for it
Who are you calling a member of
    the goat thieves' gang?
What if a sheep goes missing at Okun Apèrán?
Don't come to me about it
Who are you calling a member of
    the sheep thieves' gang?
And if a great fat cock gets lost at Okun Apèrán
Don't come to me about it
Who are you calling a member of
    the poultry thieves' gang?
What if a fine plump child goes missing
At Okun Apèrán?
Don't come blaming me for it
Who are you calling a member of
    the child-stealers' gang?
I got a great wooden dish
I used it to drink buffalo broth from
I want to go and deliver the message
You sent me on.

*(Song)*
You have forgotten
You have forgotten
You have forgotten the day of your eternal rest.

We don't want to bore you with too much dancing, we want to get on to the real business of the evening straight away: *Gbangbá dẸkùn, Kederé Bẹ̀ ẹ́ Wò* [The secret is out, exposed to view].

SOLO:    That you say you don't know
CHORUS:  That you say you don't know
SOLO:    Here we are, the ones that you say
             you don't know
CHORUS:  That you say you don't know.
SOLO:    Here we are, the ones that you say
             you don't know
CHORUS:  That you say you don't know.

## THE SECRET IS OUT

### SCENE 1

*Asínde's house. Wúrà, a young and beautiful woman, is on stage.*
*Asínde, her husband, enters. He is a diffident, serious-looking man,*
*modestly but respectably dressed. He speaks to Wúrà with courtesy.*
*All her speeches to him, by contrast, are sharp, impatient, and disdainful.*

ASÍNDE: Wúrà . . .

WÚRÀ: What is it?

ASÍNDE: Come here. I just wanted to tell you . . . The boys that I got to do that job, Adé and the rest . . .

WÚRÀ: Well?

ASÍNDE: I want to go and see what they're doing.

WÚRÀ: I see.

ASÍNDE: I thought I should tell you, when I finish there I'll be going on to see that boy who's doing that house for me, the contractor.

WÚRÀ: Thanks. Is that all? Or is there more?

ASÍNDE: No, well, I just wanted to say good-bye to you.

WÚRÀ: So? I'm listening.

ASÍNDE: No, I mean that's what I wanted to tell you, I said I'm going to see the people I told you about.

WÚRÀ: Aren't you ashamed of yourself?

ASÍNDE: Why should I be?

WÚRÀ: Your habit of going out at all hours hasn't changed.

ASÍNDE: What do you mean?

WÚRÀ: All this time that I've been telling you, why haven't you ever taken it in?

ASÍNDE: Taken what in, what do you mean . . . ? *(Enter Contractor.)*

CONTRACTOR: Good afternoon.

ASÍNDE: Hello, how are you?

WÚRÀ: Hello.

ASÍNDE: So you've come.

CONTRACTOR: That's right.

ASÍNDE: How about the work I gave you, how are you getting on?

CONTRACTOR: I've finished it.

ASÍNDE: You've finished it?

CONTRACTOR: All the laborers are on the point of stopping work.

ASÍNDE: And that wall that bulges outwards, that I said you should straighten up, have you seen to it?

CONTRACTOR: Yes.

ASÍNDE: So if I go and inspect it, you're certain that everything will meet with my approval?

CONTRACTOR: I've done everything, it's all O.K.

ASÍNDẸ: So it's all done?

CONTRACTOR: Yes, sir.

ASÍNDẸ: I could see that you were a good man, that's why I gave the contract to you.

CONTRACTOR: Oh, I wouldn't cheat you sir.

ASÍNDẸ: Well, so what are you after now?

CONTRACTOR: I need something, that's why I'm here. Two thousand.

ASÍNDẸ: Two thousand?

CONTRACTOR: Yes, sir.

ASÍNDẸ: And what do you need it for this time?

CONTRACTOR: Oh, there was a lot of work in that house, sir. And my laborers, well, I've nothing left to pay them with.

ASÍNDẸ: Wúrà . . . All right, wait a minute.

CONTRACTOR: O.K. *(Asínde goes out.)*

WÚRÀ: What on earth have you been doing about that house all this time? You ought to have finished it long ago.

CONTRACTOR: There's a lot of work in it.

WÚRÀ: You're just swallowing our money up.

CONTRACTOR: There's a lot of work in it.

WÚRÀ: He's soft on you, that's why you . . . *(Asínde comes in with a wad of money.)*

ASÍNDẸ: Here you are, my friend. Make sure that the job's finished off properly, do you hear? I'll be coming over to see you there later on. Do you hear? I'll be coming over to see you. Wait for me there. *(Contractor goes.)*

WÚRÀ: Really, you do give jobs to the most peculiar people.

ASÍNDẸ: Do I indeed.

WÚRÀ: Well, that's—

ASÍNDẸ: He came to collect some money.

WÚRÀ: That's your business.

ASÍNDẸ: Well I'm off, I'm going where I said.

WÚRÀ: Where are you going?

ASÍNDẸ: I told you, I'm going to inspect the, the—yes, the houses . . .

WÚRÀ: Oh yes, I forgot. It slipped my mind. About what we were discussing earlier—because when that man came in it stopped me from finishing what I had to say . . .

ASÍNDẸ: I'm listening, go on.

WÚRÀ: Don't you know that you're a respected man in this town?

ASÍNDẸ: Yes, I know.

WÚRÀ: And there's no end to the houses that you've built here.

ASÍNDẸ: That's true.

WÚRÀ: So why is it that when other important people invite you to a do, when they insist on your presence, you go wearing one pattern of cloth and I go wearing a different one?[8] Why is that?

ASÍNDẸ: Wúrà . . .

WÚRÀ: Well?

ASÍNDẸ: How can you say that? Don't you know that my work gives me a lot of trouble? Think of the day when I went to supervise that building, remember what time I got home. All that kind of thing hasn't given me time to bother with things like matching clothes. But I will do in future, I promise.

WÚRÀ: All right, forget about that one. So why was it that when I told you I wanted to do my mother's second burial,[9] you contributed money for two cows?

ASÍNDẸ: What do you mean?

WÚRÀ: Don't you know that I'm someone that millions flock after?[10] Don't you realize it wasn't enough to go round? Don't you know how bad that is? It's shaming.

ASÍNDẸ: Look, there's nothing you ask for that I'll refuse.

WÚRÀ: Ha. So you say.

ASÍNDẸ: All right, I'm off now.

WÚRÀ: Is going away the only answer you have left?

ASÍNDẸ: Look, I told you, anything you ask for I'll give you. The matching cloth you want us to wear, all right, we'll wear it!

WÚRÀ: Good. And there's something else bothering me.

ASÍNDẸ: What?

WÚRÀ: You say "What?" Well, important as you are, there are other people, less important than you in this town, who have bought cars for their wives! So why haven't you bought one for me?

ASÍNDẸ: Listen . . .

WÚRÀ: Well?

ASÍNDẸ: Well, since you bring it up . . .

WÚRÀ: Yes?

ASÍNDẸ: Even before you'd hit on the idea, I'd already made up my mind to give you one, it's just that I haven't presented it to you yet.

WÚRÀ: Well, I'd never have guessed from your behavior.

ASÍNDẸ: Well, I have, I've arranged everything, it's just that it isn't ready yet. I didn't want to tell you yet, before it was ready. But I've been going there continually.[11]

WÚRÀ: What if I'm old and incapable before it's ready?

ASÍNDẸ: I said I'll keep going there! You just wait and see.

WÚRÀ: In that case, good-bye, don't be long.

ASÍNDẸ: All right.

WÚRÀ: Bye-bye.

ASÍNDẸ: I'm on my way.

WÚRÀ: Don't be long.

ASÍNDẸ: All right.

WÚRÀ: Watch how you go . . . *(Asínde goes)* Mr. Terribly Important Person . . . Mr. Bridegroom. He's rich but his money never stays in this house.[12] What's the matter with him? *(Enter Fosko dressed in expensive robes)* Ah, so it's you.

FOSKO: Please, Wúrà . . .

WÚRÀ: Welcome.

FOSKO: O.K., just a second. I left a boy outside . . . I'm coming.

WÚRÀ: Sit down. I understand . . . *(Calls to the boy)* Where are you? You come in too. *(To Fosko)* Tell him to come in. Tell him to come in.

FOSKO: "Father and son are never so close that they don't have a boundary in their farmland."[13] Sit down, sit down. I've told him to wait outside.

WÚRÀ: Have you?

FOSKO: Yes. "There's no danger in the farm, except the whirring of bush-fowl."[14] Hello, Wúrà.

WÚRÀ: Here I am.

FOSKO: How are you today?

WÚRÀ: I'm fine.

FOSKO: How's everything going?

WÚRÀ: Everything's fine. Just fine.

FOSKO: "It's the eyes that speak." Turn round . . . let me enjoy . . . look at me. Just keep looking at me, you have such expressive eyes. How is our little matter coming on? Let all the important people know about it straight away! Don't let me waste my breath, let them know where I come from. I've a good mind to go inside, and deal with that wimp. But you'll be scared.

WÚRÀ: Go inside where?

FOSKO: Inside this house.

WÚRÀ: Oh, don't do that!

FOSKO: What is it?

WÚRÀ: Well, what are you going to say you came for?

FOSKO: You mean in Asínde's house? *(They laugh)* He's not as important as I am.

WÚRÀ: I didn't say you weren't important, but after all, he is the owner of his own house.

FOSKO: I've got money; I've got medicine; I've got status.

WÚRÀ: Thanks for the money you spent the day before yesterday.

FOSKO: Did I spend money? You ain't seen nothing yet.

WÚRÀ: Is that right?

FOSKO: And how many hundred did I give you when we went out? After all, when we walk we stumble, and we drop a few coins.

WÚRÀ: Oh yes, you did spend money!

FOSKO: "There's no danger in the farm . . ."

WÚRÀ: You spent a lot.

FOSKO: So let them know about it, what do you say?

WÚRÀ: You mean about what's between us?

FOSKO: Answer quickly, and say it in proper Yorùbá.[15]

WÚRÀ: Well, you say you want to marry me, and I am ready to marry you too.

FOSKO: It's not a case of wanting to marry, I will marry you. I'll take you away from this man's house . . .

WÚRÀ: Well, that's good.

FOSKO: I don't want you to suffer. How many houses has he built by now?

WÚRÀ: About fourteen.

FOSKO: Yet he's not well known—he hasn't become any better known than before.[16]

WÚRÀ: Because he doesn't go out. He never goes out.

FOSKO: He's not a chameleon like me, always changing colors!

WÚRÀ: He never goes out.

FOSKO: His prestige hasn't increased at all. He's building fourteen houses, yet he never changes his clothes!

WÚRÀ: Houses without number . . .

FOSKO: Yet they never invite him out. So that's how it is. Now, shall I expect you tomorrow?

WÚRÀ: Expect me a little after four. Because he'll be at home all day until about four o'clock. But a little after four, he'll go to the sites of the houses he's building.

FOSKO: I want you to know my house, so you'll know whether I'm the type who just puts up a good show in public, or whether I'm important from inside the household outwards! You know you said you'd call the other day when you were passing, but you didn't. I'll be expecting you.

WÚRÀ: So, all right, do expect me . . .

FOSKO: Wúrà Wúrà!

WÚRÀ: That's me!

| FOSKO: *(Sings)* | Haa, money |
| | Money, visit my house |
| | Children, visit my house. |
| WÚRÀ: *(Sings)* | All hail to money! |
| | Money, call in at my house. |
| | Children, call in at my house. |
| | All hail to money! |
| | Please, money, |
| | Money, call at my house, |
| | Children, call at my house. |

Thank you. *(Fosko goes)* Well, that's settled. No one can tell me not to go with that man, we're going to [live and] die together!

## SCENE 2

*Fosko's den. Snakehead comes in followed by Adéṅtọ́ọ́ and Rẹ̀sọ̀nà.[17]*
*Adéṅtọ́ọ́ is a cheery, cheeky youth, with a husky voice. He is dressed in rags.*
*Rẹ̀sọ̀nà, a big thuggish young woman, is dressed in an army uniform with*
*trousers, jacket, and cap. Snakehead is a tall, thin older man.*

SNAKEHEAD: 'Déṅtọ̀ọ́! No good will come of this boy . . . Ádé Àdè!

ADÉṄTỌ́Ọ́: Snakehead.

SNAKEHEAD: The Rẹ̀sọ̀nà!

ADÉṄTỌ́Ọ́: How's tricks?

SNAKEHEAD: Things are looking good—for me.

ADÉṄTỌ́Ọ́: Hey—for me too!

SNAKEHEAD: O.K., O.K. . . . Rẹ̀sọ̀nà!

RẸ̀SỌ̀NÀ: That's me, folks.

SNAKEHEAD: So what's on your mind, kid?

RẸ̀SỌ̀NÀ: I want to know what you got up to last night, I mean your movements last night have me baffled. When I got home—you know I'm the greatest—[18]

SNAKEHEAD: Well, my movements yesterday, you know my movements are never hard to follow. Get it? When I took the market road, then I turned by the bus stop, and that's the way I came home . . . you dig?

RẸ̀SỌ̀NÀ: Sure thing, baby. 'Déṅtọ̀ọ́! 'Déṅtọ̀ọ́!

ADÉṄTỌ́Ọ́: What have I done now?

RẸ̀SỌ̀NÀ: What were your movements last night?

ADÉṄTỌ́Ọ́: My movements?

RẸ̀SỌ̀NÀ: Yeah.

ADÉṄTỌ́Ọ́: God help me, my movements, they were enough to make a person weep.

RẸ̀SỌ̀NÀ: To make a person weep!

ADÉṄTỌ́Ọ́: You see before I came to work for the Boss, he paid the money I owed on some *gaàrí* . . .

RẸ̀SỌ̀NÀ: True enough.

ADÉṄTỌ́Ọ́: And he asked me if I could do his kind of work all right. Well, when you're starving you'll do anything. I didn't ask what kind of work, I said I'd do it. When he sent me to do the bus-stop job the other day . . . well, there was this bloke, when I put my hand in his pocket he didn't even give me time to reach to the bottom, my hand had hardly touched his pocket when he gave me a massive slap in the face! I was on the point of calling on the Lord [to take me from this world] . . . he gave me a real beating . . . and after all he didn't have any money any more than I did! There was only a shilling in his pocket. And he wouldn't even let me touch that one shilling. Oh my, this work of ours—may God give us some profit from it.

SNAKEHEAD: You're not experienced. And you're just being childish.

ADÉNTÒÓ: I'm not experienced!

SNAKEHEAD: You know the kind of bad experience you just had, that you're making such a big deal of, well we've all been through it.

ADÉNTÒÓ: Slaps!

SNAKEHEAD: Isn't that right, Résònà?

RÉSÒNÀ: It sure is.

ADÉNTÒÓ: You've been through it all! But I'm not used to it.

SNAKEHEAD: When you've toughened up a little, you'll know it's true.

RÉSÒNÀ: Let me ask you something, 'Déntòó, when that man you were talking about slapped you, did you still take the money, or not?

ADÉNTÒÓ: He didn't give me a chance to get my hand in his pocket before he laid into me!

SNAKEHEAD: He didn't give you a chance to get your hand in . . .

ADÉNTÒÓ: Well I'd almost got it in, when WHAM! He hit me with the back of his hand. Look, this work is tough.

RÉSÒNÀ: Snakehead, you haven't even asked me about my trip.

SNAKEHEAD: So, tell.

RÉSÒNÀ: Well, you see, I came out down opposite that river, and I started by crouching down low, do you get my drift?

SNAKEHEAD: Go on, I'm listening.

RÉSÒNÀ: I waited a bit. I pinned [English] him down like this. He's in Fosko's hands now. Fosko knows I'm the tops.

ADÉNTÒÓ: And me, they slap in the face.

RÉSÒNÀ: Of course they slap you in the face, you're too impatient. (Sings)

> They'll be ridiculed
> Anyone who insults us
> It's a fact
> They'll be disgraced in this world.
> They'll be ridiculed
> Anyone who insults us
> It's a fact
> They'll be disgraced in this world.
> We won't respect anyone any more
> Only people who respect us
> Will we respect
> We won't respect anyone any more.

SNAKEHEAD: Good on you, baby.

RÉSÒNÀ: Good on you too. Best of luck to you. (Enter Fosko, dressed in hunter's gear. He exudes menace. The others come to attention and rally round to greet him.) Baba "Moló"!

FOSKO: I'm with you. Snakehead, how's tricks?

SNAKEHEAD: All's well.

FOSKO: How are you?

SNAKEHEAD: Keep swinging!

FOSKO: No more suffering for us! Adéṅtọ́ọ́!

ADÉṄTỌ́Ọ́: Yes, here I am, boss.

FOSKO: Did you bring back the goods too?

ADÉṄTỌ́Ọ́: I was going to get the goods, but then I got slapped like . . .

FOSKO: You must expect to be slapped a little.

ADÉṄTỌ́Ọ́: I was practically knocked into the ground. With the flat of the hand. As I tried to drop back, he said,"Is anything the matter?" and I said there was nothing the matter, but then, WHAM on my ear! Well, I'm getting used to it little by little.

FOSKO: You need your wits about you . . .

ADÉṄTỌ́Ọ́: Yes, it's a question of wits.

FOSKO: At the beginning, when I rescued you from your slough of debt, and I asked you if you could work for me . . . It's not for nothing I'm well respected by the public.

ADÉṄTỌ́Ọ́: But I didn't know it would be this kind of work then.

FOSKO: It's best not to inquire what kind of work it is. It's best not to inquire. "At the root of riches lies a shameful secret." And if you're going to grow tall, your legs will get thin.[19] Or don't you know that?

ADÉṄTỌ́Ọ́: I know.

FOSKO: Yeah. I wear all kinds of clothes, I drive all kinds of different cars, I'm well respected by the public . . . it's not for nothing.

ADÉṄTỌ́Ọ́: I suppose because I've just started, that's why they slap me.

FOSKO: Soon you'll get used to it. That's how it is.

ADÉṄTỌ́Ọ́: CRASH into another ditch! It's hard. This work of ours is hard.

FOSKO: Yes, it's a hard kind of work. It's hard. But lucrative work is never easy.

ADÉṄTỌ́Ọ́: That's true.

FOSKO: So let's plan another outing. You *(to Snakehead),* you had a good trip three days ago.

SNAKEHEAD: It was great.

FOSKO: So you enjoyed it?

SNAKEHEAD: I sure did.

FOSKO: That young woman I spent money on like mad—

SNAKEHEAD: The fair one, Asíndẹ's wife?

FOSKO: That's the one. I spent money that day!

SNAKEHEAD: The money the boss spent on her that day—it was a mess!

FOSKO: Well, she's got herself a new husband—she says she wants to marry me!

SNAKEHEAD: She's going to marry us?

RẸSÒNÀ: Should we take her?

SNAKEHEAD: Let's take her. Let's take her on approval. Or what? Should we take her?

FOSKO: Just quiet down now, pay attention! Don't ask questions that'll get you slapped. Understand?

SNAKEHEAD: We understand. That man has money.

FOSKO: Asíndẹ has money all right. He's building houses like mad. He's building houses like a nesting ant.[20]

RÉSÒNÀ: He even built one right in the river!

FOSKO: But he can't please that woman. He bought a car for her, he did everything for her. But on the very first day that I spent money on her, she lost her head. And now she says she's coming here at four o'clock today.

SNAKEHEAD: Let's put her through it.

RÉSÒNÀ: Right on.

FOSKO: You lot get inside and keep out of the way.

RÉSÒNÀ: You want us out of the way?

FOSKO: (To Résònà) No, you stay with me here, after all you're a woman. You're the one who's going to do the job. One woman to ruin another, that's a great idea. Go and put on a miniskirt, then you're going to peep out at me, and when I call you, you'll run to me.

RÉSÒNÀ: O man of might!

FOSKO: You've got to treat me with great respect. You have to call me "senior brother." And if I get a bit carried away, I might give you a slap or two.

RÉSÒNÀ: That's O.K. by me.

SNAKEHEAD: All right, hurry up and get changed.

FOSKO: And whatever name I call you by, you've got to answer to. It could be Bínpé, it could be Moní—

ADÉNTÒÓ: So you don't . . . you don't want me there?

FOSKO: Don't you show your face.

ADÉNTÒÓ: There's one thing I don't understand, and you said I should ask when I don't understand something. None of us have facial marks, but you have.

SNAKEHEAD: Get out of here.

ADÉNTÒÓ: I mean, is she supposed to be related to you as a member of your extended family, or as a full sister?[21]

RÉSÒNÀ: Have you gone out of your mind? Does that mean you haven't been listening to anything he said? (They slap him.)

FOSKO: Get inside, go on, get inside.

ADÉNTÒÓ: You really know how to make people suffer. Oh God!

SNAKEHEAD: O Man of Might! (Adéntòó, Snakehead, and Résònà go out. Wúrà appears.)

FOSKO: Wúrà, come in, don't just peep in from outside! Or who is that, creeping along the wall like that? A child is never afraid of its father's house.

WÚRÀ: I thought you had company . . .

FOSKO: I sensed you were coming. I knew it was you. Wúrá Wùrà, my dear young lady, sit down. *(He laughs)* Hello.

WÚRÀ: Hello.

FOSKO: So you found your way here without any trouble. Didn't I tell you it's not hard to find?

WÚRÀ: Where are you going? — You're all dressed up to go out.

FOSKO: So you've noticed that my clothes are different today.

WÚRÀ: They really are very different.

FOSKO: It's for when I want to go hunting and so on.

WÚRÀ: Oh, so you go hunting!

FOSKO: I like to eat bush-meat. So you thought I always wear those great robes of *òfì* and so on. Well. Bínpé! *(Rẹ́sọ̀nà runs in, wearing a dress.)*

RẸ́SỌ̀NÀ: Yes sir, yes brother.

FOSKO: Well don't hang back, come out, come over here.

RẸ́SỌ̀NÀ: *(To Wúrà)* Greetings to you.

WÚRÀ: Hello.

FOSKO: Look, girl, when you see a visitor arrive, you don't have to wait to be called, you should come straight out and welcome them.

RẸ́SỌ̀NÀ: Yes sir, yes brother.

FOSKO: *(To Wúrà)* This is my little sister, the one I told you has been wanting to meet you for a long time. *(To Rẹ́sọ̀nà)* This is your new wife, that I told you was coming here today.[22]

WÚRÀ: Pleased to meet you. How do you do.

RẸ́SỌ̀NÀ: May I offer you something to eat?

WÚRÀ: Oh, nothing for me, thanks.

FOSKO: Have you got something ready, or have you just thought of it now?

RẸ́SỌ̀NÀ: There's food ready in the house, sir, brother, there's food ready in the house, sir.

FOSKO: There's food in the house. So don't bother to ask, just bring a table out. Bring it! You should have arranged all this before. I shouldn't have to be teaching you everything now.

RẸ́SỌ̀NÀ: Yes sir, brother.

FOSKO: What the hell's the matter with you? Bring a table out, bring the food. You shouldn't wait to ask, you should have just brought out the food straight away.

RẸ́SỌ̀NÀ: What should I bring her?

FOSKO: *(To Wúrà)* Would you like rice?

RẸ́SỌ̀NÀ: There's rice in the house. Feel at home, don't be shy.

WÚRÀ: It's not that I'm shy, I just don't want to eat.

FOSKO: Because she hung around asking you instead of . . . This is Wúrà, my new wife that I told you about.

RÉSÒNÀ: Yes sir. I know.

FOSKO: There's this man who's not treating her right, a lovely girl like this, it's Asíndẹ. For someone as beautiful as this to find herself among such people . . .

RÉSÒNÀ: It's a shame.

FOSKO: And we're going to tell him so, since she and I have hit it off. I've decided to take her from him. I've decided to take her. No one will be able to say a word.

RÉSÒNÀ: Yes sir.

FOSKO: That's how it is.

RÉSÒNÀ: Yes sir. Nice to meet you. (She starts to leave.)

FOSKO: Don't go far.

RÉSÒNÀ: No sir.

WÚRÀ: You know, I didn't like what you did just now.

FOSKO: What was that?

WÚRÀ: The way you gave her a hard time because of me.

FOSKO: After you've gone, I'm going to tie her down! I'm teaching her a lesson, that's all. When she gets married, she'll behave as she's learned to here.

WÚRÀ: Oh but please, don't tie her down!

FOSKO: So what have you done about your luggage?

WÚRÀ: I've packed already. I've packed everything.

FOSKO: So we should come and fetch it from there for you?

WÚRÀ: Well, all right, but you know your sister, well, as you know, you yourself have said that women know each other's business . . .

FOSKO: Just a minute, just a minute. Bínpé! (Résònà returns.)

RÉSÒNÀ: Yes, brother.

FOSKO: Say it in front of her so that she can . . .

WÚRÀ: I was saying that, as you know, women understand each other's business . . .

FOSKO: That's true.

WÚRÀ: So she can come to our house. She can come and carry the luggage for me.

FOSKO: Which day do you want her to come?

WÚRÀ: Oh, you could come tomorrow, or you could even come this evening.

FOSKO: O.K., let her come this evening.

WÚRÀ: Let's wait till tomorrow.

FOSKO: Do you hear? Tomorrow, take that van that we use for transporting goods—after all, you do know how to drive—

Rẹ́sọ̀nà: Yes.

Fosko: Go and collect her luggage, so that she can come and enjoy herself here, so that she can come and have fun with us.

Rẹ́sọ̀nà: All right. See you.

Wúrà: Thanks. *(Rẹ́sọ̀nà makes to leave.)*

Fosko: Don't go far, I'll want you to escort her when she leaves. So that's settled, Wúrà.

Wúrà: It's all right.

Fosko: When this girl's finished collecting your luggage, you can expect me, I'll be coming round too.

Wúrà: What are you coming round for?

Fosko: I just want to go inside your house.

Wúrà: Don't come.

Fosko: "There's no danger in the farm . . ."

Wúrà: I said don't come!

Fosko: Well if I do come, you won't know it's me.

Wúrà: Why, how will you look?

Fosko: Oh Lord, you're really going to see something! Just behave as if you don't know me. I want to have a friendly chat with that husband of yours. I've heard that he never welcomes visitors, so I just want to try him and see. There won't be any trouble, I just want to get into his house and have a bit of fun with him, that's all.

Wúrà: In that case, I'll be expecting you.

Fosko: Bínpé!

Rẹ́sọ̀nà: Sir, my brother!

Fosko: Show your visitor out.

Rẹ́sọ̀nà: Yes sir. *(To Wúrà)* Are you ready to go?

Wúrà: I'm on my way.

Rẹ́sọ̀nà: Thank you for coming.

Wúrà: Thank you very much, ma.

Fosko: Wúrá Wùrà!

Rẹ́sọ̀nà: And you haven't had a bite to eat!

Wúrà: Thanks, I don't fancy eating. *(Wúrà and Rẹ́sọ̀nà go out. Snakehead and Adéǹtọ́ọ́ come rushing in.)*

Snakehead: O mighty man!

Fosko: Keep swinging.

Snakehead: I was listening through the wall. I heard the sermon you were preaching. And what a sermon! It went deep into my heart. *(Rẹ́sọ̀nà returns, having escorted Wúrà out of the house.)*

Rẹ́sọ̀nà: She said I should lose no time in coming to collect her luggage! *(They laugh.)*

ADÉNTÒÓ: My God, wow, you're good at telling lies! *(More laughter)* She was so thrilled, she was waving her head about like a sympathizer at a funeral! And then you said that "auntie" here should go with the van!

FOSKO: Yeah.

ADÉNTÒÓ: Do we have a van? And he said you know how to drive! Well, I'm learning a bit about how to tell lies.

FOSKO: Ha, you call this telling lies? It's just a way to make a living, that's all.

SNAKEHEAD: There's no harm in making a living.

FOSKO: Résònà, you go and change. Go and collect the luggage.

RÉSÒNÀ: Yes sir.

FOSKO: You go and do that, the rest of us will divide out some other jobs amongst us. Snakehead . . .

SNAKEHEAD: Cheers, boss.

FOSKO: You go and get ready too. When she's brought the luggage, we'll all make an appearance at that house.

SNAKEHEAD: We'll go and pay a visit! O mighty man!

FOSKO: We'll go and visit Asínde.

SNAKEHEAD: But we'll have changed our clothes!

FOSKO: He's going to treat his visitors generously. . . . And you *(to Adéntòó)*, you wait for us at home.

ADÉNTÒÓ: Aren't you going to take me with you so that I can . . .

SNAKEHEAD: You! Not until you know how to go out on your own. *(Sings:)*

> Or can you become a spinning top
> One whose waist gyrates in the dance so thrillingly?

*He dances to the bàtá drum. All leave on their various errands.*

## SCENE 3

*Asínde's house. Wúrà is at home. Résònà arrives.*

WÚRÀ: Oh, hello, so you've come.

RÉSÒNÀ: Hello. My brother said I should come and collect your luggage.

WÚRÀ: Sit down. So how are you? I hope he didn't beat you after I'd gone?

RÉSÒNÀ: He didn't, not after you told him not to.

WÚRÀ: Well, what would you like to eat?

RÉSÒNÀ: I don't want anything. My brother told me not to be long.

WÚRÀ: Oh, you must eat!

RÉSÒNÀ: No, I don't want anything.

WÚRÀ: Is it because I didn't eat anything at your place?

RÉSÒNÀ: No, no, it's not because of that. My brother told me to be quick. He said I should hurry up and bring your luggage over.

WÚRÀ: All right, come along and help me to carry it.

RÉSÒNÀ: Yes, ma.

WÚRÀ: Watch how you go. This way.

RÉSÒNÀ: Is that the lot?

WÚRÀ: It'll do. Tell him I'll be expecting him. Have you got that?

RÉSÒNÀ: Yeah, I've got it.

WÚRÀ: Thanks.

RÉSÒNÀ: So, don't be long.

WÚRÀ: I won't be.

RÉSÒNÀ: And I'll get something ready for you before you come.[23]

WÚRÀ: That'll be nice.

RÉSÒNÀ: Good-bye.

WÚRÀ: Thanks. Good-bye. Don't drive too fast, take it easy. *(Résònà exits with the luggage.)*

WÚRÀ: That's a relief. There's nothing to worry about any more. *(Asíndẹ comes in from outside.)*

ASÍNDẸ: Wúrà, Wùrà. I know, I'm late. You know, that man has really put his back into the job. You remember all the places where I said—

WÚRÀ: What's the matter? Why are you pawing me like that?[24] What's up?

ASÍNDẸ: Is this how you receive me after a hard day at work? And it was all for your sake anyway—after I finished at the site, I went to see about your car.

WÚRÀ: *(Mocking)* Well done, loverboy. Is that all or is there more?

ASÍNDẸ: Your car's in the back yard, so what's all this about?

WÚRÀ: Is this the right time to be coming home?

ASÍNDẸ: But I told you, it was because of you!

WÚRÀ: So where's the car key?

ASÍNDẸ: You think I'm lying to you? Would someone like me tell lies?

WÚRÀ: So let's see it. If it's the truth, let's see it.

ASÍNDẸ: Go and look out of the window, you'll see your car. And here's the key. *(Wúrà goes to look.)*

WÚRÀ: *(Still disdainful)* Oh, thanks ever so much. Thanks. You're very generous. Thanks.

ASÍNDẸ: You really think someone like me would tell lies—someone of my status?

WÚRÀ: No wonder you were late! Well, thanks.

*A sound of handbells is heard outside. Fosko, Snakehead, and Résònà enter, disguised as Aláduùrà preachers. They are singing a hymn:*

FOSKO & CO.:

> Hallelujah!
> Help me glorify Jesus

> Hallelujah
> Help me glorify Jesus
> Hallelujah!
> Leader of the Heavenly army
> Hallelujah.
>
> Help me raise Jesus on high
> Hallelujah!
> Help me raise Jesus on high
> Hallelujah.
> Leader of the Heavenly army
> Hallelujah.

FOSKO: Cry Hallelujah!

THE REST: Hallelujah!

FOSKO: Are you Mr. Asíndẹ?

ASÍNDẸ: Yes, I am.

FOSKO: Do we meet you in health and peace?

ASÍNDẸ: You do, you do.

FOSKO: We're very happy to see you. We are going on our rounds, bringing the good news of salvation. And, well, we've picked out your house for a special visit, to come and pray for you.

WÚRÀ: Thank you.

FOSKO: Please, could I ask you, is that lady your wife?

ASÍNDẸ: Yes, she's my wife.

WÚRÀ: Yes, yes.

FOSKO: Could you both sit down together, please, I want her to hear our message too. Health and peace to this house. You don't know us, but we know you. We're paying visits to all the important people like you, one by one. Just as we go from one house to another, so we go from one country to another, to bring the good news of salvation, because, my friends, the world is in a state of confusion. He that hath ears, let him hear, because of the day of final rest. But good people are as hard to find as ostrich eggs. Cry "Hallelujah!"

THE REST: Glory Hallelujah!

FOSKO: Mr. Asínde, kneel down so that we can pray for you, and your wife as well, please kneel down. Take off your cap. Peace has entered this house today! We will not spend long with you today, because when we leave here we will go to the next house, and likewise we will go to other countries. He that hath ears to hear, let him hear. Now, close your eyes. Father, have mercy on us.

THE REST: Amen.

FOSKO: Father, forgive them.

THE REST: Amen.

FOSKO: Whatever they undertake, may it go smoothly.

THE REST: Amen. May it be so. Amen.

FOSKO: Have mercy on them.

THE REST: Amen.

FOSKO: Let them not be disgraced.

THE REST: Amen.

FOSKO: Let them not walk in inauspicious ways.

THE REST: Amen.

FOSKO: Let not evil eyes look upon them.

THE REST: Amen.

FOSKO: Let not evil feet enter their house.

THE REST: Amen.

FOSKO: Help me pray for them.

THE REST: Amen.

FOSKO: Help me pray for them.

THE REST: Amen.

FOSKO: Let it be so.

THE REST: Amen.

FOSKO: Open your eyes. Mr. Asínde, as I was praying, I saw some strange things. You have embarked on some enterprise, we don't know what kind. In my dream, workers come to see you at the crack of dawn. They ask for money, and lo! you give it to them. You have no time to stay at home and eat. You have no time to change your clothes. You have to go out. We pray that you may complete this undertaking you have begun, with joy and happiness. We don't know what kind of work it is, but we see workers, many many workers.

ASÍNDE: I build houses.

FOSKO: Ah, you build houses. Cry "Hallelujah"!

THE REST: Hallelujah!

FOSKO: So you build houses.

ASÍNDE: That's right.

FOSKO: As you have begun the work on the houses, so you will finish it, with joy and happiness.

ALL: Amen. Amen.

FOSKO: "There is no one who wants one to be rich, except one's own Orí."[25] One's own full brother doesn't want one to die—but if he gets a chance he'll carry off one's wealth!

ASÍNDE: That's true.

FOSKO: Only one's mother and father truly wish one well. Where a person's treasure is, there his heart is too. Is this where you live?

ASÍNDE: Yes, this is where I live.

FOSKO: With all your property?

ASÍNDE: Yes.

Fosko: Get the keys to your front door and to your own room, give them to your wife, let her put them in a bowl of water, throw them in, and then pour the water outside the house, because of wicked people. May every enterprise of yours flourish until the end of your days. *(Sings:)*

> Pagans perish every day
> But Christians can't say anything
> What could you say?
> The same criticisms
> That apply to you
> Apply to them too.[26]
> Rescue those who are perishing!
> Rescue those who are perishing!
> Rescue those who are dying!
> Rescue those who are perishing!

Fosko: These two are enough. The front door key and the bedroom key. We'll pray some more for you. Kneel down once more, and your good lady should please take off her cap. Father, have mercy on them! *(As he prays, he hastily makes an impression in soap of the two keys.)*

The rest: Amen.

Fosko: Forgive them their sins.

The rest: Amen.

Fosko: Whatever they undertake, may it succeed.

The rest: Amen.

Fosko: May evil eyes not look upon them.

The rest: Amen.

Fosko: May evil feet not arrive at their house.

The rest: Amen.

Fosko: Help me pray for them.

The rest: Amen.

Fosko: Let them not do wrong.

The rest: Amen.

Fosko: Any work he begins, may he finish it in joy.

The rest: Amen.

Fosko: Any work he begins, may it come to a good conclusion.

The rest: Amen.

Fosko: No one wants one to be wealthy except one's own Orí. Let his work flourish until the end of his days.

The rest: Amen.

Fosko: Let him profit in his work.

The rest: Amen.

Fosko: Let it be so.

The rest: Amen.

FOSKO: Have mercy upon them.

THE REST: Amen.

FOSKO: Open your eyes. Peace be with you. . . . Sprinkle a little of the water on the ground every morning. . . .

ASÍNDẸ: I see, all right.

FOSKO: Now your life has turned to one of joy. We'll call on you again very soon. *(Song. As they sing, the "preachers" leave.)*

> You will rejoice
> Your life has turned to one of joy
> You have given thanks.
> Your life has turned to one of joy
> Your life has turned to one of joy
> Peace be with you.

WÚRÀ: Well, that was odd.

ASÍNDẸ: It was astonishing.

WÚRÀ: How did he know your name?

ASÍNDẸ: That's what I couldn't understand.

WÚRÀ: But how did he know it?

ASÍNDẸ: How did he know about the houses I'm building? How did he know about all my worries?

WÚRÀ: Gosh, he really had vision. He had vision.

ASÍNDẸ: He certainly did. Well, I'm going in, I haven't been inside since I got home.

WÚRÀ: What would you like to eat?

ASÍNDẸ: Oh I can't eat anything now, I'll be back.

WÚRÀ: O.K., don't be long. *(Asíndẹ goes into the inner part of the house. He calls sharply from there:)* Wúrà!

WÚRÀ: What is it?

ASÍNDẸ: Where have you put your luggage?

WÚRÀ: Luggage?

ASÍNDẸ: Yes.

WÚRÀ: What luggage?

ASÍNDẸ: Your luggage.

WÚRÀ: My luggage?

ASÍNDẸ: Yes, your own luggage.

WÚRÀ: Go inside and have a look. My luggage! Or do you not know what you're saying? Go on, go inside. Cretin. Creep. My luggage! You've a short memory. So you think you'll make inquiries about my luggage do you? Fat chance.

ASÍNDẸ: Wúrà!

WÚRÀ: Is anything the matter?

ASÍNDẸ: Do you take me for a child?

WÚRÀ: Oh no, you're an old man.

ASÍNDE: I tell you I can't see your luggage anywhere in the house. You said go and look, I went and looked, and I can't find it.

WÚRÀ: Have you looked under your own bed? Did you know I'd spring-cleaned my room? I moved my luggage out and put it under your bed. Go and have a look. Go and look. What's all this about anyway? You're just giving yourself trouble for nothing. He's going to kill himself for nothing, and the living will go on enjoying life. What do you expect? Lover boy!

ASÍNDE: Wúrà!

WÚRÀ: Yes?

ASÍNDE: I don't like this, I don't like it. Why are you lying to me?

WÚRÀ: Are you saying I'm lying?

ASÍNDE: I asked you where your luggage was. And you lied to me. You deceived me high and low.

WÚRÀ: Are you implying that I'm a liar?

ASÍNDE: I've looked under your bed, I've looked under mine too, and I can't see anything there.

WÚRÀ: Really?

ASÍNDE: For God's sake, what else do you want me to do for you?

WÚRÀ: Is that the lot?

ASÍNDE: Where's your luggage?

WÚRÀ: Oh, what eloquence! Is that it, or is there more? After all, I've been telling you for a long time—

ASÍNDE: Telling me what?

WÚRÀ: You have eyes haven't you? Or don't you use them for seeing?

ASÍNDE: What do you mean?

WÚRÀ: Don't you realize I've been telling you, I've been dropping hint after hint. . . .

ASÍNDE: I said telling me what?

WÚRÀ: You're a Yorùbá, aren't you? Haven't you had the wit to catch on? In all this time?

ASÍNDE: What nonsense is this you're talking?

WÚRÀ: I'm through. So I'm talking nonsense. Very well, then, but I'm through.

ASÍNDE: Through with what?

WÚRÀ: I'm going.

> *A song sounds from the wings, as Wúrà slowly gathers*
> *her things and goes. Asínde watches in disbelief.*

> Quickly pack your things, wife
> To go to the house of sweet delight

Quickly pack your things, quickly
Go to your husband
Don't drag your feet.
Quickly pack your things, wife
To go to the house of sweet delight
Quickly pack your things, quickly
Go to your husband
Don't delay.

If it was your Destiny that sent you
It was a bad destiny
Those women who go from husband to husband
Will live to regret it.
Compare the wife in a good house
And the wife at the crossroads
Compare the wife in a good house
And the wife at the crossroads

Wúrà, come and look at the farm
When I arrive I'll write a "reminder"
To you to go—
Pack your luggage and go.

SOLO:      Wife
CHORUS:    Be off with you, pack your load and go.
SOLO:      Wife
CHORUS:    Be off with you, pack your load and go. . . .

## SCENE 4

*Fosko's headquarters. Adéṅtọ́ọ́ comes in carrying a heavy load on
his head. He calls to Snakehead, who is already on stage.*

ADÉṄTỌ́Ọ́: Come here, help me lift it down. Or have you become a total
layabout? When you see someone carrying a load as huge as this! Help
me put it down.
SNAKEHEAD: Who are you calling a layabout? Thickhead.
ADÉṄTỌ́Ọ́: Just help me lift it down!
SNAKEHEAD: Aren't you clever enough to know that, ever since you arrived here, if you're going to carry a load like that by yourself, you've got
to be able to put it down by yourself as well? Stay where you are! *(Rẹ̀sọ̀nà
comes in.)*
RẸ̀SỌ̀NÀ: Do you mean to say you haven't put down your load yet?
ADÉṄTỌ́Ọ́: How on earth am I to put down a huge load like this on my
own?

RÉSÒNÀ: Can't you put this one down by yourself? When I used to go to the farm, I never had anyone to help me down with my loads.

ADÉÑTÒÓ: Yes, well, you think a lot of yourself.

RÉSÒNÀ: I brought those loads home by myself (points to a pile of Wúrà's luggage.)

> Adéñtòó struggles with the huge load and finally manages to
> dump it on the ground. Snakehead and Résònà watch.

SNAKEHEAD: Ádé Àdè, shake my hand! So if you can do it by yourself, what were you bothering us for? Here, shake my hand.

ADÉÑTÒÓ: What's the matter with your hand?

SNAKEHEAD: The matter with my hand?

ADÉÑTÒÓ: Yeah, what's the matter with it? You want me to shake it?

SNAKEHEAD: Yeah.

ADÉÑTÒÓ: It's like a leper's hand. You dare stretch it out to me! Pox on your hand.

SNAKEHEAD: You talk to me like that, 'Déñtòó?

ADÉÑTÒÓ: May you never buy sugar to eat![27]

SNAKEHEAD: The cheek!

ADÉÑTÒÓ: Just get on with dividing the loot. (They open the load) So that's what's in it! Nothing but women's clothes!

SNAKEHEAD: The Reso!

RÉSÒNÀ: Oro City![28]

ADÉÑTÒÓ: Chuck it over to me!

SNAKEHEAD: Résònà! (He throws her a garment.)

RÉSÒNÀ: May God bless you!

SNAKEHEAD: D.D.![29]

ADÉÑTÒÓ: Yeah, chuck it over here so I can catch it.

SNAKEHEAD: How long since you last caught something like this?

ADÉÑTÒÓ: I've caught a few in my time.

SNAKEHEAD: I'm taking possession of this one.

ADÉÑTÒÓ: You're what?

SNAKEHEAD: I'm taking possession of this one, and that one is Résònà's share.

ADÉÑTÒÓ: "Excuse sa," don't take possession of something that will land you in the nick.

SNAKEHEAD: You're talking about me?

ADÉÑTÒÓ: Yeah. Who are you giving this one to? (Referring to a garment Snakehead has thrown to him.)

SNAKEHEAD: Well who's holding it?

ADÉÑTÒÓ: So I get trousers picked from a rack,[30] that I'd use as a carry-ing-pad to bring the rest of my load home! I'm given these!

SNAKEHEAD: That's your share.

ADÉNTÒÓ: Right, and I've not got to say a word, right? You'll have to put a knife to my throat. Look, take your time and divide it up again. Otherwise you'll bring down trouble on your own heads.

SNAKEHEAD: Are you referring to us?

ADÉNTÒÓ: Yes. One of you might even die in jail, that's the lengths I'll go to. *(Fosko enters.)*

SNAKEHEAD: "Boss-o-mine"!

FOSKO: Well done, boys and girls.

RÉSÒNÀ: O mighty one!

FOSKO: What have you been doing all this time?

SNAKEHEAD: Don't say I'm jumping the gun, seeing as you're hardly into the room: but this boy has gone much, much too far.

FOSKO: What happened?

SNAKEHEAD: If I wasn't so well behaved I'd have settled his hash before you came. You see, as we were putting this load on top of the second box in the inside room—

FOSKO: Yes?

SNAKEHEAD: We said, "This belongs to the boss."

FOSKO: That goes without saying.

SNAKEHEAD: Then I gave this one to Résònà as her share.

RÉSÒNÀ: Baba, this is mine.

SNAKEHEAD: Then I took possession of this one. I gave that one to 'Déntòó as his share. And 'Déntòó said we'd get ourselves into trouble.

FOSKO: Is that right, 'Déntòó?

SNAKEHEAD: He said he wasn't happy with it.

ADÉNTÒÓ: Ye Gods! Did I say that? Ah. I've been framed!

RÉSÒNÀ: Are you going to claim you never said that?

ADÉNTÒÓ: I didn't.

RÉSÒNÀ: What?

SNAKEHEAD: You didn't?

ADÉNTÒÓ: Just a moment. Just let me talk to the boss.

FOSKO: Well?

ADÉNTÒÓ: When I got here, I had to unload that box all by myself, they wouldn't help me.

FOSKO: Go on.

ADÉNTÒÓ: So I managed eventually to get it down. Then they said—in fact they knocked me over here, and I ended up here . . .

FOSKO: Go on.

ADÉNTÒÓ: Then they divided the load, and they gave me these trousers. I said, "Oh, thank you, may we continue to prosper, may we make ever greater profits. . . . Could you possibly find just a little something extra to add to this?" You see, I'm getting to know how things are done around here, so that's what I said.

FOSKO: That's enough, that's enough, stop right there.

SNAKEHEAD: How dare you talk like that?

FOSKO: You asked them to add something else?

ADÉNTÓÓ: Yes, so that our enterprise will prosper in future.

FOSKO: Your big mouth has landed you in the shit. It's not for you to tell them to add extra for you. I ought to find you on your belly, prostrating your thanks. "Let him add . . ."—that shows that you're not satisfied with what you've been given.

ADÉNTÓÓ: I've split my shin too.

FOSKO: You dare tell him to add more? Whose son are you? I met you deep in debt, they [your creditors] were dragging you from pillar to post; I brought you here, and as soon as you get here you begin throwing your weight about. You said they'd get into trouble.

SNAKEHEAD: That's what he said.

FOSKO: As I remember, you told me on the day you arrived that you were the son of a hunter. So go and fetch all your father's medicines and lay an ambush for these people with them. Why don't you get your gun and just go hunting? When you first came to me, you were destitute, that's why we took you in. They found work for you, yet you said they'd get themselves into trouble.

SNAKEHEAD: That's what he said, I was really surprised at him.

FOSKO: This boy ought to be punished.

RÉSÒNÀ: Boss, let's teach him a lesson. What if I put out my cigarette in his eye, for instance?

SNAKEHEAD: Leave him be, boss, let him off.

FOSKO: Take the luggage inside, please.

SNAKEHEAD: *(To Adéntóó)* Go on, take it inside.

ADÉNTÓÓ: Help me lift it up then.

RÉSÒNÀ: You want me to help you lift it!

*Adéntóó jerks the load toward the inner room, pushing Résònà along with it.*

RÉSÒNÀ: Just look at that!

FOSKO: And right in front of my eyes!

ADÉNTÓÓ: They say "We don't show off our strength if we've found a helper."[31]

FOSKO: Calm down, Résònà. All right, for the next three months you're not to go out with them again. You can guard the house. You'll be the watchman while they're out. When they bring back the goods, you'll keep your head down and button up your mouth like a baboon's backside. You thought you were going to share the loot with them! When you've toughened up a bit, maybe in three months or so, if you're very good, they'll take you out with them. You've offended me, I'm angry with you. Let's wait and see whether we can find any use for you. Résònà!

RÉSÒNÀ: O mighty one.

FOSKO: What did that young woman say, when you went to fetch her luggage?

RÉSÒNÀ: She said she was coming here herself.

FOSKO: She's coming to her husband's house?[32]

RÉSÒNÀ: She'll be here any minute, O mighty one.

FOSKO: Make yourself scarce. Don't let her see you here.

RÉSÒNÀ: Father Làkúú!

FOSKO: Snakebite!

SNAKEHEAD: Here, boss, at your service.

FOSKO: Take this boy with you, you're going to do a little performance when the young lady arrives.

SNAKEHEAD: I know what you mean, boss.

FOSKO: If she asks for Èdá, say there's no one of that name here. You know she won't recognize you, she hasn't seen you here before.

SNAKEHEAD: She'll not know me from Adam.

FOSKO: But you know her, I take it?

SNAKEHEAD: Oh yeah, I know her, from the day we met at that do.

FOSKO: And you'll recognize her?

SNAKEHEAD: Sure thing.

FOSKO: She's left Asínde. And there's nowhere for her to go.

SNAKEHEAD: She'll not find anywhere else to go.

FOSKO: That's how I planned it.

SNAKEHEAD: O mighty one!

FOSKO: Have a bit of fun with her first, when she comes. Ask her if she knows where she is. And if she doesn't take herself off at once . . . *(Someone whistles nearby)* Don't kill her, just cut her about a little. Take this one with you, you may be able to find a use for him.

SNAKEHEAD: O mighty one!

ADÉÑTÒÓ: Oh, I know how to tease people, sir, I can make a game of her like nobody's business.[33] I'll be of use to you there! Yeah, boss. And they say she's left Asínde!

SNAKEHEAD: Adé!

ADÉÑTÒÓ: And she'll not get a chance to come into this house!

SNAKEHEAD: No way. *(Fosko goes out.)*

ADÉÑTÒÓ: Look, let's be frank with each other. The Hausa call a compliment . . . "Mala." The British call a compliment . . . "Yes kè." I'm paying you a compliment. Everything you were doing in front of the boss, I'm wise to it.

SNAKEHEAD: You've got a nerve.

ADÉÑTÒÓ: It was me that the boss told off. He opened his mouth wide like an old wooden door[34] and named my father!

SNAKEHEAD: Cretin.

The Èdá Theatre: Adéǹtòó and Snakehead playing cards. Photograph
© Elio Montanari. Used by permission.

ADÉǸTÒÓ: Bad cess to you. Bad cess to you for ever. (Takes up a threatening posture) I'm waiting for you.

SNAKEHEAD: Adé . . . (He cringes.)

ADÉǸTÒÓ: God blight your big mouth. May you never have money to buy sugar in your life. What a show you're going to make with your suffering! Prostrate! Wait, I won't even make you prostrate, I'll do worse, I'll make you jump. To add to your agony.

SNAKEHEAD: Adé, behave like an elder, don't be mad.

ADÉǸTÒÓ: Say please.

SNAKEHEAD: I said, don't be mad.

ADÉǸTÒÓ: I want to hear you say "Please, sir."

SNAKEHEAD: You didn't look properly at the thing I gave you, I gave the same to the boss.

ADÉǸTÒÓ: That doesn't concern me—even if it had been your own father. Say "Please sir."

SNAKEHEAD: O.K., please. Please.

ADÉǸTÒÓ̩: Say "Please sir."

SNAKEHEAD: Just please! Ha!

ADÉǸTÒÓ̩: Say "Please sir."

SNAKEHEAD: "D.D."!

ADÉǸTÒÓ̩: Say "Please sir," I've no time to waste.

SNAKEHEAD: All right. Please, sir.

ADÉǸTÒ̩: Ha, aha, haha! Sit down, sit down. So you can't fight? You've got your eye on this knife? Go on, sit down.

SNAKEHEAD: O.K., give it here, give it here, you could do someone an injury with your horseplay.

ADÉǸTÒ̩: Don't play with me. Come and fight. If you can stand up and fight, good. If not, you'll never have money to buy sugar in your life.

SNAKEHEAD: O.K., bring out the thing [a deck of cards]. What have you got? Have you got any "machine"?

ADÉǸTÒ̩: Oh no, I've not saved enough to buy a machine [motorbike].

SNAKEHEAD: You've no "rug"?

ADÉǸTÒ̩: Rug, schmug.

SNAKEHEAD: You still don't understand the lingo after all this time? It means money, in case you didn't know.

ADÉǸTÒ̩: You mean Naira?

SNAKEHEAD: Yeah.

ADÉǸTÒ̩: You call it "machine"? No wonder that kind of money doesn't stick. You people really set a lot of store by slang. Come on. *(They begin a game of Snap.)*

ADÉǸTÒ̩: You turn money into "machine." And next minute you're talking about "rug." What's "rug"? You with your head as big as a sacrificial pudding! Rotten slang.

SNAKEHEAD: Shut the hell up.

ADÉǸTÒ̩: I wasn't insulting you. Everyone has to carry the parcel of his own mouth about.

SNAKEHEAD: I've got you, mate [in the game]. I've tasted you!

ADÉǸTÒ̩: You're wrong. It's a bit dark here. You've a quick hand. Look, I want you to change my name. I want you to call me "Mister."

SNAKEHEAD: You, "Mister"!

ADÉǸTÒ̩: Mister.

SNAKEHEAD: From me!

ADÉǸTÒ̩: Mister Adé.

SNAKEHEAD: Don't you know that I'm much older than you?

ADÉǸTÒ̩: "There are no elders on a rat-hunt."[35] That's two fives.

SNAKEHEAD: You thief, you've taken a six with a five!

ADÉǸTÒ̩: It was a mistake.

SNAKEHEAD: You're playing "either-or" [guessing].

ADÉǸTÒ̩: I'm not playing "either-or"! God will make you play "either-or."

*The Èdá Theatre: Adéntòọ́, Snakehead, and Résọ̀nà. Photograph © Elio Montanari. Used by permission.*

*(Wúrà enters.)*

WÚRÀ: Hello there!

ADÉNTÒỌ́: *(Ignoring her)* God will make you play "Hello there."

SNAKEHEAD: You're chicken. Go and play "Hello there" with her, hello there, hello there. Are you her equal?

ADÉNTÒỌ́: Did you "Snap"?

WÚRÀ: It's you I'm greeting!

ADÉNTÒỌ́: Did you "Snap"? . . . *(to Wúrà)* Oh my goodness, I hope you're not offended? Please, please. Have you been standing behind us for long? I hope you're not annoyed? Oh, Heavens, we should be more observant.

Thank God I noticed. . . . You see, it was the heat from your nostrils blowing down my neck that made me realize someone was standing behind me. I do implore you not to be offended. You see what we're doing? We're playing Snap. So sorry. Are you looking for someone?

WÚRÀ: You two are beginning to try my patience. Well I've heard what you have to say, and you don't seem too bright, but what about this one? *(indicates Snakehead.)*

ADÉÑTÓỌ: *(In paroxysms of laughter)* Holy shit! I'm going to die! She said I don't seem too bright . . . don't you know the meaning of that Yorùbá? She means we're both thick. And if I'm as short as a surveyor's peg, you're as long as a trouser drawstring!

SNAKEHEAD: Young lady, did we have a quarrel before?

WÚRÀ: It's not a question of a quarrel. But I kept greeting you, and you didn't answer.

SNAKEHEAD: Are you looking for someone?

WÚRÀ: Yes.

SNAKEHEAD: What kind of person?

WÚRÀ: It's, umm . . .

SNAKEHEAD: I'll be with you in a minute, hang on. 'Déñtọọ . . .

ADÉÑTÓỌ: Yes indeed.

SNAKEHEAD: She's looking for someone.

ADÉÑTÓỌ: Ah, the way you're addressing me now makes me very happy!

SNAKEHEAD: Adé.

ADÉÑTÓỌ: So you're looking for someone? Do you know the owner of these premises?

WÚRÀ: I know him.

ADÉÑTÓỌ: Is that so. What kind of facial marks has he got?

WÚRÀ: I'm actually asking for Ẹ̀dá Fosko. He said if I came here and asked for him, you would be able to show me his new place, where he's just moved to.

ADÉÑTÓỌ: Yah, yah, "correcti," "correcti." And do you recognize this lady, mate?

SNAKEHEAD: Oh, yes.

ADÉÑTÓỌ: She's looking for you.

SNAKEHEAD: "Oh yes." How've you been? Are you looking for me?

WÚRÀ: You mean . . . It's not someone like you I'm looking for. Just take a look at yourself!

ADÉÑTÓỌ: I'm dying! Oh God keep us out of trouble! *(To Snakehead, laughing)* Arms ought to be of a reasonable length, you see for yourself how you've stretched them, see how long they are.[36]

SNAKEHEAD: *(Laughing)* If I do like this . . .

ADÉÑTÓỌ: *(To Wúrà)* About the man you're looking for, well you know there are all sorts . . .

WÚRÀ: That's true.

ADÉNTỌ́Ọ́: Is he dark or light, or short and a bit dark, and not light at all, but a bit tall, does he have facial marks? *(Snakehead beats a tattoo with his mouth)* Oh God, I'm no use to myself any more!

SNAKEHEAD: Sorry about all this. You see, when we have a visitor from outside who doesn't yet know us, we start by putting on a show for them. We start by putting on a real show for them.

WÚRÀ: Just hold your horses. Do you mean to say neither of you has one of my kind at home [i.e., a wife]?

ADÉNTỌ́Ọ́: Should I answer the lady? I have one of your kind. But they say people all have doubles. And the one of your kind that I have is not a "Yellow Fever" like you![37] *(They laugh uproariously)*

WÚRÀ: I don't deny I look like that. You understand? But the way you talk is really stupid.

ADÉNTỌ́Ọ́: She says the way we talk is stupid. Oh let me answer her! Come here, "Madam, Madam," we're hungry.

WÚRÀ: Don't you have any work to do?

SNAKEHEAD: Sorry, you see this game of Snap that we're playing, we use it to make money. And if we're in the middle of a game, and if we get carried away like this . . .

ADÉNTỌ́Ọ́: Holy mackerel!

SNAKEHEAD: Otherwise, no visitor could speak to us without us answering.

WÚRÀ: Well, you seem a bit better than the other one. As for him, I don't think . . . you're not well at all, are you?

SNAKEHEAD: It's true, there was a time when he wasn't well.

ADÉNTỌ́Ọ́: I was "sick." [English]

SNAKEHEAD: You were terribly "sick."

ADÉNTỌ́Ọ́: Let's hurry up and take you to where you say you're going.

WÚRÀ: Do you mean you'll give me directions?

ADÉNTỌ́Ọ́: Yeah.

SNAKEHEAD: We were just fooling around entertaining you all this time. We never pick fights. All the time you were insulting us, we weren't even annoyed.

ADÉNTỌ́Ọ́: No, we weren't annoyed. God forbid. "The innards are used for childbearing, not for anger."[38] Just show her the way so that she can go.

SNAKEHEAD: You show her.

ADÉNTỌ́Ọ́: I thought you knew the place.

SNAKEHEAD: Isn't it that house, you know, over there . . .

ADÉNTỌ́Ọ́: Yeah.

SNAKEHEAD: Adé.

ADÉNTỌ́Ọ́: Yeah.

SNAKEHEAD: D.D.

ADÉNTỌ́Ọ́: Yeah.

SNAKEHEAD: She says she's taking you. Show her the way. *(Adéntòó begins to take Wúrà's things from her.)*

WÚRÀ: What, why?

ADÉNTÒÓ: What's this? What's this? What's this?

WÚRÀ: Please, please.

SNAKEHEAD: Get her handbag.

ADÉNTÒÓ: Her handbag.

SNAKEHEAD: And that shiny thing she wears on her head . . . *(Wúrà runs away, leaving her bag and head-tie behind)* Look at her stumpy legs, like the legs of a new-born baby!

ADÉNTÒÓ: What are you looking at? Come on, give it here.

*Fosko enters with Rẹ̀sònà, who immediately sees what has been going on and snatches Wúrà's handbag.*

SNAKEHEAD: Mighty.

ADÉNTÒÓ: O mighty one!

SNAKEHEAD: "Brother Tomèè"!

FOSKO: What's this?

RẸ̀SÒNÀ: They've taken all the money that was in it, I just wanted you to see the bag. This fellow's got the money *(indicating Adéntòó).*

FOSKO: Give me the money you've taken. *(Adéntòó ignores him.)*

RẸ̀SÒNÀ: Or are you out of your mind?

FOSKO: If I wanted to give it to you as a present, that would be another matter. We don't do that in Yorùbáland.

ADÉNTÒÓ: Say please, say please to the boss.

RẸ̀SÒNÀ: But it's you who's got the money!

ADÉNTÒÓ: Me! Holy mackerel! If you search my pockets and don't find the money, what will you do then?

FOSKO: Leave him alone, if he won't give it to you.

SNAKEHEAD: But he's got the money. . . . Get out.

ADÉNTÒÓ: If you "charge" me *[English]* and then don't find the money, what will you do?

FOSKO: Leave him alone, leave him alone, if he won't give it to you.

SNAKEHEAD: He's got the money. I don't like this at all.

ADÉNTÒÓ: If you "charge" me and then don't find the money on me, you'll go to jail.

RẸ̀SÒNÀ: Turn out his pockets.

ADÉNTÒÓ: I'm not a baby! Here's my pocket. *(Turning it out.)*

RẸ̀SÒNÀ: He's got no money on him.

ADÉNTÒÓ: I've no money on me. Rotten troublemakers you are. Me, with money on me? *(Laughs derisively.)*

FOSKO: 'Déntòó!

ADÉNTÒÓ: Sa! *(Fosko searches Adéntòó roughly and finds the money.)*

FOSKO: Here's what you've got in your pocket!

SNAKEHEAD: How could that have happened?

ADÉ̀NTÒ̩Ó̩: It got stuck in the corner.

SNAKEHEAD: Got stuck, how?

ADÉ̀NTÒ̩Ó̩: It got stuck here.

FOSKO: Did it really? O.K., I'll believe your story. Now, Snakehead.

SNAKEHEAD: O mighty one!

FOSKO: You're doing well, you're doing well. I'm glad that this lad's beginning to learn. Instead of the three months I said we'd keep him at home, let's change it to one month.

SNAKEHEAD: He's a real thief is that lad, he's no good.

FOSKO: Leave him alone, leave him alone. *(To Adéǹtò̩ó̩)* Look, we're going to get on just fine. You're beginning to get the hang of things. I didn't know you were ready for the battlefront already! At first your mouth was getting you into trouble, don't let that happen again. You're to spend another couple of weeks at home, to give you time to toughen up. Don't ask any more questions that'll get you into trouble. *(To the others)* After two weeks, you can take him out.

SNAKEHEAD: O mighty one, it shall be done.

FOSKO: One work spurs you on to do another. Sing a rousing song, dance, there's food, drink plenty of good palm wine. Then when you're ready . . . You, come here. Where are those two keys? Let me know how far you've got with that job.

SNAKEHEAD: I just have to finish the edges. I showed them to Ré̩sò̩nà yesterday.

RÉ̩SÒ̩NÀ: I saw them yesterday, mighty one.

FOSKO: Go and fetch them so I can see.

SNAKEHEAD: Why do you say that?

FOSKO: I said go and fetch them. I can't afford to fail in that job. Look, I don't want the kind of key that you have to keep turning and turning in the lock before it'll open.

SNAKEHEAD: Baba, you know very well that it's not the first time, nor the second nor the third, that I've made this kind of key.

FOSKO: *(Agreeing)* And they worked instantly! Ré̩sò̩nà.

RÉ̩SÒ̩NÀ: O mighty one.

FOSKO: Entertain yourselves. These boys have done a good job. Have fun. Let me find you something to drink.

ADÉ̀NTÒ̩Ó̩: Great. May you never be disgraced!

FOSKO: *(Hands Ré̩sò̩nà his walking stick)* Hold this for me, Ré̩sò̩nà.

ADÉ̀NTÒ̩Ó̩: Brothers International! *(They play a record, dance to it, and drink.)*

ADÉ̀NTÒ̩Ó̩: "It's all right," sa.

FOSKO: "Of Ejo." *(Offers Snakehead a drink.)*

SNAKEHEAD: This is great, mighty one!

ADÉNTÒ̩ó̩: I just want to taste it. Let me see what his tastes like.

RÉ̩SÒ̩NÀ: Don't let him drink it all, cos he's no good.

ADÉNTÒ̩ó̩: I'm not warmed up yet.

RÉ̩SÒ̩NÀ: You're going to get really warmed up!

FOSKO: Enjoy yourselves, enjoy yourselves. Ré̩sò̩nà, bring me my stick. Thanks. Now, I want to say something to you. Enjoy yourselves. Those keys . . . I'm pleased with the job you've done. What about the food? Eat your fill! Now let me say something. Come on, Ré̩sò̩nà, sit down. 'Déǹtò̩ó̩, sit down, sit down.

ADÉNTÒ̩ó̩: If I sit down, that drink will do me a mischief!

FOSKO: That's enough, I want to speak to you. *(Adéǹtò̩ó̩ drunkenly lurches over to Ré̩sò̩nà and sits on her lap.)*

RÉ̩SÒ̩NÀ: Is he out of his mind?

FOSKO: Take no notice of him.

RÉ̩SÒ̩NÀ: Look out, don't trample on me, are you mad?

FOSKO: That's enough, I want to talk to you. Stop it! What's the matter with you? Now, we three will go to Asínde̩'s house. *(To Snakehead)* Go and take off that record. Take off that record, please.

ADÉNTÒ̩ó̩: Don't mess about! If you don't want me to go to jail for life, "MISIK" [music]!

FOSKO: Don't be childish. Have you lost your senses?

ADÉNTÒ̩ó̩: "Misik"! What do you mean by turning off the "misik"?

FOSKO: I told him to go and turn it off.

ADÉNTÒ̩ó̩: How could you? What made you tell him to turn it off?

RÉ̩SÒ̩NÀ: The boss told him to go and turn it off.

ADÉNTÒ̩ó̩: And the apprentice says he should go and turn it on again! If you have a chance to enjoy life and don't, other people will take it and enjoy it for you. Just when we were dancing to that record . . .

> "Making whoopee is good
> Making whoopee will be the ruin of me!"

You numbskull, you had to go and turn off the "Misik"!

FOSKO: You're out of your mind.

ADÉNTÒ̩ó̩: You went and turned off the "Misik." What do you mean?

FOSKO: I won't tell you off. I wanted you to enjoy yourselves, after all.

ADÉNTÒ̩ó̩: "Nonsense."

FOSKO: Go and sleep if you're drunk.

ADÉNTÒ̩ó̩: What me? I'm not drunk! I'm just having fun.

FOSKO: Shut up, go inside and sleep.

ADÉNTÒ̩ó̩: Let me take off my cap. Right, now I'm the boss. I'm your boss now. Call me "Fosko," because I'm your boss. I'm playing with you. . . . I'll take your cap. You're no fun to play with.

RÉ̩SÒ̩NÀ: Are you mad?

FOSKO: Leave him alone.

ADÉNTÒÓ: It's your mother who's mad. Bad cess to you. When I'm ready to slap your face, I'll slap it, I'll slap your face and your mouth together. "Misik"! Go and put on the "Misik"!

> "I want to go and rest
> I want to go and rest in peace"

*(Coughs)* This stuff's choking me.

FOSKO: Go inside. Go.

ADÉNTÒÓ: Any chance of another bottle?

RÉSÒNÀ: Not likely!

ADÉNTÒÓ:  "Whoopee is good for me
Whoopee will be my ruin"

Don't wake me up if I fall asleep, anyone who wakes me up . . .

RÉSÒNÀ: Don't worry, we'll let you lie forever.

ADÉNTÒÓ: Come and take this bottle. If a rich man throws his cigarette end down, a poor man's going to step on it. If I drink liquor, one of you derelicts can take the bottle. Look how she's staring at me, like a frog on the river bank! Useless. Can't fight. I'm going to "rest in peace."

RÉSÒNÀ: Next time we won't give him anything to drink.

SNAKEHEAD: I'll tap palm wine from his side if he's not careful!

FOSKO: You're not being sensible. There's always a wild one in any bunch of people. People can't all be the same after all. Leave him alone, let him go and sleep. Leave him alone. As I was saying before, if we keep him at home for about another week . . .

RÉSÒNÀ: You said two weeks before!

FOSKO: There won't be anything he can . . . Look, you mustn't go into his room and wake him up.

RÉSÒNÀ: Who's going to wake him up? That boy's going too far, he doesn't know who his equals are. A boy who came here as a debtor, and now he's throwing his weight about! He's a useless bastard. If I put my fag out in his face it'll sting like fire.

FOSKO: You've not got to wake him up. He's asleep. You two go and have a nap as well. When it's time I'll come and wake you and we'll get ready to go to Asínde's house.

SNAKEHEAD: O mighty one!

FOSKO: Do you hear?

RÉSÒNÀ: We hear and we obey.

FOSKO: We three will go to Asínde's house. Don't wake that boy up. When he's come to his senses tomorrow, he'll know that drink destroys you with the things that are already inside you.[39]

SNAKEHEAD: He'll have to explain himself.

FOSKO: He'll have to explain himself properly to me. Let me give you a prayer before we go to Asíndẹ's house.

RÉSÒNÀ: O mighty one, give me a drink, drink is good for the head.

FOSKO: *(Ignoring her)* We must go well and return well.

RÉSÒNÀ: O mighty one.

FOSKO:  The chicken returns immaculate from
    the clinging creeper patch
  The *ayò* seeds grow up unscathed in the middle
    of the thorn patch[40]

RÉSÒNÀ: May it be so.

FOSKO: You will go well. You will return well.

RÉSÒNÀ: May it be so, O mighty one.

FOSKO: Who's going to go in front? Snakehead, you go first.

RÉSÒNÀ: Oró [pain] will go first, we will follow.

FOSKO: Keep your mouths shut. When you get there, "the angry ones did not send you on our case—"

SNAKEHEAD: I accept.

FOSKO: *(Chants:)*

  Divination was done for the *babaláwo* Tìòtí[41]
  When he was about to go on a divination trip to Ìwó
  He said the rain should threaten.
  Rain threatened.
  He said rain should fall.
  Rain fell.
  On the day the pillar falls
  That's the day they stopped being angry.
  Go like that. There is no danger. Go, go, go.

RÉSÒNÀ: O mighty one.

FOSKO: If the place turns out to be too fierce, call me.

RÉSÒNÀ: Baba, it won't be fierce.

SNAKEHEAD: It won't be hard.

FOSKO: Asíndẹ's house will be rewarding. There are goods in Asíndẹ's house. Bring them.

RÉSÒNÀ: You too, don't be long where you're going.

FOSKO: There's no danger on the farm.

RÉSÒNÀ: O mighty one, we'll report back to you.

*Résònà and Snakehead leave for Asíndẹ's house; Fosko goes inside. After a pause, Adéntòó comes out from his room, completely sober.*

ADÉNTÒÓ: They called me a drunken madman. Bad cess to every one of you forever. So you thought you'd leave me behind at home. I hope the

*The Èdá Theatre: Adéǹtóó. Photograph © Elio Montanari. Used by permission.*

bogeyman gets you![42] This is how they live. They stole the luggage from off the bride's head. Then they could think of nowhere better to go on with their work than in her husband's house. It was by paying for my *gaàrí* that they turned me into their employee. That's the kind of help that leads to trouble. Slaps! They'd slap me whenever they felt like it. You know, one of them tried to pick my nose with a knife! What a world! See what they've done to me. This is what they use in their work. *(He examines some clothes and implements in Fosko's box.)* Wow! Here it is. Just look at that. Hunters' shorts. Anyone who fires a gun at them will find the gun becomes a toy in his hands. He has medicines all right. He festoons himself in them from head to foot. Loads of them. Well, he's going to be completely disgraced. I say he's disgraced. I'll make sure I lead him right to the bottom of the river. I'm having nothing more to do with their line of work ever again. God forbid that I should ever work as a thief again. I won't do it any more! It's enough. I know that if they haven't got this *[a magical charm]* they won't be able to go to Asínde̩'s house. I'll make sure they can't go. And they won't go, by the grace of God! They want to destroy Asínde̩'s household. Shall I take it or not?

AUDIENCE: Take it! Take it!

ADÉṄTÒ̩Ó̩: Bless you for that. Some people would say I shouldn't take it. Anyone who thinks I shouldn't take it please say so!

AUDIENCE: Take it!

ADÉṄTÒ̩Ó̩: Don't tell them then. Or are you going to tell?

AUDIENCE: We won't tell. *(Adéṅtò̩ó̩ goes out with the magical charm.)*

## SCENE 5

*At the Elékóto shrine outside the town. White-robed devotees surround the shrine. They salute the god, led by Olúode̩, the head of the hunters who is also the chief priest.*

OLÚO̩DE̩: All hail!

DEVOTEES: All hail!

> On the day that I go to Ìwéré-town
> On the day that I go to Ìràwò̩[43]
> The calabash-bearer[44] will bear calabashes of soap
> Isalawè̩[45] will bear sponges
> I too will go with a staff of lead[46]
> With a staff of lead
> I'll come out in gorgeous array.

OLÚO̩DE̩: We have brought Elékóto!

DEVOTEES: Elékóto!

OLÚO̩DE̩: We cut the okro from the stem

DEVOTEES: Elékóto.

OLÚO̩DE̩: We cut the snail from its shell

DEVOTEES: Elékóto.

OLÚO̩DE̩: We enter the sea from a pool

DEVOTEES: Elékóto

OLÚO̩DE̩: If we don't go through the middle of the river

DEVOTEES: Elékóto

OLÚO̩DE̩: The water will carry Róngbé away

DEVOTEES: Elékóto, Elékóto

OLÚO̩DE̩: Olóṅsé is the mother of the young ones

DEVOTEES: Elékóto

OLÚO̩DE̩: I've brought Elékóto

DEVOTEES: Elékóto
OLÚODE: Yes, I've brought Elékóto
DEVOTEES: Elékóto
On the day that I go to Ìwéré town
On the day that I go the old Ìràwò . . .

OLÚODE: Hail!
DEVOTEES: Hail!
OLÚODE: Greetings for this festival. May we live to celebrate many more.
DEVOTEES: May it be so.
OLÚODE: The festival of Elékóto that we're celebrating today, the god, the god Elékóto, will bring happiness to you all.
DEVOTEES: May it be so!
OLÚODE: Your prayers will be answered.
DEVOTEES: May it be so.
OLÚODE: When I was in my own backyard and I heard your voices, I was happy, I was elated, and I felt proud. Hear me—all of you who are seeking children will find them.
DEVOTEES: May it be so, may it be so.
OLÚODE: All of you who desire pregnancy will become pregnant.
DEVOTEES: May it be so. May it be so.
OLÚODE: Now then, I want everyone to speak the truth at the shrine of the òrìsà. Because this òrìsà here has been worshipped for a long time in this area, and it has been good for us.
DEVOTEES: That's true.
OLÚODE: So each one of you must propitiate this òrìsà with truth in your heart. Do you hear? Ìyá-olórìsà!
PRIESTESS: I'm here.
OLÚODE: Don't let this festival be a failure.
PRIESTESS: I hear.
DEVOTEES: All hail!
PRIESTESS: *(Sings)*

        Ìkórìkótó oh[47]
        Don't let my child die
DEVOTEES: Goddess of the young ones[48]
        Don't let my child die
PRIESTESS: Ìkórìkótó
        Don't let my child have fever
DEVOTEES: Goddess of the young ones
        Don't let my child have fever . . .

OLÚODE: Ah, Ìyá-olórìsà, may you live in happiness.
PRIESTESS: May it be so.

OLÚ̩ODĘ: And may you enjoy good health.

PRIESTESS: May it be so.

OLÚ̩ODĘ: When I'm at the shrine, if I see you here, all sorrow departs.

PRIESTESS: That is good.

OLÚ̩ODĘ: You too will not experience sorrow.

DEVOTEES: May it be so.

OLÚ̩ODĘ: There's one thing about this *òrìṣà*, I want to ask you to do something. When you come to the shrine of the *òrìṣà*, I want you to worship it with truth in your hearts. Then what you ask for will come about.

DEVOTEES: That is true.

OLÚ̩ODĘ: Anyone who's asking for a child will get a child.

DEVOTEES: May it be so.

OLÚ̩ODĘ: Anyone who's asking for money will get money.

DEVOTEES: May it be so.

OLÚ̩ODĘ: Do you hear? And those of you who are out of work, you will get work.

DEVOTEES: May it be so.

OLÚ̩ODĘ: Because when you're at the shrine, you have to tell the truth. The *òrìṣà* wants nothing but the truth. Some people come and tell lies at the shrine. They forget that the *òrìṣà* hears them. That's the kind of *òrìṣà* we have in this area—one that was being worshipped before my great-grandfather was born.

PRIESTESS: That's true.

OLÚ̩ODĘ: And it has never deceived me. In my capacity as Ọ̀dọ̀fin of this town—and you know, I'm also the head of the town's hunters—

DEVOTEES: That's right.

OLÚ̩ODĘ: —the propitiation of this *òrìṣà* devolves on me.

*A man rushes in in distress, with a woman following him.*

MAN: Baba o, baba o!

OLÚ̩ODĘ: What is it?

MAN: You're an elder in this town—

OLÚ̩ODĘ: What's happened?

MAN: So don't let things go wrong in it.

OLÚ̩ODĘ: What's happened?

MAN: You know the house down by the river, I met this young lady there, and she said they'd been robbed!

DEVOTEES: Ha. Thieves!

MAN: Baba, it's in your hands.

OLÚ̩ODĘ: Thieves!

MAN: Yes, thieves, that's what I discovered. Look at him staring like a groundnut—can't you say anything?[49]

A GIRL: Baba, didn't I tell you that that's how they robbed Tijani's house too, the day before yesterday?

OLÚODE: There are hunters in the town, and yet Tijani's house is robbed![50] And I, the Olúode, the Head of the Hunters, was not told!

MAN: Baba, take care of this town. This town is going wrong. Let's take care of the town.

OLÚODE: We'll take care of it. I'll call all the hunters.

SOMEONE ELSE: Did you hear that? The thieves are back. They've come back. When there are hunters in the town!

OLÚODE: I'm going to call all the young hunters. The thieves can do their worst, this town will not be destroyed in my lifetime.

DEVOTEES: May it be so.

MAN: It won't be easy, baba. (Adéntòó comes in.)

OLÚODE: Ah! Son of Jagun!

ADÉNTÒÓ: Greetings for the festival. Many happy returns.

DEVOTEES: Thank you.

ADÉNTÒÓ: May we continue to celebrate it. There will be nothing in our lives needing to be discarded except the afterbirth of newborn babies![51]

DEVOTEES: May it be so.

ADÉNTÒÓ: We won't be found huddling at home during the festival.[52]

DEVOTEES: May it be so.

ADÉNTÒÓ: We will not become soggy and watery.[53]

DEVOTEES: May it be so.

ADÉNTÒÓ: We will not have any venereal diseases!

DEVOTEES: May it be so.

ADÉNTÒÓ: This festival will bring us blessings.

DEVOTEES: May it be so, may it be so.

ADÉNTÒÓ: So, why don't you tell me I'm late?

DEVOTEES: You are a bit late.

ADÉNTÒÓ: There's a reason for it, baba. They say "If theres no reason for it, no woman will be called Kúmólú."[54]

DEVOTEES: That's true.

ADÉNTÒÓ: And if there's no reason for it, no woman is allowed to carry a corpse.

DEVOTEES: That's true.

ADÉNTÒÓ: If things were not as they are, then a woman could be called Salawu. If she's called Salawu, she'll have to pay tax.[55]

OLÚODE: Your father was the Jagun of this town before he died.

ADÉNTÒÓ: Yes, that's right.

OLÚODE: So we look on you too as Jagun. Your father used to kill animals at the Ògún shrine here. But you—is it right that you should leave it as late as this before you come?

ADÉNTÒÓ: I didn't mean to be this late. But what I've just experienced has affected me seriously.

DEVOTEES: What was it? What's happened now?

ADÉNTÒÓ: It's very serious. But if I tell you about it here, it might mean that this festival has to be cancelled. I don't want that to happen.

OLÚODE: Don't let it be cancelled.

ADÉNTÒÓ: The habit of a lifetime can't be broken as easily as that. *(Sings)*

> Elékóto, greetings for the festival
> Evil people attacked okro in the old days
> And okro became overripe.[56]

DEVOTEES: That's right.

ADÉNTÒÓ:     And they did the same to garden egg
        And made it go blood red
        They did it to sweet potato . . .

DEVOTEES: All hail!

ADÉNTÒÓ: We will not have anything to be ashamed of in our celebration of Elékóto.

DEVOTEES: May it be so.

ADÉNTÒÓ: You see, the matter that brought me here is heavy on my tongue, and when that happens what do we do? We say it anyway. Because in the age of Olúgbón this ritual was not spoiled . . .

DEVOTEES: That's true.

ADÉNTÒÓ: And in the age of Arèsà it wasn't spoiled.[57]

DEVOTEES: That's true.

ADÉNTÒÓ: And it will not be spoiled in your time.

DEVOTEES: May it be so!

ADÉNTÒÓ: None of your people will be stricken with grief.

DEVOTEES: May it be so.

ADÉNTÒÓ: *(Sings)*

        Ìkórìkótó, don't make my dear one weep
THE REST:   *Òrìsà* of the young ones
        Don't make my dear one weep.
ADÉNTÒÓ:    Ìkórìkóto, don't make my dear one weep
THE REST:   *Òrìsà* of the young ones
        Don't make my dear one weep.

ADÉNTÒÓ: Well, baba, they say "Things have come to a head, the rich man of Apòmù."[58] You see, the thing I've come about is hard: yet it's not hard. It depends on you.

OLÚODE: What is it?

ADÉNTÒ́Ọ́: Thieves have almost succeeded in destroying this town. If you've been keeping your ears open, you'll know that a house was burgled the other day.

DEVOTEES: That's true, it was Tijani's house.

ADÉNTÒ́Ọ́: God bless you. May God protect your children. You'll have more to your name. Tijani was burgled, "that was just one out of many that God has."[59] I was in my own home, and I went out at the crack of dawn, I went to the foot of the wall to have a pee. As I was standing there, I caught a glimpse of a "toigilaisi" [torchlight], a huge one, shining, so I hid behind the door. I lurked there. The people with the light were coming closer. When it pleased God to deliver them up to me, just in front of the spot where I'd been peeing, then they began to talk. They said, "Today, we're going to do a real job." They said, "The place where we're going, it's 'if the calabash can be opened, we'll open it; if not, we'll break it.'"[60] Then they said some things I couldn't follow; and then they said "What shall we take from there?"

A DEVOTEE: What's the meaning of that, "What shall we take from there?"

ADÉNTÒ́Ọ́: Well, God decreed that they should explain it! They kept talking and in the course of their conversation they said they would go there today, and if he didn't surrender they would kill him!

DEVOTEES: What!!!

ADÉNTÒ́Ọ́: When by God's will the secret was exposed, and they said they were going to Asínde's house.

A DEVOTEE: What! That nice Mr. Asínde, what have they got against him?

ADÉNTÒ́Ọ́: They said he's rich.

A DEVOTEE: Oh, the world is hard.

OLÚỌDE: Listen, listen, son of Jagun, son of Jagun.

ADÉNTÒ́Ọ́: Yes?

OLÚỌDE: In this very town! While I am here in the town as Ọ̀dọ̀fin?

ADÉNTÒ́Ọ́: You are in the town . . .

OLÚỌDE: And I'm the Head of the Hunters in the town. And there are people here arming themselves to the teeth and swearing to terrible plans. Tell me exactly what you heard.

ADÉNTÒ́Ọ́: All right.

A DEVOTEE: Here in our town?

ADÉNTÒ́Ọ́: Yes, right here in our town.

A DEVOTEE: By the power of Olúkóto [Elékóto], this town will not be spoiled.

DEVOTEES: May it be so.

ADÉNTÒ́Ọ́: It's to prevent that that I'm here. If we hang around here much longer, it seems to me that those thieves we're talking about could nick our very caps from off our heads.

DEVOTEES: What!

OLÚQDE: Well, I think we'll cope with them. Is it tonight they said they'd go to Asíndę's house?

ADÉ̀NTÒ̩Ó̩: Yes, tonight.

OLÚQDE: This very night. Well, there's no help for it: In my capacity as Ò̩dòfin and Olúọdę of this town, I too am going to prepare.

ADÉ̀NTÒ̩Ó̩: "Whatever happens in a town concerns the head of the town."

OLÚQDE: I'll go there myself.

ADÉ̀NTÒ̩Ó̩: Are you sure?

OLÚQDE: Listen, just calm down for a moment—you're going with me!

ADÉ̀NTÒ̩Ó̩: Who?

OLÚQDE: You.

ADÉ̀NTÒ̩Ó̩: Is that so? And do you want us to go this very minute?

OLÚQDE: Wait, just listen.

PRIEST: Let me know so that I can go and get ready.

OLÚQDE: Everybody's going to get ready.

ADÉ̀NTÒ̩Ó̩: They say the truthful person in the town is the cruel person in the town.[61]

DEVOTEES: That's true.

ADÉ̀NTÒ̩Ó̩: When I came and told you about the thieves . . . because my father was a hunter . . .[62]

OLÚQDE: 'Déǹtò̩ó̩, 'Déǹtò̩ó̩, it's not like that. No, you're doing just what a person should do if he has the interests of the town at heart.

DEVOTEES: That's right.

OLÚQDE: We know you have the interests of the town at heart. After all, we didn't hear anything, you found out about it and came and told us.

DEVOTEES: That's right.

OLÚQDE: Now, just as we know you in this town, so we knew your father, we knew him well as the Jagun of this town.

DEVOTEES: That's right.

OLÚQDE: Now, you yourself must do your father's work.

ADÉ̀NTÒ̩Ó̩: That's right.

OLÚQDE: Go and change, everybody go, then we'll go together to Asíndę's house and keep watch there.

ADÉ̀NTÒ̩Ó̩: Er, baba, they say that "Every matter concerns the head of the town." If there's something that concerns the townspeople, and the head of the town says it doesn't concern him, then he's leaning his back against empty air.

DEVOTEES: Very true. Very true.

ADÉ̀NTÒ̩Ó̩: Because, if there aren't trees behind the garden fence, the fence is an "empty barrel."[63]

DEVOTEES: Yes—

ADÉ̀NTÒ̩Ó̩: It'll fall down!

DEVOTEES: That's right.

ADÉNTÒÓ: If something happens to make the schoolchildren dance to the *gangan* drum, and the teacher dances—then the children will dance themselves practically to death![64]

OLÚODE: Yes.

ADÉNTÒÓ: Did you hear that? If you take action, I won't stand by and watch. If you've all agreed that I should go—

OLÚODE: You'll go.

ADÉNTÒÓ: And that I should take my father's powers with me, and my own powers that God has bestowed on me, then fine, let's go there. I'll go. This town will not be ruined.

DEVOTEES: Àṣe. Àṣe.

OLÚODE: Listen, everyone who's celebrating this festival—the festival has had to be postponed.

ADÉNTÒÓ: Stop, now wait, don't do that! If I sing a song and you all immediately disperse—won't that suggest that I said something bad in my song? *(Sings:)*

|  |  |
|---|---|
| | People of the world, make my life good for me |
| DEVOTEES: | People of the world |
| | With a small flat flop |
| ADÉNTÒÓ: | Grant me all my wishes |
| DEVOTEES: | People of the world |
| | Falls with a small flat sound[65] |

*(They sing and dance their way out.)*

## SCENE 6

*Outside Asínde's house. Asínde brings out a deck chair and lies in it, complaining to himself.*

ASÍNDE: It's too bad that air conditioner that we bought isn't cooling the house, it's blowing hot air. Why things should be so difficult, only God knows. *(A boy enters.)*

BOY: Good evening.

ASÍNDE: Hello. Is anything wrong?

BOY: I'm here to prevent that. The Olúode told me to come and wait for him here.

ASÍNDE: But why?

BOY: He just said I should come and wait for him here.

ASÍNDE: Well that's surprising, since I've never seen you here before.

BOY: I know.

ASÍNDE: So what's happened?

BOY: He just said I should come and wait for him here.

ASÍNDE: And the hunters . . . You're not having me on?

Boy: Oh no, never, how could I be having you on, sir?

Asíndè̩: So the hunters are coming too?

Boy: Yes, they're on their way, they'll be here any minute. (*Olúo̩de̩ arrives with group of men.*)

Asíndè̩: Head of the Hunters!

Olúo̩de̩: Yes. Things are really tough in the town!

Asíndè̩: And what brings you here to my house?

Olúo̩de̩: Haaa. Asíndè̩. The time has come for the medicine man to use his medicines. You see, the thieves have held a meeting and decided to visit your house tonight, whether we like it or not.

Asíndè̩: My house—tonight!

Olúo̩de̩: So, don't sleep out here tonight, take your chair inside and sleep in your bedroom. If you hear gunfire . . .

Boy: Don't come out.

Olúo̩de̩: That'll be the hunters at work, don't come out.

Asíndè̩: Oh, Olúo̩de̩, save me, save me, Olúo̩de̩!

Man 1: Just go indoors.

Asíndè̩: Oh, please save me!

Olúo̩de̩: So the son of Jagun hasn't come here?

Man 1: Not yet.

Olúo̩de̩: Well there's nothing for it—ah, there's a drum. The son of Jagun has arrived. (*Adé̩ǹto̩ó̩ arrives in haste.*)

Adé̩ǹto̩ó̩: Where is he?

Boy: He's gone indoors.

Adé̩ǹto̩ó̩: Didn't you tell him we're going to put on a real show tonight?[66] When he saw this business was serious enough to bring out an elder like you, wasn't he amazed?

Olúo̩de̩: He certainly was.

Adé̩ǹto̩ó̩: The defeat of these thieves depends on you. Only a very brave person would dare point his gun at them. Anyone who's not so brave will raise his hand to strike only to drop it again helplessly.[67] But we've got the antidote to their poison now.

Olúo̩de̩: And we are hunters.

Adé̩ǹto̩ó̩: And the rat's tail has snapped off in their hands.[68]

A boy: That's right.

Adé̩ǹto̩ó̩: Where do you want us to stand?

Olúo̩de̩: Son of Jagun, you crouch down here. This boy should stand over there. When they've gone into the house, follow them a little way. Let them get quite a way inside. Then raise the alarm and come out again. I'm going inside myself, I'll lie in wait inside the house.

> They take up their positions and there is silence. Then a penetrating whistle is heard. Fosko's men enter. Snakehead begins an incantation.

*The Èdá Theatre: Snakehead and Adéǹtòọ́ in the final battle of
incantations. Photograph © Elio Montanari. Used by permission.*

SNAKEHEAD:  What we say to the *ogbọ́* shrub
　　　　　　The *ogbọ́* shrub hears[69]
　　　　　　What we say to the fence
　　　　　　The fence accepts[70]
　　　　　　The climbing rope goes right round the palm tree
　　　　　　I say you should sleep!

RÉSÒNÀ: Who else is reciting that with you? Ha. *(She sees one of the hunters.)* Give me your gun!

　　　　　　The okro was forgetful
　　　　　　The okro became overripe

The garden egg was forgetful
The garden egg donned a blood-red garment[71]
The dog was forgetful
So the dog has no horns.

Give that gun to me!

ADÉNTỌ́Ọ́: Ha, go back from there. Where's your boss?

SNAKEHEAD: 'Déntọ̀ọ́! A curse on your mouth.

ADÉNTỌ́Ọ́:    You are load-carriers.
              You are load-carriers
              I and your master are traders
              Call your boss here,
              So that we can trade together.

SNAKEHEAD: This from you, 'Déntọ̀ọ́?

ADÉNTỌ́Ọ́: I said it and I mean it.

RẸ́SỌ̀NÀ: What!

ADÉNTỌ́Ọ́: Today is not yesterday.

SNAKEHEAD: You dare to do this?

ADÉNTỌ́Ọ́: Oh yes, I dare. *(A drum sounds. Fosko arrives.)*

ADÉNTỌ́Ọ́: Who's there?

FOSKO: Isn't that 'Déntọ̀ọ́?

ADÉNTỌ́Ọ́: And who do you resemble?

FOSKO: Watch your head! I'll box your ears.

ADÉNTỌ́Ọ́: I'll pay you back with interest.

FOSKO: This to me?

ADÉNTỌ́Ọ́: I said it and I mean it.

FOSKO: What did I tell you about this traitor? What did I tell you? When I couldn't find my luggage anywhere in the house, what did I say?

SNAKEHEAD: You said it must be him who stole it.

FOSKO: What did I tell you? When I wash my eyes with medicines I can foresee the future. You stole my property and then had the nerve to turn up here?

ADÉNTỌ́Ọ́: The person who has the scabbard has the sword.[72]

FOSKO: Just shut your mouth or I'll strike it.

ADÉNTỌ́Ọ́: You shut yours too. You should be asking yourself what you're worth. Can you use your name to get goods on credit?[73]

FOSKO: 'Déntọ̀ọ́!

ADÉNTỌ́Ọ́: When I strike your face, there'll be a thunderclap!

FOSKO: I'll get this girl to perform her feats on you . . . *(Rẹ́sọ̀nà makes a grab at Adéntọ̀ọ́'s hunting bag.)*

ADÉNTỌ́Ọ́: Leave me alone! *(Rẹ́sọ̀nà seizes a charm from the bag and hands it to Fosko.)*

Fosko: Ha, here's my property.

Adéntòó: You can have it, it's mine.[74]

Fosko: What about the powers that are innate, not acquired?

Adéntòó: There's no innate power that I don't know about.

Fosko: You . . . !

Adéntòó: I say it and I mean it.

Résònà: I'll make kebabs out of him! I'll turn him into *suya!*[75]

Adéntòó: Get out of my way. Ha! You're holding the sword by the blade, I'm holding the hilt. This is the Olúọde standing here.

Fosko: The Olúọde of dogs or of goats?

Olúọde: *(Chants)* One who rushes to the market
    Ofenlete terrifies the elders.
    You are the one who brought the dry land to the world
    You said [he should be like] a little child, just learning to walk
    The diviner is wishing evil upon me
    But the evil only rebounds upon him.

    Give me your gun!
Résònà: What gun?

Olúọde: *(Chants)* Give me your gun
    Give me your gun
    Give me your gun!

Fosko: Did this treacherous boy tell you to come and meet me here?

Adéntòó: Don't say another word about that!

Fosko: You, treacherous boy, you're looking at Èdá Fosko. *(Fosko prepares medicines.)* So he told you to come and meet me here. . . . We're going to enter Asínde's house.

Adéntòó: Never.

*(Chants)*

What we say to the *ogbó* bush
The *ogbó* bush hears
What we say to the fence
The fence accepts
The climbing rope encircles the palm tree completely
The grass we pluck with the right hand
Stays in the right hand
The grass we pluck with the left
Remains in the left.
The proposal made by the chameleon
Is accepted by the Òrìsà of the Hill

Go back!

> The snail is calm and cool

Come over here, you can't enter there.
FOSKO: And I tell you: *(Chants)*

> "Anger in the heart
> No one sent my case to you
> Violent temper
> No one offered my case to you"
> Did divination for the *babaláwo* Adéòtí
> When he was traveling and divining
> As far as Ìwo town
> He said rain should threaten
> And rain threatened
> He said the rain should fall
> The rain fell.
> The wall opens its mouth but never talks
> On the day that the mud-pillar falls
> On that day the anger dissolved.

Give me my gun back! I tell you!

> Ògún builds a house—

I say give it back!

> If it should be
> That you are talking to me
> Eriwo-tiwo is the name
> That they call Ifá . . .
> I do what I have said
> Let the followers of Èṣù say so.

ADÉŃTÒÓ: Ha, I've told you, you'll turn back. I said you'll turn back.
You'll turn back. If you so much as stick your head inside [the house],
you'll burn to a cinder.
FOSKO: *(Struggling to retain control)* Who . . . why . . . you have the courage? You have the courage of a sacrifice-eater?[76] *(To Résònà)* Have a game
with this one—till his hair falls out of his head!

RÉSÒNÀ:　　The okro was forgetful
　　　　　　The okro became overripe
　　　　　　The garden egg was forgetful
　　　　　　The garden egg donned a blood-red garment
　　　　　　The dog was forgetful
　　　　　　So the dog has no horns.

FOSKO: It must not have!

RÉSÒNÀ: Everything that all of you are thinking will disappear from your memory!

ADÉNTÓÓ: If it's your mother who taught you, tell her the ingredients [of her magic] are one leaf short. Did you ever see the like? I say that you are mere porters. I and your master would like to do business together, and Olúọde too.

SNAKEHEAD: Stop there.

> They say "Running very swiftly"
> Is the name they call the witches by
> "Walking along gently"
> Is the name they call the denizens of heaven by.
> I said
> "Running very swiftly"
> Is the name they call the witches by
> "Walking along gently"
> Is the name they call the denizens of heaven by.
> What we say to the *ogbó* bush
> The *ogbó* bush hears
> What we say to the fence
> The fence accepts
> The climbing rope encircles the palm tree completely
> "Let it come to pass" is the word of the snail[77]
> The *ibéjì* statue has no eyesight.
> I say the elephant spear[78]
> Is telling you to run all round the house
> The basket[79] is telling you to shake with fear
> If the partridge sees the farmer
> It goes clucking off into the bush
> "There's no chance of survival"[80]
> "There's no chance of survival"
> That's the sound that chicks make.

ADÉNTÓÓ: Stop there.

> The squirrel holds its hands up in front
> The *sìgìdì*[81] holds its sword up in vain
> When the squash plant puts forth its shoots
> They lie flat on the ground
> The squirrel holds its hands up in front
> The *sìgìdì* holds its sword up in vain
> When the squash plant puts forth its shoots
> They lie flat on the ground

> When the pumpkin puts forth its shoots
> They lie flat on the ground.
> The proposals made by the chameleon
> Are always accepted by the Òrìsà of the Hill
> What we say to the *ogbọ́* bush . . .

Look, I want to say something to you. You are little children, it's your boss I want to do business with.

FOSKO: I told you not to say that again.

ADÉǸTỌ̀Ọ́: I shall say it all the same. Women gave birth to you people here, and when you were born they washed you with soap.[82] So everything I say will happen, will happen to you. When you were born, your mothers used sponges to wash you. So whatever I say will strike home to you.[83]

> No needle ever disobeyed the cloth
> No frog ever disobeyed the river

Start spinning, so that I can see how well you spin! Don't stop! The water in the palm-oil vat is used to spinning.

FOSKO: Who do you say should spin?

ADÉǸTỌ̀Ọ́: I say your boys and girls should spin.

> The water in the palm-oil vat is used to spinning.
> So start spinning, start turning and whirling!

> *Rẹ̀sònà and Snakehead begin to spin on the spot. When*
> *they fall down exhausted, Olúọdẹ's men tie their hands.*

FOSKO: But you should know that my way is the way of:

> The child will not [recoil]-
> If it puts its hand in the fire
> The child will not recoil
> If it puts its hand in the snake's mouth
> The snake cleaves the pool with its head, head-first
> The crab mounts the *ìrókò* tree with its head, head-first

OLÚỌDẸ: One who sees death and does not flee
> One who sees disease and does not scuttle off
> What I've said makes me fearless
> I am not afraid
> I shall not meet the like of you
> And fail to conquer you.

Give it to me.

FOSKO: *(Wavering)* What do you want to do with it?

OLÚỌDẸ: Just give it to me.

FOSKO: I said what do you want to do with it?

OLÚO̩DE̩: Give it to me.

FOSKO: Your mouth's hanging open, go and shut it.

OLÚO̩DE̩: *(Keeping up the pressure)* Give it to me.

FOSKO: Did that just slip out by accident?

OLÚO̩DE̩: Give it to me.

FOSKO: My gun?

OLÚO̩DE̩: That's right. Put it in my hand.

BOY: Put it in baba's hand.

FOSKO: *(Weakening)* What does he want to do with it?

ADÉ̩N̩TO̩Ó̩:  Like air,
The spider's web is light as air.
Whatever I say
You will listen to.
Put the gun you're holding into my hand
The snail is soft and cool and damp

It is so. Put it in my hands of your own accord. . . . Give me the fire [gun] in your hand. . . . Put it down here.

OLÚO̩DE̩: Son of Jagun . . . there's nothing left but to tie him up!

ADÉ̩N̩TO̩Ó̩: Come here. Come here. You've been caught. Come over here, come over here. There is no shortcut to the top of a palm tree. Yes, young man, come over here. Stay as you are, I want to tie you up. Hold your hands out. "Fully, fully the chameleon stretches its hands out to dance." Come here, come here. Come closer.

FOSKO: To do what?

ADÉ̩N̩TO̩Ó̩: For me to tie you up. You're going to come closer. . . . Come closer. Gently, gently. You're not going to be angry with me, the farmer is never angry when the cotton bursts its pod, the mother never hears her child crying without pricking up her ears. Come closer. *(Fosko is drawn slowly and reluctantly toward Adé̩n̩to̩ó̩.)*

Hold out your hands.

FOSKO: My hands?

ADÉ̩N̩TO̩Ó̩: That's what I said.

FOSKO: It slipped out of your mouth by accident.

ADÉ̩N̩TO̩Ó̩: No, I said it and meant it.

FOSKO: They've thrown sacrifices at you.[84]

ADÉ̩N̩TO̩Ó̩: God has not allowed that.

FOSKO: And if I do stretch out my hands, will you be able to tie them?

ADÉ̩N̩TO̩Ó̩: God's my witness, I'll tie them!

FOSKO: When you tied the others up I freed them.

ADÉ̩N̩TO̩Ó̩: They're still tied up. I know that you are a man as I am, but even you will agree that however many cloths a young man has, he can never have as many rags as an elder.

FOSKO: You realize that?[85]

ADÉŇTÒÓ: I know it.

FOSKO: "Anger did not send your case to you . . ."

ADÉŇTÒÓ: You bought yours; I inherited mine. Ẹ̀dá Fosko, you are a man. I know you are a man. A cutlass is a male . . .

FOSKO: A cutlass is a male . . .

ADÉŇTÒÓ: But it's come to the point where the medicine man must use his medicine.

FOSKO: That's right.

ADÉŇTÒÓ: I'm telling you. You acquired yours with money, I inherited mine. You must pay attention to what I'm going to say:

> "No needle ever rejected the cloth
> No frog ever rejected the river
> Whatever the chameleon suggests
> The Òrìsà of the Hill accepts"
> Did divination for the *babaláwo* of yesteryear
> He said he was going into the forest
> He asked, what would happen if he went into the forest?
> He said he was going to do divination
> For the diviners
> But which *babaláwo* should he do divination for?
> He said as he entered the forest without hesitation
> So he entered the grassy plain
> The clumps of grass were thick there
> Fallen leaves in the forest were thick on the ground.
> The vulture lurking there
> Will come out.
> The hornbill lurking there
> Will come out.
> They'll come out, they'll come
> And see me in the open.
> Two hundred forked branches hold up the house
> Two hundred people hold up the housepost.
> Sàngó is one that all rush to hold up[86]
> The whole world holds up the Ọba.
> All the people of the town
> Right
> Left
> They are holding me up.
> They say I should come and catch you today
> You've been caught!
> You've been caught today.

> The words I utter
> You cannot reject.
> I say it and I mean it!

OLÚODE: Tie him, tie him, tie him.

ADÉNTÒÓ: Hold out your hands. Hold out your hands in front. Hold out your hands. . . . Come over here. Come over here. Come closer. . . . I shouldn't have to say more than that to you. Stretch them out, stretch them out. Throw down the staff you're holding. Drop it. Drop it, so that I can tie your hands.

FOSKO: You want me to throw this staff down? What do you want to do with it? *(He drops his staff. Adéntòó picks it up and hands it to the Olúode.)*

ADÉNTÒÓ: Olúode, here you are. Now I'll tie him up.

FOSKO: "Try it" was the origin of the rat's suffering.

ADÉNTÒÓ: I'll tie them. *(Adéntòó slowly ties Fosko's hands while Fosko glares terrifyingly but is unable to resist.)* Now, quick, young hunter, run inside and tell Asínde to come. Then go and call the townspeople, tell them to come and have a look at the villains.

> *Young hunter goes. Asínde and the townspeople rush in.*
> *Wúrà is among them, dressed in rags.*

TOWNSPEOPLE: Where are they?

OLÚODE: There they are.

TOWNSPEOPLE: Ha! Heaven help us! A woman among them! Thieves! *(Song:)*

| SOLO: | Behold the thief! |
|---|---|
| CHORUS: | Thief! |
| SOLO: | Behold the thief! |
| CHORUS: | Thief! |
| SOLO: | Other people's money |
| CHORUS: | Thief! |
| SOLO: | Other people's clothes |
| CHORUS: | Thief! |

OLÚODE: That's enough, that's enough. Come here, all of you.

ADÉNTÒÓ: Because if I fire at you, you'll think Sòpònnón is enveloping you.[87] That's them. That's them.

ASÍNDE: Listen, Olúode, this man came to my house as a preacher not long ago.

OLÚODE: A preacher? A preacher!!!

ASÍNDE: Yes. He took all my keys outside, saying he was going to pray over them for me. You've been caught now, God has caught up with you. Ha!

OLÚODE: "He who goes, only to make the owner cry."[88]

ADÉNTÒÓ: "He who spoils the world." Come here. Come here. *(To Wúrà)* Woman, do you know them?

WÚRÀ: Ha.

OLÚODE: Here are the thieves. Do you know them?

WÚRÀ: It's them all right.

OLÚODE: Yes, it's them.

ADÉNTÒÓ: Robbers. That's who they are.

ASÍNDE: Olúode—

OLÚODE: Yes.

ASÍNDE: Do you know this woman?

OLÚODE: Ha!

ASÍNDE: This is Wúrà, my wife who left me.

OLÚODE: Ah, Wúrà!

ASÍNDE: Are these the people you said used to stop to talk to you when you went out? God has caught up with you. God has caught up. . . . I did everything I could to please this woman. I did everything she asked. But it wasn't enough. She went off and fell into the hands of the type of people who pass pennies off as shillings.[89] God's hand has got you now.

OLÚODE: Son of Jagun, son of Jagun, come over here.

ADÉNTÒÓ: Yes, baba.

OLÚODE: Well?

ADÉNTÒÓ: They say that "When a hunter stands to attention it's as if an *àgèrè* drum could come to blows with him." If they call this man a preacher—

OLÚODE: Well?

ADÉNTÒÓ: They wouldn't be lying.

OLÚODE: How do you mean?

ADÉNTÒÓ: If they call him a mallam—

OLÚODE: Yes?

ADÉNTÒÓ: They wouldn't be lying. And if they call him a *babaláwo,* they wouldn't be lying.

OLÚODE: How come?

ADÉNTÒÓ: He can turn his hand to anything. He's a real man all right. But they say that a day is a day, but one of these days will be the thief's last. Let those whom it concerns understand this. Things have gone out of his control today. That's all I need to say.

OLÚODE: Well.

ADÉNTÒÓ: As far as this woman's concerned . . .

OLÚODE: Yes?

ADÉNTÒÓ: God has caught up with her. They say "String of beads, break in the house, don't break outside: the string of beads is bound to break somewhere."

OLÚ̩ODE̩: That's true.

ADÉ̩N̩TÒ̩Ó̩: But when the string of beads broke, it broke into the river![90] This is the man she wanted to marry.

OLÚ̩ODE̩: What! A robber!

ADÉ̩N̩TÒ̩Ó̩: Yes. That's where she went. Some women don't know the meaning of "What is your work? What kind of trade do you do?" As long as they see that the man is loaded. If he has fancy shoes . . . wears lace every day . . . She won't bother to ask "What is your work?" She'll just go off with him! Well, God has punished this one. At least she still has the clothes she stands up in. That's all she has left, what she's wearing now. And she hasn't even got any shoes any more. *(To Wúrà)* No one is going to punish you, you've already been punished enough.

OLÚ̩ODE̩: That's right.

ADÉ̩N̩TÒ̩Ó̩: That was what was troubling her.

ASÍNDE̩: Thank you for saying that.

ADÉ̩N̩TÒ̩Ó̩: Er, baba—

OLÚ̩ODE̩: Yes?

ADÉ̩N̩TÒ̩Ó̩: Let me shoot these ones.

OLÚ̩ODE̩: Shoot them.

ADÉ̩N̩TÒ̩Ó̩: *(To townspeople)* Get out of the way. Let me shoot them. I'll wipe them out.

OLÚ̩ODE̩: Wipe them out. *(Adé̩n̩tò̩ó̩ fires his gun at the thieves but no one falls.)*

OLÚ̩ODE̩: Have you got another [gun]? Take this one.

ADÉ̩N̩TÒ̩Ó̩: Where's the horsetail that I gave you?[91] That's right. I know that you too are a man. Ha, Ifá o! *(Adé̩n̩tò̩ó̩ fires his gun again.)*

RÉ̩SÒ̩NÀ: Oh agony! *(They all die except Fosko.)*

ADÉ̩N̩TÒ̩Ó̩: Are you ready?

FOSKO: You and who?

ADÉ̩N̩TÒ̩Ó̩: You and me.

FOSKO: To do what?

ADÉ̩N̩TÒ̩Ó̩: Ha, don't you see your companions?

FOSKO: What about them?

ADÉ̩N̩TÒ̩Ó̩: They're lying on top of one another.

FOSKO: Me against you?

ADÉ̩N̩TÒ̩Ó̩: That's right.

FOSKO: If a diviner is going to throw his Ifá away, it won't be in front of a layman. That is what I've got to say to you.

ADÉ̩N̩TÒ̩Ó̩: *(Laughs derisively)* We know you're a man.

FOSKO: I mean it. I'll go to my house.

OLÚ̩ODE̩: You will fall to the ground. Fall.

ADÉ̩N̩TÒ̩Ó̩: So, go! *(Laughs)* The ground. *(Slowly, Fosko sinks to the ground.)* Thief. Thief. *(Fosko dies.)* You see how wicked the world is? *(Song:)*

ALL:   The secret is out
Exposed to plain view
Your gang was not like a flock of doves
Or of pigeons

You burgled other people's houses
You killed other people's children
Other people's wives could not walk
Without fear of disappearing.
Look up and then look down
This wickedness has reached its end.

*Lérè Pàímọ́, playing Fosko, now gets up and addresses the audience.*

LÉRÈ PÀÍMỌ́: If you see people building one house after another, buying more land every day, [remember that] at the root of riches is a shameful secret. Don't you go that way, let us wait our turn, the good things of life that are due to us will not pass us by, God willing. You see, someone who does not know how his mates are getting rich will run himself almost to death [trying to catch up]. Don't go that way. They may shine [with wealth] every day; by the power of God, we too will be blessed in our time. When you watch the plays of Lérè Pàímọ́—*Èdá, Onílé Ọlá*—and laugh, please also always learn from them.

*Song by the whole company:*

The secret is out
Exposed to plain view
Your gang was not like a flock of doves
Or of pigeons
You burgled other people's houses
You killed other people's children
Other people's wives could not walk
Without fear of disappearing.
Look up and then look down
This wickedness has reached its end.

We'll keep saying it
If you like, listen;
Even if we said it over and over and over
Many more times than that
Those with cloth ears
Will never listen.

LÉRÈ:   I've delivered the message you sent me with
Yes, I've delivered the message you sent me with.

Ìkòyí soldiers don't call each other by name[92]
But I've delivered the message you sent me with.

The secret is out
Exposed to plain view

Your gang was not like a flock of doves
Or of pigeons
You burgled other people's houses
You killed other people's children
Other people's wives could not walk
Without fear of disappearing.
Look up and then look down
This wickedness has reached its end.
Yẹmí went, but Yẹmí is back again
CHORUS:    We have arrived
LÉRÈ:       Yẹmí went, but Yẹmí is back again
CHORUS:    We have arrived.
LÉRÈ:       The *igbegbe* bird never stays long
                where it goes to look for food
CHORUS:    We have arrived
LÉRÈ:       Let us give thanks to God.
CHORUS:    We have arrived.
LÉRÈ:       Ah, the danger of fire never kills the hawk
CHORUS:    Oh hawk, greetings for escaping!
LÉRÈ:       Well, I've delivered the message you sent me with
                I've delivered the message you sent me with.

Thank you, thank you for spending money. God will replace the money you spent tonight with plenty more. This year will be a year of laughter and joy for us all. By the power of God, we will meet again next year. We'll meet again in joy. And we'll bring a new play to you. We greet all our guests.

### NOTES

1. "do remarkable shows": The Yorùbá phrase is *ṣe bẹbẹ*, which recalls the great Bẹbẹ festival of old Òyó, held as a jubilee once in his reign only by an Aláàfin who lived to a great age: in other words a rare and magnificent event.

2. "All your games with the girls / Have come to an end": These lines are in the voice of a bride, who is warning her husband that his carefree bachelor life is over.

3. "Onílé-Olá had two wives": This verse refers to the story of another play in the Èdá Theatre's repertoire, entitled *Onílé Olá*. The song was originally composed

for that play but later included in the collection of opening glee songs that can be performed before any play.

4. Èdá is Everyman, the famous role in which Lérè Pàímó first made his name as an actor in Dúró Ládiípò's theatre company in the 1960s. The name stuck and became a permanent alias, by which audiences always recognized him. The verse suggests that Lérè had been absent from the theatre circuit for some time, because of illness or the attacks of enemies, but has withstood the ordeal and is now back in fine form.

5. "the house of Olúfón": The house of the king of Ifón. This expression is an idiom used to suggest something that happened in times of antiquity: the Olúfón is associated with two other primordial kings, Asèdá and Akódá, both of which mean "Founder."

6. "Òpó" [Housepost]: This is the emblem of one of the great scattered quasi-kin groups, called clans in the anthropological literature, which identify themselves by claiming common origin in an ancient, named town. In this case the town of origin is Ìwàtá. This "clan" is associated with the weaving of cotton cloth and with a story about an ancestor who was plagued by repeated swarms of locusts. The chant is a performance of *oríkì orílè*, the praise poetry of places of origin. The "clan" being praised and identified in this way is named by Lérè Pàímó as his mother's own.

7. "the post wears a wrapper / the post ties a sash": These lines of *oríkì* allude to a funeral custom still prevalent among groups of Ìwàtá origin in which a short carved post is erected in the house of the deceased and wrapped in rich cloths as an emblem of his or her group identity. The post wrapped in cloth combines the two themes of housepost and weaving, important in the *oríkì*, and also alludes to a story about an ancient king of Ìwàtá who carved 200 houseposts for the Aláàfin in the image of the Aláàfin's dead mother. The Aláàfin wrapped them in cloth to commemorate her.

8. "You go wearing one pattern of cloth and I go wearing a different one": The fashion is for men and wives, or whole families, or all the members of an association or club, to wear outfits made of the same cloth on important occasions. These matching outfits are known as *aso ebí*, "family cloth."

9. "Do my mother's second burial": Lit. *Yí èhìn òkú ìyáà mi padà:* to turn my mother over (in the grave). It's another excuse for spending money conspicuously as well as doing honor to the memory of the dead.

10. "someone that millions flock after": Lit. *elérò*, "owner of crowds." One of the greatest signs of success in Yorùbá culture is the ability to attract huge numbers of people to one's celebrations.

11. "I've been going there continually": I.e., he's been going to the car dealers to urge them to get him a suitable car, a necessary step in a country of shortages where all transactions depend on the exertion of personal influence.

12. "his money never stays in this house": I.e., he must be spending the money outside, on other people (she suspects him of not going to the building site but to a lover).

13. "Father and son are never so close . . .": A proverb, meaning that however kind he is to the boy, there are some things he won't let him share.

14. "There's no danger in the farm . . .": A proverb, meaning that there's nothing to fear.

15. "proper Yorùbá": This means to talk as elders do, wisely, with forethought and mastery of the subject.

16. "he hasn't become any better known than before": I.e., however many houses he builds, if he does not use his wealth to make himself socially visible, they will not add to his prestige.

17. Fosko, Oríẹ̀jò, Adéǹtòọ́, Résọ̀nà: All these names say something about the character of the people who bear them. Fosko is one of the boss's many nicknames, which also include Baba Moló, "Bros International," and "Ìgbóyà bàbá" (courage father, translated here as "mighty one"). The name Fosko is associated with the American underworld, appearing as the name of a villain in Wilkie Collins's *The Woman in White*, but even to members of the audience who don't know this, it is unmistakably imported and non-Yorùbá. Oríẹ̀jò means snake's head. This character is also sometimes called Oró-ejò, "snake's venom" or the pain caused by a snakebite. Adéǹtòọ́ [Adé rìn tò ọ́] is a good royal Yorùbá name meaning "The crown is following you" i.e., you can expect to be Ọba soon. Résọ̀nà is the Yorùbá version of a brand name of a popular type of imported soap, Rexona, and is therefore associated with the good life.

18. "You know I'm the greatest": The word used is the Hausa *megida*, meaning a high-ranking, estimable man. Many Hausa words, including this, have been adopted by Yorùbá speakers in informal speech but still retain an air of foreignness. (Many others, however, have become basic Yorùbá words not recognized as Hausa loan words.)

19. "If you're going to grow tall, your legs will get thin": This is an idiom, meaning that someone who intends to achieve much in life will have to suffer first.

20. "like a nesting ant": *aládi*, a small black ant that builds nests in trees.

21. "as a member of your extended family, or as a full sister": People of the same lineage usually have the same facial markings. Adéǹtòọ́ thinks Wúrà will see through the deception if Résọ̀nà is presented to her as Fosko's sister, because he has marks and she doesn't.

22. "your new wife": All the natal members of a lineage, including the daughters, are identified together as a solidary block when marriages are negotiated. The women that marry into the compound are referred to as the "wives" of all its members. So Fosko's sister would treat his new wife Wúrà as "her" wife and would be referred to as Wúrà's "husband."

23. "I'll get something ready for you": Conventionally this would mean to prepare something nice to eat for her, which is how Wúrà understands it. What Résọ̀nà means, however, is that they're planning a horrible reception for Wúrà.

24. "Why are you pawing me like that?": The Yorùbá is *teFá láraà mi*, the literal meaning of which is "marking Ifá figures on my body." A diviner casting Ifá will mark patterns in a tray of sawdust with two fingers of his right hand, to produce one of the 256 *odù* or divination figures. The process is long drawn-out: she means a prolonged pawing.

25. "There is no one who wants one to be rich, except one's own Orí." Orí is Head, Luck, Destiny, principle of success, one's closest "adviser" and only trusted friend, even closer than one's *òrìsà* (deity). This formulation is a standard philosophical one used in praise poems, or quoted as a proverb; it sums up an important theme in Yorùbá thought, the idea that every individual is surrounded by potential enemies and must be watchful and self-reliant.

26. "The same criticisms / That apply to you / Apply to them too": I.e., you're each as bad as the other.

27. "May you never buy sugar to eat": A modern colloquial curse: *súgà* (local or imported sugar) represents the good things of life not only because of its sweetness but because it is associated with foreign things, modern ways of life, and luxuries.

28. "Oró City": One of Oríẹ̀jò's alternative names is Oró-ejò (snakebite, snake's venom). Résọ̀nà is punning on the word *oró* (venom) which sounds like the name of the town, Òro.

29. "D.D.": For 'dé 'dè, i.e., Ádé Àdè, in turn short for Adéǹtòọ́.

30. "Trousers picked from a rack": Good quality new clothes are always made to measure. Ready-made clothes bought from market stalls are usually ultra-cheap, bulk-imported, second-hand, and of low quality.

31. "We don't show off our strength if we've found a helper": A proverb. You only make a show of strength when you have no alternative, i.e., when there's no one else to do the job for you or with you. Since Résònà and Oríejò refused to help Adéǹtòó lift the load to his head, he made the best of a bad job and gave it a mighty push.

32. "She's coming to her husband's house": "To come to the house of" a man is to marry him.

33. "like nobody's business": What he actually says is "to the point of *wálà láálí naha*," this Arabic phrase being taken from Islamic prayers. Islamic praying is thought to be excessive by non-Muslims, so the quotation suggests something like "to excess," "to the highest degree."

34. "Like an old wooden door": *ìlèkùn abógundé* is an old-fashioned thick round wooden door used in traditional mud-built compounds.

35. "There are no elders on a rat-hunt": A proverb, meaning that when people go hunting, seniority is of no concern—everyone joins in the chase together.

36. "see how long they are": Wúrà has criticized Snakehead's appearance without specifying what's wrong with it. Adéǹtòó pretends to think the problem is the length of Snakehead's arms, which he has willfully stretched to inelegant lengths.

37. "a 'Yellow Fever' like you": Slang to describe someone with a very light, yellowish complexion. The expression was popularized by Felá Aníkúlápó-Kútì's Afrobeat album of that title.

38. "The innards are used for childbearing, not for anger": This expression turns on a pun: to be angry is *bínú* [*bí inú*]; to bear children is *bí omo*. The word *inú*, embedded in the verb *bínú*, means "innards," "stomach," "inside."

39. "Drink destroys you with the things that are already inside you": I.e., your own faults of character come out under the influence of drink and ruin you.

40. "The chicken returns immaculate from the clinging creeper patch / The *ayò* seeds grow up unscathed in the middle of the thorn patch": These lines are *ofò* (incantations) which are intended to bring about a state of affairs in real life analogous to the ones described in the poetry. A chicken's shiny feathers do not pick up burrs from creepers, and the smooth round seeds used in playing the game *ayò* are not scratched by the thorns which may surround them where they grow. In the same way, the robbers will come back unscathed from Asínde's house.

41. "Divination was done for the *babaláwo* Tíòtí": This is a characteristic formulation from an Ifá divination verse. Here it is being used as *àyájó*, another form of incantatory and efficacious poetic utterance which draws heavily on Ifá.

42. "I hope the bogeyman gets you!" The Yorùbá expression *kélé gbé o* [or the variant *gbóró gbé o*], "Kélé's caught you" is used in a children's game rather like "What time is it Mr. Wolf?" When the person who is "it" manages to catch someone else who is stalking him, he shouts "Kélé's got you."

43. Ìràwò: The town especially associated with the worship of Òrìsà Oko (deity of the farm, who is also a hunter and river deity).

44. Calabash-bearer: A ritual office held by a young virgin in the Òsun cult. Òsun is the deity of the river of that name, especially associated with Òsogbo.

45. Isalawè: An office held in the Òrìsà Oko cult.

46. "I too will go with a staff of lead": Lead ornaments are associated with the worship of the "white deities" clustered around the central figure of Òrìsàálá/Obàtálá.

47. Ìkórìkótó: A variant of Elékóto.

48. "Goddess of the Young Ones": In Yorùbá, *Òrìsà Èwe*, another name for Elékóto.

49. "staring like a groundnut": A strange and uncommon metaphor, presumably intended to suggest the vacant gaze of someone who is at a complete loss.

50. "There are hunters in the town, and yet Tijani's house is robbed": Hunters traditionally had the task of protecting the town against marauders and thieves. In wartime they kept watch for the enemy and trained the town's young men in the use of magical weapons and incantations.

51. "except the afterbirth of newborn babies": This prayer means that there will be nothing bad (= what is discarded) except the "bad" part of a birth, i.e., the afterbirth. When a woman gives birth successfully she is said to have delivered "both bad and good" i.e., both afterbirth and baby. So there will be nothing bad in our lives except the "bad" that has to accompany the greatest blessing of all, a new child.

52. "huddling at home during the festival": The only reasons for "huddling at home" would be illness, bereavement, or a terrible loss of some other kind.

53. "soggy and watery": The Yorùbá expression *pin yìnkìn*, used to describe what happens to *èko*, cornstarch loaves, when they are a few days old and have begun to deteriorate inside their leaf wrappings.

54. "If there's no reason for it, no woman will be called Kúmólú": A proverb meaning that there is always a good reason for an unusual occurrence ("no smoke without fire"). Kúmólú ("Death has taken the lord") is a man's name, appropriate for someone who inherits an important town title on the sudden death of the previous incumbent. The unusual circumstances leading to a woman's being called Kúmólú might be a regency held by a woman: a rare but not impossible occurrence.

55. "If she's called Salawu, she'll have to pay tax": Salawu is a typical man's Muslim name. "She'll have to pay tax" harks back to the early days of colonial rule when only adult males paid tax. If she bears a man's name she must shoulder a man's burdens—which only goes to show how impossible it is that a woman should be "Salawu." All this is Adéntòó's flippant way of talking, but also announces the inevitability of his reason for being late.

56. "okro became overripe": This is a standard Yorùbá poetic idiom. Okro is paired with *ikàn* (garden egg) and the development cycle of each is used to illustrate a wide variety of behavior among humans. See Barber (1991:179–82).

57. "In the age of Olúgbón . . . in the age of Arèsà": This is an idiom, meaning in the days of old.

58. "Things have come to a head, the rich man of Apòmù:" An idiom used to indicate the crisis or high point of an activity. People I asked did not know who the original "rich man of Apòmù" was or how his case was relevant to situations of crisis.

59. "that was just one out of many that God has": A saying used to comment on a misfortune when there has been a whole succession of them—it shows the speaker is fed up.

60. "if the calabash can be opened, we'll open it; if not, we'll break it": I.e., they'll do it by hook or by crook, by force if necessary.

61. "the truthful person in the town is the cruel person in the town": A saying, meaning that because the truth is often painful the person who speaks the truth will be seen as unkind.

62. "because my father was a hunter . . .": Adéntòó doesn't express his thought in full, but the Olúode immediately knows what he's getting at. Adéntòó thinks the townspeople connect the thefts of earlier times with his father, who was a great hunter and could have provided thieves with magical powers.

63. "if there aren't trees behind the garden fence, the fence is an 'empty barrel'": Adéntòó is mixing his metaphors as well as his languages. The Yorùbá proverb says "If there were no trees behind the garden fence, the fence would fall": i.e., to succeed, everyone must have a more important person quietly lending his sup-

port. He then adds the expression "empty barrel" in English to reinforce the idea of the uselessness and helplessness of a man without supporters.

64. "If something happens . . . practically to death": I.e., if the head of the town bestirs himself, the townspeople at large will be spurred on to far greater efforts.

65. "Falls with a small flat sound": Probably a nonsense line.

66. "put on a real show tonight": Lit. "The masquerade is going to dance."

67. "raise his hand to strike only to drop it again helplessly": Because he can't withstand the thieves' superior magical powers. There is a medicine which empowers a fighter to command the enemy to drop their weapons, freeze, turn their backs, etc., without using any physical weapon.

68. "the rat's tail has snapped off in their hands": There is a folk story in which Leopard chases Rat right to its burrow and manages to seize it, only to find that it has shed its tail and escaped into the hole.

69. "What we say to the *ogbọ́* shrub / The *ogbọ́* shrub hears": *ogbọ́* is a glabrous shrub with round black fruits. It is used in this incantation because of the syllable *gbọ́* which is identical in sound to the verb *gbọ́*, to hear.

70. "What we say to the fence / The fence accepts": *ogbà* (an enclosure, or garden fence) is used because of the syllable *gbà* which is identical in sound to the verb *gbà* to accept, agree.

71. "The okro . . . the garden egg": A common lexical pair. See note 56.

72. "The person who has the scabbard has the sword": I.e., he has both destructive medicine and its antidote. He has every advantage.

73. "Can you use your name to get goods on credit?": Only very important people can buy things on tick simply on the strength of their reputation.

74. "You can have it, it's mine": Fosko is referring to magical substances he claims Adéǹtọ́ọ́ stole from him and is now using against him. Adéǹtọ́ọ́ answers that Fosko can take them if he likes, because they belong to him (Adéǹtọ́ọ́) and will not harm their owner even if they fall into an enemy's hands.

75. "I'll turn him into *suya*!": *suya* is a kebab, strongly spiced with ginger and pepper, sold in Yorùbá markets and motor parks by Hausa people.

76. "You have the courage of a sacrifice-eater": Someone who takes the food that has been left at shrines as an offering, and eats it, is risking the wrath of the òrìṣà for whom the offering was intended. Such a person must be brave to the point of foolhardiness.

77. "'Let it come to pass' is the word of the snail": *Ilákòṣe* is a type of small snail, chosen in this formulation because of the syllable *ṣe*, which is identical in sound to the verb *ṣe* to come to pass, to happen as predicted or requested.

78. "I say the elephant spear": Elephant spear (*aṣá* or, in Ọ̀yọ́ dialect, *aṣá*) is used in this context for the syllable *sá*, identical in sound to the verb *sá* to run.

79. The basket: Basket (*agbọ̀n*) is chosen for the syllable *gbọ̀n*, which is identical in sound to the verb *gbọ̀n*, to shiver or shake.

80. "There's no chance of survival": In Yorùbá this is *Kò síyè*, which when repeated is felt to sound like the clucking of chicks.

81. The *ṣìgìdì*: A clay image made by a person who wishes to send harm to his enemy. He will make sacrifices to it and utter incantations over it, thus empowering it to go by night in a dream to the victim and inflict harm on him.

82. "they washed you with soap": Soap (*ọṣẹ*) is brought in here because its second syllable is identical in sound to the verb *ṣẹ* meaning to come about, to happen as predicted or commanded.

83. "When you were born, your mothers used sponges to wash you": So whatever I say will strike home to you. Sponge (*kàn-ìn-kàn-ìn*) is brought in here because the syllables *kàn-ìn* resemble the words *kàn 'ín*, "strike you, affect you."

84. "They've thrown sacrifices at you": Fosko is referring to the kind of sacrifice that is made to avert disaster by redirecting it away from the human community.

If the offering is thrown at a scapegoat, the evil will be diverted to him. The statement has the force of a curse as well as an insult.

85. "However many cloths a young man has, he can never have as many rags as an elder": A proverb meaning, in this context, that newly acquired property cannot be compared to long-standing property. Adéntòó is referring to medicine: Fosko has a lot of charms and incantations, but Adéntòó's are more effective because as well as those acquired by himself, he also has those inherited from his father. Fosko attempts to reverse the application of the proverb, by claiming that he is superior because he is older than Adéntòó and therefore has medicines of longer standing.

86. "Sàngó is one that all rush to hold up": He means the Sàngó priest, who when possessed during the festival does all kinds of amazing stunts, and is supported by a retinue of chanting, drumming devotees.

87. "You'll think Sòpònnón is enveloping you": Sòpònnón is the god of smallpox, and to be covered or enveloped by him is to be afflicted with the disease.

88. "He who goes, only to make the owner cry": A nominalized phrase like an epithet of oríkì (praise poetry), coined to describe thieves.

89. "people who pass pennies off as shillings": Lit. "Those who fill up the hole in a penny with èbà (a foodstuff made from cassava meal) and tell you it's a shilling." In the early days of colonial rule, pennies in Nigeria had a hole in the middle to make it possible to string them like cowries, the pre-colonial currency.

90. "When the string of beads broke, it broke into the river": The best place for a string of beads to break is inside the house where they can be easily retrieved. The worst possible place is over water. Adéntòó is saying that Wúrà would eventually have left Asínde whatever he did (the beads are bound to break) but she threw herself at the worst possible new husband (the beads broke into the river).

91. "Where's the horsetail that I gave you?": The allies are trying to find a weapon that will kill the robbers, who are tied up but are still able to resist normal gunfire. Olúode offers Adéntòó another gun, but he asks for his horsetail, a magically endowed charm which Olúode is holding for him. This charm weakens Oríejò and Résònà enough for the next shots to kill them, but Fosko still holds out.

92. "Ìkòyí soldiers don't call each other by name": Ìkòyí was the headquarters of the Aláàfin's military forces. They are professionals, and know better than to reveal each others' names, which enemy soldiers could use in incantations directed against them. The phrase as used here suggests a meaning like "We don't need to spell it out," "You can all take a hint," "We have delivered our message and it is up to you to interpret it."

# BIBLIOGRAPHY

Agblemagnon, F. N. 1984. *Sociologie des sociétés orales d'Afrique noire: les Eve du Sud-Togo*. Paris: Silex [1st edition 1969, Paris: Mouton].

Akam, Noble, and Ricard, Alain (eds.). 1981. *Mister Tameklor, suivi de Francis le Parisien, par le Happy Star Concert Band de Lomé*. Paris: SELAF/ORSTOM.

Awoonor, Kofi. 1974. *Guardians of the Sacred Word: Ewe Poetry*. New York: Nok.

Bame, K. N. 1985. *Come to Laugh: African Traditional Theatre in Ghana*. New York: Lillian Barber Press.

Barber, Karin. 1982. "Popular reactions to the petro-naira," *Journal of Modern African Studies* 20, 3.

Barber, Karin. 1986. "Radical conservatism in Yorùbá popular plays," *Bayreuth African Studies Series*, 7.

Barber, Karin. 1987. "Popular Arts in Africa," *African Studies Review*, 30, 3.

Barber, Karin. 1988. "Ethnies, état et littérature populaire Yoruba," *Politique Africaine* 32.

Barber, Karin. 1991. *I Could Speak Until Tomorrow: Oríkì, Women and the Past in a Yorùbá Town*. Edinburgh: Edinburgh University Press for the I.A.I.

Barber, Karin. 1995. "Literacy, improvisation and the public in Yorùbá popular theatre," in Stewart Brown (ed.), *The Pressures of the Text: Orality, Texts and the Telling of Tales*. Birmingham: Birmingham University African Studies Series, 4 (6–27).

Barber, Karin. forthcoming (1997). "Introduction," in Karin Barber (ed.), *Readings in African Popular Culture*. London: James Currey/Bloomington: Indiana University Press for the International African Institute.

Barber, Karin, and Ogundijo, Bayo. 1994. *Yorùbá Popular Theatre: Three Plays by the Oyin Adéjobí Company*. Atlanta: ASA Press.

Barber, Karin, and Waterman, Christopher. 1995. "Traversing the global and the local: fújì music and praise poetry in the production of contemporary Yorùbá popular culture," in Daniel Miller (ed.), *Worlds Apart*. London: Routledge.

Caldwell, J. C. 1969. *African Rural-Urban Migration*. London: Christopher Hurst.

Chartier, Roger. 1989. "Texts, printings, readings," in Lynn Hunt (ed.), *New Cultural History*. Berkeley: University of California Press.

Chernoff, John Miller. 1979. *African Rhythm and African Sensibility*. Chicago: University of Chicago Press.

Chernoff, John Miller. 1985. "Africa come back: the popular music of West Africa," in Geoffrey Hayden and Dennis Marks (eds.), *Repercussions*. London: Century.

Clark, Ebun. 1979. *Hubert Ogunde: The Making of Nigerian Theatre*. Oxford: Oxford University Press.

Clifford, James, and Marcus, George. 1986. *Writing Culture*. Berkeley: University of California Press.

Collins, E. J. 1976a. "Comic opera in Ghana," *African Arts* 9, 2. Reprinted in Richard Priebe (ed.), *Ghanaian Literatures*. Westport, Conn.: Greenwood Press, 1988 (61–72).

Collins, E. J. 1976b. "Ghanaian highlife," *African Arts* 10, 1 (62–68 and 100).

Collins, John (E. J.). 1985. *Music Makers of West Africa*. Washington, D.C.: Three Continents Press.

Collins, E. J. 1986. *E. T. Mensah, King of Highlife*. London: Off the Record Press.

Collins, E. J. 1987. "Jazz feedback to Africa," in *American Music* (Illinois Press) 5, 2 (176–93).

Collins, John [E. J.], and Richards, Paul. 1982. "Popular music in West Africa: suggestions for an interpretative framework," in David Horn and Philip Tagg (eds.), *Popular Music Perspectives*. International Association for the Study of Popular Music: Goteborg and Exeter. Reprinted as "Popular Music in West Africa" in Simon Frith (ed.), *World Music, Politics and Social Change*. Manchester: Manchester University Press, 1989.

Collins, John [E. J.]. 1992. *West African Pop Roots*. Philadelphia: Temple University Press.

Collins, John [E. J.]. 1992. "The Concert Party: popular entertainment and the Ghanaian school syllabus," in Ad Boeren and Kees Epskamp (eds.), *The Empowerment of Culture: Development Communication and Popular Media*. The Hague: CESO Publications no. 17 (171–7).

Collins, John [E. J.]. 1994. "The Ghanaian Concert Party: African Popular Music at the Crossroads." Ph.D. diss., SUNY Buffalo.

Collins, John [E. J.]. 1994. *Highlife Time*. Accra: Anansesem Publications Ltd.

Coplan, David. 1978 . "'Go to my town, Cape Coast!': the social history of Ghanaian highlife," in Bruno Nettl (ed.), *Eight Urban Musical Cultures*. Urbana: University of Illinois Press.

Drewal, M. T. 1991. "The state of research on performance in Africa," *African Studies Review* 34, 3 (1–64).

Duvignaud, Jean. 1965. *L'Acteur—Esquisse d'une Sociologie du Comédien*. Paris: Gallimard.

Etherton, Michael. 1982. *The Development of African Drama*. London: Hutchinson.

Euba, Akin. 1970. "New idioms of music drama among the Yoruba," *Yearbook of the International Folk Music Council*, 2.

Fabian, Johannes. 1978. "Popular culture in Africa: findings and conjectures," *Africa* 48, 4.

Fabian, Johannes. 1990. *Power and Performance: Ethnographic Explorations Through Proverbial Wisdom and Theater in Shaba, Zaire*. Madison: University of Wisconsin Press.

Fafunwa, A. Babs. 1974. *History of Education in Nigeria*. London: Allen and Unwin.

Fagborun, J. Gbenga. 1994. *The Yoruba Koiné—Its History and Linguistic Innovations*. Munich/Newcastle: Lincom Europa.

Götrick, Kacke. 1984. *Apidan Theatre and Modern Drama*. Stockholm: Almqvist and Wiksell International.

Gray, Anne. 1994. *Video Playtime*. London: Routledge.

Gugler, Josef, and Flanagan, William G. 1978. *Urbanisation and Social Change in West Africa*. Cambridge: Cambridge University Press.

Hannerz, Ulf. 1987. "The world in creolization," *Africa* 57, 4 (546–59).

Haynes, Jonathan. 1994. "Structural adjustments of Nigerian comedy: Baba Sala," *Passages* (Northwestern University), 8.

Hopkins, A. G. 1973. *An Economic History of West Africa*. London: Longman.

Horton, Christian Dowu. 1984. "Popular bands of Sierra Leone: 1920 to the present," *The Black Perspective in Music* (Cambria Heights, N.Y.), vol. 12, 2.

Ijimere, Obotunde. 1966. *The Imprisonment of Obatala and Other Plays*. London: Heinemann Educational Books.

Jenkins, Ray. 1990. "Intellectuals, publication outlets and 'past-relationships'. Some observations on the emergence of early Gold Coast/Ghanaian historiography in the Cape Coast-Accra-Akropong 'triangle': c. 1880-1917," in P. F. de Moraes Farias and Karin Barber, *Self-Assertion and Brokerage: Early Cultural Nationalism in West Africa*. Birmingham: Birmingham University African Studies Series, 2.

Jeyifo, Biọdun. 1984. *The Yoruba Popular Travelling Theatre of Nigeria.* Lagos: Nigeria Magazine Publications.

July, Robert W. 1968. *The Origins of Modern African Thought.* London: Faber.

Kavanagh, Robert Mshengu. 1985. *Theatre and Cultural Struggle in South Africa.* London: Zed Books.

Ladipọ, Duro. 1970. *Èdá/Everyman.* Transcribed and translated by Val Ọlayẹmi. University of Ìbàdàn, Institute of African Studies, Occasional Publication no. 24.

Ladipọ, Duro. 1972. *Ọba Ko So/The King Did Not Hang.* Transcribed and translated by R. G. Armstrong, Robert L. Awujọọla, Val Ọlayẹmi. University of Ibadan: Institute of African Studies.

Leonard, Lynn. 1967. "The Growth of Entertainments of Non-African Origin in Lagos From 1866 to 1920 (With Special Emphasis on Concert, Drama, and Cinema)." M.A. thesis, University of Ibadan.

McWilliam, H. O. A. 1959. *The Development of Education in Ghana.* London: Longman.

Mda, Zakes. 1993. *When People Play People: Development Communication Through Theatre.* London: Zed Books/Johannesburg: Witwatersrand University Press.

Mlama, Penina Muhando. 1991. *Culture and Development: The Popular Theatre Approach in Africa.* Uppsala: Scandinavian Institute of African Studies.

Moraes Farias, P. F. de, and Barber, Karin (eds.). 1990. *Self-assertion and Brokerage: Early Cultural Nationalism in West Africa.* Birmingham: Birmingham University African Studies Series, 2.

Obiechina, E. N. 1972. *Onitsha Market Literature.* London: Heinemann Educational Books.

Ọlajubu, Oludare. 1978. "The sources of Duro Ladipọ's *Ọba Ko So,*" *Research in African Literatures* 9, 3.

Peel, J. D. Y. 1968. *Aladura: A Religious Movement among the Yorubas.* Oxford: Oxford University Press.

Peel, J. D. Y. 1989. "The cultural work of Yoruba ethnogenesis," in E. Tonkin et al. (eds.), *History and Ethnicity,* London and New York: Routledge.

Ricard, Alain. 1974. "The concert party as a genre: the Happy Stars of Lomé," *Research in African Literatures,* 5, 2.

Ricard, Alain. 1986. *L'Invention du Théâtre et les Comédiens en Afrique Noire.* Lausanne: Editions L'Age d'Homme.

Rouch, Jean. 1973. "Essai sur les avatars de la personne du possédé, du magicien, du sorcier, du cinéaste et de ethnographe," in *La Notion de Personne en Afrique Noire,* Paris: CNRS.

Schicho, Walter, and Mbayabo Ndala. 1981. *Le Groupe Mufwankolo.* Vienna: Afro-Pub (Beitrage zur Afrikanistik, vol. 14, Institut für Afrikanistik).

Sutherland, Efua. 1970. *The Original Bob: The Story of Bob Johnson, Ghana's Ace Comedian.* Accra: Anowa Educational Publications.

Turner, H. W. 1967. *History of an African Independent Church.* Oxford: Oxford University Press.

Waterman, C. A. 1990. *Jùjú: A Social History and Ethnography of an African Popular Music.* Chicago: University of Chicago Press.

Westermann, Diedrich. 1907. *Grammatik der Ewe Sprache.* Berlin: Reimer.

Willis, Paul. 1990. *Common Culture.* London: Routledge.

Zinsou, Senouvo A. 1987. *La Tortue Qui Chante.* Paris: Hatier.

Zinsou, Senouvo A. 1987. *L'Africaine de Paris.* [French translation of Happy Stars' Ewe concert play.] Lomé: Nouvelles editions du Golfe.

Zumthor, Paul. 1983. *Introduction à la poésie orale.* Paris: Editions du Seuil [available in English as *Oral poetry: An Introduction,* trans. Kathryn Murhpy-Judy. Minneapolis: University of Minnesota Press, 1990].

# INDEX

Italicized locators refer to illustrations.

KARIN BARBER is Senior Lecturer at the Centre of West African Studies, the University of Birmingham. She has published extensively on Yorùbá oral literature, religion, and popular culture and worked and traveled with a Yorùbá theatre group in the early 1980s. Barber is author of *Yorùbá Dùn ún So: A Beginner's Course in Yorùbá (Part 1), I Could Speak Until Tomorrow: Oríkì, Women and the Past in a Yorùbá Town,* and (with Bayọ Ogundijọ) *Yorùbá Popular Theatre: Three Plays by the Oyin Adéjobi Company,* and editor (with P. F. de Moraes Farias) of *Discourse and Its Disguises: The Interpretation of African Oral Texts* and *Self-assertion and Brokerage: Early Cultural Nationalism in West Africa.*

JOHN COLLINS is Head of Bokoor Recording Studio, Ghana, and Technical Director of a joint German/Ghanaian music archive redocumentation project at the Institute of African Studies, University of Ghana, Legon. He plays guitar, harmonica, and Ghanaian percussion and has been involved in the West African music and entertainment scene as a musician, band leader, and music producer. Collins has written many articles and books on African popular entertainment, including *Music Makers of West Africa* and *West African Pop Roots.*

ALAIN RICARD is Research Professor with the French National Center for Scientific Research (CNRS) of the African Studies Center of the University of Bordeaux, specializing in African languages and literatures, including drama and popular literature. He has taught at the University in Lomé and was a researcher in residence with the Togolese National Theatre Ensemble. His books include *Théâtre et nationalisme, L'invention du théâtre, Wole Soyinka, l'invention démocratique,* and *Littératures d'Afrique noire: des langues aux livres.* He has also produced two films on concert party, *Agbeno Xevi* and *The Asihu Principle.*